THE
ENCYCLOPEDIA
OF
MEMORY
AND
MEMORY DISORDERS

THE
ENCYCLOPEDIA
OF
MEMORY
AND
MEMORY DISORDERS

Richard Noll, Ph.D.,
and
Carol Turkington

Facts On File®

AN INFOBASE HOLDINGS COMPANY

The Encyclopedia of Memory and Memory Disorders

Library of Congress Cataloging-in-Publication Data
Noll, Richard.
  Encyclopedia of memory and memory disorders / Richard Noll and Carol
Turkington.
        p. cm.
  ISBN 0-8160-2610-6
    1. Memory—Encyclopedias.   2. Memory disorders—Encyclopedias.
  I. Turkington, Carol.   II. Title.
  BF371.N55   1994
  153.1′2′03—dc20   94-1590

Printed in the United States of America

BP VC 10 9 8 7 6 5 4 3 2 1

This book is printed on acid-free paper.

CONTENTS

FOREWORD

The phenomenon of human memory is, and always has been, perhaps the most central problem of philosophy and psychology because it is at the root of the mystery of human consciousness: the continuity (or discontinuity) of the experience of the self. How is it that despite numerous developmental changes through the life span and daily exposure to novel stimuli that clearly influence us in a myriad of ways that we still, despite it all, experience a continuous "self" through time? Paradoxically, how is it that we all also experience a discontinuity of the experience of the self due to alterations in consciousness such as sleep or hypnosis, or perhaps in more unfortunate circumstances such as neurological insult or disease (such as Alzheimer's)? From philosophical, experimental psychological, neurological and biochemical researchers we continue to receive a steady stream of new information that helps us to understand, piece by piece, the perplexing nature of human memory.

In this volume, we provide a wealth of complex information about human memory in plain language for the general reader, the journalist, the family member of a person with a memory disorder such as Alzheimer's, and even the medical or mental health professional who is lacking the expertise to understand the highly technical professional literature on human memory. Whereas other "encyclopedias" of memory and learning are aimed at the still relatively small circle of scientists who also need to keep abreast of such information, these volumes are incomprehensible to those who do not read or speak the language of "neurobiologese." This book gives all of us a chance to enter the exciting world of these scientists through explaining, in simple terms, the most important concepts and issues currently under investigation in laboratories all over the globe. Additionally, we provide many entries that summarize the most important ideas about human memory that have been proposed since the times of Plato and Aristotle. Twenty-first–century students of the history of science who may wish to make sense of the cognitive science revolution of the last quarter of the twentieth century may very well wish to refer to this volume to begin to develop their basic knowledge of the vocabulary of learning and memory research.

I welcome the reader who consults this volume to simply browse its pages and follow his or her own interests as they are sparked by the material we provide.

Richard Noll, Ph.D.
Department of the History of Science
Harvard University
Cambridge, Mass.

INTRODUCTION

Throughout history, the meaning of memory has worn many guises. To the ancient Greeks and Romans, memory was the key to political success. To later memory experts, it was the path to spiritual fulfillment. To countless preliterate tribes, memory carried the key to the history of their people.

With the advent of the alphabet, of the written word, of typewriters and computers and satellites, memory no longer holds the mystical spiritual magic it offered our ancestors. For many in today's world, a good memory is nothing more than a sort of intellectual shorthand, an easier way to study, to succeed in business, to live an organized life.

But in a deeper sense, there is far more to memory than recalling dates, finding car keys or cramming for a history final. It is our memory that transforms a series of unconnected moments into a continuous unified whole, linking us to our past and pointing the way into the future.

We are compassionate because we remember what it is to feel pain. We buttress our lives against disaster because we remember what disaster has cost in the past. Our memory gives us a future more secure than creatures who are doomed to repeat their past simply because they cannot remember it. And it can rescue us from a fate that awaits those destined to obliteration because they cannot adapt to changed circumstances.

Our memory has made possible the development of philosophy and science and song. More personally, it is the repository of our deepest emotions and our most compelling experiences. After all, it is our memory that holds the scent of the sea wind, the sound of a child's laughter, the image of the beloved. In the final analysis, it is our memory that makes us fully human, because it distills the rich diversity of experience into the essence of the soul.

Carol Turkington
Morgantown, Pa.

ENTRIES A–Z

A

abaissement du niveau mental   A term meaning "lowering of the level of consciousness" invented by French psychiatrist Pierre Janet to describe the weakening control of consciousness prior to DISSOCIATION. Today this term usually refers to ALTERED STATES OF CONSCIOUSNESS.

Janet believed this altered state of consciousness was found not just in dissociation but also in multiple personality, trances and automatic writing. He used the term to describe the weakening of willful control of consciousness and the subsequent dissociation into autonomous parts that might not be aware of each other.

Swiss psychoanalyst Carl Jung picked up Janet's term to describe schizophrenia; Jung believed this lowering of consciousness was the root of the mental disorder. In 1902 in Paris Jung became a student of Janet and was influenced by Janet throughout his life.

While Janet wrote widely in French, very few of his works have been translated into English. (See also JANET, PIERRE.)

abreaction   Emotional release or discharge after recalling a painful experience that has been repressed because it was consciously intolerable. A therapeutic effect sometimes occurs through partial discharge or desensitization of the painful emotions and increased insight. (See also REPRESSED MEMORIES; REPRESSION.)

absentmindedness   Failure to register information because of preoccupation with other thoughts. This kind of forgetting is not the same thing as the inability to recall information, which means that the information has been registered and stored. In absentmindedness, the information was never registered in the first place, so it can't be recalled.

While everyone may be absentminded occasionally, as people age they tend to become more absentminded. The phenomenon occurs most often in familiar surroundings, during habitual automatic activities that don't require much attention and when the mind is distracted or preoccupied with outside stress.

If absentmindedness is due primarily to not paying attention, it can be averted by putting more energy into registering information. People who always forget where they put their keys might try saying out loud, "I'm putting my keys down HERE," as they set them down. Then the keys should be looked at, while noticing what is being done. The only cure for absentmindedness is finding better ways to pay attention to daily activities.

abstract memory   This term refers to a person's general store of knowledge. This type of memory has a huge capacity for storing meanings of events and objects. Its center is believed to be located in the CORTEX, the brain's outer gray layer. Damage to the temporal, parietal and occipital cortex affects abstract memory in different ways.

acalculia   A specific impairment in dealing with arithmetical concepts.

accident neurosis   See AMNESIA, SIMULATED.

acetylcholine   A type of neurotransmitter (a chemical that transmits messages between nerve cells) that may play a role in learning and memory by helping brain cells in the CORTEX retain the imprint of incoming information. (See NEUROTRANSMITTERS.) Acetylcholine is vital for the transmission of messages from one nerve cell to another, and the neurotransmitter is found at all nerve-muscle junctions as well as at many other sites in the nervous system. Its action is called cholinergic.

Scientists discovered its role in memory when studying ALZHEIMER'S DISEASE patients, whose memory problems underlie their disease. Scientists speculate that Alzheimer's patients forget because their brains contain low levels of acetylcholine.

acetyl-L-carnitine (ALC)   A molecule found naturally in the body responsible for carrying fats into the mitochondria (the energy-producing part of the cells) and regarded by some scientists as one of the most promising chemicals for the treatment of ALZHEIMER'S DISEASE.

Long-term administration of ALC, which is found in many common foods (including milk), has preserved spatial memory in aged rats. Some studies suggest that ALC also may play an important part in protecting the brain from the effects of aging. One study has found that ALC helps nourish certain receptors in the brain that are important for learning. In addition, other animal research suggests that ALC interferes with the formation of lipofuscin, a substance that is associated with a reduction of cognitive ability in the aged.

In human studies, ALC has been found to increase short-term memory, attention span and alertness of those with Alzheimer's disease and other forms of senility. It also is said to increase the brain levels of choline acetyltransferase and to increase dopamine activity. (Dopamine deficiencies in the brains of Alzheimer's patients are believed to be the primary reason behind low levels of ACETYLCHOLINE, which can lead to muddy thinking, confused memory, slow reflexes and DEPRESSION. [See DEPRESSION AND MEMORY LOSS.])

After studying 30 Alzheimer's patients and ALC, researchers at Columbia University concluded that ALC may retard the deterioration in some cognitive areas in patients with Alzheimer's disease.

ALC has been available in Italy since 1986, where it is classified as a nootropic drug (see NOOTROPICS) and is used to treat Alzheimer's disease and age-associated memory impairment. Recent studies at the University of Modena in Italy found that ALC improved cognitive performance in 279 elderly patients and that the cognitive gains persisted long after the treatment ended. In tests of cognitive function, emotional state and relational behavior, patients showed gains on all measures when compared to a placebo group. (See also CHEMICALS AND MEMORY LOSS.)

Barnes, C.A., et al. "Acetyl-L-carnitine, 2: Effects on Learning and Memory Performance of Aged Rats in Simple and Complex Mazes." *Neurobiological Aging* 11, no. 5 (September–October 1990): 499–506.
Bonavita, E. "Study of the Efficacy and Tolerability of L-acetylcarnitine Therapy in the Senile Brain." *Journal of Clinical Pharmacology, Therapy and Toxicology* 24 (1986): 511–16.
Bowman, B. "Acetyl-carnitine and Alzheimer's Disease." *Nutrition Review* 50, no. 5 (1992): 911–16.
Ghirardi, O., et al. "Active Avoidance Learning in Old Rats Chronically Treated with Levocarnitine Acetyl." *Physiological Behavior* 52, no. 1 (July 1992): 185–87.
Rai, G., et al. "Double Blind, Placebo Controlled Study of Acetyl-L-carnitine in Patients with Alzheimer's Dementia." *Current Medical Research and Opinion* 11, no. 10 (1990): 638–47.

acquisition   The process of encoding or recording information in the first stage of the memory process (followed by storage and retrieval/recall). If a person can't remember something, it may be because the information was never recorded in the first place (a failure of acquisition), although it is most likely a problem of retrieval.

acrostic   A mnemonic technique (also called first-letter mnemonics) in which the first letters from a word or phrase are used to create a new phrase that is easier to remember. To remember the names of the Great Lakes, an acrostic would be: Happy Old Mares Exercise Some (Huron, Ontario, Michigan, Erie, Superior). (See also FIRST-LETTER CUEING; MNEMONICS; MNEMONIC STRATEGIES.)

ACTH (adrenocorticotropic hormone)
A hormone that aids in memory retention
and concentration. Produced by the anterior
part of the pituitary gland, ACTH stimulates
the adrenal cortex to release various corticosteroid hormones. ACTH also is necessary
for the maintenance and growth of adrenal
cortex cells.

A combination of ACTH and melanocyte-
stimulating hormone (MSH) have been studied as a possible "memory pill" helpful in
treating some types of mental retardation,
hyperactive children and adults with SENILE
DEMENTIA; however, its use also has serious
side effects.

ACTH stimulates the adrenal cortex to
increase production of the hormones hydrocortisone, aldosterone and androgen. ACTH
production is controlled partly by the hypothalamus and partly by the level of hydrocortisone in the blood; when ACTH levels are
too high, hydrocortisone production is increased, which suppresses the release of
ACTH from the pituitary gland. If levels
are too low, the hypothalamus releases its
hormones, stimulating the pituitary gland to
increase ACTH production. ACTH levels
increase in response to stress, emotion, injury, infection, burns, surgery and a decrease in blood pressure.

adenosine triphosphate (ATP)   Called
the "universal energy molecule," this substance is created in the mitochondria of a
cell with the energy from dietary food. All
cellular activities in the body use the energy
released by splitting ATP.

ADH   See VASOPRESSIN.

Ad Herennium   The standard Roman text
on memory written by an unknown author
in 80 B.C., this is the earliest existing how-
to book on rhetoric. The text, which includes
a section on MNEMOTECHNICS, was written
for rhetoric students and had a profound
influence on some of the greatest thinkers of
the ancient world.

Rhetoric students learned effective communication, especially effective public
speaking. Since paper and books were expensive and scarce, rhetoric students had
to learn ways to remember their speeches
without referring to notes. In the *Ad Herennium*, the author describes an astonishing
system of recalling facts, known as the
METHOD OF LOCI, in which people can recall
facts by arranging scenes in a space they
have committed to memory and placing
the things to be remembered in those
rooms.

Students would first imagine a space in a
quiet building they knew well. (Often rhetoric students searched for very large buildings
with interesting architecture and committed
these buildings to memory.) Then students
would mentally lodge associative images in
this space. When they wanted to recall information, they would take an imaginary walk
through the space, looking at the images and
remembering the associations. For example,
if a lawyer wished to memorize details of a
case, he might begin with an intruder hitting
his victim. In order to remember this, he
would imagine himself walking into his
memory palace, stopping at the first architectural detail—a staircase—and imagining a
picture of the intruder standing on the steps,
hitting the victim. He would proceed
through the memory palace, lodging other
facts throughout the building. When it came
time to call up the facts of the case, he
would simply enter the memory palace in
his mind; when he encountered the staircase,
he would immediately remember the *association* of the intruder standing on the steps,
hitting the victim.

The book discusses one of the classic
rules of artificial memory: The aids must
be unusual—even bizarre—in order to be
memorable. The book's author notes that
things in life that are boring, banal and
ordinary are soon forgotten because the mind
has not been stirred; but we are likely to
remember the marvelous or novel, the base,
dishonorable, unusual, great or ridiculous.

The *Ad Herennium* is the only complete source for the Roman and Greek art of memory, and was the primary transmitter of this classical art to the Middle Ages and the Renaissance, where the book enjoyed great popularity because it was thought to have been written by CICERO.

While the *Ad Herennium* gives general rules for memory systems, however, it does not give many concrete examples of images that a person could use to aid memory. The book's author apparently believed that a person should generate his or her own images and not use the pictures or associations or others.

Yates, Frances. *The Art of Memory.* Chicago: University of Chicago Press, 1966.

adrenaline See EPINEPHRINE.

adrenocorticotropic hormone (ACTH) See ACTH.

advance knowledge and witness perception Having some sort of knowledge about an event before it happens can influence how people view that event—what they see and what they pay attention to. (See also AGE AND EYEWITNESS ABILITY; EYEWITNESS TESTIMONY; MEMORY FOR EVENTS.)

age and eyewitness ability A slight decline in recall and recognition ability may begin to occur at about age 60. Eyewitnesses over age 60 perform more poorly than do somewhat younger people, and some decrease in performance has been found on many tasks between ages 40 and 60.

But although some tasks, such as memory for details, may weaken slightly with age, other cognitive skills are maintained. In addition, there are great individual differences among people. Therefore, while performance on some tasks may decline somewhat as people age, performance on others—memory for logical relationships or the ability to make complex inferences, for example—does not deteriorate.

In addition, age may affect whether a witness is susceptible to potential biases and misleading information. Researchers always have believed children are both highly suggestible and particularly inaccurate, and studies suggest that younger children are very much more suggestible than older children or adults. (See also CROSS-RACIAL WITNESS IDENTIFICATION; EYEWITNESS TESTIMONY; GENDER AND EYEWITNESS ABILITY; MEMORY FOR EVENTS.)

age-associated memory impairment (AAMI) A medical condition first recognized by the National Institute of Mental Health in 1986. AAMI is believed to affect 20 percent of Americans over age 50 who suffer from a gradual loss of memory to the point that it interferes with everyday life. To reach a diagnosis of AAMI, memory loss must be unrelated to injury, stroke or dementing disease such as Alzheimer's. (See also AGING AND MEMORY.)

age regression, hypnotic A hypnotic technique that directs the subject mentally to return to childhood; it is not uncommon for the subject to take on childlike qualities, with changes in voice, handwriting and gestures. Often the subject of age regression spontaneously may relive a painful or traumatic experience of childhood.

The first published report of age regression appeared in 1883 in the *Revue Philosophique* by Charles Richet, who suggested to a subject that he was six years old again. This report set off a plethora of age-regression suggestions, which became popular during the 1890s as one type of "personality alteration" (similar to the "double personality" also being explored at that time).

Estimates are that about 43 percent of individuals respond positively to age-regression suggestions, much higher than the 15 percent of people who are considered to be highly hypnotizable.

Many researchers now believe that any

time age-regression techniques are used to elicit memories, the subsequent memories may be either fact or fantasy—or a mixture of both. Clinically, therapists don't really care whether the memory is fact or fiction, since it is believed that treating a person's fantasies of the past can be just as effective as treating the documented reality of that past.

Hypnotized subjects are not consciously lying, according to memory expert Martin Orne, M.D. When subjects are regressed to age five, they really believe they are children and they will respond as they believe five-year-olds would. While subjects feel they are children, they are not really children; instead, the subjects are role playing with all of their heart, Orne says—but not all of their mind.

One of the hallmarks of HYPNOSIS is translogic, or a decrease in critical judgment. It is translogic that causes a hypnotized subject to copy down a complicated dictation in a childish scrawl—but with perfect spelling beyond the capability of any child. An adult who is consciously trying to mimic a child would not make the mistake of copying a complicated paragraph without inserting some spelling errors.

Scientists can test hypnotic memories by testing the reactions of regressed subjects and comparing them to actual behavior exhibited by children of the same "age." Most regressed subjects demonstrate that they react as they expect children of that age would react, not as true children act.

aging and memory   As a person ages, the functioning of the memory process begins to slow down, affecting different types of memory in different ways. There could be a whole host of reasons why this memory deterioration occurs: malnutrition, depression, medications—or a range of organic problems in the aging brain itself.

Causes   Researchers have come up with several possible reasons for this age-related memory deterioration, although none has been proven conclusively. First of all, there are a range of reversible reasons for an age-related loss: depression, medications (especially the BENZODIAZEPINES used to treat anxiety), dietary irregularities, thyroid deficiency, alcohol and marijuana.

But there are also a wide range of organic reasons that underlie this type of memory loss. While scientists once thought that age brought an irreversible loss of cells in the cerebral cortex, they have now completely changed their minds. Today researchers believe that major cell loss appears to be in a tiny region toward the front of the brain called the basal forebrain and in the HIPPOCAMPUS and AMYGDALA, which control memory and learning. Loss of these cells causes a drop in the production of the neurotransmitter ACETYLCHOLINE, vital to memory and learning. Alzheimer's disease patients, for example, have marked decreases in this vital neurotransmitter.

Unfortunately, the hippocampus—probably one of the most important brain structures involved in memory—is highly vulnerable to aging. Studies have found that up to 5 percent of the nerve cells in the hippocampus evaporate with each decade past middle age. This could mean a loss of up to 20 percent of total hippocampal nerve cells by the time people enter their 80s.

Damage to this area of the brain may be a result of stress hormones such as cortisol, made in the adrenal glands. Research with rats at Stanford University and the University of Kentucky have found that stress-induced increases in cortisol prematurely age the hippocampus. Excessive amounts of free radicals (toxic forms of oxygen) also can build up as a person ages, damaging the hippocampus.

It may be that as the brain ages, the speed with which information is processed decreases so that retrieving stored material takes longer. Or memory problems may occur because of dying neurons or decreased production of neurotransmitters (chemicals like acetylcholine that allow brain cells to communicate with each other).

Memory problems also may be linked to the fact that as a person ages, the brain shrinks and the cells become less efficient, according to neuroscientist Mark Shapiro, M.D., of the Neuroscience Laboratory of the National Institute of Aging in Bethesda, Maryland. In addition, things can happen to the brain to accelerate its decline—a person can be genetically unlucky, be exposed to toxins such as lead or make bad choices in life, as by smoking and drinking to excess. All those things will accelerate memory decline.

Or it could be that an aging person's ability to retrieve memories may be impaired directly. Studies have shown that older people may have problems recalling a list of words but have no problem picking out those previously seen words from a longer list. Because they can recognize these previously seen words, it is obvious that the memory of the words has been stored somewhere in the brain—it is just harder to retrieve them (remember) than recognize them (picking from a list). In this case, a list may serve as a visual cue to help a person retrieve the memory.

Age-related memory problems also may be due to differences in ENCODING (storing information). Those people with the best ability to remember at any age tend to cloak new information with details, images and "cues." When they are introduced to a new acquaintance, for example, they notice the physical appearance of the person and link it in some way to the person's name, fitting the introduction into a context they already understand. Researchers have discovered that with age, a person is less able to organize this information effectively, perceiving less and noticing fewer details. In fact, researchers have documented a drop in effective encoding strategies during the 20s and traced a further, more gradual decrease over the life span. For these reasons, older people have the most difficulty when attempting unfamiliar tasks that require rapid processing—such as learning how to program a videocassette recorder or operating a computer.

About half of elderly men and women with severe intellectual impairment have ALZHEIMER'S DISEASE; another fourth suffer from vascular disorders (especially multiple strokes) and the rest have a variety of problems, including BRAIN TUMOR, abnormal thyroid function, infections, pernicious anemia, adverse drug reactions and abnormalities in the spinal fluid. (See STROKE.) A good diagnosis is important because all of these other disorders can be treated.

Symptoms The chief decline in mental ability among healthy older people is in "executive function"—the ability to perform several tasks at once or to switch back and forth rapidly between tasks.

And while semantic memory (general vocabulary and knowledge about the world) often stays sharp through the 70s, memory for names (especially those not used frequently) begins to decline after age 35. While short-term memory does not decline as a person ages, long-term and episodic memory (remembering the time and place something occurred) does deteriorate.

The elderly also suffer from SOURCE AMNESIA (forgetting where something was learned). Spatial visualization skills (the ability to recognize faces and find one's car) already has begun to wane by the time a person enters the 20s.

An older person's ability to recall memories from long ago does not necessarily have anything to do with memory; the memories are not being remembered from long ago, but merely from the last time the story was told. This is why memories that have been retrieved many times may be distorted.

The Good News While some specific abilities do decline with age, overall memory remains strong through the 70s; research studies have shown that the average 70-year-old performs as well on such a test as do 25 to 30 percent of 20-year-olds. In fact, many older people in their 60s and 70s score significantly better in verbal intelligence than young people.

There is significant proof that memory loss is not an inevitable part of aging, according to experts at Harvard University. Studies of nursing home populations controlled for age bias and excess anxiety showed that patients were able to make significant improvements in memory through rewards and cognitive challenges.

While some memory loss is common, it is usually benign and memory function diminishes only slightly with the years. Physical exercise and mental stimulation improve mental function in some people. Animal studies in California reveal that rats living stimulating lives, with plenty of toys in their cages, have larger brain cells and longer dendrites.

"One may not learn or remember quite as rapidly during healthy late life, but one may learn and remember nearly as well," says Dennis Selkoe, M.D., co-director of the Center for Neurologic Diseases at Brigham and Women's Hospital in Boston.

So while it is true that the brain does become less effective as a person ages, it is generally because of disuse rather than disease. And just as it's possible to strengthen a muscle by lifting weights, it's also possible to challenge the brain to become more efficient.

"The use-it-or-lose-it principle applies not only to maintaining muscular flexibility, but to high levels of intellectual performance as well," says psychologist K. Warner Schaie, Ph.D., director of the Gerontology Center at Pennsylvania State University. Dr. Schaie, who's been tracing the mental meanderings of 4,000 people for more than 30 years, is an international authority on mental stimulation and the aging brain. He believes that by running through some daily mental drills—sort of like practicing scales on a piano—a person can prevent intellectual breakdown. In fact, he's discovered that you can reverse

a downward mental slide through a combination of mental gymnastics and problem-solving skills.

Only recently have scientists figured out that a person's brain doesn't gradually self-destruct during aging—that there is some choice over when, and how much, mental ability is lost, says gerontologist Robert Butler, M.D., director of the National Institute of Aging and winner of the Pulitzer Prize for his book *Why Survive? Being Old in America* (1985). "There is no overall decline with age," Butler says. "In fact, judgment, accuracy and general knowledge may increase."

Researchers once thought that by age 13 a person's brainpower began a slow downward spiral until—by about age 70 or 80—there would be barely enough brain cell wattage to power a penlight. More recent studies have exploded that myth.

Schaie's long-term study has looked at how older people handle skills ranging from identification of a rotated object to finding the square root of 243. He found that after about age 30, most people reach a plateau that is usually maintained until about age 60; after that, there are small declines depending on ability and sex. It's not until the 80s that any sort of serious mental slowdown occurs.

The capacity to focus on a task or follow an argument remains strong throughout life. The bad news, according to some neuropsychologists, is that memory may decline by 50 percent between ages 25 and 75. But the good news is that wisdom does not decline.

Putting Off Memory Problems   It is possible to slow down a memory decline, some experts say. Evidence from animal research suggests that stimulating the brain can not only stop cells from shrinking, it can actually increase brain size. Studies show that rats living in an enriched environment had larger outer brain layers, with larger, healthier neurons. The rats also had brains with more cells responsible for providing food for the neurons. Those rats kept in a barren cage with nothing to play with were listless and had smaller brains.

Some scientists now believe that humans can also improve their brain function and even reverse a decline by challenging themselves with active learning or by living in an "enriched" environment. In fact, stimulating environments can even counteract the brain shrinkage due to old age.

In addition, research has found that exercised brain cells have more DENDRITES (the branchlike projections that allow the cells to communicate with each other). With age, a stimulating environment encourages the growth of these dendrites, and a dull environment lowers their number. That's why scientists believe that a person's socioeconomic status often predicts mental decline, since people who don't have a lot of disposable income often can't afford very stimulating environments. Researchers conclude that fewer, smaller brain cells is the price a person pays for failing to stimulate the brain.

In the Future Someday, researchers suggest, it will be possible to go to a doctor and get a personally designed "exercise plan" for the brain to prevent mental skills from deteriorating, much the way a physical therapist might devise a treatment plan to help a trick knee or bad back.

Interestingly, researchers have discovered that older people best remember things and events that occurred from the ages of 25 to 40 rather than after age 50. This is probably because most of a person's life goals were begun during those years: jobs, relationship, children, marriage. It's not that life gets dull in middle age, but it has become routine—and the brain is far better at remembering details of a wedding day than thoughts during a bridge game last Tuesday. This is related to the FLASHBULB MEMORY phenomenon, in which an extremely emotional event is remembered clearly years later. Everyone remembers what he or she was doing when President Kennedy was shot, although not much will be remembered about the day before or after.

Part of the reason why momentous events are imprinted so strongly in the brain is that it's more than likely that a person was paying attention when they occurred. As generations of students have found out, no matter how well material is presented, if they are not paying attention they probably won't remember it. This is also why most people immediately forget a person's name when introduced—they are so busy looking at the new person, making initial judgments and trying to make pleasant conversation, that they forget the name quickly.

There are probably as many memory aides as there are things to be remembered. As far back as the late 19th century, psychologist William James was busy coming up with ways to put some pizzazz into his brain cells. He came to the conclusion that it's possible to improve memory by improving the way facts are memorized . . . which is why every music teacher since has translated the notes of the scale (E, G, B, D, F) into "Every Good Boy Does Fine."

But no matter what method is used to remember the name of the new neighbor, a zip code or the third law of quantum mechanics, the amount of time spent trying to remember is crucial. Researchers have found it's always better to sit down once or twice a day to try to remember things than to try to cram ten hours of study in at one time. People pay attention to what interests them. If older people must read and remember something, they should try to find a room where they can read without too many distractions. Also, it helps to be an active reader, reading a sentence as a critic would, ready to locate an inconsistency, checking against what is already known.

If a memory problem is caused by any sort of brain disease, memory strategies aren't going to help. But if the brain is structurally healthy, odds are these strategies will provide some improvement in memory and problem-solving skills.

Normal Memory Changes with Age

- *Reduced attention span:* **Problems paying attention and ignoring distractions in the environment**
- *Slowed thinking process:* **Particularly apparent when dealing with new problems or a problem that needs an immediate reaction**
- *Fewer memory strategies:* **Older people don't use as many cues and associations as younger people**
- *Longer learning time*

Memory That Doesn't Normally Change

- *Short-term memory*
- *Semantic memory*
- *Retention of well-known information*
- *Searching technique:* **Searching may take longer, but the technique doesn't change**
- *Interference:* **New information in one area competes with original information, which makes it hard to break old habits**

Adler, Tina. "Memory software explains failings." *APA Monitor* (December 1989): 6.

Dean, Ward, and Morgenthaler, John. *Smart Drugs & Nutrients*. Santa Cruz, CA: B&J Publications, 1991.

Harvard Editors. "When to Worry About Forgetting." *Harvard Health Letter* (July 1992): 1–3.

agnosia A neurological condition in which patients fail to recognize objects even though they show no signs of sensory impairment. The problem in recognizing objects is often restricted to particular types of stimuli, such as colors or objects, and may take quite subtle forms. For example, in facial agnosia (PROSOPAGNOSIA) patients cannot recognize a familiar face, but they can recognize the person's voice. Even odder, some facial agnosics can't recognize their own faces in a mirror, although their concept of self is intact; it is just that the face in the mirror and the connection to the self has vanished. There are indications that patients with facial agnosia also may have problems recognizing other classes of stimuli (such as makes of cars or species of birds).

Because an object can be recognized only if the sensory information about it can be interpreted, a person must be able to recall memorized information about similar objects. Agnosia is caused by damage to those parts of the brain responsible for this necessary interpretative and memory recall. The most common causes of this type of brain damage are stroke and head injury. In addition, tumors of the parietal lobe of the cerebral hemispheres also frequently cause agnosia.

Sigmund Freud invented the term "agnosia," meaning "state of not knowing." It can be contrasted with APHASIA (inability to recall words and construct speech).

In addition to facial agnosia, there are other types: In *visual agnosia,* the patient is unable to verbally identify visual material, even though he or she may be able to indicate recognition of it by other means (such as gestures). In *color agnosia,* a patient can't recognize colors; if asked to pick out a blue sweater, he or she cannot do so. There is nothing wrong with a color agnosic's eyesight and he or she is not color blind; it is just that colors are devoid of meaning.

There are a wide variety of agnosias for sound (sensory agnosia): These can include *pure word deafness,* the inability to recognize spoken words although the patient can read, write and speak, and react to other sounds. In *cortical deafness,* the patient has problems discriminating all kinds of sounds.

Somatosensory agnosia is the inability to recognize objects by shape or size. ANOSOGNOSIA is the inability to recognize the fact that you are ill; a patient may feel sick but cannot make the connection between the symptoms and the perception "I'm sick."

Reduplicative paramnesia, or CAPGRAS SYNDROME, is a rare disorder in which patients fail to recognize other people and places they know well. The effect can be induced by showing a patient a picture and then, a few minutes later, producing the same picture again. A patient with reduplicative paramnesia may say she has seen a similar picture but insist that it is definitely not the one she is now looking at. This disorder is believed to have a psychological origin, although more recent research suggests there may be an organic cause. It is typically associated with CONFABULATION, speech problems and a denial of illness.

agraphia The loss or reduction of the ability to write, despite normal hand and arm muscle function, as a result of brain damage to the part of the brain concerned with writing.

Writing requires a complex sequence of mental processes, including the selection of words, recall from memory of how these words are spelled, formulation and execution of necessary hand movements and visual checking that written words match their representation in the brain.

Researchers believe these processes take place in a number of connected brain areas; damage to any of these areas (usually within the left cerebral hemisphere) can cause an agraphia of different types and severity. The most common reasons for such damage are head injury, stroke and brain tumors.

Agraphia rarely occurs on its own, but often is accompanied by alexia (loss of the ability to read) or expressive APHASIA (general disturbance in speaking).

While there is no specific treatment for agraphia, some of the lost writing skills may return some time after the stroke or head injury. (See also ALEXIA; APRAXIA; DYSPHASIA.)

AIDS dementia A percentage of AIDS patients in advanced stages of the disease develop symptoms of an organic mental disorder (dementia) due to the direct infection of the brain by the human immunodeficiency virus (HIV).

Early symptoms of AIDS dementia are not specific; they include the usual signs of dementia (forgetfulness, poor concentration, confusion, slow thinking), but they also include movement problems (unsteady gait, leg weakness) and more serious psychiatric symptoms of apathy, depression, agitation and mania of psychosis. Estimates suggest that 30 percent of AIDS patients will go on to develop dementia.

In fact, the AIDS dementia complex first described in 1986 is the presenting symptom of the disorder in about 25 percent of all patients. Based on this information, the Centers for Disease Control in the United States has modified the diagnostic criteria for AIDS to allow a diagnosis of the disease solely on the basis of dementia in a person who is HIV-positive, without any evidence of other opportunistic infection or Kaposi's sarcoma.

Although dementia is fairly common in advanced stages of AIDS, scientists disagree on whether people who test positive for HIV but who have no symptoms are already mentally impaired. However, HIV carriers do not generally exhibit signs of AIDS dementia. In fact, the World Health Organization has stated that being HIV-positive does not indicate a person has neurological or neuropsychological abnormalities, and there is no evidence of such abnormalities in HIV-infected people without symptoms. Studies have shown that less than 1 percent of those who are HIV carriers but have no symptoms have AIDS dementia.

The figures for AIDS dementia, however, are much higher in children: About 60 percent go on to develop the disorder. It is suspected that this is because children tend to resist opportunistic infections better than adults and therefore live long enough to develop dementia.

akashic records   This concept is a description of "divine memory" described in ancient texts from Tibet, Egypt and India. It refers to a cosmic data bank of all universal happenings recorded on a sort of "ether"— an invisible unmanifested medium through which visible light passes as a manifestation of vibration. The name comes from the Sanskrit word *Akasha,* meaning "unshining light" or black light of radiation, referring to primordial substance.

According to psychics, it is to this etheric record that many seers, including Edgar Cayce, claim they have access in order to obtain detailed information about a person's past lives.

alcohol amnestic disorder   See KORSA-KOFF'S SYNDROME.

alcohol and memory   Alcoholism is one of the most serious and prevalent medical problems in the United States, and brings with it serious memory problems. Statistics suggest that at least 12 to 15 percent of the population may be alcoholics, and even a few drinks four times a week will lower the ability to remember.

Short-term memory loss is a classic problem among patients who abuse alcohol, which impairs the ability to retain new information. This potential deficit is based not on the number of ounces drunk per day but on each individual's tolerance for alcohol. In studies at the University of California at Los Angeles, scientists discovered that people over age 40 experienced the most memory problems after drinking—but even people age 21 to 30 experienced some memory loss.

In addition, women appear to be more susceptible to the toxic effects of alcohol, especially in relation to their short-term memory performance. Among alcoholics, women also seem to suffer from both verbal and spatial cognitive problems, whereas men seem to be affected only by spatial cognitive difficulties.

Chronic alcohol abuse may result in WERNICKE'S ENCEPHALOPATHY, a condition characterized by the sudden onset of confusion, coordination problems, loss of sensation and impaired reflexes. The level of consciousness progressively decreases, and without treatment, this syndrome may lead to coma and death.

If treatment is not begun early enough, Korsakoff's psychosis (or syndrome) may result. With this disorder, sufferers experience severe amnesia, apathy and disorientation. Recent memories are affected more than distant memory; often patients cannot remember what they did even a few moments ago, and they may make up stories to cover for their loss of memory.

Some researchers believe that people who are frequently drunk and sober may experience state dependency (also called compatibility); that is, things learned in one state or context are impossible to remember in another. For example, on the following day an alcoholic will not remember activities at a party while drunk—but can recall them when drunk again. This type of state dependency is why witnesses are sometimes brought to the scene of a crime to help them remember details.

Most alcohol-induced memory problems seem to disappear when the person stops drinking, although a lifetime of abuse may cause irreversible damage. When investigators tested alcoholics after four or five weeks of treatment, their memory performance was much better. (See also BLACKOUTS, ALCOHOLIC; KORSAKOFF'S SYNDROME; STATE-DEPENDENT LEARNING.)

Herrmann, Douglas. *Supermemory.* Emmaus, PA: Rodale Press, 1991.
Kra, Siegfried. *Aging Myths.* New York: McGraw-Hill, 1986.

Minninger, Joan. *Total Recall*. Emmaus, PA: Rodale Press, 1984.

Parkin, Alan J. *Memory and Amnesia*. Oxford: Basil Blackwell, 1987.

alcohol idiosyncratic intoxication   A marked behavioral change (usually to aggressiveness) caused by drinking an amount of alcohol insufficient to induce intoxication in most people. This behavior change, which is usually atypical for the person, is usually followed by AMNESIA for the period of intoxication.

Some experts believe the phenomenon is really a dissociative disorder in which aggressive and destructive behaviors are likely to be prominent. (See also ALCOHOL AND MEMORY; BLACKOUTS, ALCOHOLIC; KORSAKOFF'S SYNDROME.)

alexia   The inability to recognize and name written words by a person who had been literate, severely disrupting the ability to read. The disability is caused by brain damage from stroke or head injury to a part of the cerebrum. It is considered to be a much more serious reading disability than dyslexia. (See also AGRAPHIA; APHASIA; APRAXIA; DYSLEXIA AND MEMORY; DYSPHASIA.)

alphabetical searching   A type of verbal method for improving memory in which the subject works through the alphabet in the hope that a particular letter will act as a retrieval cue for a forgotten word or name. Alphabetical searching is believed to be effective only when the person already has a great deal of information about the word (its length, whether it is common, the number of syllables, etc.).

altered states of consciousness   Qualitative alterations in the overall pattern of mental functioning, so that the person feels consciousness is radically different from the way it normally functions.

Alzheimer, Alois (1864–1915)   German neuropathologist who first diagnosed the disease that bears his name in 1906 during the autopsy of a 55-year-old patient who had died with severe dementia. Alzheimer's, a disease characterized by progressive loss of memory, had never before been isolated as a brain disorder.

During the autopsy, Alzheimer noted two abnormalities in the woman's brain—neuritic plaques and NEUROFIBRILLARY TANGLES.

Alzheimer worked with colleagues Emil Kraepelin and Franz Nissl in the research lab at the Psychological Clinic of the University of Munich, where they conducted research on the underlying disease processes in the nervous system that caused DEMENTIA PRAECOX. While Nissl invented new staining techniques to better study nerve cells, Alzheimer discovered the disease process for Alzheimer's disease. Alzheimer also served as a professor at Breslau University in Poland from 1912 until he died in 1915.

Alzheimer's Association   A national, nonprofit organization dedicated to research for the prevention, cure and treatment of ALZHEIMER'S DISEASE and related disorders and to providing support and assistance to afflicted patients and their families.

In 1980 seven independent caregiver groups joined to form the Alzheimer's Disease and Related Disorders Association to help families who endure the financial, physical and emotional tolls of Alzheimer's disease. The association has become the nation's leading nonprofit health organization with an annual $30 million budget devoted to the disease. In 1988 the organization changed its name from ADRDA to the Alzheimer's Association.

The goals of the group include research into the cause, prevention, treatment and cure; education of the public; and information services to health care professionals. The group also helps set up chapters at the local level, advocates for improved public policy and legislation and provides patient and family service to help present and future victims and caregivers.

Through its national chapter and volunteer network, the association sponsors 1,600 support groups and other services for America's 4 million patients, families and caregivers.

The association publishes a quarterly *Alzheimer's Association Newsletter* for 650,000 concerned readers nationwide and produces educational brochures, books and publications for patients, family members and professionals.

Through its medical and scientific advisory board, the association promotes and funds research; its Autopsy Assistance Network helps families make the difficult decision about autopsy to confirm the diagnosis of Alzheimer's disease.

In addition to its Chicago headquarters, the association maintains an office in Washington, D.C. to ensure that the needs of patients and families are taken into consideration as legislation and public policy are developed. Each year the association presents Congress and the president with a National Program to Conquer Alzheimer's Disease.

For more information, contact the Alzheimer's Association, 919 North Michigan Avenue, Suite 1000, Chicago, IL 60611-1676; phone (312) 335-8700; fax (312) 335-1110; TTD (312) 335-8882. A nationwide 24-hour hotline—(800) 272-3900—provides information and referrals to local chapters.

Alzheimer's Association Autopsy Assistance Network, The A network designed to assist families with the difficult decision of autopsy, which is the only way to confirm the diagnosis of ALZHEIMER'S DISEASE (AD). The network provides families with information regarding autopsy and helps in obtaining a confirmed diagnosis. It also provides tissue for AD research and establishes diagnosis for the purpose of clinical and epidemiological studies. The network was established because families needed support and guidance in making the decision and planning for an autopsy.

There are two major reasons for autopsy. One is the ongoing research need for tissue. Also, to aid in more reliable studies and statistics on the prevalence of dementia, it is important that the cause of death be listed accurately on the death certificate.

The Alzheimer's Association Medical and Scientific Advisory Board recommends that the body organs of the patient with Alzheimer's disease *not* be donated for transplant purposes.

All states require a signed autopsy permit; in some states, it is possible to presign a permit, but the decision for brain autopsy must be confirmed verbally at the time of death. Permit forms are available from the pathologist or hospital. The pathologist will arrange the details of the autopsy.

Family members can expect a written autopsy report from the pathologist, neuropathologist or research center within a reasonable time after the patient's death.

Legally, the next of kin or guardian is the person to make the autopsy decision. If the spouse is deceased, the oldest child is considered next of kin. In instances where Alzheimer's disease is suspected, only the brain tissue is examined for diagnosis.

The autopsy is performed in the hospital, if that is where death occurs; if the patient dies in a nursing home, the pathologist will make other arrangements.

Alzheimer's disease The most common form of dementia in which cognitive functions are progressively lost. This fatal disorder affects the cells of the brain, producing intellectual impairment in up to 4 million Americans usually in the sixth decade of life; about 60,000 are between 40 and 60. The disease kills about 120,000 Americans each year and is the fourth leading cause of death among the elderly (behind heart disease, cancer and stroke).

About half of elderly men and women with severe intellectual impairment have Alzheimer's disease; another fourth suffer from vascular disorders (especially multiple strokes), and the rest have a variety of problems, including BRAIN TUMOR, abnormal thyroid function, infections, pernicious anemia, adverse drug reactions and abnormalities in the spinal fluid (hydrocephalus). A good diagnosis is important because all of these other disorders can be treated.

Alzheimer's disease, which is the most common of the more than 70 forms of dementia, is characterized by abnormal fibers in the CORTEX (or "gray matter"), which appear under the microscope as a tangle of filaments (NEUROFIBRILLARY TANGLES). These tangles were first described in 1906 by German neurologist Alois Alzheimer, M.D., who discovered them after performing an autopsy on the brain of a 55-year-old woman afflicted with dementia. Newer diagnostic techniques indicate there are other brain changes common in Alzheimer's disease, including groups of degenerated nerve endings in the cortex (called plaques) that disrupt the passage of electrochemical signals in the brain. The larger the number of plaques and tangles, the greater the disturbance in intellectual functioning and memory.

The early-onset form of the disease has been linked to genes on chromosomes 21 and 14; recently scientists at Duke University identified a cholesterol-processing gene pair called apolipoprotein E-type 4 (apoE-4) that carries a 90 percent risk of the disease by age 80. This gene is located on chromosome 19; a person may have up to two copies of the apoE-4 allele—and the more copies, the higher the risk of getting Alzheimer's, according to researchers. The more apoE-4 alleles, the earlier in life individuals are affected.

The gene is fairly common; 15 percent of the overall population has one apoE-4 allele, and 1 percent has two of the alleles. But not everyone with apoE-4 will develop the disease.

While researchers have made great strides in untangling the mystery, scientists still don't know how to prevent or cure Alzheimer's disease. Some scientists suspect that an imbalance between different kinds of apoE proteins may cause plaque formation. If Alzheimer's disease is related to a protein imbalance, it may be possible to alter diet or lower the protein that is too high.

The findings lead researchers to believe they will be able to develop a diagnostic tool that could screen for the gene, enabling counselors to make judgments about whether a person's likelihood of getting the disease is high or low, early or late. Researchers caution that their conclusions about the gene can be applied only to families where members have late-onset Alzheimer's, the most common form of the disease.

Symptoms   The disease can affect anyone, and because its symptoms vary from patient to patient, its course is impossible to predict. In the early stages, there is usually a kind of selective memory loss, often accompanied by some loss of previously well-established memory and a worsening short-term memory. The disease may last between three to 15 years before the patient dies.

There is a difference, however, between AGE-ASSOCIATED MEMORY IMPAIRMENT (AAMI) and Alzheimer's disease. AAMI may remain unchanged for years, but Alzheimer's disease is progressive, interfering with the normal activities of daily life. In addition, Alzheimer's disease affects more than memory; it affects the ability to use words, compute figures, solve problems and use reasoning and judgment. It also may result in changes in mood and personality.

Although Alzheimer's disease begins with signs of forgetfulness, it soon becomes a far more profound memory loss than simply misplacing keys or forgetting a name. The difference is this: If a patient misplaces his glasses, that's normal forgetfulness; if he can't remember that he *wears* glasses, it could be a sign of Alzheimer's.

Forgetfulness usually begins with the short-term memory, resulting in a tendency to forget recent events. The patient may neglect to turn off the oven, may recheck to see if jobs are done and may repeat already-answered questions. As the disease worsens, the signs become more pronounced. The patient's conversation becomes more and more senseless and judgment begins to be affected. The person may begin to wander from home and not be able to find the way back. Others get lost inside their own house.

As mental ability declines, daily activities become more difficult—and then impossible. Patients can't concentrate, and they begin to forget about bathing, dressing, brushing their teeth and shaving. Emotions begin to deteriorate as well, and patients become anxious, hostile and depressed.

Patients forget to eat, can't remember where or even who they are. They no longer recognize friends or members of their own family. They may hallucinate and become completely incapacitated and disoriented. Finally, Alzheimer's disease patients become incontinent and lose all verbal skills; at this point, deterioration is almost complete.

While the symptoms are progressive, there is a great deal of variation in the rate of change from person to person. Some patients may decline rapidly, but more commonly many months pass with little change. In later stages, the patient's immobility may result in pneumonia and other physical illnesses, shortening the remaining life expectancy by as much as one-half.

Etiology   Alzheimer's disease is a disorder of the brain that is linked to a gene pair in susceptible families, but why the plaques and fibers suddenly develop is not yet known. And while scientists have been able to identify the gene, they don't know why some people with the gene don't develop the disease and some do. However, it's not caused by hardening of the arteries or stress, and it's not contagious. A wide range of causes have been studied, although no conclusions have been reached.

In addition to the Alzheimer's gene, there is some evidence that some forms of the disease may be due to a "slow virus"; it's also possible that the disorder is caused by an accumulation of toxic metals in the brain or by the absence of certain kinds of brain chemicals.

Toxins   Research has found accumulated amounts of aluminum within the affected nerve cells of subjects having the classic neurofibrillary tangles of Alzheimer's disease. Other studies have shown high amounts of aluminum, iron and calcium in the brains of Chamorro natives of Guam who died of amyotrophic lateral sclerosis or parkinsonism dementia, both of which were previously suspected to be transmitted by a slow-acting virus. Now scientists wonder if there is a link between the Chamorros' environmental deficiency in calcium and magnesium and excess of aluminum and other metals. The studies are important because of the similarity between parkinsonism dementia and Alzheimer's disease.

Mercury, selenium, zinc and other elements also have been studied to see whether there is a link with Alzheimer's disease, but so far no proof has been found.

Other investigations are looking at excitotoxins, chemicals that overstimulate nerve cells to the point of killing them. Some excitotoxins are found in certain foods, such as the cycad seed eaten on the island of Guam; others occur naturally within the body. Under certain conditions, the neurotransmitters GLUTAMATE and aspartate (contained in the artificial sweetener ASPARTAME) can become toxic to nerve cells, although scientists do not yet know why.

Gene Defect   A wide range of studies have investigated links to particular genetic defects. In addition to the apoE-4 cholesterol-processing gene found on chromosome 19, which must be inherited from both parents in order to produce the disease, British researchers have identified a genetic defect associated with an inherited form of Alzheimer's disease that occurs in only a fraction of Alzheimer's patients.

The defect, located on chromosome 21, causes cells to insert a single incorrect amino acid while manufacturing a substance called amyloid precursor protein. In the British study, family members not affected by the disease and 100 unrelated, normal individuals from the local population lacked the genetic error. DNA analysis of 18 individuals with early-onset Alzheimer's in 16 other families revealed that two members of one family bore the same mutation. The finding adds fuel to the assumption that there are many underlying causes of Alzheimer's disease.

The link between chromosome 21 and Alzheimer's disease was discovered because nearly all people with Down's syndrome (who have a defect on the same chromosome) who live to their late 30s develop brain degeneration similar to that of Alzheimer's disease.

Other studies suggest that the gene for amyloid precursor protein (APP) is on chromosome 21, and a few cases of Alzheimer's disease are linked to a defective APP gene.

However, a large number of Alzheimer's disease patients have no family history of the disease; these sporadic cases suggest that there may be multiple factors influencing the development of the disease.

Chemical Abnormality All brain function depends on chemical messages transmitted from cell to cell by a carrier (or "neurotransmitter"). In Alzheimer's patients, scientists have identified a striking reduction of up to 90 percent in a brain enzyme called choline acetyltransferase, which is involved in the passage of nerve signals. In addition, scientists have found low levels of the neurotransmitter ACETYL-CHOLINE, important in the formation of memories in the same areas of the brain where plaques and tangles occur. This finding could have great value in potential treatment of the disease, since a problem in

chemical process rather than destruction of cells would be far easier to treat.

Research also has discovered that the disease affects other neurotransmitter systems. Some scientists are focusing on abnormal proteins—especially beta-amyloid, a major component of neuritic plaques. Beta-amyloid is a fragment of the normal protein APP; in Alzheimer's disease patients, an unknown malfunction cuts APP in an abnormal place, producing beta-amyloid. It is suggested that this beta-amyloid may have either growth-related or toxic effects on nerve cells. If doctors can block the steps that create these beta-amyloids, the progression of the disease may be halted.

Slow Virus Some researchers believe that the disease could be caused by a slow-acting virus producing symptoms years after a person is exposed. Unlike most viral diseases, however, Alzheimer's disease is not transmissible to animals, and it is not similar to other viral disease patterns. If it is caused by a virus, then, it is not a conventional one.

Other rare dementias are caused by unconventional viruses, including CREUTZFELDT-JAKOB DISEASE, kuru and Gerstmann-Straussler syndrome. Because these dementias have similar brain changes to Alzheimer's disease, scientists hope that studying them may reveal clues about how a slow-acting virus may play a role in brain disease.

Diagnosis With the discovery of the apoE-4 genetic pair in late-onset Alzheimer's disease, scientists believe they will be able to screen for the defect and predict with precision who will go on to develop the disease. Otherwise, the only way to make a definite diagnosis is by examining brain tissue at autopsy, looking for the characteristic tangles and plaques. A probable diagnosis can be up to 90 percent accurate when performed by experienced physicians and specialists.

Before a diagnosis of Alzheimer's disease is made, other diseases must be ruled out. It must be clear that the memory problems are not the result of mild, occasional forgetfulness caused by normal aging. Depression, which can affect memory, also must be ruled out. Any patient suspected of having Alzheimer's disease should have physical, neurological and psychiatric tests.

Brain imaging can take a picture of the brain without resorting to surgery. Some techniques include computerized tomography (CT scan), electroencephalography, PET (positron emission tomography) and SPECT (single photon emission computed tomography).

Occasionally special studies of the spinal fluid are required for a diagnosis. Blood studies, including tests for detecting several metabolic disorders, must be ordered as part of the evaluation.

If other diseases have been ruled out, a diagnosis of Alzheimer's disease usually can be made based on medical history, mental status and the course of the illness. An electroencephalogram may show a general slowing of the brain waves that may help confirm the presence of Alzheimer's disease. Periodic neurological exams and psychological testing help evaluate the progress of the disease.

Risk Factors   Age is the most clearly established risk factor; most victims of Alzheimer's disease are over 65. Family history is another risk factor; many studies show that those with relatives with Alzheimer's disease are more likely to develop the disease than someone with no family history. Other potential risk factors include toxins, head injury and gender.

Treatment   As yet, doctors can neither prevent nor cure Alzheimer's disease, although it's possible to ease some of the symptoms. It is imperative that the patient be under the care of a physician (a gerontologist, psychiatrist, internist or family physician) who can consult with a neurologist.

Other treatments target behavioral problems, including anxiety, aggression, wandering, depression and sleep problems. While no drug yet has been found that will cure the disease, judicious use of tranquilizers can lessen anxiety, agitation and unpredictable behavior, improve sleeping patterns and treat depression.

Recent trends in behavioral management are moving away from the use of drugs and focusing on nondrug management, including better environmental design, patient monitoring systems, organized activities and programs tailored to individual needs. Proper nutrition is very important, although special diets usually are not needed.

Most drugs being tested today in the treatment of the disease try to treat the cognitive symptoms, including memory loss, confusion and problems in learning, speech and reasoning. A number of these drugs are being tested in multicenter clinical trials in the United States, but the first-ever drug approved for use with Alzheimer's disease is called tacrine, or THA (tetrahydroamainoacridine; trade name: Cognex). Although tacrine is not a cure, it has proved to have some effect on Alzheimer's devastating symptoms. In two trials it has shown to provide small but meaningful improvement in memory and reasoning ability for some patients suffering from mild to moderate Alzheimer's disease. Tacrine blocks the function of enzymes that normally break down excess acetylcholine, making more of the neurotransmitter available to brain cells.

Its manufacturer, Warner-Lambert Co. of Morris Plains, New Jersey began selling the drug in late 1993. It costs about $1,500 a year.

Other drug researchers are excited about a substance called hyperzine A, a chemical found in a type of tea brewed with club moss (Huperzia serrata) that for hundreds of years the Chinese have insisted improved memory. Chemists at the Mayo Clinic in Jacksonville, Florida have been studying hyperzine A, a potent and selective acetylcholinesterase inhibitor. Acetylcholinesterase is an enzyme that breaks down acetylcholine, a key chemical messenger in the brain involved in awareness and memory; an acetylcholinesterase inhibitor interferes with this acetylcholine-harming chemical. Like the drug tacrine, hyperzine A prevents acetylcholinesterase from breaking down acetylcholine, thus raising levels of acetylcholine in the brain and improving memory. Researchers say that hyperzine A is a more effective, more specific agent than tacrine; drug companies are seeking permission from the Food and Drug Administration to test the compound on humans in 1994.

Other experimental strategies include the use of certain substances such as an infusion of the hormone NERVE GROWTH FACTOR directly into the brain; this hormone is found in healthy brains but is deficient in Alzheimer's patients. In the treatment, a catheter is surgically implanted under the skin and scalp, leading into a hole drilled in the skull to allow a catheter tip to enter the brain. The catheter infuses the drug directly into the brain at a set rate from a refillable pump implanted under the skin in the abdomen. The pump is powered by a battery that lasts about two years. Tissue transplants also may stimulate nerve cell growth.

While it's helpful if patients can continue a daily routine and be encouraged to do a little more than they feel can be done, when the condition becomes severe, a special setting with professional staff and full-time care may be required.

Dean, Ward, Morgenthaler, John, and Fowkes, Steven. *Smart Drugs II: The Next Generation.* Menlo Park, CA: Health Freedom Publications, 1993.

Mace, Nancy, and Rabins, Peter. *The 36-Hour Day: A Guide to Caring for Persons with Alzheimer's Disease and Related Dementing Illnesses.* Baltimore: Johns Hopkins University Press, 1991.

Wuethrich, B. "Higher Risk of Alzheimer's Linked to Gene." *Science News* 144, no. 7 (August 14, 1993): 108.

Alzheimer's Disease and Related Disorders Association   Former name of the ALZHEIMER'S ASSOCIATION.

Alzheimer's disease in youth   While the disease is generally thought of as an older person's problem, Alzheimer's disease (AD) can strike those in their 30s, 40s or 50s. The behavioral symptoms are the same no matter when the disease strikes, but the younger patient with AD *is* different.

Younger patients may have more problems expressing thoughts and feel even more frustration at the situation. In addition, while the symptoms may be noticed, they will often be confused with psychiatric disorders or thought of as some sort of "midlife crisis." This preconceived idea that AD is an "old person's disease" may lead even the physician to disregard AD as a possible diagnosis. In this event, a second opinion should be obtained from a physician who is familiar with the diagnosis of dementia-type illnesses.

Families are encouraged to seek legal advice as soon as possible after receiving a diagnosis; this is even more important for the family of younger patients, because of the possibility of children still living at home.

While a person with AD finds that friendships often fade away as the disease progresses, younger patients may find friends breaking away even sooner because they are faced with the reality that AD can strike someone their own age.

The Alzheimer's Association provides a brochure, "Dealing with the Younger Alzheimer's Patient," that describes expected changes in the younger patient's physical and emotional behavior. For a free copy or for referral to a family support group, the association can be called: (800) 272-3900.

Alzheimer's Disease Research Center Program   The National Institute of Aging currently funds 12 Alzheimer's Disease Research Centers in a program designed to understand the disorder's etiology and treatment.

Each center serves as the site for new, expanded studies of the basic clinical and behavioral aspects of Alzheimer's disease. The centers also train scientists and health care professionals new to the field and serve as the link between research and the public. Centers include Duke University, Mt. Sinai School of Medicine, Harvard Medical School/Mass. General Hospital, University of California at San Diego, The Johns Hopkins Medical Institutions, University of Kentucky, University of Pittsburgh, University of Southern California, Case Western Reserve University, University of Washington, Washington University and University of Texas, Southwestern Medical Center.

aminergic   Those neurons that use an amine as neurotransmitter (a catecholamine such as norepinephrine). (See NEURON.)

amino acids   Any organic acids containing one or more amino groups. Amino acids are integral parts of proteins and are precursors of brain NEUROTRANSMITTERS.

amnesia   A memory disorder featuring the loss of the ability to memorize and/or to recall information. In most cases of amnesia, the storage of information in long-term memory and/or the recall of this information is impaired.

In many types of amnesia, the patient experiences a gap in memory extending back for some time from the moment of onset of the cause (usually a head injury). Called RETROGRADE AMNESIA, this is principally a deficit of recall, which usually shrinks over time. In addition, a patient may not be able to store information right after damaging the brain; this resulting gap in memory is called ANTEROGRADE AMNESIA. It extends from the onset of amnesia to the time when long-term memory resumes. This gap in memory is usually permanent.

Many theories explain the underlying mechanism of amnesia. It can be caused by damage from a head injury (including concussion) in areas that are concerned with memory function (TRAUMATIC AMNESIA). Other possible causes include degenerative disorders such as ALZHEIMER'S DISEASE or other DEMENTIA, infections (such as encephalitis [see ENCEPHALITIS AND MEMORY]) or a thiamine deficiency in alcoholics leading to KORSAKOFF'S SYNDROME. Amnesia with an organic basis also could be caused by a BRAIN TUMOR, STROKE or a SUBARACHNOID HEMORRHAGE, or certain types of mental illness for which there is no apparent physical damage.

Transient Global Amnesia   This type of uncommon amnesia refers to an abrupt loss of memory from a few seconds to a few hours without loss of consciousness or other impairment. During the amnesia period, the victim cannot store new experiences and suffers a permanent memory gap for the time of the amnesic episode.

There also may be a loss of memory encompassing many years prior to the amnesia attack; this retrograde memory loss gradually disappears, although it leaves a permanent gap in memory that does not usually extend backward more than an hour before onset of the attack. Attacks of transient global amnesia, which may occur more than once, are believed to be caused by a temporary reduction in blood supply in certain brain areas. Sometimes they act as a warning sign for an impending stroke.

The attacks, which usually strike healthy, middle-age victims, may be set off by many things, including sudden temperature changes, stress, eating a large meal or even sexual intercourse. While several toxic substances have been associated with transient global amnesia, it is believed that the attacks are usually caused by a brief loss of blood flow to regions of the brain involved in memory.

Posthypnotic Amnesia   Amnesia also may occur after HYPNOSIS either spontaneously or by instruction, leaving the memory of a hypnotic trance vague and unclear, much the way a person remembers a dream upon awakening. If a hypnotized subject is told that she will remember nothing upon awakening, she will experience a much more profound posthypnotic amnesia. However, if the patient is rehypnotized and given a countersuggestion, she will awaken and remember everything; therefore, experts believe the phenomenon of posthypnotic amnesia is clearly psychogenic.

The amnesia may include all the events of the trance state or only selected items—or it may occur in matters unrelated to the trance. Memory for experiences during the hypnotic state also may return (even after a suggestion to forget) if the subject is persistently questioned after awakening. This observation led Sigmund Freud to search for repressed memories in his patients without the use of hypnosis.

Psychogenic Amnesia   Several types of amnesia belong in a different class from those caused by injury or disease; called PSYCHOGENIC AMNESIAS, they are induced by hypnotic suggestion or occur spontaneously in reaction to acute conflict or stress (usually called hysterical). They also may extend to basic knowledge learned in school (such as mathematic), which never occurs in organic amnesia unless there is an accompanying aphasia or dementia. These types of amnesia are completely reversible, although they have never been fully explained.

In one type of MIXED AMNESIA, organic factors may also be involved in the development of psychogenic amnesia, and an accurate diagnosis may be difficult. This complex intermingling of a true organic memory defect with psychogenic factors can prolong or reinforce the memory loss. It is quite common for a brain-damaged patient to experience a hysterical reaction in addition to brain problems. For example, one patient who developed a severe amnesia that impaired the formation of new memories after CARBON MONOXIDE POISONING went on to develop a HYSTERICAL AMNESIA that continued to sustain the memory loss.

In psychogenic amnesia, there is no fundamental impairment in the memory process, registration or retention—the problem lies in accessing stored or repressed (usually painful) memories. This inability to recall painful memories is a protection against bringing into consciousness ideas associated with profound loss or fear, rage or shame.

Usually psychogenic amnesia can be treated successfully by procedures such as hypnosis. Under traumatic conditions, memories can become detached from personal identity, making recall impossible. Modern accounts of hysterical amnesia have been heavily influenced by Sigmund Freud, who attributed it to a need to repress information injurious to the ego.

Freud believed that the memory produces a defense reaction for the individual's own good. This explains why psychogenic amnesia occurs only in the wake of trauma and is consistent with the high incidence of depression and other psychiatric disorders in those who go on to develop psychogenic memory problems.

There are four types of recall problems following trauma: *localized amnesia, selective amnesia, generalized amnesia* and *continuous amnesia.*

Localized amnesia: The failure to recall all the events during a certain period of time (usually the first few hours after a disturbing event).

Selective amnesia: The failure to recall some, but not all, of the events during a certain period of time.

Generalized amnesia: The inability to recall any events from a person's entire life.

Continuous amnesia: Failure to recall events subsequent to a specific time, up to and including the present. (See also ALCOHOL AND MEMORY; AMNESIA, CHILDHOOD; AMNESIA AND CRIME; AMNESIC SYNDROME; ANESTHESIA, MEMORY WHILE UNDER; ANTERIOR COMMUNICATING ARTERY ANEURYSM AMNESIA; BLACKOUTS, ALCOHOLIC; BRAIN SURGERY AND MEMORY; CAPGRAS SYNDROME; CHOLINERGIC BASAL FOREBRAIN; CONFABULATION; DIENCEPHALON; DISSOCIA-

TIVE DISORDERS; DRUG ABUSE AND MEMORY; ELECTROCONVULSIVE THERAPY AND MEMORY; EMOTION AND MEMORY; ENCEPHALITIS AND MEMORY; EPILEPSY; FUGUE; KLUVER-BUCY SYNDROME; KORSAKOFF'S SYNDROME; MEDIAL TEMPORAL AMNESIA; MEMORY, DISORDERS OF; SCOPOLAMINE; SOURCE AMNESIA; TRAUMATIC AMNESIA.)

amnesia, childhood The lack of memories of early childhood (usually before age four in most people). Sigmund Freud believed that repression of infantile sexuality caused this early amnesia. But many modern memory researchers believe it occurs because of a child's lack of sophisticated mental abilities, such as language, which are used to cue memory. (See also FREUD, SIGMUND; MEMORY IN INFANCY.)

amnesia, normal See AMNESIA, CHILDHOOD.

amnesia, simulated A condition related to PSEUDODEMENTIA in which head-injured victims awaiting settlement of compensation claims exaggerate the extent of their memory defect in a bid for higher compensation. It is very difficult to detect malingering, and clinicians must rely on common sense and intuition for a proper diagnosis. (See also PSYCHOGENIC AMNESIA.)

amnesia and crime According to research, between 23 and 65 percent of murderers claim to have amnesia related to their crime. A great deal of amnesia for crime has a psychogenic origin; that is, the crimes are so horrific that the criminal must not remember in order to remain sane.

But not all criminal amnesia is of a self-protective nature; some criminals do not remember their crimes because they have schizophrenia or depression. In these cases, their amnesia may be an intrinsic part of their illness. In addition, many violent crimes are committed by alcoholics during "blackouts." During such a blackout, the person is not unconscious or stuporous—just drunk. (See also BLACKOUTS, ALCOHOLIC.)

If a defendant claims amnesia for the crime with which he is charged, it could be argued that he is unfit for trial or that he can plead "automatism." This means that the behavior was carried out involuntarily and without conscious intent. Crimes committed during an alcoholic blackout are not included in this plea, since it is assumed that people are aware of the effects of alcohol and are therefore responsible for their actions while drunk.

Amnesia for a crime may be a form of emotional defense that arises after the crime has been committed; this does not therefore imply a lack of conscious involvement during the amnesic period itself.

No cases have been found in which a defendant was acquitted due to an organic amnesic state.

Parkin, Alan. *Memory and Amnesia.* Oxford: Basil Blackwell, 1987.

amnesic syndrome A permanent, global disorder of memory following brain damage from accident or illness that does not result in a general deterioration of memory function, but selectively impairs some aspects of memory while leaving others normal.

For example, patients with this syndrome score very badly on clinical memory tests but perform normally on intelligence tests, such as the Wechsler Adult Intelligence Scale. Therefore, a person with amnesic syndrome will have a memory quotient (MQ) between 20 to 40 points below the IQ. In particular, these patients score very poorly on tests of the retention of novel information (such as paired-associate learning or free recall), but they have no problem understanding a normal-length sentence—they just can't remember it for any length of time. Skills learned before the onset of the syndrome, such as riding a bike or driving, are unaffected.

The amnesic syndrome can be caused by lesions in two distinct parts of the brain: the DIENCEPHALON and the MEDIAL TEMPORAL LOBE of the CORTEX. Damage can be caused by a wide range of problems, including disease, neurosurgery, BRAIN TUMOR or HEAD INJURY, STROKE and deprivation of oxygen (ANOXIA). It also may be caused by a TRANSIENT ISCHEMIC ATTACK (TIA) that briefly blocks blood flow to the HIPPOCAMPUS.

Kra, Siegfried. *Aging Myths.* New York: McGraw-Hill, 1986.

amusia The loss of the ability to comprehend or reproduce musical tones.

amygdala A part of the brain lying within each temporal lobe that is important for memory; its primary function may well be its responsibility for bringing emotional content to memory.

Sensory stimulation from the cortical area enters the limbic system directly through the amygdala and indirectly through the hippocampus via the entorhinal cortex. Lesions to the hippocampus and entorhinal cortex lead to mild memory impairment; lesions to the amygdala and entorhinal cortex produce devastating impairment.

Researchers suggest that associative recall is established through a mechanism that requires information to be carried from the limbic system back to the sensory system—a process mediated by the amygdaloid complex. In some studies animals were required to associate an object with the location in which it first appeared; only those with an intact hippocampus were able to complete the task. This suggests, scientists say, that the hippocampus serves an associative function with regard to spatial memory.

Some researchers believe that when a perception reaches the cerebral cortex, it will be stored within the amygdala if it arouses emotions (such as fear of a dog)—but other experts disagree.

While most now believe the amygdala does not process memory, it is believed to be a source of emotions that imbue memory with meaning. For example, often the remembrance of a memory or a whole stream of recollection brings with it a burst of emotion—evidence that the amygdala has become involved. (See also HIPPOCAMPUS; MEMORY.)

amytal See SODIUM AMYTAL.

anemia A condition in which the concentration of the oxygen-carrying pigment hemoglobin in the blood is below normal. Hemoglobin molecules travel inside red blood cells and carry oxygen from the lungs to the tissues. In severe cases, anemia cuts down on the amount of oxygen carried by the blood, which cuts the amount available to the brain. Memory problems can result.

By far the most common form of anemia is caused by a deficiency of iron, an essential component of hemoglobin. But there also are many other causes of anemia, which is not a disease in itself but a symptom of many other disorders.

Normal blood hemoglobin concentrations are between 14 to 16 grams (g) per 100 milliliters (ml) for men and 12 to 14 g/100 ml for women. Concentrations below 10 can cause headaches, tiredness and lethargy. Concentrations below 8 can cause breathing problems on exercise, dizziness, heart palpitations and angina, and memory problems. Symptoms also depend on how quickly the anemia develops—its sudden development causes immediate symptoms, depending on the degree of blood loss.

Treatment, which will restore the memory to normal function, is aimed at correcting the underlying disorder.

anesthesia See ANESTHESIA, MEMORY WHILE UNDER.

anesthesia, memory while under Some anesthetized patients may comprehend enough of what is said during surgery to affect their recovery. Language understanding may continue while a person is anesthetized even though explicit recall does not.

Nearly all adequate anesthetics produce an AMNESIA that prohibits any recall of memory during surgery; at the same time, auditory function is the last sense to fade under anesthesia. When unexpected recall occurs after surgery with an apparently adequate anesthesia, it usually involves memories for meaningful events that are recalled.

Recent research has found that anesthetized patients recover faster when given positive suggestions. One group was told that they would "want to get out of bed to help your body recover earlier." According to British researchers, this group actually did recover earlier, with fewer complications than a comparison group. However, not all studies have reached the same conclusions, and some physicians are skeptical. While the effects may be subtle, researchers also warn that thoughtless remarks may have very profound consequences.

If patients do not receive sufficient oxygen during anesthesia, they can experience memory disturbances. Even under perfect conditions, memory disturbances may linger for several days after surgery until the medications are eliminated from the system. (See also "FAT LADY" SYNDROME.)

aneurysm   An abnormal dilatation of an artery or a vein that fills with blood. It is caused by pressure of the blood flowing through an area weakened by disease, injury or a defect in the artery or vein wall.

angiography   A test in which the blood vessels of the brain are filled with a radioactive medium, allowing a physician to detect circulatory abnormalities by X ray.

Angiography is used to detect diseases that change the appearance of the blood vessel, including ANEURYSMS (weakening or ballooning of the vessel walls), blockage from fatty deposits or clots. It also is used

to view the pattern of blood vessels that lead to tumors.

Carotid angiography is sometimes performed on patients suffering from TRANSIENT ISCHEMIC ATTACKS (brief symptoms of stroke) to check for a narrowing in one of the carotid arteries in the neck, which supply blood to the brain. *Cerebral angiography* can locate an aneurysm within the brain or help outline a BRAIN TUMOR prior to surgery. In *digital subtraction angiography,* computers are used to process images and remove unwanted background information, leaving only the image of the blood vessels being studied. This procedure requires a much smaller amount of contrast medium, which makes it safer.

In angiography, a contrast medium is usually injected into the vessel through a thin catheter inserted into the femoral artery in the groin or the carotid arteries in the neck. While the physician watches on an X-ray monitor, he or she guides the tip of the catheter into the vessel to be examined and injects a contrast medium. Angiography may take only a few minutes, or it can last up to three hours.

Often the contrast medium feels warm to the patient. Some patients, however, may exhibit an allergic reaction, although the risk of a serious reaction is less than one in 80,000. Digital angiography substantially reduces the risks because the catheter does not need to be passed as far into the blood vessels.

Angiography also can be used to treat, not just diagnose, disorders. Small balloons can be inflated at the tip of a catheter to expand a narrowed or blocked segment of artery (balloon angioplasty), or foreign material can be injected to shut off blood supply to a tumor. In addition, drugs can be infused directly into the blood supply to individual organs.

animal magnetism   See MESMERISM.

animal memory   Not all animals possess a memory in the sense that humans do.

Animals farther down on the evolutionary ladder possess a rudimentary perceptive memory, genetically programmed to help them survive, but a productive memory that depends on recall developed later in animal evolution.

Ants, for example, live a deceptively complex life of rigid job descriptions and interrelated socialization patterns, but they are unable to recognize each other based on a memory of past experience. Instead, they make sure of chemical signals to identify each other; they live their busy little lives based entirely on the way they interpret smells. By extracting a chemical that would normally identify larvae and attaching the chemical to fake larvae, scientists were able to prove that ants could not distinguish fakes from real larvae. To an ant, if it smells like larvae, it is larvae, and ants have no ability to adapt to any other circumstance or possibility.

Birds are farther along, evolutionarily speaking. While they are still largely guided by inborn instincts, they also are able to adapt to their circumstances using recognition based on memory. If a scientist moves eggs from one nest to another, birds can recognize their own eggs and reclaim them: The bird's past experience molds its present behavior. This is the difference between recognition based on memory and identification based on genetically programmed instinct.

Higher animals, however, rely on the adaptive value of the memory to an even greater degree. An elephant stuck in quicksand will, once freed, always remember the danger of quicksand and avoid it. This type of memory based on recognition is memory of the highest order; many animals are not capable of it, and scientists have yet to be able to program any computer to recognize other objects. Animals without such memory cannot adapt their behavior to changing circumstances; their adaptation relies only on natural selection.

aniracetam   One of a class of nootropic drugs that some studies suggest may be capable of improving cognitive performance on a number of intelligence and memory tests. (See NOOTROPICS.) Its chemical structure is similar to PIRACETAM, a drug being investigated in the treatment of Alzheimer's disease.

Aniracetam's mechanism of action is unknown, although it does not seem to act directly on the catecholamine, serotonin or acetylcholine neurotransmitter systems.

Aniracetam is not approved for distribution in any country. Other names for aniracetam include Draganon, RO 13-5057 and Sarpul.

Cumin, R., et al. "Effects of the Novel Compound Aniracetam Upon Impaired Learning and Memory in Rodents." *Psychopharmacology* 78 (1982): 104–11.
Vincent, G., Verderese, A., and Gamzu, E. "The Effects of Aniracetam on the Enhancement and Protection of Memory." *Annals of the New York Academy of Sciences* 444 (1985): 489–91.

Anna O   A young Viennese woman and hysteric patient in the late 19th century whose real name was Bertha Pappenheim. She was called Anna O by Josef Breuer and Sigmund Freud, who described her treatment in their book *Studies on Hysteria*.

Anna O was treated by Breuer from 1880 to 1882 for a range of psychosomatic problems and dissociative absences. Freud learned about her case after her treatment by Breuer, but her case led him to the technique of letting patients talk about their problems.

Breuer and Freud did not agree on the fundamental cause of dissociative absences. Breuer insisted they were a form of autohypnosis, while Freud believed they served as a defense mechanism, a protection against harmful thoughts.

Anna O was quite hypnotizable and excellent at self-hypnosis, and Breuer hypnotized her almost daily for hours at a time. Before the onset of her hysteria, she had often hallucinated an alternate world she called her private theater, a fairy-tale world in which she lived her life. If her father had not contracted a fatal case of tuberculosis, she might have spent the rest of her life in her dream world, but she was called upon to stay alert and nurse her father.

Although a bright, energetic woman, her culture expected her to live a life of quiet self-denial. She spent her time tending her dying father, never revealing any emotion and never earning a respite from her duties. Yet despite her resentment, she did not rebel openly. Her father's illness brought about a crisis in her life; she could no longer retreat into her private world, but she couldn't bear her new life, either. First, she experienced a hysterical cough while hearing an orchestra playing as she tended her father. She wished she could be at the party, and then immediately felt guilty for wanting to dance while her father lay dying. She coughed instead and continued to cough whenever she heard music. She had altered her emotional memory; she associated music with happiness, but then remembered her father and despised her wish for fun, changing the association with music.

After six months, she retreated to her bed, where she alternated between consciousness and dissociation. During conscious periods, she seemed normal except that she stayed in bed and exhibited a variety of odd behaviors—speaking only English, coughing when hearing music, and hating water. When she retreated into her dream world, she lost the abilities of recognition and perception. She did not see or hear people, although Breuer could break through to her and maintain contact by steady speech. Anna did not, however, perceive strangers.

When Breuer brought a colleague to see her, she did not perceive him, and recognized that there was another person in the room only when he blew cigar smoke at her. She looked for the source of smoke, saw the stranger and ran.

Eventually Anna O recovered apparently on her own, although her changed circumstances helped. (Her father died and she entered a sanitarium where she had no responsibilities.) While Breuer's intensive therapy relieved some of her symptoms, she developed others, and when he stopped her treatment she was no better than when she had begun two years before. Many more years passed before she was healthy, but eventually she became an important figure in Austria's feminist movement.

Anna O's case shows that emotional memory failures don't need to have an objective cause—they can be related to a patient's own perceptions. While Breuer could attempt to treat her symptoms, he couldn't address the inequities of Viennese society. (See also BREUER, JOSEF; FREUD, SIGMUND.)

anosognosia   A type of AGNOSIA in which people can't recognize that they are ill because they can't make the connection between the fact of symptoms and the perception "I'm ill."

anoxia   The complete absence of oxygen within the brain (or other body tissue). This loss of oxygen causes a disruption of cell metabolism and can be fatal to the cell unless it is corrected within a few minutes. Anoxia is very rare; hypoxia (the *reduction* of oxygen to a tissue) is far more common.

antagonist   A drug that reduces or blocks the action of another drug. For example, LEUPEPTIN blocks the neurotransmitter CALPAIN by competing with it for receptor sites in the brain. (See NEUROTRANSMITTERS.) By occupying these sites, leupeptin prevents calpain from binding to the receptors and exerting its effects.

anterior communicating artery   A short artery located in the forebrain that connects the two anterior arteries of each hemisphere. Aneurysms often occur along this artery; when they burst, AMNESIA develops. (See also ANTERIOR COMMUNICATING ARTERY ANEURYSM.)

anterior communicating artery aneurysm   An aneurysm on the anterior communicating artery. When this type of aneurysm bursts, it leads to AMNESIA. While experts are not sure of the location of the critical aneurysm, both the frontal association neocortex and the cholinergic basal forebrain may be affected. The symptoms also may vary, both in the extent of the frontal symptoms and the degree of amnesia. (See also ANTERIOR COMMUNICATING ARTERY.)

anterograde amnesia   A loss of the ability to learn, featuring very poor recall and recognition of recently presented information. This is contrasted with RETROGRADE AMNESIA, which is the very poor recall and recognition of information that was acquired before brain damage occurred. (See also AMNESIA.)

anticholinergics and memory   Anticholinergics are a group of ACETYLCHOLINE-blocking drugs that are used to treat irritable bowel syndrome and certain types of urinary incontinence, Parkinson's disease, asthma and other diseases. They also have a reputation as amnesic drugs.

These drugs act as antagonists to the actions of cholinergic nerve fibers (or cells), usually of the parasympathetic nervous system. These cholinergic nerve cells are those that use acetylcholine as their neurotransmitter. Drugs that have anticholinergic effects block the transmission of this neurotransmitter, preventing the communication between nerve cells and altering behavior. Most psychoactive drugs have anticholinergic effects in both the central and the peripheral nervous systems.

Depending on the dose, the anticholinergics SCOPOLAMINE, atropine and glycopyrrolate all can produce sedation and lack of vigilance. The most famous of the memory-clouding anticholinergics is SCOPOLAMINE, a belladonna alkaloid that is a particularly potent amnesic agent. Other anticholinergics include heterocyclic antidepressants, antipsychotics, antihistamines, antiparkinsonian drugs and some hypnotics.

Research studies suggest that after a patient has received an anticholinergic drug, memory retention remains intact but effortful retrieval is impaired. It is believed that the neurochemical processes disrupted by these drugs are not involved in maintaining information in memory; rather they control the encoding process, which leads to a deficiency of retrieval.

If a patient takes several of these drugs together—or takes too many of any one kind—the combination can cause a crisis called the anticholinergic syndrome. Symptoms of this include dry mouth, constipation, urinary retention, decreased sweating, fever, flushing, discoordination, tachycardia, confusion, delirium, disorientation, agitation, visual and auditory hallucinations, anxiety, restlessness, pseudoseizures and delusions. Treatment for anticholinergic syndrome is anticholinesterase therapy.

antidiuretic hormone (ADH)   See VASOPRESSIN.

anxiety and memory   Anxiety—the feeling of uneasiness, apprehension or dread—is one of the major causes of memory problems at any age. When anxiety becomes pronounced, it monopolizes a person's attention so that it is impossible to concentrate on anything else. Because the formation of memory is dependent on paying attention, anything that interferes with attention will impair memory.

Anxiety attacks can affect memory. These attacks are a pervasive feeling of anxiety not associated with anything in particular. In fact, this is how most definitions distinguish anxiety from fear, which usually has an object. In the midst of an anxiety attack, the sufferer withdraws from the exterior world and turns inward, focusing on internal turmoil. This is why the person fails to record information the way he or she normally would. When the thought processes are occupied exclusively with negative thoughts, there is no room for other thoughts that could cue memory.

Experts suggest that anxious patients tell themselves "I'm going to calm down and pay strict attention if I want to remember this." Together with relaxation techniques such as deep breathing, this should help calm anxiety enough to facilitate encoding and recall.

aphasia A neurological condition in which the previously acquired capacity for language comprehension or expression is disturbed due to brain dysfunction that affects the ability to speak and write and/or the ability to comprehend and read. *Aphasia* is a complete absence of these communication and comprehension skills, while *dysphasia* is merely a disturbance in these abilities. A stroke or head injury is the most common cause of brain damage leading to aphasia.

The speech expression problems found in aphasia are different from those problems caused by disease or damage to the parts of the body involved in the mechanics of speech; comprehension problems are not due to hearing or vision difficulties.

Language skills within the brain lie in the dominant cerebral hemisphere; two areas in this hemisphere (Broca's and Wernicke's areas) and the pathways connecting the two are important in language skills. Damage to these areas is the most common cause of aphasia. Other disabilities that may occur with aphasia include AGRAPHIA (writing difficulty) or ALEXIA (word blindness).

While there may be some recovery from aphasia after a stroke or head injury, the more severe the aphasia, the less chance for improvement. Speech therapy is the main remedy.

Broca's Aphasia While aphasia is a general term covering loss of language ability, there are different ways of classifying its various forms. In BROCA'S APHASIA, the patient has very disturbed speech and will often experience some comprehension problems. Speech is nonfluent, slow, labored, with a loss of normal rhythm.

Wernicke's Aphasia In WERNICKE'S (RECEPTIVE) APHASIA, the patient has fluent speech but the contents are often meaningless because of poor comprehension. There are often many errors in word selection and grammar, indicating that internal speech also is impaired. Writing may be disturbed too, and spoken or written commands usually are not understood.

Global Aphasia A patient with GLOBAL APHASIA exhibits total or near-total inability to speak, write or understand spoken or written words. The aphasia usually is caused by widespread damage to the dominant cerebral hemisphere.

Nominal Aphasia NOMINAL APHASIA is difficulty in naming objects or in finding words, although the person may be able to choose the correct name from several offered. Nominal aphasia may be caused by generalized cerebral dysfunction or damage to specific language areas. (See also APRAXIA.)

aplysia A sea slug (more accurately, sea hare) about the size of a human fist used in the study of memory and learning because of its relatively simple nervous system. This marine invertebrate contains fewer than 2×10^4 neurons; many of them are very large and can be seen with the naked eye. Sea slugs have no brain in the traditional sense; a collection of ganglia (or "subbrains") controls their functions.

apraxia Loss of previous ability to perform skilled motor acts that can't be explained by weakness, abnormal muscle tone or uncoordination. In this neurological condition patients fail to carry out skilled voluntary movements in the absence of paralysis or any defect in the peripheral muscles.

Apraxia is caused by damage to nerve tracts within the main mass of the brain (cerebrum) that translates the *idea* for a movement *into* that movement. While most patients with apraxia seem to know what they want to do, they seem to have lost the ability to recall from memory the sequence of actions they need to do to achieve the movement. A direct head injury, infection, stroke or brain tumor may have caused the damaged cerebrum.

There are several different types of apraxia, depending on which part of the brain has been damaged. A patient suffering from *ideomotor apraxia* can't carry out a spoken command to make a particular movement but at another time can be observed making those very same movements unconsciously. Other special forms of apraxia include AGRAPHIA (difficulty writing) and expressive APHASIA (severe difficulty in speaking).

Because recovery after stroke or brain injury differs widely from one patient to another, it is difficult to predict the recovery from any accompanying apraxia. In general, however, some deficit remains and the patient may need considerable patience and effort to relearn past skills. (See also ALEXIA; DYSPHASIA.)

Aquinas, St. Thomas (1225?–1274)

The patron saint of MNEMONICS, this Italian scholastic philosopher was instrumental in making the trained memory a devotional and ethical art. During the Middle Ages, monks and philosophers were the only people who used trained-memory techniques, which were basic to some religions as a way to reach heaven and avoid hell.

Aquinas was truly talented at the art. As a boy, he could remember word for word everything his priests taught him, and as a young man he confounded Pope Urban by compiling a compendium of writing by church fathers from memory.

Today the memory system he used has been lost, but his belief in the value of images has survived. Most people in the Middle Ages believed that images and everything else connected with the senses, the body and the natural world were dangerous and evil. But St. Thomas stood alone in praising the senses, explaining that people needed imagery to solidify their memories and discharge their ethical duty of keeping alive the memory of heaven, hell and church teachings. In fact, not only did he permit images—he advised his flock to cultivate them.

Aristotle (384 B.C.–321 B.C.)

Author of a lost book on MNEMOTECHNICS, this Greek scientist and philosopher believed that thinking takes place in the head, but memory resides in the heart. Although his teacher, Plato, believed that the mind was separate from the body, Aristotle was convinced that both thought and memory resided somewhere within the body. In fact, he was echoing a Chinese belief already thousands of years old at that point—the Chinese ideograph for "remember" and "memory" are the same as "heart."

The key to his belief lay in the fact that he did not feel it was possible to think without mental images. He advocated the construction of complex "memory palaces" as a way of remembering everything that had to be learned by heart. Aristotle is credited with formulating the idea of association—that if one imagines a house and associates a piece of information with a part of that house, one can start in any room and move in either direction, effortlessly calling up more and more information.

Aristotle believed that imagination and memory occupy the same place in the mind, and their strength to hold on to sense impressions is very important—because he believed that the only way we learn is through the senses. He taught that memory could be divided into two parts. One type, common to all animals, he called memory, and a second, superior action peculiar to humans he called recall or reminiscence. This "reminiscence" involved a sense of time, deliberation and the relationship of a chain of experiences to a present experience.

Aristotle went on to explain the mechanics of memory, coming up with four kinds of association he thought would stimulate memory: things near each other (such as sky and horizon), things that happen at the same time (birth and pain), things that are similar (snow and water skis) and things in contrast (young and old).

He drilled his students in the art of memory for one primary reason: to win debates. He knew that linked images will come to mind automatically in a forceful progression as an argument progresses. Therefore, he taught his students to create memory palaces and people the rooms of these imaginary edifices with all the thoughts and information they needed to memorize.

Aristotle also had a theory about memory problems. He believed that a person who is in a state of rapid transition cannot store memories. "It is like a seal stamped on running water," he asserted, noting that this was the basis for memory problems in the very young and the very old: The first are growing, and the latter are decaying.

Ars Notoria   A magical art of memory attributed to Apollonius (and sometimes to Solomon). Experts at *Ars Notoria* recited magical prayers while looking at diagrams marked with "*notae*" (notes), which were supposed to help the practitioner gain knowledge or memory of all the arts and sciences.

This tradition, which Thomas Aquinas condemned as a particularly evil form of black magic, was nevertheless taught furtively for centuries, where—as a secret knowledge—it underwent various transformations.

It is believed that *Ars Notoria* may have been a descendant of the classical art of memory—in particular, that difficult branch

of memory that used shorthand *notae*. (See also AQUINAS, ST. THOMAS.)

artificial memory   The synthesis and training of innate memory powers first developed in the Greek and Roman empires in order to run their large bureaucracies in the absence of paper or books. While the empires depended on "white-collar" workers, there was little way for the officials to keep records. Everything had to be memorized, and the bureaucrats needed a disciplined, well-trained and practiced memory.

Because a well-trained memory was such an integral part of the Roman culture, memory training was included as a standard part of education. The Romans called this memory training artificial memory and distinguished it from the inborn "natural memory" with which we remember normally. While the Romans sometimes used their artificial memory to dazzle their friends, its primary requirement was to preserve their own work—for use by lawyers, politicians and preachers. The ancients believed that artificial memory was a way to link themselves with whatever they had to remember.

The standard text on artificial memory was the Roman *AD HERENNIUM*, a book for rhetoric students written about 80 B.C. Rhetoric students learned effective means of communicating, especially effective public speaking. Since paper was scarce, rhetoric students had to learn how to memorize their speeches without referring to notes. The *Ad Herennium* provided the answer, outlining an amazing system of remembering facts by arranging them into scenes in a place that had been committed to memory.

This principle, called the method of loci, became an established part of ancient education and philosophy. (Indeed, the English word "topic" comes from the Greek *topoi*, for "place.") In the Greek and Roman systems, a "topic" was a place in the space where a memory image appeared.

As Rome's importance faded, along with the need for a well-trained memory, so did interest in artificial memory. Artificial memory was reborn during the Middle Ages, when religious leaders revived it as a way to form a personal bond between one's mind and religion. They did this by coming up with personally meaningful images of doctrine and then walking among those images, providing a means of private and intense devotion.

In 1491 the Italian author PETER OF RAVENNA published a book on how to improve memory *(The Phoenix)*, which became wildly popular—yet artificial memory was nowhere as popular as it had been. The availability of paper ended the necessity for extensive use of artificial memory.

The most radical opponents of artificial memory were the Puritans, who preferred impersonal rote memorization over the personal excitement of artificial memory. In the late 1500s and early 1600s, rising scientists such as Galileo, Descartes and Kepler understood the excitement of learning but rejected the vivid imagery, personal meaning and arbitrary order of artificial memory. The revolt was so powerful and so complete that the practice of artificial memory faded forever from the world.

Today we think of memorization exclusively as rote and we praise the ideal of scientific reasoning, forgetting completely that there had ever been any other way to understand memory and thought.

aspartame   The chemical name for NutraSweet, this artificial sweetener has been linked to memory loss, confusion and mental deterioration in sensitive individuals, according to some reports.

A synthetic chemical discovered by accident in 1965, aspartame is a combination of methyl alcohol (also known as methanol and wood alcohol) and two amino acids, phenylalanine and aspartic acid. The aspartame molecule is made up of 50 percent phenylalanine, 40 percent aspartic acid and 10 percent methyl alcohol.

The amount of aspartame in any one product can vary; some brands of diet cola contain as much as four times more aspartame than others, and orange-flavored beverages tend to have a higher content (up to 333 mg. aspartame per 12 fluid ounces).

Although aspartame was kept off the market for many years because one animal study suggested that it caused a high incidence of brain tumors, other studies failed to duplicate these results. As aspartame proved to taste better than many alternatives on the market, it was subsequently approved for use as a food additive after being subjected to rigorous safety testing.

After more than 100 studies, however, there is still controversy over its safety. Critics say that many of the studies used by the Food and Drug Administration (FDA) to approve the use of aspartame are tainted by excessive food industry support. But FDA reviews show no adverse health effects among lab animals tested.

Still, complaints about aspartame account for 80 percent of the telephone calls received on the FDA food additives hot line, second only to sulfites. In particular, more than 125 users complained to the FDA of experiencing memory loss while using aspartame products.

Critics are most concerned about aspartame because it contains phenylalanine and aspartic acid, substances that in large doses have been shown to stimulate the brain excessively. This overstimulation may damage the brain and may lead to neurological disease. Studies done on animals also suggest that children (especially infants) could be particularly vulnerable to this brain disease.

Describing research in memory loss and related areas by its scientists, G. D. Searle and Company published full-page ads in leading medical journals (such as the December 1987 issue of the *Journal of the American Medical Association*) stating that "excessive activity of the excitatory amino acids might cause nerve cell destruction resembling the changes noted in Alzheimer's disease, Huntington's chorea and other degenerative diseases." Amino acids of this type are products of aspartame metabolism. Other researchers at the London Institute of Neurology reported a striking loss of aspartate receptors in certain important brain cells of patients with Alzheimer's disease after aspartame ingestion.

As a condition of FDA approval, aspartame manufacturers are required to monitor the use of aspartame in food products.

Brayne, C., and Calloway, D. "Normal Aging, Impaired Cognitive Function and Senile Dementia of the Alzheimer's Type: A Continuum?" *Lancet* 1 (1988): 1265–66.

Procter, A.W., et al. "Glutamate/Aspartame-releasing Neurones in Alzheimer's Disease." *New England Journal of Medicine* 314 (1986): 1711–12.

Roberts, H.J. *Aspartame: Is It Safe?* Philadelphia: The Charles Press, 1990.

assessment of memory disorders   The assessment, study and treatment of memory disorders is part of neuropsychology, the subdiscipline of psychology concerned with the relationship between brain damage and psychological processes.

Disorders caused by brain dysfunction are called organic, and those with no apparent physical cause are called functional or psychogenic. Within these classes of disorders, a memory problem can be classed as either "global" or "specific."

The first step in assessing a patient with a memory disorder is to determine whether the disorder is organic or psychogenic by studying the patient's medical record. While determining the etiology of a memory problem may seem simple, the reason is not always clear-cut; sometimes psychogenic factors may overlay an organic impairment. At other times a psychogenic disorder may be complicated by a disorder such as epilepsy.

Second, it is important to determine how extensive the deficit is. While there exist many tests and procedures for evaluating a patient's memory deficit, certain basic tests should be done first. All patients should receive a preliminary screening for memory impairment using the WECHSLER MEMORY SCALE (WMS), developed by David Wechsler in 1945. The WMS is the most widely used clinical memory test today, although its value has been questioned because all but one of its subtests involve verbal memory. Because of this bias, the test may overestimate memory disorders in patients whose deficits are primarily verbal or underestimate memory impairment in those who have problems with nonverbal information.

Next, the RIVERMEAD BEHAVIORAL MEMORY TEST should be administered to obtain a more general impression of the patient's problems. Results of the WMS and the Rivermead test can give a qualitative indication of the patient's memory disorder and can then be backed up with more detailed tests aimed at specific memory functions.

These might include the Williams Scale for the Measurement of Memory (1968), which places more emphasis on nonverbal memory and past personal events. A more recent battery devised to detect minor deficits in the retention of verbal and visual information is the Recognition Memory Test (1985). It is especially useful in pinpointing right- or left-hemisphere damage.

Other memory tests could include the WISCONSIN CARD SORTING TEST, one of the most common ways to assess frontal lobe brain damage. The subject is given a deck of cards marked by a pattern with various symbol shapes, numbers and colors and asked to sort them by a particular order, such as placing all the cards with red squares in one pile. After ten correct tries, the subject must devise a new way to sort the cards. Patients with frontal lobe damage or KORSAKOFF'S SYNDROME tend to make a perseveration error when asked to change sorting styles and continue to sort the cards by the first rule. Patients with MEDIAL TEMPORAL LOBE damage usually do not exhibit the perseveration error on this test.

Questionnaires also may be useful in evaluating the impact of the disorder on patients and their families. (See also MEMORY, DISORDERS OF; ORGANIC AMNESIA; PSYCHOGENIC AMNESIA.)

association The connection of one item to be remembered with others a person already knows. For example, the easiest way to tell the difference between "stationery" and "stationary" is that you use stationery to write a letter; to remember how to spell "believe," never believe a lie. Association can be used consciously to remember information; but it also can occur unconsciously. The experience of hearing or seeing something that reminds one of something else occurs because such sounds or sights somehow were linked together in the past, so that remembering one bit of information automatically drew the other bit of information with it.

association, theories of A psychological theory that states that when any past event or experience is recalled, the act of recollection tends to bring forth other events and experiences related to this event in one or more specified ways. This general theory has been expanded to include almost everything that could happen in mental life (except for feeling an original sensation).

While the first theory of association generally is attributed to ARISTOTLE, who had proposed that there were three forms of association (similarity, contrast and contiguity), the philosophy of ASSOCIATIONISM is normally considered to be a British doctrine.

The association of ideas was first developed by John Locke in *An Essay Concerning Human Understanding* (1690), and David Hume expanded on these theories in *A Treatise of Human Nature* in 1739. Others who held various views of association included David Hartley in the 18th century and James and John Stuart Mill, Alexander Bain and Herbert Spencer in the 19th century.

In general, however, association says that knowledge is acquired through one or more of the senses, and by repetitions throughout life the original sensory data are interconnected and can be revived or reinstated as representative images or ideas.

But in 1890 the American philosopher William James suggested in *The Principles of Psychology* that the association of ideas should be replaced by an association of central nervous processes set up by overlapping (or successive) stimuli.

Thirteen years later Russian physiologist Ivan Pavlov studied what had been called association, eventually arriving at a complete description of all behavior, which he believed was derived from original and conditioned reflexes. For the next decades, various schools of thought debated the varieties of association; the Gestalt psychologists called for a total rejection of associationism as far as higher mental processes were concerned. Today very few psychologists support these theories completely, although most agree that association is an important and effective principle that affects all instances of learning through accumulated experience. (See also LOCKE, JOHN; PAVLOV, IVAN PETROVICH.)

associationism The idea that very complex ideas can be built up from extremely simple ones. This philosophy was propounded by the 19th century English philosopher John Locke, who was deeply interested in the study of memory and its laws.

association word lists A type of common mnemonic device similar to the loci system of Simonides, in which a list of associated words are first memorized; information to be memorized is then linked to this already learned list. (See MNEMONIC STRATEGIES.)

Here is a typical association list, showing how one word is associated with the next

green light

car

garage

house

shag rug

lamp

chair

bed

pillow

goosefeather

chicken

Associations between these words are established next; the power of this method depends on the cleverness of the associations between consecutive words.

For this list, the "green light" is a good way to begin, since "green light" means go. The green light means a car can go; cars use a garage; a garage is attached to a house; a house is carpeted in shag rugs; a rug is under a lamp; a lamp is beside the chair; the chair is beside the bed; and so on.

It's a good idea to try to make every fifth or tenth word stand out, so that the items to be remembered in sequence can be kept track of. In addition, both the base word list and the information to be remembered by association must be translated into striking visual images.

ATP   See   ADENOSINE   TRIPHOSPHATE (ATP).

attention   *Noticing*, or paying attention, is the first fully conscious step in the formation of a memory. It involves deciding which stimuli are worth remembering and which can be discarded and forgotten.

While some 19th-century psychologists, such as William James, focused on attention and the mind, others—such as Russian physiologist Ivan Pavlov—concentrated on attention and behavior. In his well-known experiments on dogs and bells, he noted the signs of attention in dogs and the role attention plays in the activation of conditioned reflexes in the animals.

Today researchers and psychologists consider attention against a background of unfocused awareness that can be focused if necessary. For example, while a person learns how to crochet she must devote all of her attention to the project; once the skill has been mastered, she can carry on conversations or watch TV, attending to her crocheting only if a problem occurs. This suggests that once learned, a skill is carried out in a state of unfocused awareness.

Usually the only way to tell if someone is paying attention is by studying the brain. If a person is given a signal that indicates a second signal will be coming, the electroencephalogram (EEG) shows a slow change in the negative charge of the brain's cortex. This is called the contingent negative variation (CNV) and is considered to be the clearest physical sign of attention.

With the development of computers, scientists have tried to compare attention and the way computers handle information. Called information theory, this approach focuses on the brain systems that may organize the flood of incoming data, allowing it to be attended to. These highly complex mechanisms, which appear to be located at different spots in the brain, must deal with a wide variety of information using different criteria of selection. In addition, attention also appears to be under at least partial voluntary control. (See also PAVLOV, IVAN PETROVICH.)

attention and memory   The most important thing to remember about attention is its fragility. For example, the attention span of the average audience is just 20 minutes, which is why public speakers are urged to convey the essential part of their message immediately. Once past an audience's maximum attention span, the good public speaker will resort to other ways to maintain attention—pauses, differences in tone or speed of delivery, good examples, anecdotes, humor or activity.

Attention can be measured in two ways—how well we avoid distraction and how well we can sustain concentration over a period of time. While humans are usually good at directing their attention to one source, there is evidence that information that is not attended to is still being analyzed to a considerable degree. In the "cocktail party effect," for example, a person who is concentrating on one conversation at a party will nonetheless likely notice if a nearby conversation suddenly switches to the same topic.

It is possible for humans to do more than one thing at a time—we can eat dinner and watch television, or talk and drive a car. It appears that as long as the tasks do not depend on the same mental processes, both can be handled at the same time. But if two tasks depend on the same type of mental process (such as listening to a story and reading a book), neither task can be accomplished very well.

The capacity for any one individual to pay attention to more than one stimulus at the same time varies from person to person and can be affected by alertness, age and motivation. In addition, certain brain lesions can cause severe impairments in the attentional mechanism.

There are also a number of situations in which it is difficult to sustain attention—when a person's attention is most vulnerable: when one is distracted, interrupted, tired, rushed or under stress; when one feels strong emotions, doesn't understand the material or is absorbed in an activity. People also have trouble paying attention if they are under the influence of drugs or alcohol, in familiar surroundings or doing something while on "automatic pilot."

Still, even if people are paying attention, it doesn't mean that they are going to be able to recall everything they are listening to on demand. Attention is required in order to record information, but people also must store that data along with cues for later recall, because recall is the most difficult of the three memory processes.

auditory memory The memory for sound. This type of sense memory is particularly strong among great musicians; the great conductor Arturo Toscanini, for example, could remember a score after hearing it one or two times and could write it out from memory 40 years later.

Augustine, St. (354–430) The bishop of Hippo in Roman Africa from 396 to 430 and the dominant personality in the Catholic church at the time. Recognized as the greatest thinker of Christian antiquity, Augustine pondered deeply on the problem of memory and the soul.

In the famous *Confessions,* which he wrote when he was middle aged, Augustine told the story of his own restless youth and his eventual journey to the Catholic church. He appeared to be aware at some level of the art of ARTIFICIAL MEMORY, describing in a meditation on memory a series of spacious palaces stored in the "vast court" of memory. As a Christian, Augustine sought God in memory, believing that knowledge of the divine is naturally present there.

In *Confessions,* he summarized the paradox of memory when he wrote:

> When, therefore, the memory loses something—and this is what happens when we forget something and try to remember it—where are we to look for it except in the memory itself? And if the memory offers something else instead, as may happen, we reject what this offers until the one thing we want is

presented. When it is presented to us we say "this is it," but we could not say this unless we recognized it and we could not recognize it unless we remembered it.

autistic savants Individuals who lack normal intelligence but who possess one outstanding mental ability, such as a so-called photographic memory or the ability to do complex mathematical calculations in their heads. Autistic savants were formerly called idiot savants (meaning "wise idiot"), a term invented in 1887 by J. Langdon Down, a pioneer in the study of mental retardation. Autistic savants are usually incapable of activities of daily living other than their one ability and are often unable to reason or to comprehend meaning.

The savant syndrome is six times more likely to appear in males than females. Although it is considered rare, almost 10 percent of children diagnosed with autism may exhibit this syndrome.

No matter what their particular talent, all savants share a prodigious memory; their skills may appear in a range of areas, including calendar calculating, music, rapid calculating and mathematics, art or mechanical ability.

One of the more common patterns that can be found among savants is a triad of mental retardation, blindness and musical ability.

In 1988 the movie *Rain Man* won an Academy Award for Best Picture for its portrayal of a prodigious autistic savant; the feats of this savant were based on actual clinical literature.

Treffert, D. "The Idiot Savant: A Review of the Syndrome." *American Journal of Psychiatry* 145 (1988): 563–72.

autobiographical memory A uniquely human function of early memories that be-gins at a certain point in childhood. It depends on a child's ability to speak, since it requires linguistic representations of events. The phenomenon of INFANTILE AMNESIA was first identified by Sigmund Freud, but since Freud's time, scientists have learned that as children grow older they learn to share memories with others and acquire the narrative forms of memory recounting. Such recountings are effective in reinstating experienced memories only after the children can use another's representation of an experience in language as a reinstatement of their own experience. This requires an ability to understand language that appears in the mid- to late preschool years. (See also FREUD, SIGMUND; MEMORY IN INFANCY.)

automatic gestures Habitual routines (such as locking your front door) that, because they are performed without any conscious thinking or awareness, may not be recorded in memory and therefore may not be recalled at a later date.

automatic processing Memory functions are carried out with a minimum amount of conscious attention. While it is often argued that processing activities (such as ENCODING and RETRIEVAL) require different levels of ATTENTION, automatic processing tasks are disrupted only slightly by the simultaneous performance of other more demanding tasks regardless of their precise nature—and automatic processing disrupts only minimally the performance of these other tasks. In contrast, EFFORTFUL PROCESSING is disrupted by and disrupts other demanding tasks performed at the same time.

axon The core of a nerve cell which typically conducts impulses away from the cell body, to other cells and glands.

B

background context When someone pays attention to episodic or semantic information, that information falls within a space-time framework known as background context. This context includes not only the precise spatial and temporal characteristics of events and facts but also other features of the background in which they occur; for example, colors or the objects present.

Background context and format context make up the EXTRINSIC CONTEXT, which is opposite INTRINSIC CONTEXT. Background context usually falls on the periphery of attention and may be processed automatically.

Bacon, Sir Francis (1561–1626) The English philosopher and man of letters whose *Essays* established him as a master of English prose, Sir Francis also was an expert on RHETORIC. Educated at Cambridge, he became a barrister, a member of Parliament and eventually lord chancellor of England.

At the beginning of the 17th century, Bacon was responsible for bringing science into thoughts of English oral delivery, calling for a scientific approach to the study of gesture in rhetoric.

After leaving government service, he spent his final years writing some of his most influential works.

balloon angioplasty See ANGIOGRAPHY.

barbiturates SODIUM PENTOTHAL is one of many barbiturates (a group of sedative drugs) that have been found to facilitate the recall of emotionally disturbing memories. Scientists believe that these drugs reduce anxiety so that the patient can tolerate the recollection of experiences that are too painful to recall in the normal conscious state. Other than pentothal, the most common barbiturate is SODIUM AMYTAL (amylbarbitone).

Bartlett, Sir Frederic C. (1896–1969) An English psychologist who believed that the brain stores information by using what it already knows and placing a new pattern over a similar old one.

Bartlett's work was a departure from the popular theories and style of psychologist Hermann Ebbinghaus, who tested his own ability to memorize nonsense syllables. This memorization could be called rote learning, but modern researchers understand that what Ebbinghaus was really studying was rote learning without arousal—in other words, factual memory for events that have no emotional importance. And because rote learning without arousal is a poor way to construct memory, it is not surprising that Ebbinghaus and his colleagues concluded that memory doesn't work very well or endure for a very long time.

While Bartlett developed his technique as a way of sidestepping problems in memory study, it limited his ability to understand memory. He believed that memory was simply a storage bin for objective items that were either retained or not—a point of view that eventually was challenged by psychologists who believed that subjective factors also are vital to memory systems.

Bartlett did not believe that only objective factors should be studied; his work during the 1930s was designed to test the way people usually use their memories. As he described in his book *Remembering: A Study in Experimental and Social Psychology* (1967), Bartlett believed that remembering is active; it is not the reactivation of memory traces that have been filed away but an imaginative reconstruction built out of the relationship of the attitude toward a mass of organized past reactions and to little details. Therefore, he noted, memory is hardly ever exact, and he agreed with Sigmund Freud that personal view greatly affects memory.

Instead of memorizing nonsense syllables, Bartlett asked his subjects to look at pictures and remember stories he told them, coming up with personal associations, earlier experi-

strict controls to guarantee a uniform basis of comparison, at the time many of his colleagues criticized his work for being too vague and complex.

In one of his most famous studies, he told an American Indian war story filled with unusual details; when it was over, subjects were asked to repeat the story after 15 minutes and then after four and six months. As time passed, the story grew shorter and shorter, and its Indian point of view disappeared. What Bartlett's study revealed was that memory alters information, omitting and distorting facts depending on personal prejudices and turning a puzzling but emotionally rich story into something that is dull but understandable.

Bartlett believed that what was going on was the operation of something he called a schema—an underlying subjective organizing principle. A person's memory of the Indian tale changed over time to conform with that person's underlying personal schema.

In *Remembering:* Bartlett explained that memory was based on the general impression that results from combining recalled details with the overall sense an individual forms of what has occurred. That overall sense, in turn, is affected by a person's general knowledge and the expectations that result from that knowledge. (See also EBB-INGHAUS, HERMANN.)

Bolles, Edmund. *Remembering and Forgetting: An Inquiry into the Nature of Memory.* New York: Walker and Company, 1988.
Minniger, Joan. *Total Recall.* Emmaus, PA: Rodale Press, 1984.

basal ganglia The group of large paired nerve cell clusters buried deep in the forebrain and including the CAUDATE NUCLEUS, putamen and globus pallidus. These nerve cells sit above the brain stem and under the cerebrum.

The basal ganglia play an important role in control of movement and may help medi-ate the development of skills and habits. Diseases or degeneration of the basal ganglia and their connections may lead to the appearance of involuntary movements, trembling and weakness such as those found in PARKINSON'S DISEASE. (See also BRAIN DAMAGE; CARBON MONOXIDE POISONING; CAUDATE NUCLEUS; HUNTINGTON'S DISEASE.)

behavioral treatments of memory disorders Techniques to improve memory that include chaining (breaking up a task into smaller units taught one at a time), flooding or modeling. Behavioral treatments of memory problems work well because they are adaptable to a wide range of patients, the goals are small and specific and treatment can be tested continually and easily.

The theoretical approaches underlying behavioral therapy draw upon a number of fields within psychology. While behavioral treatments have been used in rehabilitation for years, only recently have they been tried for amelioration of acquired cognitive impairments.

A behavior program for patients with memory problems should specify the behavior to be changed, state the goals of treatment, measure deficit to obtain a baseline, plan/begin treatment, monitor progress and change the procedure if needed.

benzodiazepines A class of psychoactive drugs which includes diazepam (Valium) and lorazepam (Ativan), that can be used to promote sleep or reduce anxiety—but that also can impair memory and other aspects of mental function. For example, when Ativan is taken at night for sleep, patients experience a small memory impairment the next morning.

Under certain circumstances, benzodiazepines can induce a temporary amnesic state with a marked ANTEROGRADE AMNESIA. But since neither Valium nor Ativan has any effect on the recall of information presented shortly before giving the drug, researchers believe that memory impairment following the drug administration is caused by some aspect of acquisition.

The ability of the benzodiazepines to induce this type of amnesia can be used to the patient's advantage in a medical setting; some dentists use intravenous Valium for their patients who fear dental surgery, for example. Not only does the drug reduce anxiety, but patients have difficulty recalling the surgery itself, which is helpful if they need to face further surgery at a later date.

Binet, Alfred (1857–1911) This noted French psychologist and co-developer of the Binet-Simon standardized intelligence test that bears his name also was interested in children's memory. It was Binet who suggested that children remember the basic idea or the underlying message of long passages. The popularity of the behavioral viewpoint during the first part of the 20th century diminished the impact of Binet's work.

biofeedback A technique in which a person uses information about a normally unconscious body function such as blood pressure, to gain conscious control over that function. Biofeedback may help in the treatment of stress-related conditions such as hypertension or migraine.

The subject is connected to a recording instrument that can measure one of the unconscious body activities—blood pressure, pulse rate, body temperature, muscle tension, sweat on the skin, brain waves or stomach acidity. The subject receives the information (feedback) on the changing levels of the body activities from alterations in the instrument's signals (flashing lights, fluctuating needle, changing sounds).

With practice, the person starts to become aware of how he or she is feeling whenever there is a change in the recording instrument's signal. Relaxation techniques also may be used to bring about a change in the signal; the instrument's response may indicate which methods of relaxation work best.

Eventually the subject learns to change the signal by consciously controlling the body function being tested. Once learned, control can be exerted without the equipment.

Many at-home versions of biofeedback machines are now available, including a home blood pressure monitoring kit for measuring blood pressure with the fingertip.

blackouts, alcoholic Blackouts are a common phenomenon among alcoholics and normal drinkers who overindulge, involving a loss of memory during the drunken state. During a blackout, the individual is not unconscious or incapacitated, and usually possesses most of his or her faculties.

In one form of alcoholic blackout, called en bloc, the person experiences AMNESIA that has a clear beginning and end; in this form, the patient knows there has been a "lost period." In a second form of blackout, the person is not aware of any amnesia and also may have exhibited memory problems while drinking without any recollection of them.

Experts once believed that blackouts were a form of state-dependent forgetting, that is, a person can remember information learned in a state only when in that state. In other words, a person who commits a crime while drunk would only remember that crime while drunk. However, at least one research study did not support this theory. In a study of five convicted murderers who had committed their crimes while drunk and claimed amnesia for their activities, the murderers were allowed to become drunk. None recalled their crimes while drunk, and when they were sober again all had varying degrees of amnesia for the experiment.

The researchers believe that alcoholic blackouts occur because the original level of alcohol intoxication was enough to disrupt the physiological processes involved in forming memories.

Boston remote memory battery The most extensive test for RETROGRADE AMNESIA, devised by Marilyn Albert in 1979.

Its three components each have "easy" and "hard" questions; the easy questions reflect information that might be answered on the basis of general knowledge, while the hard questions reflect information whose recollection relies much more on remembering a particular time period.

Unfortunately, the test is considered to be culture-specific and cannot be used with patients outside the United States. (See also ASSESSMENT OF MEMORY DISORDERS.)

brain abscess A collection of pus inside inflamed brain tissue that is almost always caused by the spread of infection elsewhere in the body; about 40 percent of abscesses are caused by middle ear or sinus infections. Among other symptoms, brain abscesses can cause memory problems due to raised pressure and local damage to nerve tracts. The most common sites of brain abscesses are the FRONTAL and TEMPORAL LOBES of the cerebrum. Other causes of brain abscess include infection following a penetrating brain injury and multiple abscesses from blood-borne infections, such as endocarditis and some immunodeficiency disorders.

Besides memory problems, the most common symptoms are headache, drowsiness and vomiting, together with vision problems, fever, epileptic seizures and symptoms caused by local brain damage (partial paralysis and speech problems).

A brain scan (computerized tomography or magnetic resonance imaging) may suggest a diagnosis. Abscesses are treated with high doses of intravenous antibiotics, but because antibiotics alone may not cure an abscess, surgery may be required. After the operation, antibiotics are usually given for one or two months.

In the surgery, a section of the skull is opened to provide access to the abscess and to facilitate drainage. If the abscess has penetrated any area of the skull, some of the affected bone may be removed. Locating and removing all traces of infection is some-

times difficult, and recovery may be complicated by reinfection.

Brain abscesses are fatal in about 10 percent of cases, and surviving patients often suffer some residual brain dysfunction. Because many patients experience epilepsy after brain abscesses, anticonvulsant drugs are often administered after removal or drainage of the abscess.

Brain abscesses are relatively rare today because the widespread use of antibiotics controls many infections in the early stages.

brain cell See NEURON.

brain damage Degeneration or death of nerve cells and tracts within the brain, which may be localized in particular areas (causing specific defects) or more diffuse, causing mental problems or severe physical handicap. Memory is very sensitive to brain damage, since it is dependent on such a wide range of interacting processes; even limited brain damage may affect some of these processes. Many brain structures seem to be involved in the process of memory, including the HIPPOCAMPUS, hypothalamus, THALAMUS and TEMPORAL LOBE. Damage to any of them can cause memory problems.

Most people with organic amnesia will have experienced one of the following: HEAD INJURY, cerebral vascular accident, progressive DEMENTIA, BRAIN TUMOR, toxic disorder, brain surgery or nutritional disorder. (See CEREBRAL VASCULAR ACCIDENTS [CVAS].)

Memory deficits may be a lifelong handicap for brain-damaged patients and their families. Such patients are liable to a greater risk of personal danger (by forgetting a lighted cigarette or a pot on the stove), increased annoyance from others by repeatedly failing to remember and social isolation.

Localized Brain Damage This form of brain damage can occur as a result of a head injury (especially those that penetrate the skull) or from a STROKE, brain tumor or

BRAIN ABSCESS. It also may be caused by damage to the brain at birth from jaundice (excess bilirubin levels). The BASAL GANGLIA also may be damaged by CARBON MONOXIDE POISONING.

Diffuse Brain Damage This more severe type of brain damage may result from hypoxia (lack of oxygen in the brain) that may occur during birth; from cardiac or respiratory arrest; or from poisoning, drowning, electric shock or prolonged convulsions. It also may be caused by the accumulation of toxic substances in the brain, as occurs in phenylketonuria or galactosemia, or of environmental poisons (such as lead or mercury). Other possible causes include brain infections (such as encephalitis) or, rarely, a reaction after immunization. In addition, there is some evidence that the tips and undersurface of the temporal lobes may be more susceptible to traumatic damage than other parts of the brain; if so, then memory problems following diffuse brain damage may in fact indicate hippocampal damage. Encephalitic patients, too, may suffer extensive temporal lobe lesions (although the virus does not always attack this area).

Patients who have suffered head injury or stroke are likely to experience memory problems in addition to other symptoms. Unlike nerves in the limbs or trunk, nerve cells and tracts in the brain and spinal cord do not recover their function if they have been destroyed. However, patients may improve somewhat after brain damage as they learn to use other parts of the brain to compensate for the loss.

The ability to store and recall memories following brain injury may be affected in quite different ways from one patient to the next. This is because there is not just one kind of memory, but many—verbal and nonverbal memory, visual and auditory memory, short-term and long-term memory, episodic and semantic memory. Moreover, even in the same patient, some memory functions may work fine while others show more disruption.

There are three main ways to improve memory performance for brain-damaged patients—physical treatment (such as medication) and internal and external aids.

Internal aids include mnemonics, rehearsal strategies or anything a patient does mentally to the information to be remembered. External aids include diaries, notebooks and calendars, alarm clocks, gadgets and computers. Environmental aids also may be used to help mold behavior in patients with severe memory problems, for example, lines may be painted on the ground to help them find their way around. One hospital geriatric unit reduced its incontinence problem among patients by painting all the lavatory doors a different color from other doors.

The effectiveness of external aids is related to the attitude toward their use; in some cases patients need counseling before they will accept the aids. One of the most effective aids is the combination of a digital alarm watch and a notebook with the day's activities; whenever the alarm goes off, the patient consults the notebook.

The ability of a brain-damaged patient to recover memory depends on the cause and site of the damage, the individual's personality and how motivated he or she is to recover. Indeed, researchers agree there is little evidence that practice by itself will significantly improve a brain-damaged person's memory. (See also MEMORY FOR FACES; VISUAL IMAGERY METHOD.)

brain injury See BRAIN DAMAGE.

brain scans A group of specialized tests that chart brain function using a variety of chemical, electrical or magnetic technologies ranging from POSITRON EMISSION TOMOGRAPHY to SQUIDS (superconducting quantum interference devices). Each type of brain scan has its pros and cons; some are so precise they can distinguish structures as small as a millimeter but are so slow they can't differentiate between neurons. Others can track brain function but can't resolve structures less than half an inch apart.

The computerized scanning equipment introduced over the past 15 years has revolutionized diagnostic neurology. The two most commonly used scans are COMPUTED TOMOGRAPHIC (CT) SCANning and MAGNETIC RESONANCE IMAGING (MRI), also known as NMR or nuclear magnetic resonance.

While the computerized scanning techniques of CT and MRI are similar and noninvasive, they rely on two distinct methods of producing an image. CT scans use an ultrathin X-ray beam; MRI uses a very strong magnetic field. During CT scans, an X-ray beam passes through the body; various tissues absorb different amounts of the beam, and the intensity of the beam that emerges from the body is measured by an X-ray detector. On the scan, tissues appear as various shades of gray; bone—appearing white—is at one end of this spectrum, and air is at the opposite end (appearing black).

During an MRI scan, each hydrogen atom in the body responds to the magnetic field produced by the device; a magnetic field detector measures the responses of the atom. The degree of response depends on the type of tissue or its water content. There is no radiation in an MRI scan, but the magnetic field may affect heart pacemakers, inner ear implants, brain aneurysm clips or embedded shrapnel.

Both CT and MRI scans are done by taking detector measurements from thousands of angles all over the body while the patient lies on a special table; these data are then processed by computer to create a composite three-dimensional representation of the body. Any particular slice can be selected from this representation and displayed on a TV screen for examination, and still photos also can be produced.

CT scans show internal structures much better than conventional X rays. They are particularly useful for brain disorders such as strokes, hemorrhages, injuries, tumors, abscesses, cysts, swelling, fluid accumulation and dead tissue.

MRI scans are especially useful for imaging areas where soft and hard tissue meet and areas affected by stroke that can't be seen well on a CT scan. They also are used to diagnose nerve fiber disorders (such as multiple sclerosis).

Other brain scan technology includes ELECTROENCEPHALOGRAM (EEGs) and SPECT (single-photon emission computerized tomography).

"Mapping the Brain." *Newsweek,* April 20, 1992.

brain structure and memory Many brain structures seem to be involved in the process of memory, including the HIPPOCAMPUS, hypothalamus, THALAMUS and TEMPORAL LOBES. Damage to any of them can cause memory problems.

Hippocampus It was in the hippocampal area that the best-documented link to memory was discovered in the case of HM, an epileptic whose temporal lobes were destroyed to alleviate his seizures. After surgery, he was unable to learn any new information and showed symptoms of a classic amnesic syndrome. From these data, scientists realized that an intact hippocampus was essential for normal memory function. Further research has suggested that removing the left temporal lobe causes verbal memory deficits and removing the right lobe impairs nonverbal memory (such as remembering mazes, patterns or faces).

However, memory problems following damage to the hippocampal structures does not occur only after surgery; injury following a stroke can also cause a profound SHORT-TERM MEMORY problem.

Thalamus One of the main parts of the DIENCEPHALON, the thalamus was involved in many cases of memory disorder in WERNICKE-KORSAKOFF SYNDROME patients. One of the best-known cases of thalamic damage and memory problems is NA, a man who was stabbed in the thalamic region at age 22 and suffered extensive memory deficits as a result. Other cases of thalamic tumors have been reported, which can lead to a rapidly developing dementia.

Temporal Lobes Because the temporal lobes may be more easily damaged, memory problems following diffuse brain damage may in fact indicate hippocampal damage. Encephalitic patients, too, may suffer extensive temporal lobe lesions (although the virus does not *always* attack this area).

Stimulating various areas of the cortex produces a range of responses from patients; however, only stimulation of the temporal lobes elicits meaningful, integrated experiences, including sound, movement and color, that are far more detailed, accurate and specific than normal recall. In fact, some scientists believe the phenomenon of DÉJÀ VU is a disturbance of the temporal lobe of the brain.

brain surgery and memory Operations on one TEMPORAL LOBE (when there has been unsuspected damage in the other lobe) can cause a severe and persistent general memory defect very similar to postencephalitic amnesia. This memory loss is especially pervasive for SHORT-TERM MEMORY and in learning with a RETROGRADE AMNESIA involving at least the past several years of a patient's life before surgery.

It's also possible, during open brain surgery, to stimulate the temporal lobes with an electrode and produce hallucinogeniclike memories. This was first discovered in the 1950s by Canadian neurosurgeon Wilder Penfield, whose patients reported meaningful, integrated experiences including sound, movement and color while Penfield held the electrode in certain parts of their brain. Sometimes his patients did not recall the memories after the operation; often the memories were far more detailed, specific and accurate than normal recall. Stimulating one particular part of the brain brought back the memory of a mother calling her child or a certain song. Stimulating the same point brought back the same memory every time. (See also AMNESIA; ANESTHESIA, MEMORY WHILE UNDER; ENCEPHALITIS AND MEMORY; MEDIAL TEMPORAL LOBE; PENFIELD, WILDER.)

brain tissue transplants Initial research with rats has suggested the possibility of restoring some types of memory using fetal brain tissue transplants. However, the moral and philosophical issues surrounding their use in humans presents many problems. Moreover, the fact that successful transplants depend on the availability of fetal brain tissue adds to the ethical and legal dilemma.

One of the greatest problems in treating BRAIN DAMAGE is the fact that the brain cannot regenerate very well. And when particular areas of the brain are damaged, other regions do not always take over the function of the disabled sections.

Scientists destroyed connections in the septo-hippocampal region of young rats who had already learned several mazes. Following the damage, the rats' performance was impaired. After being given grafts of septo-hippocampal tissue taken from rat fetuses, the rats went on to show improvement in their maze-learning tasks. This suggests that the grafts had become effective parts of the animals' memory system. Other studies showed that the neural tissue taken from the same region in rat fetuses could improve the age-related learning impairments in rats.

Scientists are already transplanting fetal brain cells into the brains of Parkinson's disease patients, hoping that the new cells will begin to churn out dopamine, a key brain chemical that is deficient in the disease. Early results have been encouraging, and some patients have shown some improvement, although not total health.

Someday soon scientists hope they will be able to tackle some of the most intractable diseases of the brain, including Alzheimer's disease, that short-circuit brain cells and destroy memory and personality—and with it, the essence that makes us human.

Genetically altered cells, and genes themselves, can be injected into the brain to combat or reverse damage caused by degenerative diseases. The new approaches rely on the same basic strategy: using living tissue instead of drugs to supply chemicals crucial to brain function. Scientists at Brown University, for example, are developing a way to encapsulate small clumps of cells that produce desired chemicals, letting out the substances through holes in the plastic capsule that are too small to let antibodies in. In that way, the body's immune systems can't reject the cells when the capsule is implanted. The technique has been used to reverse memory impairment and Parkinson-like damage in rats.

In other studies, Harvard scientists have put new genes in rat brains by linking the new DNA to a weakened herpes virus; the virus splices in the new genes when it infects neurons. While scientists aren't sure whether the genes can be "turned on" to work effectively, the number of potential uses could be limitless.

brain tumor An abnormal growth that destroys brain tissue and puts pressure on neighboring brain structures. Tumors causing particular memory problems are often found on the floor of the third ventricle, adjacent to diencephalic structures; tumors in this area produce amnesia resembling KORSAKOFF'S SYNDROME. In fact, in a study of 180 cerebral tumors, more than half the patients with marked memory impairment had tumors involving the third ventricle.

Patients suffering from a wide variety of tumors are likely to exhibit memory deficits. For example, frontal lobe tumor patients have memory problems comparable to patients with Korsakoff's syndrome and other diencephalic amnesias. Patients with corpus callosum tumors also are likely to show a severe memory impairment, which rapidly progresses to general intellectual deficits.

This type of general impairment is often seen in patients with temporal lobe tumors, but parietal tumors are less likely to result in memory problems. Occipital tumors, however, can lead to memory problems.

Tumors of the parietal lobe of the cerebral hemispheres also frequently cause AGNOSIA (loss of the ability to recognize objects or people), while tumors of the parietal lobe of the dominant cerebral hemisphere can cause AGRAPHIA (loss of ability to write, a form of aphasia).

Fifty-seven percent of patients with temporal lobe lesions exhibit memory problems; 50 percent of patients with frontal lobe lesions, 45 percent of patients with occipital lobe lesions and 25 percent of patients with parietal lobe lesions do so.

Tumors of the posterior fossa (that is, the cerebellum, cerebellopontine angle and brain stem) are less likely to cause cognitive deficits than tumors just described, unless the increase in intracranial pressure causes hydrocephalus.

Estimates suggest that 15 percent of all patients suffering from brain tumors were initially diagnosed with dementia, which gradually interfered with writing, reading and calculations. In fact, frontal lobe tumors are the most likely to be confused with dementia, especially when both lobes are involved and the tumor develops in the midline. In addition, slow-growing tumors often mimic the symptoms of Alzheimer's disease, but a cancer spreading from another area of the body (such as the lung or breast) may cause memory impairment as well.

In the United States, about six new cases of primary brain tumor per 100,000 are diagnosed each year, occurring most often around the age of 50.

Symptoms In addition to memory problems, compression of brain tissue or nerve tracts near the tumor may cause muscle weakness, vision loss, sensory disturbances, speech problems and epileptic seizures. An expanding tumor can raise pressure inside the skull, causing headaches, vomiting, visual disturbances and impaired mental function.

Diagnosis Common diagnostic tests for brain tumors may include a myelogram, angiogram (or arteriogram), pneumoencephalogram, brain scans, spinal tap or electroencephalogram (EEG). The most accurate diagnostic procedure, however, is a biopsy of tumor tissue.

Treatment While any surgical operation carries risk, a skilled surgeon can operate on many parts of the brain without destroying important functions. However, surgery in the temporal lobes is extremely difficult because intellectual functions (memory, speech, ability to comprehend abstractions) can be profoundly reduced by cutting into this center. Other treatments besides surgery include radiation and chemotherapy with anticancer or corticosteroid drugs.

If a tumor is inaccessible or too large to be removed, as much of it as possible is cut away to relieve pressure on the brain, but the outlook in these cases is poor; fewer than 20 percent of such patients survive for one year.

Wilson, Barbara. *Rehabilitation of Memory*. New York: Guilford Press, 1988.

Breuer, Josef (1842–1925) An Austrian physician and physiologist who was acknowledged by Sigmund Freud and others as the principal developer of psychoanalysis. In 1880 Breuer was able to relieve the symptoms of hysteria in "Anna O" after he had induced her to recall unpleasant past experiences under HYPNOSIS. Breuer concluded that neurotic symptoms result from unconscious processes and disappear when those processes become conscious.

He later described his methods and results to Freud, and referred patients to him; together the two wrote *Studien uber Hysterie* (1895), in which Breuer described his treatment of hysteria. Breuer and Freud eventually became enemies, however, over disagreements on basic theories of therapy. (See also ANNA O; FREUD, SIGMUND.)

Brierre de Boismont, Alexandre (1798–1881) A noted French *alieniste* (psychiatrist) who studied hallucinations during HYPNOSIS (which he called "magnetic visions") in mental illness, religious experiences and other ALTERED STATES OF CONSCIOUSNESS. He published *Hallucinations Or, the rational history of apparitions, visions, dreams, ecstasy, magnetism and somnambulism* in 1853.

Broca, Paul (1824–1880) A French surgeon whose study of brain lesions contributed significantly to the understanding of the origins of APHASIA (the loss or impairment of the ability to form or articulate words).

Broca founded the anthropology lab at the École des Hautes Études in Paris in 1858 and the Société d'Anthropologie de Paris in 1859, where he developed his research into the comparative study of the craniums of the races of mankind, studying the form, structure and topography of the brain.

In 1861 he announced his discovery of the seat of articulate speech, located in the left frontal region of the brain, since known as the convolution of Broca. With this discovery, Broca provided the first anatomical proof of the localization of brain function. (See also BROCA'S APHASIA.)

Broca's aphasia An expressive disorder that affects both written and spoken speech, producing nonfluent, slow, labored and arrhythmic speech. Patients usually retain reasonably good comprehension of some words, such as nouns, and the few words they can utter tend to be meaningful.

Broca's aphasia is caused by a lesion in the left frontal cortex, although a lesion serious enough to produce a permanent disorder probably also affects parts of the BASAL GANGLIA. (See also APHASIA; BROCA, PAUL; WERNICKE'S [RECEPTIVE] APHASIA.)

Brown-Peterson task This commonly used test of recall over delays of a few seconds features items presented to subjects (usually in threes), after which the subject engages in some interfering activity (such as counting backward) until the end of the retention interval. At that point subjects are asked to recall the items just presented.

Although recall usually declines steeply after a 30-second delay, researchers believe that the interfering tasks makes recall more difficult but does not completely prevent it. Patients with ALZHEIMER'S DISEASE and some with AMNESIA usually perform badly on this test.

Bruno, Giordano (1548–1600) An Italian philosopher, astronomer, mathematician and occultist who believed in an infinite universe and the multiplicity of worlds; he also was extremely interested in the art of MEMORY and in MNEMONIC STRATEGIES.

While he is best known for being burned at the stake during the Inquisition for supporting Copernicus's theory that the earth circles the sun, there were other reasons for his unpopularity. He was burned for the overarching heresy of his belief in extraordinary memory systems, which many at the time considered black magic.

Bruno's systems were extremely complex; his book of seals (symbolic emblems often used in Renaissance memory systems) was a masterwork. The seals included pictures of a man with astrological symbols on appropriate body parts (such as Aries the Ram on the head). Bruno tried to imbue his seals with emotional intensity, as they were talismans designed to evoke astral and artistic energies, to be contemplated and internalized.

He tried a great variety of other memory systems until he hit upon the idea of putting memory images in motion on revolving wheels. In this system, the inner wheel held all the astrological and astronomical images (150 houses, decans and planets), all recombining as the wheels turned. As this wheel revolved in memory, around it rode other wheels, each bearing 150 images. In all his work and writing, Bruno tried to develop the memory of a divine human that would restore the transcendental nature.

In 1582 Bruno published three mnemotechnical works in which he explored new means to attain an intimate knowledge of reality. In 1591, at the invitation of Venetian patrician Giovanni Mocenigo, Bruno participated in discussions with progressive Venetian aristocrats. But Mocenigo, disappointed by his private lessons from Bruno on the art of memory, denounced him to the Venetian Inquisition in May 1592 for heretical theories.

Bruno was arrested and tried, then was extradited to Rome for trial by the Roman Inquisition in 1593; he was sentenced to death in 1600 and was burned at the stake.

C

caffeine and memory While the amount of caffeine in coffee or tea is a mild stimulant and may keep one awake enough to pay attention, it also may make one too jittery to learn, and is just as likely to have a negative effect on memory as a positive one.

Studies have shown that a person who is already wide awake and rested will not find much of a memory boost from caffeine. But too much coffee (and the exact amount varies from person to person) can bring on the jitters, insomnia and memory problems. For a habitual user, however, omitting this stimulant will have the same negative effect.

Effects Caffeine acts on the brain, affecting coordination, concentration, sleep patterns and behavior. The gastrointestinal tract absorbs almost all the caffeine and distributes it to all tissues and organs within minutes of consumption; maximum blood levels are reached within 45 minutes. While it may improve simple motor tasks, it may disrupt more complex tasks involving fine motor coordination and quick reactions. Of course, any drug's effect depends on the amount consumed, how often, how much the body absorbs and how quickly it is metabolized.

Some research has shown that administering small amounts (two or more cups of regular coffee) did not affect performance when compared with subjects drinking the same amount of decaffeinated coffee. In addition, one study suggests that caffeine may interfere with memory only in women. No information is available about possible memory-enhancement possibilities of nonprescription caffeine-based stimulants.

A separate study of healthy college students found that their ability to remember lists of words they had just heard was diminished following the administration of caffeine. And a 1983 study found that combining caffeine and alcohol actually slowed the reaction time of eight subjects, making subjects more drunk than the alcohol alone.

In any case, caffeine may be hard to avoid. A staggeringly large number of products in the United States contain caffeine; in addition to food and beverages, caffeine is found in over-the-counter stimulants, analgesics, cold preparations, antihistamines and prescription drugs. In fact, more than 2,000 nonprescription drugs and 1,000 prescription drugs contain caffeine or caffeine-type stimulants.

Dean, Ward, and Morgenthaler, John. *Smart Drugs & Nutrients.* Santa Cruz, CA: B&J Publications, 1991.
Herrmann, Douglas. *Supermemory.* Emmaus, PA: Rodale Press, 1991.
Watson, Ronald R. "Caffeine: Is It Dangerous to Health?" *American Journal of Health Promotion* 2 (Spring 1988): 13–21.

calcium The most abundant mineral in the body, this substance has been implicated as both a possible cause of mental decline and as (through its release of CALPAIN) a memory enhancer. Calcium is essential for proper cell function, muscle contraction, nerve impulse transmission and blood clotting.

The drug NIMODIPINE, which blocks excess calcium in the part of the brain associated with memory and learning, has been used successfully to improve memory loss in STROKE victims. In addition, conditions that result in a flood of calcium in the brain lead to memory problems, which some researchers believe is caused by a release of too *much* protein-eating calpain. At the same time, normal levels of calcium release calpain, which seems to improve memory by improving cell-to-cell communication.

The main dietary sources of calcium are milk and dairy products, eggs, fish, green vegetables and fruit. The amount of calcium in the body is controlled by the action of two hormones, parathyroid hormone and calcitonin. When the level of calcium drops, the parathyroid glands release more parathyroid hormone, raising blood calcium levels by helping to release calcium from reservoirs in bones.

calendar calculators See AUTISTIC SAVANTS.

calpain One of several brain chemicals called NEUROTRANSMITTERS currently being studied for their role in memory. Released by CALCIUM in the cells, calpain can digest protein and appears to clean up blocked receptors and let neurons communicate more easily with each other. Some researchers suspect that reduced calcium levels in older patients may be one reason that senior citizens so often experience memory loss.

To test this hypothesis, researchers used a calpain blocker called LEUPEPTIN to interfere with the level of calpain in rats and then tested the animals' ability to solve an eight-sided maze. In the experiment, a rat is placed in the middle of a maze with eight tunnels; at the end of each is food. Rats quickly learn to run to the end of one tunnel, get the food and move on to the next alley without returning to the chambers where they had already eaten the reward. While the rats appeared to be normal and clearly recognized their surroundings, they had a hard time actually remembering which paths they had visited, especially if they were removed in the middle of the experiment and returned a few moments later. The calpain blocker seemed to be interfering directly with their ability to form memories. But other researchers have disagreed with these findings, since not a great deal is known about leupeptin.

Camillo, Giulio (1480–1544)   Given the title "divine" by his contemporaries, Camillo built a "memory theater" in Venice such as the world had not seen before or since. The purpose of the memory theater was to waken a person to the memory of his or her own divine legacy.

Camillo's memory system was based on archetypes of reality that were placed around a traditional neoclassical theater. His views on memory were grounded in the teachings of PLATO; he tried to construct an artificial memory based on truth. Allegedly, Camillo had whispered the secret of his memory theater to King Francis I of France, but the king never revealed the secret.

Camillo was a memory master and magician, and described his wooden memory theater masterpiece as "a constructed mind and soul" or a "windowed mind." He filled the theater with exquisite images—Apollo, the Three Gorgons, Pasipha and the Bull, Prometheus. The theater reversed the usual perspective, so that a guest standing on the stage looked out into the fan-shaped rows of the "audience," crowded with memory images.

On the first level were the seven world-empowering ideas that sprang from the divine abyss symbolized as Cabalistic Sephiroths, archangels and planets. The influence of each of the seven moved up the auditorium through the crowded seven rings of exis-tence, from supercelestial to the material arts of man. Memory images were connected organically to achieve unified, cosmic memory.

The theater also was built upon an understanding of Renaissance magic. The architecture reflected the sacred geometry of the zodiac and the earth, a type of sacred architecture designed to focus cosmic energy and create resonant space. Camillo crafted his images following the belief that certain patterns and proportions align with the universe and induce the flow of astral energies—energies that alter mind and matter. He believed this was how the ancient Egyptians made their statues come alive.

Capgras, Jean Marie Joseph (1873–1950)   A well-known French psychopathologist who first identified the delusional syndrome called reduplicative paramnesia (or CAPGRAS SYNDROME) that today bears his name.

Capgras and J. Reboul-Lachaux first noted the syndrome in 1923 in a female patient with a chronic paranoid psychosis who also insisted that various individuals involved in her life had been replaced by doubles. Capgras and Reboul-Lachaux called the condition *l'illusion des sosies* (the illusion of doubles).

Capgras syndrome   One form of reduplicative paramnesia, this is a delusional condition also called the syndrome of "doubles," in which a patient fails to recognize well-known people or places, believing that doubles have replaced them. The delusion is often quite strong and can be deeply disturbing to family and friends whose identity is constantly denied. Generally, the person accused as an "imposter" also is believed to have harmful intentions toward the patient.

The effect can be induced by showing patients a picture and then, a few minutes later, producing the same picture again. The patients will probably say they have seen a similar picture, but insist it is definitely not

Levels of Carbon Monoxide Poisoning

Carbon Monoxide Concentration	Symptoms
Less than 35 ppm (cigarette smoke)	None, or mild headache
0.005% (50 ppm)	Slight headache
0.01% (100 ppm)	Throbbing headache
0.02% (200 ppm)	Severe headache, irritability, fatigue
0.03%–0.05% (300–500 ppm)	Headache, confusion, lethargy, collapse
0.08%–0.12% (800–1200 ppm)	Coma, convulsions
0.19% (1,900 ppm)	Rapidly fatal

the one they are now looking at. This disorder is believed to have a psychological origin, although more recent research suggests there may be an organic cause. It is typically associated with CONFABULATION, speech disorders and denial of illness.

It was first described by Jean Marie Capgras and J. Reboul-Lachaux in 1923, who discussed a female patient with a chronic paranoid psychosis who also insisted that various individuals involved in her life had been replaced by doubles. Capgras and Reboul-Lachaux called the condition *l'illusion des sosies* (the illusion of doubles).

Capgras syndrome is one of a group of MISIDENTIFICATION SYNDROMES that can occur in psychotic patients. It also may occur as a result of brain injury. Although the precise cause of this unusual syndrome is uncertain, it may involve extensive cerebral damage, probably with extensive frontal lesions.

Frontal lesions may cause problems in the integration of different kinds of information, and when these problems are combined with perceptual and memory deficits from other brain lesions, reduplicative paramnesia or Capgras syndrome may result. (See also CAPGRAS, JEAN MARIE JOSEPH.)

carbon monoxide poisoning   Poisoning with carbon monoxide, a tasteless, colorless, odorless gas, can lead to profound cognitive impairment (including memory loss).

ANOXIA (lack of oxygen to the brain) causes brain damage, particularly to the BASAL GANGLIA. Common sources of exposure to carbon monoxide include smoke inhalation in fires, automobile exhaust fumes, faulty or poorly ventilated charcoal, kerosene or gas stoves, cigarette smoke and methylene chloride. Several minutes of exposure to 1,000 parts per million (0.1 percent) may cause fatal poisoning.

People exposed to carbon monoxide complain of headache, dizziness and nausea; patients with heart problems may experience angina or myocardial infarction. More severe exposures bring on impaired thinking, coma and convulsions. Survivors may suffer numerous neurological problems, such as parkinsonism and personality and memory disorders.

Treatment includes the administration of oxygen in the highest possible concentration (100 percent); some experts support the use of hyperbaric chambers, which can enhance the elimination of carbon monoxide. Such treatment may be useful to patients exposed to very high levels of carbon monoxide and who are reasonably close to a chamber. (See also CHEMICALS AND MEMORY LOSS.)

Olson, Kent, M.D. *Poisoning & Drug Overdose.* Norwalk, CT: Appleton & Lange, 1990.

catecholamine   A class of neurotransmitter including norepinephrine, epinephrine and dopamine. (See NEUROTRANSMITTERS.)

catharsis   The therapeutic release of ideas through talking about conscious material, accompanied by an appropriate emotional reaction. Cartharsis also refers to the release into awareness of repressed material from the unconscious. (See also REPRESSED MEMORIES; REPRESSION.)

caudate nucleus   A part of the BASAL GANGLIA often referred to as the enostriatum. The deterioration of this part of the brain results in HUNTINGTON'S DISEASE.

centrophenoxine   A drug (trade name: Lucidril) that is believed to improve various aspects of memory function. It is believed to remove LIPOFUSCIN deposits, the material of which "age spots" are made. Lipofuscin buildup in heart, skin and brain cells appears with age; decreased deposits have been correlated with improved learning ability.

In some studies centrophenoxine appears to remove these deposits and repair synapses. In the bloodstream, centrophenoxine breaks down into dimethylaminoethanol (DMAE), a naturally occurring nutrient found in seafood that is normally present in the brain in small amounts. DMAE also is believed to enhance brain function.

Scientists have shown that centrophenoxine can protect the brains of animals against lack of oxygen and may be of value in treating diseases in which tissue oxygenation is lowered (such as DEMENTIA or STROKE). While centrophenoxine does not seem effective in the treatment of ALZHEIMER'S DISEASE, it may help in cases where the brain is not getting enough oxygen.

Centrophenoxine should not be used by patients who are easily excitable, hypertensive or subject to convulsions or involuntary musculoskeletal movements.

cerebral cortex   See CORTEX.

cerebrovascular accident (CVA) Sudden rupture or blockage of a blood vessel within the brain (also called stroke) resulting in serious bleeding or local obstruction to blood circulation. Several researchers have reported AMNESIA after a blockage in the posterior cerebral artery (a blood vessel that supplies the HIPPOCAMPUS); less often, CVAs may cause amnesia by damaging the diencephalic structures.

Cause   Blockage may be due to a clot formation (thrombosis) or an embolism, and rupture of different blood vessels may cause different patterns of bleeding.

About 8 percent of cerebral vascular accidents are due to a SUBARACHNOID HEMORRHAGE, which usually affects younger people who are less likely to suffer from widespread cerebral vascular disease. The usual cause of such a hemorrhage is the rupture of a brain ANEURYSM (ballooning of an artery), which bleeds into the subarachnoid space surrounding the brain.

The anterior communicating artery (located between the frontal lobes) often is associated with ruptured aneurysms. Other common sites are the middle cerebral artery and the posterior communicating artery.

While a hemorrhage sometimes may be caused by a ruptured benign tumor, in about 20 percent of cases no structural cause is known. Shortly after the hemorrhage, symptoms similar to those found in Korsakoff's syndrome may occur, including disorientation, CONFABULATION and impaired memory. Memory impairment following a subarachnoid hemorrhage may be temporary or permanent.

Finally, TRANSIENT GLOBAL AMNESIA almost always is due to a cerebral vascular cause, with a sudden onset of symptoms in an otherwise normal patient. The episode may begin with a brief clouding of consciousness, and the amnesia usually lasts for several hours, ending in complete recovery.

Wilson, Barbara. *Rehabilitation of Memory*. New York: Guilford Press, 1988.

cerebropathia psychica toxemica   The original term for KORSAKOFF'S SYNDROME used by Russian psychiatrist Sergey Sergeyevich Korsakoff, who first described it in 1887. (See also KORSAKOFF, SERGEY SERGEYEVICH.)

cerebrum   The largest area of the brain, the cerebrum is arranged in two hemispheres (or halves), called the right and left cerebral hemisphere. It is the part of the brain responsible for higher-order thinking and decision making. The right side of the cerebrum controls the left side of the body, and the left side of the cerebrum controls the right side of the body.

The outer layer of the cerebrum is called the CORTEX (or "gray matter"); the inner portion is the white matter. Indentations (called fissures) divide each cerebral hemisphere into four lobes: the frontal lobe, parietal lobe, TEMPORAL LOBE and occipital lobe. Functions involving memory are thought to take place within the frontal lobe, the parietal lobe and the temporal lobe.

chaining   A behavioral method for helping patients with memory problems handle everyday tasks. In this method, a particular task is broken down into a series of smaller units and taught one at a time. (See also BEHAVIORAL TREATMENTS OF MEMORY DISORDERS.)

chemicals and memory loss   A wide variety of drugs and other substances have been implicated in memory problems, including calcium and many other medications and substances. (See also PHYSIOLOGICAL CAUSES OF MEMORY LOSS.)

Calcium   Calcium has been implicated as a possible cause of mental decline over time. The drug nimodipine, which blocks excess calcium in the part of the brain associated with memory and learning, has been used successfully to improve memory loss in stroke victims.

Choline Acetyltransferase   Choline acetyltransferase is deficient in the brains of Alzheimer's patients and is believed to be the primary reason behind their deficiency of ACETYLCHOLINE.

Carbon Monoxide Poisoning   Survivors of CARBON MONOXIDE POISONING can be left with profound cognitive impairment; carbon monoxide poisoning may also damage the BASAL GANGLIA.

Lipofuscin   Buildup of lipofuscin, of which "age spots" are made, has been linked to decreased learning ability.

chemistry of memory   The language of memory is written with chemicals, the basis of memory itself, although details about the complex pattern of neuronal activity that underlies memory function is not yet known.

When a person remembers, the work is done by NEUROTRANSMITTERS such as ACETYLCHOLINE, which help pass nerve signals from cell to cell over a network of SYNAPSE bridges. At a synapse, the impulse triggers release of other neurotransmitters. Most scientists today believe that memory is a result of functional changes in these synapses, which arise from the effects of external stimuli prompted by education or training.

The communicating nerve cells (or neurotransmitters) are found throughout the brain but especially in the HIPPOCAMPUS. Deficits in many of these neurotransmitters, such as acetylcholine, interfere with learning and can lead to muddy thinking and poor memory. Aging interferes with the manufacture of acetylcholine; in fact, the gradual reduction of acetylcholine and other neurotransmitters in the aging brain is the primary culprit in the slowdown in mental function.

As evidence of acetylcholine's importance in memory, scientists have discovered that when drugs that block the action of acetylcholine (such as SCOPOLAMINE) are administered, subjects experience problems in tasks requiring retention over long periods of time.

Research into the biochemical basis of memory itself was first begun during the 1950s, when studies suggested that the complex molecule RNA (ribonucleic acid) served as a chemical mediator for memory. Rat studies showed that when animals were trained to do certain tasks, RNA in certain cells changed; further, if an animal's RNA was destroyed, it could no longer remember the task it had learned previously. Apparently blocking the rats' RNA interfered with long-term memory, although no change was apparent in short-term memory. In addition, active learning that involves the use of memory seems to cause the brain to produce increased amounts of RNA, which in turn increases the amount of protein production. Swedish researchers have discovered that the brains of rats undergoing a learning experience produce up to 40 percent more RNA than the brains of control rats that have not learned anything. To erase memory of a task completely, a drug that blocks RNA had to be injected into many areas of the brain instead of only one specific place. This research suggests that the RNA and protein increases that result from learning expand the neuron network and enable memory of the task to spread out over the cortex. Even more intriguing, when RNA cells from a trained rat were injected into an untrained rat, the untrained rat suddenly "remembered" tasks that it had never been trained to do before.

Other memory-enhancing chemicals being studied include CALPAIN, NOREPINEPHRINE, d-amino-d-arginine vasopressin (DDAVP) and adrenaline.

Calpain seems to be able to digest protein and unblock receptors, facilitating neuronal communication. Calpain is released naturally by calcium in the cells, which leads scientists to wonder if calcium deficiency may decrease enzyme activity in older people, leading to memory loss.

Norepinephrine, a neurotransmitter associated with stress, also appears to be linked to memories (especially those associated with stress). By blocking the production of norepinephrine, it's possible to block fearful memories, according to rat studies done at the University of California at Irvine.

While DDAVP is used to balance water content in the body, it also can improve temporarily the ability to recall in normal humans and some animals.

Adrenaline appears to be a key to locking memories in place in the brain, since rats that can't produce adrenaline have poorer recall ability than those that can produce the hormone. And rats that get a booster shot of adrenaline after learning something can remember the information better. This fact may support the idea that hormone deficiency in older people contributes to memory loss.

Scientists theorize that hormones like adrenaline act as fixatives, locking up memories of exciting or shocking events, which allows the brain a way to remember important information while discarding trivial bits. Hormones may act directly on the brain, or they may alter body chemistry so some other substance can reach the brain and lock in the memory.

chess   When it comes to memory for the game of chess, studies have shown that chess masters don't have superior memories, but they have better memories for meaningful, properly structured information in their particular knowledge domain. Experts perceive board positions in terms of relations between groups of pieces. Whereas amateur players must memorize the position of each individual piece, experts only have to remember the group. Experts organize information into chunks in accordance with the relational patterns resulting from the attacking and defensive moves that occur in the game.

child abuse, memory of   In general, research has shown that the more psychodynamically important a memory, the more likely it is to be either warped or utterly forgotten. In fact, early childhood memories are highly malleable and susceptible to a wide range of distortions, even among siblings raised in the same home.

Symptoms of Possible Childhood Abuse

The following signs could mean a person was abused but has repressed or forgotten the memory:

Compulsive Habits   These habits, which could include overeating, drinking to excess or abusing drugs, may follow a traumatic incident.

Uncontrollable anger   More common in men, the habit of regularly flying into rages over nothing may be a strong indication of repressed trauma.

Recurrent unexplainable medical problems   Tension in the neck or shoulders may be rooted in repressed trauma.

Strong aversions   Aversions to smells or food, which are usually intense to the point of nausea or vomiting, may indicate repressed trauma.

Intense fears of harming your own children   These fears, sometimes occurring along with panic attacks, may be in fact memories of a person's own childhood abuse.

Usually a child forgets abuse because remembering is simply too painful. During the experience, experts believe, a small part of memory disassociates or splits off. It can suddenly reemerge during adulthood, coming into consciousness after it is triggered by something—such as a dream, hypnosis or therapy.

In one Massachusetts study of 53 women who had been abused as children, the earlier, longer and more violent the incest, the more likely it was to have been forgotten. The extent of the incest was known only because other individuals revealed the experience to the women.

The sudden recollection of abuse, particularly childhood sexual abuse, is controversial, however. Victims themselves often agonize over their memories, and—in the case of incest—the accused family members often deny any guilt. According to memory expert Elizabeth Loftus, Ph. D., memories are highly susceptible to imagination or suggestion. Loftus, who researches false memories, says she can implant a false memory into the minds of people in the laboratory and they will believe the memory is real.

While the memories Loftus studies are unimportant ones, not emotional traumas,

she also believes that some people use the "memory" of abuse to explain painful symptoms they don't understand.

Whether these memories are real becomes very important when the issue comes to court. Until 1988, most states ruled there was a statute of limitations for sexual abuse in civil suits lasting three years after a person reached age 21. But since memory of abuse often doesn't surface until many years later, most cases never went to court.

The first state to change that law was Washington, which changed its statute in 1988 to allow victims to bring suit three years after the memory of abuse returned. Since then 14 states have passed similar laws.

Goleman, Daniel. "In Memory, People Re-Create Their Lives to Suit Their Images of the Present." *New York Times*, June 23, 1987.

childhood memories   Virtually no one remembers events from childhood before age four, but the reason why this is so is still debated. Sigmund Freud believed this childhood amnesia was caused by the repression of infantile sexuality, but many modern memory researchers say it is due to the lack of development of various mental abilities (such as language) used to cue memory.

The first memories that a person can remember may have important implications for later psychological development, since a person's earliest memories also may reveal information about overall psychological makeup, according to Alfred Adler, one of Freud's early disciples.

Other memory researchers believe that earliest memories are not true memories at all, but retrospective inventions or selections that reveal some psychological truth about a person's life. In fact, studies show that a person's earliest memories sometimes change as psychotherapy progresses and interpersonal conflicts are resolved.

Relationships that are reflected in these early memories often repeat themselves throughout a person's life, according to a University of Missouri/St. Louis study. This research revealed that college students who had reached the fullest psychological maturity (such as achieved commitments after a period of doubt and searching) tended to have early memories reflecting striving and mastery. But those who had adopted parental values without independently seeking an identity had highly dependent early memories revolving around a need for nurturance, safety and compliance with authority. (See also MEMORY IN INFANCY.)

Goleman, Daniel. "In Memory, People Re-Create Their Lives to Suit Their Images of the Present." *New York Times*, June 23, 1987.

choline   This dietary substance is the forerunner of ACETYLCHOLINE (a brain compound necessary for transmitting nerve impulses) and has been implicated as a possible aid to improving memory by increasing the amount of acetylcholine in the brain.

In one federal study, a single 10-gram dose of choline significantly improved both memory and recall in healthy subjects; those with the worst memory were the ones most helped by the choline. Other tests suggest that choline may improve thinking

ability, muscle control and the nervous system.

Repeated studies of administering choline to treat the memory problems of ALZHEIMER'S DISEASE patients have resulted in conflicting evidence, although the majority found that giving choline was not helpful. Other studies suggest that choline might be useful in heading off some deterioration in the early stages of the disease.

Still other studies have suggested that egg yolk (a dietary source of choline) may be useful to patients suffering from memory problems. Alcoholics and drug addicts also seem to show an improvement. The major dietary source of choline is LECITHIN; foods rich in lecithin include eggs (average size), salmon and lean beef.

While some researchers dismiss the idea that eating these foods can significantly improve memory, other scientists note at least that a "normal" level of lecithin in the diet may not be enough as people age.

The body uses phosphatidyl choline to make cell membranes, where most of the important electrochemical activities arise. Nerve and brain cells especially repair and maintain themselves with large quantities of this substance.

In research at the University of Ohio, scientists noted that levels of choline drop as a person ages and that levels are especially low in people with Alzheimer's disease.

Kra, Siegfried. *Aging Myths*. New York: McGraw-Hill, 1986.

Minninger, Joan. *Total Recall*. Emmaus, Pa.: Rodale Press, 1984.

Ostrander, Sheila, and Schroeder, Lynn. *Supermemory*. New York: Guilford Press, 1988.

choline acetyltransferase (ChAT)   An enzyme in the brain that is a crucial ingredient of the chemical process that produces ACETYLCHOLINE, a neurotransmitter involved in both learning and memory.

cholinergic   Refers to those neurons that use ACETYLCHOLINE as a neurotransmitter. (See NEUROTRANSMITTERS.)

cholinergic basal forebrain   Nuclei in the deep regions of the forebrain containing neurons that release the neurotransmitter ACETYLCHOLINE. The cholinergic basal forebrain includes the medial septum, which projects to the HIPPOCAMPUS; the band of Broca, which projects to the hippocampus and amygdala; and the nucleus basalis of Meynert, which projects to the neocortex and AMYGDALA. Damage to these structures of the brain is believed to contribute to organic amnesia.

cholinergic hypothesis of Alzheimer's disease   There is a link between memory loss and the decrease in the activity of the enzyme CHOLINE ACETYLTRANSFERASE (CHAT) in the brain of Alzheimer's patients. (See ALZHEIMER'S DISEASE.)

ChAT is a crucial ingredient in the chemical process that produces ACETYLCHOLINE, a neurotransmitter involved in learning and memory. There has been a link between this decrease in neurochemical activity and changes in memory loss and disorientation and the physical appearance of Alzheimer brains (especially in the number of plaques).

Researchers have found a marked loss of nerve cells among Alzheimer's patients in a part of the base of the brain called the nucleus basalis; some patients with classical Alzheimer's disease have been shown to lose as many as 90 percent of these cells. The nucleus basalis produces acetylcholine, and uses it and its enzymes to communicate with the brain's cortex.

cholinomimetic   agents   Drugs that mimic the activity of the neurotransmitter ACETYLCHOLINE, which is important in both learning and memory. The cholinomimetic agents include arecoline, which enhances learning in normal humans and aging primates. Researchers have found that cloni-

dine, a substance that promotes the activity of catecholamines, improves the learning capability of aging monkeys and a few KORSAKOFF'S SYNDROME patients. Still, treatment aimed at replacing or stimulating cholinergic activity has had little success in improving memory in Alzheimer's disease patients.

Arnsten, A.F.T., and Goldman-Rakic, P.S. "a2-Adrenergic Mechanisms in Prefrontal Cortex Associated with Cognitive Decline in Nonhuman Primates." *Science* 230 (1985): 1273–76.

Bartus, R.T., et al. "The Cholinergic Hypothesis of Geriatric Memory Dysfunction." *Science* 217 (1982): 408.

McEntee, W.J., and Mair, R.G. "Memory Enhancement in Korsakoff's Psychosis by Clonidine: Further Evidence for a Noradrenergic Deficit." *Annals of Neurology* 7 (1980): 466–70.

chunking, process of   Grouping several separate bits of information into larger chunks in order to better remember them; often organizing them in a particular way, such as according to sound, rules of grammar, rhythm and so on, helps a person to recall them. For example, it's easier to remember a phone number broken up into chunks of three, three and four digits (215-555-1328) than to remember a ten-digit number: 2155551328.

Cicero (106 B.C.–43 B.C.)   One of the greatest of the Roman orators and a devoted mnemonist and teacher of memory systems and rhetoric, Cicero also believed (as did PLATO) that humans possess divine memory. He wrote that the memories of the lawyers and orators of his time were aided by systems and training that he used himself.

Oratory was an important career in Cicero's time, and the ancient Greeks and Romans realized that memory training could help the thinking process itself. In fact, a papyrus fragment dated to 400 B.C. extols the value of a trained memory.

In addition to the classical memory method of loci (building memory palaces),

Cicero also learned how to make mental notes and remember words verbatim, but this memory system of Cicero's is lost; the AD HERENNIUM considered it to be too hard to use—and Cicero agreed. However, Cicero did borrow from his system to introduce to Rome a new way of writing called shorthand, which the church of the Middle Ages believed was grievous heresy and condemned as springing from the devil.

Yates, Frances. *The Art of Memory*. Chicago: University of Chicago Press, 1966.

cigarettes and memory   See SMOKING AND MEMORY.

circadian rhythm and memory   A person's strength for memory tasks is cyclical, rising and falling during certain times of the day and of the week. Although most people experience a period of "peak" efficiency somewhere between 11 A.M. and 4 P.M., every person's internal body clock is different. As the day progresses, a person gets more involved in activities, but by lunchtime tiredness sets in. The daily biological cycles (body temperature, respiration and pulse rate) vary the power of attention and, therefore, of memory ability.

People who go to bed and wake up early learn more readily at the beginning of the day, while those who have a later schedule experience the opposite. Those who work a night shift probably experience different cyclical peak times from those who work a nine-to-five schedule.

In addition, research has shown that for some reason, memory ability tends to be at its best on Friday and Saturday, probably because the anticipation of the weekend improves a person's outlook and mood.

Disruptions to a person's normal cycle interfere with learning and memory ability. A new parent whose baby wakes every few hours all night long will experience memory problems due to chronic sleep interruption. Jet lag also can affect memory efficiency.

circulation and memory   The proper function of memory requires a steady supply of blood and oxygen to the brain. Excess antihypertensive medication can lower the blood pressure to the point where it isn't sufficient to pump the blood to the brain, especially when a patient stands up. This causes a lack of blood supply in the brain that can produce a loss of memory. However, this memory loss only occurs when the brain has been subjected to low blood pressure repeatedly for several months. It usually affects patients over age 70.

classical conditioning   A type of learning in which a previously neutral stimulus elicits a response. The most famous example of classical conditioning is Ivan Pavlov's dogs, which were trained to salivate (an existing response) when hearing the sound of a bell (neutral stimulus) because it had previously been associated with food. (See also PAVLOV, IVAN PETROVICH.)

Amnesic patients can learn through classical conditioning; when two amnesic patients acquired a conditioned eye-blink response to a buzzer and puff of air, the patients showed no recollection of the conditioning procedure but maintained the conditioned response.

Classical conditioning is the type of learning most often studied by scientists trying to locate the source of memory in the brain.

clioquinol   An active component of many antidiarrhea drugs until it was banned, clioquinol also may cause memory problems. In 1966 clioquinol was distributed in Japan to treat dysentery after widespread flooding; soon thereafter more than 100 people reported a TRANSIENT GLOBAL AMNESIA. Other sporadic cases have occurred in Europe.

Clioquinol is still contained in creams, lotions and ointments as an antibacterial and antifungal, but it should not be taken internally.

coexistence hypothesis   A theory about eyewitness memory that explains why people report incorrect facts after witnessing an event. According to the hypothesis, both the original memory and the false postevent memory exist in the brain, as two competing alternatives. When a witness is asked about the event, he or she usually responds with the false version because it is the more recent memory and is therefore more accessible. However, even if a person produces a false memory, the original is recoverable, according to the coexistence hypothesis. (See also EYEWITNESS TESTIMONY; MEMORY FOR EVENTS.)

coexistence vs. alteration of memories
See MEMORY FOR EVENTS.

cognition   The processing of information by the brain; specifically, perception, reasoning and memory.

cognitive development   The acquisition of intelligence, conscious thought and problem-solving skills beginning in infancy and progressing throughout life. (See also MEMORY IN INFANCY; PIAGET, JEAN.)

Cognitive Failures Questionnaire   A test that assesses a person's susceptibility to slips of action and other failures of memory and perception. On the test, subjects are asked to assess the frequency with which they experienced specific examples of cognitive failure, such as: "Do you forget whether you've turned off the stove?" The test then gives a five-point scale ranging from "never" to "very often."

Scores from this test are not related to performance on tests of immediate and delayed memory or to perception as measured by performance on a word-identification test. The test scores are related to a person's ability to perform two tasks at the same time; the inability to pay attention and allocate processing resources effectively is associated with frequent slips of action as well as other forms of memory deficits.

Test scores are also related to forward digit span (ability to repeat back a sequence of digits in the correct order), which is involved in carrying out action sequences, such as remembering to turn off the stove. (See also ASSESSMENT OF MEMORY DISORDERS.)

cognitive map   A person's internal method of remembering how to find directions in unknown locations.

cognitive triage   The tendency to recall hard-to-remember items first in a series of lists of items. Scientists speculate that cognitive triage may be an unconscious adaptive strategy for getting weakly remembered items to surface first.

A widely held psychological theory is that when people try to recall several items, they remember easily recalled items first. But new research by scientists at the University of Arizona at Tucson suggest that by as early as age six, people asked on memory tests to recall lists of items in any order first remember items they previously had trouble recalling.

If the theory of cognitive triage is correct, researchers say, police officers interrogating children who have witnessed crimes might obtain more information by asking questions about critical and disturbing events first rather than starting out with easy questions in order to relax the children.

Bowers, Bruce. "Weak Memories Make Strong Comeback." *Science News* 13 (July 21, 1990): 36.

collective unconscious   A term coined by Swiss psychiatrist Carl Jung (1875–1961) to indicate a portion of shared ideas in the unconscious common to all people; also called racial unconscious or racial memory. Jung regarded the foundation of such mythical images as positive and creative (compared to Sigmund Freud's more negative view of mythology).

As part of his theory on the collective unconscious, Jung postulated a theory of archetypes—broadly similar images and symbols that occur in myths, fairy tales and dreams around the world. Jung believed these archetypes were inherited from experiences in our distant past, and that they are present in each person's unconscious, controlling the way he or she views the world. Jung believed the human psyche has an in-built tendency to dwell on certain inherited motifs, and that the basic pattern of these archetypes persists, however much details may vary.

While Jung also believed that every person had a personal unconscious of life experiences, he felt that the collective unconscious was superior. His aim in therapy was to put the patient in touch with the profound insight of the collective unconscious, particularly through dream interpretation.

combat amnesia   Once called combat fatigue, this is a type of traumatic AMNESIA occurring after combat in which the amnesia has a straightforward origin—a distressing event during war. One method of treating combat amnesia is by the SODIUM PENTOTHAL interview, in which a slow intravenous injection of the drug relieves the patient's anxiety to the point of drowsiness. Then the injection is stopped, and the therapist can begin to question the patient about the traumatic incident. The recall at this point is often profoundly disturbing to the patient, who reaches the height of the reaction and then collapses, then often is able to pick up the story at a more less traumatic point. One interpretation of this type of treatment is that the narcosis allows the patient to reinstate the extreme emotion felt during combat itself, unlocking the forgotten event.

A range of BARBITURATES, including sodium pentothal, have been used to facilitate the recall of emotionally disturbing memories; the most common alternative to sodium pentothal is SODIUM AMYTAL (amylbarbitone).

compensation neurosis   See ACCIDENT NEUROSIS.

complex   A group of associated ideas having a common, strong emotional tone. These are largely unconscious and significantly influence attitudes and associations.

computerized axial tomography (CAT)   See COMPUTERIZED TOMOGRAPHY (CT) SCAN.

computerized tomography (CT) scan Commonly known as a CAT (computerized axial tomography) scan, this is a quick and accurate diagnostic technique utilizing a computer and X rays passed through the brain at different angles to produce clear cross-sectional pictures of the tissue being examined. The CT scan provides a clearer and more detailed picture of the brain than X rays alone, and it tends to minimize the amount of radiation exposure.

Before the scan is performed, a contrast dye may be injected to make blood vessels or abnormalities show up more clearly. A number of low-dose X-ray beams are passed through the brain at different angles as the scanner rotates around the patient.

Using the information produced by the scanner, a computer constructs cross-sectional pictures of the brain, which are then displayed on a TV screen and can reveal soft tissue, including tumors, more clearly than normal X rays. CT scans are particularly useful in scanning the brain because they sharply define the ventricles (fluid-filled spaces).

The first scanner was developed as a brain research tool and was used clinically in 1972. Since then CT brain scans have improved the diagnosis and treatment of strokes, head injuries, tumors, abscesses and brain hemorrhages.

computer use and memory Because of the computer's ability to focus attention without distraction, recent research suggests that playing computer games and using computers may influence memory and cognition, especially in the elderly. In a preliminary study in Rockville, Maryland, 50 nursing home residents in their 70s, 80s and 90s were introduced to video games modified so they would have a greater chance of success. Other than those with severe mental impairment, residents—even those with Alzheimer's or Parkinson's disease—were able to participate and sharpen their memory skills.

concealing memories See SCREEN MEMORIES.

concussion Brief unconsciousness (usually for only a few seconds) following a severe blow to the head or neck caused by a disturbance of the electrical activity in the brain. The impact creates a sudden movement of the brain within the skull, which can produce a wide range of injuries including a loss of memory for experiences just before and during the accident that caused the concussion. However, memory loss may encompass a few weeks or, rarely, months before the accident. The recovery of memory usually progresses from the more distant past to the recent experience. (See RIBOT'S LAW.)

There is no evident structural damage to the brain with a concussion, although there may be cuts or bruises on the skin outside the skull.

About a third of all those with concussion have a combination of symptoms called postconcussion syndrome for some time after a HEAD INJURY. Recent research has suggested that postconcussion syndrome can include significant memory problems, dizziness and behavioral changes that can disturb patients for as long as six months to a year following the head injury. Precisely why these symptoms occur in some people is not known.

Concussions usually are caused by traffic or industrial accidents, falls and physical assaults. Accidents are the leading cause of death from men under age 35, and more than 70 percent involve head injuries.

Symptoms Common symptoms immediately following a concussion include confusion, inability to remember events immediately before the injury, dizziness, blurred vision and vomiting. Partial paralysis and shock are also possible. The longer the period of unconsciousness, the more serious and persistent symptoms tend to be. During the 24 hours after the injury, symptoms may include headache, vomiting, increased pulse rate and anxiety. Initial symptoms usually begin to fade within a few days, but if they fail to do so a physician should be consulted.

A physician should be seen after any loss of consciousness, since the possibility of serious bleeding within the skull could require emergency surgery. Symptoms of serious damage may be immediately obvious or may not appear for some time.

Diagnosis Diagnosis could include X rays or CT scans. A patient who has experienced concussion should be confined to bed for 24 hours in a hospital or at home under observation, and should not drive a car or play sports. If new symptoms develop (drowsiness, breathing problems, repeated vomiting or visual disturbances), they should be reported to a physician immediately since they indicate potential damage to the brain or bleeding between the skull and the outside of the brain.

Treatment While generally no treatment is needed, acetaminophen or a stronger painkiller may be prescribed for headache. Aspirin is not generally recommended because it can contribute to bleeding. Rest and relaxation with no activities requiring concentration or vigorous movement will speed recovery within a few days.

Repeated concussions such as the blows boxers experience can damage the brain, impair concentration, slow thinking and slur speech. Initial symptoms usually begin to fade within a few days, although it is not uncommon for symptoms to last up to six months to a year. Concussed athletes should have a medical evaluation before returning to their sport. (See also PARKINSON'S DISEASE; PUNCH DRUNK SYNDROME.)

conditioning   The formation of a specific type of response or behavior to a specific stimulus in the environment. Conditioning theories have been advanced in part by the psychologists Ivan Pavlov and B. F. Skinner, whose names are associated with classical conditioning.

If a stimulus that is known consistently to produce a response is paired consistently with a second "neutral" stimulus, eventually the second stimulus alone will produce the response. The most famous example of this type of conditioning was devised by Pavlov; each time food was presented to a dog, making it salivate, a bell was rung. Eventually the dog would salivate in response to the bell alone. Pavlov noted that the response would generalize to similar stimuli; thus, a dog conditioned to salivate when shown a round object also would salivate (although not as much) when shown an elliptical one. Pavlov also discovered that the conditioned response would fade if not reinforced occasionally with the original neutral stimulus.

In *operant conditioning*, behavior is determined by rewards and punishments. Skinner placed a hungry rat in a box; it moved randomly about the cage, but once in a while it accidentally pawed a lever that released a pellet of food. Eventually the rat learned to press the lever whenever it wanted food; thus, it became conditioned.

Behavioral psychologists believe that all behavior is learned this way, and they regard psychiatric problems as learned behavior patterns. They base treatment for psychiatric disorders on the same principles, since a behavior that has been learned can be unlearned by reinforcing a more appropriate

form of behavior. (See also CLASSICAL CONDITIONING; PAVLOV, IVAN PETROVICH.)

confabulation   The production of false recollections. Confabulation is very common in psychiatric disorders and occurs especially in memories with a tinge of grandiosity. Confabulation memories also may borrow from fantasy or dream.

This problem was once thought to be a product of a person's embarrassment at losing memories, but many patients with severe AMNESIA do not confabulate. There appears to be no relationship between the severity of the amnesia and the tendency to confabulate; instead, the tendency may be related to personality traits in force before the onset of amnesia. People who are outwardly sociable but inwardly secretive are particularly prone to produce these false memories. Patients with the greatest tendency toward confabulation, however, are those with the least insight into their own memory disorder and who deny that a problem exists.

consciousness and memory   The consciousness or awareness of self shows most clearly the intimate relationship between memory and consciousness. In order to be perceived as continuous, the self requires continuity of memories.

Some researchers, including neurological expert Endel Tulving, have postulated that there are three varieties of consciousness: noetic, autonomous and anoetic. Noetic consciousness implies a semantic memory, since it involves thinking about objects and events and relationships among them in their absence. Autonomous consciousness is self-knowing; it is related to episodic memory that recognizes events as in the personal past. Anoetic consciousness is the state of nonknowing, but it is still consciousness because it allows appropriate behavioral responses to aspects of the environment.

Some scientists believe that the perception of consciousness occurs when nerve cells fire at similar frequencies, which imposes a "global unity" on nerve cells in different brain areas.

consolidation   A change in the structure of memory, other than the forgetting that occurs with the passage of time after learning.

Modern theories of consolidation can be traced to the work of Donald Hebb (1904–1985), who believed that new information is first represented by a temporary trace, a specific pattern of activity within a group of interconnected neurones (which Hebb called a cell assembly). At this stage, any disruption in the pattern of activity will cause the information to be lost completely. But if the activity is maintained for enough time, structural changes in the cell will occur, causing a permanent memory trace. Once this trace is formed, there is no more need to maintain the initial pattern of activity, and the information is then in "passive storage."

Many scientists believe that the structural change underlying consolidation involves an altered pattern of synapse activity. It has been estimated that the brain has 10^{13} synapses that could handle the levels of information storage in memory.

The exact way that synapses change is not known, although scientists speculate that it may involve how much neurotransmitter is released at the synapses.

context   The placement of information under consideration. There are three types: semantic context, which determines the meaning of the information; situational context—details of the physical setting in which the information was received; personal context—emotions, state of health and levels of arousal at the time the information was received.

continuous amnesia   A type of PSY-CHOGENIC AMNESIA in which the patient cannot recall events subsequent to a specific time up to and including the present. (See also HYSTERICAL AMNESIA.)

contrecoup effects   Damage to the side of the brain opposite the point of impact following a closed HEAD INJURY. Contrecoup effects are especially likely to occur in the temporal and orbital regions of the brain and may destroy neurons which later results in subcortical demyelination. Lesions in the corpus callosum following head injury also have been reported.

conversion   An unconscious defense mechanism by which conflicts that would otherwise cause anxiety are instead given symbolic external expression. The repressed impulses and the defenses against them are converted into a variety of symptoms involving the nervous system, which may include paralysis, pain or loss of sensory function.

cortex   The home of the most lofty abilities in the brain, the cortex is a quarter-inch-thick pad of grooved tissue running from the eyebrows to the ears, with a right and left hemisphere, each of which has four distinct lobes. The lobes are connected by a pathway of fibers called the corpus callosum.

Research studies have pinpointed scores of regions within the cortex that seem to specialize in different jobs, especially in the diffuse storing of memories. The cortex stores a person's abstract memory, a huge jumble of events and objects. Damage to the temporal, parietal or occipital cortex affects abstract memory in different ways. For example, damage to the left temporal or parietal lobe produces problems in reading, writing, speaking and simple arithmetic skills, but other mental abilities and memory remain intact. However, damage to the right temporal or parietal lobe causes subjects to become lost easily even in familiar surroundings; they cannot negotiate simple mazes, use or draw maps, match or copy the slant of a line, copy simple shapes or arrange blocks to form required patterns, or judge size, distance and direction of objects.

The sensory and motor areas of the cortex take up relatively little space, compared with the huge areas occupied by the association parts of the brain. The sensory areas of the cortex receive sensations of the muscles, skin and organs, such as temperature or touch. These sensory areas are responsible for locating the area in the body from which feelings are coming. Motor areas of the cortex send out messages that control muscles or muscle groups, which make the body move. The association areas of the cortex link the sensory areas with motor areas; these association areas are the true seat of the personality, intelligence, language, judgment, emotions and memory. In essence, the association areas of the brain allow the brain to think.

Creutzfeldt-Jakob disease   A very rare infectious viral disease of the nervous system caused by a transmissible infectious organism, probably a slow virus, that causes a progressive dementia with seizures. (See SLOW VIRUSES OF THE BRAIN.) It usually can be distinguished from other dementias by its rapid course—it takes only months from onset of symptoms until death.

The first symptoms involve a sudden progressive memory loss, bizarre behavior, reasoning problems and visual distortions of objects, hallucinations and mental confusion, and a lack of coordination. As the disease progresses, mental deterioration becomes pronounced, involuntary movements and muscle jerks appear, and the patient may become blind and develop weakness in the arms or legs, and ultimately lapses into coma. Bedridden, unconscious, Creutzfeldt-Jakob disease patients usually die from infections.

Infected patients can transmit the disease to monkeys, cats and guinea pigs, but the disease is not contagious between humans. However, infection has been linked to brain surgery with contaminated instruments or transplantation of an infected cornea. There are also indications that there may be a genetic link to this condition.

An autopsy is required for an accurate diagnosis. At present, there is no treatment for Creutzfeldt-Jakob disease.

cross-racial witness identification   People are better at recognizing faces of those of their own race than those of a different race, even if subjects have had extensive contact with other races. But this cross-racial identification problem is not related to the fact that people have greater prejudices or less experience with members of the other race. All studies, which include ones of black and white subjects as well as Asians and students from India, report the same findings.

Researchers suspect that members of a different race often have distinctive features in common. For example, most Asians have distinctive eyes; when a white person sees an Asian for a few seconds, the distinctive eyes stand out, attract the viewer's attention and take up most of the processing time. When later asked to pick an Asian out of a group of Asians, the one feature that was attended to—the eyes—aren't helpful in discriminating one Asian from another. (See also AGE AND EYEWITNESS ABILITY; EYEWITNESS TESTIMONY.)

cryptococcosis   A rare infection caused by inhaling the fungus *Cryptococcus neoformans*, which is found throughout the world (especially in soil and pigeon droppings). This fungus can lead to MENINGITIS, an inflammation of the coverings of the brain that can cause DEMENTIA if untreated. Most cases occur among people with a compromised immune system. Untreated, the disease can cause increasing memory loss, irritability, collapse and death.

Those most susceptible are patients with weakened immune systems, patients taking corticosteroids or AIDS patients. Symptoms may include low-grade fever, chest pain and a cough, but more serious cases resemble bronchitis and lead to meningitis, with symptoms of headache, stiff neck, fever, drowsiness, blurred vision, mental deterioration and staggering gait.

The infection is diagnosed from spinal fluid, which reveals the presence of yeast-type cells; an X ray may be needed to detect lung damage. If the disease has affected the brain, treatment includes a combination of the antifungal drugs flucytosine and amphotericin B for six weeks. Relapses can occur.

cryptomnesia   A phenomenon in which experiences that originally make little conscious impression are nonetheless filed away in the brain and only later are remembered suddenly in graphic detail as "hidden memories." Some brain experts believe that irregular or "supernatural" experiences such as alien abductions, satanic kidnappings, channeling of spirits and recall of past lives are all evidence of cryptomnesia.

One well-known example of this occurred to a young Helen Keller, who—at the age of 11—wrote a short story entitled "The Frost King" as a birthday present to the president of the Perkins School for the Blind. The story was so delightful and so packed with visual imagery that the educator published it in one of the school's reports; it was then reprinted in a weekly magazine.

Eventually, however, it became clear that Keller's story was closely patterned after the short story "The Frost Fairies," written by Margaret Canby before Keller's birth. The theme and some of the passages of the two stories were so close that it was clear Keller's story was derived from the earlier work, but both Keller and her teacher Anne Sullivan denied that Sullivan had "read" her the story.

Eventually Sullivan stated that a family friend whom Keller had visited three years earlier had a copy of Canby's book and had indeed "read" it to the girl, although Keller had no memory of having "heard" it. (In a separate account, the young Helen was alleged to have confided that Sullivan did, in fact, "read" her the story.)

In any case, recent research has suggested that people can retrieve recently acquired information from memory without experiencing the information as the recall of a memory. This suggests that there is an important distinction to be made between something remembered and the experience of remembering something. In fact, the experience of remembering when there is nothing to remember is a problem called CONFABULATION, or false memories.

Pettinati, Helen. *Hypnosis and Memory*. New York: Guilford Press, 1988.

CT scan   See COMPUTERIZED TOMOGRAPHY (CT) SCAN.

cue-dependent forgetting   An explanation of forgetting that centers around problems in retrieval. With cue-dependent forgetting, the memory does not fade away, nor is it displaced by other information; instead, it merely depends on using the right cue to retrieve it.

With the right cue, the information can be retrieved from memory; if the item is "forgotten," it is because the wrong cue has been used. An example of cue-dependent forgetting is when a person can't remember a fact until something "jogs" his or her memory.

Cushing's syndrome   A hormonal disorder caused by an abnormally high circulating level of corticosteroid hormones. The abnormal level of hormones may be produced directly by an adrenal gland tumor, by prolonged administration of corticosteroid drugs or by enlarged adrenal glands resulting from a pituitary tumor. Sometimes a malignant tumor of the lung or other organ will cause Cushing's syndrome. While possible at any age, it is most common during middle years.

Symptoms   Named for Harvey Cushing, an early 20th-century American surgeon, the disease often produces multiple abnormalities, including memory loss, agitation, depression and delusions. Patients have a humped upper back, wasted limbs, an obese trunk and the face has a characteristic round, reddened appearance. Frequent or spontaneous bruising on the arms and legs is another symptom; acne develops and purple stretch marks may appear on abdomen, thighs and breasts. Women may become more hairy, and patients may be more susceptible to infection and experience ulcers.

Diagnosis   An endocrinologist may order tests including examination of blood and urine for the presence of higher-than-normal amounts of steroid hormones; a computerized tomography (CT) scan of the pituitary and adrenal glands may also be ordered.

Treatment   The successful removal of a benign pituitary or adrenal tumor will probably cure the disorder, although long-term hormone therapy may be necessary. If left untreated, this syndrome eventually may end in death. If the symptoms are caused by excess steroids, the medication is decreased and then stopped; *sudden discontinuation of steroids may aggravate the underlying disorder*.

If Cushing's syndrome is caused by a tumor, removal of the tumor or the entire gland may be necessary. Radiation therapy may be an option if the tumor is located in the pituitary gland. If the treatment inactivates the adrenal glands, oral drugs must be taken to replace the missing hormones.

CVAs   See CEREBRAL VASCULAR ACCIDENTS (CVAS).

D

decay   One of many theories of FORGETTING that suggests memories leave a physical trace in the brain that gradually fades away with time after a period of nonuse. (See also TRACE DECAY.)

declarative memory   The type of memory network responsible for memory of facts, as opposed to PROCEDURAL MEMORY, the memory for procedures—learning *what* versus learning *how*. Scientists believe that the HIPPOCAMPUS is critical to storing facts but not procedures. An amnesiac with a damaged hippocampus can still learn simple skills (such as reading reversed print in a mirror), but she can't remember anything about the training session.

Likewise, riding a bicycle involves *procedural* memory; after learning to ride the bike, people can't articulate the knowledge they have learned; all the micromovements that go into riding a bike are stored implicitly throughout the central nervous system as processes, not fact. (See also HM.)

defense mechanism   The unconscious process that provides relief from emotional conflict and anxiety. Conscious efforts often are made for the same reasons, but the true defense mechanism is unconscious. Some of the common defense mechanisms include compensation, CONVERSION, denial, DISPLACEMENT, DISSOCIATION, idealization, identification, incorporation, introjection, projection, rationalization, reaction formation, regression, sublimation, substitution, symbolization and undoing.

dehydroepiandrosterone (DHEA)   A steroid hormone produced in the adrenal gland from the metabolism of cholesterol, where it is then converted into all the other steroid hormones. DHEA, the most common steroid in the human body, may be an important part of cognitive enhancement.

Research suggests that DHEA may protect brain cells against Alzheimer's disease and other forms of senility, since nerve degeneration occurs most often when DHEA levels are low. Recent research suggests that adding DHEA to nerve cell tissue cultures could increase the number of neurons, their ability to establish contacts and their differentiation. DHEA also has been shown to improve long-term memory in mice.

Alzheimer's disease patients have only about half as much DHEA as their same-aged counterparts without the disease; studies have been looking at the possibility of using DHEA to enhance their cognitive abilities. (See also PREGNENOLONE.)

Bologa, L., Sharma, J., and Roberts, E. "Dehydroepiandrosterone and Its Sulfated Derivative Reduce Neuronal Death and Enhance Astrocytic Differentiation in Brain Cell Cultures." *Journal of Neuroscience Research* 17, no. 3 (1985): 225–34.

Flood, J.F., and Roberts, E. "Dehydroepiandrosterone Sulfate Improves Memory in Aging Mice." *Brain Research* 447, no. 2 (1988): 269–78.

Sunderland, T., et al. "Reduced Plasma Dehydroepiandrosterone Concentrations in Alzheimer's Disease." *Lancet* 2 (1989): 1335–36.

déjà vu   French for "already seen," this is the haunting sense or illusion that one is seeing what one has seen before. Almost all people at some point in their lives have had the sense of recognition and familiarity when they come upon a new landscape and feel sure they have been there before. The sense of familiarity is sometimes so vivid that it almost seems like a hallucination.

Examples of déjà vu have been recorded for millennia; but while descriptions of the experience have been traced as far back as St. Augustine, no one has yet come up with the definitive theory about what causes it. Plato argued that déjà vu is a real memory of events that took place in a previous existence and that prove the theory of reincarnation. Nineteenth-century Romantic poets also believed the déjà vu experience supported the idea of reincarnation, but modern scientists believe it is a disturbance of the temporal lobe of the brain.

Other scientists suggest déjà vu is really a false memory, triggered by a current experience that has some features in common with an earlier one. They believe that memories are stored in the brain in the form of holograms and that any part of the hologram

has enough information stored in it to reproduce the whole picture.

This theory helps explain how memories can be brought forward by stimulating a section of the brain and why the memory may remain even after that section is surgically removed. This fact implies that—just as with a hologram—there is enough information in any one cluster of brain cells to evoke the entire memory.

In cases of déjà vu, then, while clumps of holographic data may form entirely different memories, portions of them may be identical. This could fool us momentarily into thinking we are reexperiencing something.

Freud expressed the idea of déjà vu in relationship to consciousness and unconsciousness; a conscious experience touching on a repressed memory, he said, would set off the feeling of déjà vu. More modern psychoanalysts believe that feelings of déjà vu occur during moments of anxiety, as a means of reassurance.

delayed matching to sample   A task developed to test memory in nonhuman primates. The animal sees an object and then, after a delay, sees two objects—the one already shown and a new one. The animal receives a reward by choosing the familiar object.

delayed nonmatching to sample   A task developed to test memory in nonhuman primates. Animals see a single object and then, after a delay, see both the recently presented object and a new one. The animal earns a reward by choosing the second, new object.

delirium   Acute mental confusion, usually brought on by a physical disease. Symptoms mimic those of disordered brain function, and include the failure to understand events or remember what has been happening, mood swings and physical restlessness. Delirious patients may experience hallucinations or panic attacks and resort to violence or shouting. Symptoms are usually worse at night because of sleep disturbance and the fact that darkness and quiet make visual disturbances more likely.

While delirium may be caused by any severe illness, high fever and disturbances of body chemistry are usually the prime factors. Children and older people are most prone to delirium, especially after major surgery or in the presence of a preexisting brain disturbance such as DEMENTIA. Drugs, poisons and alcohol also may cause delirium.

Delirium is treated by easing the underlying disorder and appropriate care to relieve anxiety, together with calm environment, seclusion, clear communication and trusted attendants. The patient must get enough fluids and good nutrition, but tranquilizers (such as chlorpromazine, haloperidol or thioridazine) often are necessary to ease restlessness. Antibiotic treatment to control infection has made delirium less of a problem than it was in the past.

delirium tremens (DTs)   An acute brain disorder characterized by a state of confusion together with trembling and vivid hallucinations usually experienced by chronic alcoholics after withdrawal or abstinence from alcohol. DTs often occur after hospital admission and are fatal in 10 to 15 percent of untreated cases.

Symptoms, which usually develop within 24 to 96 hours after stopping drinking, include restlessness, agitation, trembling and sleeplessness, with rapid heartbeat, fever, widened pupils, profuse sweating, confusion, visual or auditory hallucinations, illusions, delusions, paranoia terror and convulsions. Symptoms usually subside within three days.

The condition often is accompanied by nutritional deficiencies. Treatment includes rest, rehydration and sedation (chlorpromazine or chlordiazepoxide) with vitamin injections (especially thiamine), since some of the features of delirium tremens seem linked with thiamine deficiency.

DTs are caused by the withdrawal of alcohol after the brain and other organs have become accustomed to tolerating elevated levels of ethanol.

demand characteristics hypothesis   A theory about eyewitness memory that explains why people report incorrect facts after an event they have witnessed. The theory, similar to the COEXISTENCE HYPOTHESIS, says that when false information is provided about an event, both incorrect and correct memories about an event exist and both are equally accessible. Supposedly people produce the false memory because they think it is the one that is demanded of them, not because it is more accessible. When eyewitness expert Elizabeth Loftus tested this theory by asking subjects who witnessed an event to recall both the original and the false memory versions, very few subjects could produce both. (See also EYEWITNESS TESTIMONY; MEMORY FOR EVENTS; SUBSTITUTION HYPOTHESIS.)

dementia   A class of degenerative brain disorders with many different causes, all of which produce a gradual decline in intellectual function and almost always a significant deterioration of memory.

Loss of memory is usually the first sign, with patients asking the same question, forgetting to turn off the stove and so on. As dementia continues, symptoms worsen, including more and more confused episodes, and more drastic impairments (such as language problems) begin to appear. Because of similar symptoms, it is often difficult to diagnose particular forms of dementia, but a number of distinct forms have been recognized.

The term "dementia" is not used to indicate a particular loss of mental function, such as occurs in amnesia, aphasia, agnosia or apraxia; in dementia, the decline usually involves memory, other cognitive capacities and adaptive behavior without any major change in consciousness.

The patient may or may not be aware of the condition, but in almost all cases the loss of memory is accompanied by defects in one or more areas of intellectual function, such as language, spatial or temporal orientation, judgment and abstract thought. While some criteria for dementia require defects in one or more of the components of intellect, others require that the defect involve all components of intellectual function.

Cause Dementia is a result of dysfunction of the brain, especially in those parts of the cerebrum known as the association areas, which combine perception, purposeful action and thought to enable a person to adjust and survive in his or her environment. Dementia is not the same thing as mental retardation, although a person with mental retardation may become demented upon losing intellectual abilities he or she once had. Dementia is also not the same thing as psychosis; a demented patient may or may not be psychotic, and a patient with psychosis may or may not be demented.

Although it occurs at all ages, the chance of dementia increases with advancing age; its highest rate is in the population over age 75. According to recent estimates, dementia in costs the United States more than $40 billion.

Symptoms The onset of dementia is usually gradual; it begins with mild forgetfulness, restlessness or apathy followed by an increasing tendency to misplace things and small inconsistencies in some of the ordinary daily living tasks. Words or actions may begin to be repeated. As the dementia worsens, the cognitive dysfunction worsens and patients may begin to have problems at work, lose their way in their own neighborhoods, fail to recognize friends or family and reverse sleep cycles.

These symptoms may be followed by hallucinations, delusions, paranoia, or inappropriate or antisocial behavior. Depending on the cause of the dementia, there may or may not be indications of organic brain disease in addition to the intellectual or behavioral changes, such as problems with balance, senses or vision.

Diagnosis Proper identification of the cause of dementia is critical to treatment, since some diseases that produce dementia can be treated or reversed. (These include benign brain lesions, intoxication, infections and metabolic and nutritional disorders.) It is likewise important to differentiate the early stages of dementia from nonprogressive cognitive changes found in normal aging—but it's not always possible. The best way to tell the difference is through a series of observations over a period of time; still, diagnoses of many of the most common dementing diseases can be confirmed only upon autopsy.

The patient's history is the most important component of the initial evaluation, and should be obtained from the patient and the family. Family members most often in contact with the patient should be interviewed first, followed by other family members, friends and neighbors. Important objective information also can be provided by community health workers, social workers and nurses. Previous medical records should be reviewed. A chronological account of the patient's current problems—symptoms, duration of disease and specific intellectual and behavioral changes—should be noted. The medical history should include inquiries about relevant systemic diseases, trauma, surgery, psychiatric disorders, nutrition, alcohol and substance abuse.

The two most common forms of dementia in old age are multi-infarct dementia and ALZHEIMER'S DISEASE, but the many different diseases capable of producing dementia can be divided into two main groups. The first group includes those disorders that appear to be primary in the brain and that inevitably produce dementia, such as Alzheimer's disease, HUNTINGTON'S DISEASE and Parkinson-dementia complex.

The second group are those that are outside the brain and affect it secondarily, and may or many not produce dementia depending on how the brain is affected—liver disease, certain metabolic disorders and infectious disorders such as syphilis or AIDS.

In addition, there are a great number of reversible causes of dementia.

Reversible Causes of Dementia

Intoxication Overdose of medication or chemicals is capable of causing a dementia; neuroactive and psychoactive drugs, opiate analgesics and the adrenocortical steroids are the most common causes. However, some often-used drugs may cause or aggravate dementia, including anticholinergic medicines used in the treatment of movement disorders, allergic reactions or gastrointestinal disorders; and drugs used to treat heart problems, such as high blood pressure. Almost all street drugs (from heroin to glue) can cause dementia, as can a range of common chemicals such as carbon monoxide, carbon disulfide, lead, mercury and manganese. While all these chemicals may have irreversible or fatal effects, they are often the cause of arrestable or reversible dementia.

Infections Any infection that involves the brain is capable of producing dementia. Dementia from infections such as leptomeningitis and encephalitis, if they are treated early, can be prevented. Chronic infectious diseases such as syphilis, Whipple's disease or cryptococcus affect the brain, but the dementia can still be stopped—and sometimes reversed—at least to a degree. Chronic viral illnesses such as AIDS often produce dementia, but it is not known whether drugs that retard the AIDS process can stop or reverse changes in the nervous system that lead to dementia. The agents responsible for diseases such as Creutzfeldt-Jakob disease and progressive multifocal leukoencephalopathy do not respond to any kind of treatment. Postinfectious encephalomyelitis sometimes can result in dementia.

Metabolic Diseases Chronic diseases of the thyroid, parathyroid and adrenal glands and the pituitary are easily diagnosed and the resulting dementia can be reversed. A number of inherited metabolic diseases that appear in adult life, including Wilson's disease, metachromatic leukodystrophy and neuronal storage diseases, also cause a reversible dementia.

Nutritional Disorders Wernicke-Korsakoff's encephalopathy is caused by a loss of thiamine, which can lead to Korsakoff's dementia. Once established, this form of dementia is irreversible, although there may be periods of remission. Thiamine deficiency usually is seen in alcoholic patients, but it also can be found among pregnant women with chronic vomiting and depressed patients. Pernicious anemia sometimes can produce irreversible dementia. (See WERNICKE-KORSAKOFF SYNDROME.)

Cardiovascular Disorders High blood pressure is one of the most frequent causes of MULTI-INFARCT DEMENTIA, by causing frequent blood clots in the brain. Other causes are some forms of arteriosclerosis (a group of disorders causing thickening of artery walls), vasculitis (inflammation of blood vessels) and blood clots. The inability of the heart to pump blood efficiently also can produce dementia by single or repeated episodes of ischemia (insufficient supply of blood to the brain), which cuts off oxygen to the brain. Chronic blockage of arteries leading to the brain does not cause dementia if brain tissue has not been damaged by loss of oxygen.

Lesions A chronic subdural hematoma (large blood clot in the space between the dura, the tough outer layer of covering of the brain [meninges] and the middle meningeal layer) can produce dementia, a not-uncommon cause of dementia in older patients. Benign tumors of the brain, especially those on the orbital surface of the frontal lobe or on the medial surface of the temporal lobe, also can cause dementia, depending on their size and location. Obstructive hydrocephalus (spinal fluid on the brain) may produce dementia when certain benign lesions such as some neurofibromas press on the brain. Malignant tumors of the brain also often produce dementia; only rarely does this type of dementia respond to treatment.

Normal Pressure Hydrocephalus A rare cause of dementia, normal pressure hydrocephalus usually occurs together with balance disturbances and incontinence.

Affective Disorders Some patients may be so depressed that a true cognitive deficit results; it can be reversed with treatment. In addition, depression is often found among patients with dementia—especially those with Alzheimer's disease.

Progressive Degenerative Diseases Most of the progressive degenerative diseases that cause dementia are not treatable; they originate primarily in the brain and may or may not cause other neurological signs. Alzheimer's disease is the most common of these diseases. Progressive degenerative diseases causing dementia that appear with other prominent neurological signs include diseases of the BASAL GANGLIA (Parkinson's and Huntington's diseases), cerebellar and spinocerebellar degenerations, and amyotrophic lateral sclerosis (Lou Gehrig's disease).

Treatment If there is a diagnosis of a curable cause of dementia, the doctor will be able to recommend the best treatment. Even if the diagnosis is one of the irreversible disorders, much can be done to help the patient and family. Careful use of drugs can lessen agitation, anxiety and depression and improve sleeping patterns, if needed. Proper nutrition is particularly important, although special diets or supplements usually are not necessary.

Daily routines, physical activities and social contacts are all important. Often, stimulating the individual by supplying information about time of day, place and what's going on in the world encourages the use of remaining skills and information. This keeps brain activity from failing at a faster rate. In the same way, providing memory cues helps people help themselves—these cues might include a visible calendar, a list of daily activities, written notes about simple safety measures and directions to and labeling of commonly used items.

Prevention Developing interests or hobbies and becoming involved in activities that keep the mind and body active are among the best ways to avoid problems that can mimic irreversible brain disorders. Certain physical and mental changes seem to occur with age even in healthy people, but senility is by no means a given past age 65.

dementia, evaluation of The purpose of testing a patient for dementia is to rule out treatable causes of the impairment; therefore, an accurate diagnosis is important. There are a wide range of treatable causes of dementia, including depression, drug reactions, vitamin B_{12} deficiency, thyroid abnormalities, alcoholism, drug abuse or systemic disease.

Evaluation of the patient begins with a detailed history of symptoms and physical and neurological examinations together with a battery of lab tests. A mental status exam is often part of the neurological evaluation; this is not a test of sanity, but assesses various mental functions such as memory, attention, language and perception.

In particular, memory may be tested exhaustively, since memory problems are a prominent feature of dementia. Tests should include an assessment of a person's ability to learn both verbal and nonverbal information and the ability to recall items from the remote past. The patient may be asked to construct objects by drawing or recall these drawings later.

In addition, an assessment usually will include a battery of standardized tests of intelligence (such as the Wechsler Adult Intelligence Scale, or WAIS), memory (the Wechsler Memory Scale), language (Boston Diagnostic Aphasia Examination) and prior academic achievement (the Wide Range Achievement Test).

Lab tests may be run to rule out diseases with certain brain disorders, such as tumors, abscesses, strokes, fluid accumulations, heart and lung disorders, liver disease, kidney disease, infections such as AIDS or SYPHILIS. Other tests that look for these disorders might include a brain scan (magnetic resonance imaging or computerized tomography), electrocardiogram, chest X ray, blood chemistry and urine tests and drug screening, electroencephalography (EEG), lumbar puncture or radioisotope studies.

If all other diseases and injuries are ruled out, the patient may be suffering from ALZHEIMER'S DISEASE; there is no specific test that can uncover Alzheimer's, which is diagnosed only after all other possibilities have been exhausted. An absolute diagnosis can be made only with autopsy.

dementia praecocissiima A form of DEMENTIA PRAECOX diagnosed before puberty. The term was first used in 1905 by Italian psychiatrist Sante De Sanctis.

dementia praecox This term refers to a markedly rapid mental disintegration into senility in younger patients that usually occurs only in very old or brain-damaged individuals.

The term *"demence precoce"* was first used in 1852 by Benedict Augustin Morel in his book *Etudes cliniques*. It was used 46 years later by noted psychiatrist Emil Kraepelin in his textbook *Psychiatrie* to describe the progressively degenerative mental disorder accompanied by acute or subacute mental disturbance. Kraepelin noted that dementia praecox began in late adolescence or early adulthood and that half his cases began between ages 16 and 22. He believed that the disease might be caused not only by heredity but by an organic brain disease that was degenerative and not reversible.

dendrite One of several branched fibers extending out of a nerve cell (neuron) that receives impulses from another NEURON.

denial An unconscious defense mechanism used to resolve emotional conflict and allay anxiety by disavowing thoughts, feelings, wishes and needs that are consciously intolerable. This behavior is often seen in those with psychotic disorders; in its extreme form, denial can appear to have an almost delusional quality.

deprenyl A drug (trade names: Eldepryl, Jumex) that has been used as a treatment for PARKINSON'S DISEASE and is currently being studied for the treatment of ALZHEIMER'S DISEASE. Some researchers also are studying the drug as a life span extender and a memory enhancer.

The treatment of choice in Parkinson's disease, deprenyl also has been said to improve cognition in some patients, improving attention, memory and reaction times. The disease has a much slower progression in newly diagnosed Parkinson patients who receive deprenyl.

Deprenyl is chemically related to phenylethylamine, a substance found in chocolate, and to amphetamine. A monoamine oxidase (MAO) inhibitor, these drugs can correct the age-related decrease in neurotransmitters. Deprenyl is the only drug that researchers know that stimulates the substantia nigra, a tiny brain region rich in dopamine-using brain cells. (A deficiency of dopamine can result in Parkinson's symptoms.) But degeneration of the neurons in the substantia nigra also has been associated with the aging process.

Therefore, deprenyl protects against the age-related degeneration of the substantia nigra and the nervous system.

In an Italian study, administration of the drug to ten Alzheimer's patients improved memory, attention and language ability compared to those who received a placebo. Another study of 20 Alzheimer's patients for six months also showed significant improvements in memory and attention. A third study of verbal memory and deprenyl in Alzheimer's disease showed a significant improvement in verbal memory and improved information-processing abilities and learning strategies at the moment of acquisition.

Deprenyl was more effective than oxiracetam, another drug being tested for use with Alzheimer's patients, at improving higher cognitive functions and reducing impairment in daily living, and better short- and long-term memory and attention. Other studies also found deprenyl to be slightly more effective than ACETYL-L-CARNITINE and more effective than PHOSPHATIDYLSERINE in measures of cognition in Alzheimer's disease patients.

Finali, G., et al. "L-deprenyl Therapy Improves Verbal Memory in Amnesic Alzheimer Patients." *Clinical Neuropharmacology* 14, no. 6 (1991): 523–36.

Knoll, J. "Deprenyl Medication: A Strategy to Modulate the Age-related Decline of the Striatal Dopaminergic System." *Journal of the American Geriatric Society* 40, no. 8 (August 1992): 839–47.

Letters to the Editor on Deprenyl in Parkinson's Disease. *New England Journal of Medicine* 322 (May 24, 1990): 1526–27.

depression and memory Severe depression is accompanied by physical symptoms, such as sleep disturbances and loss of interest in food and sex—but it is also associated with a memory deficit that is in some ways similar to the loss shown by some patients with schizophrenia and by those with lesions in the frontal lobe. Depression alters brain chemistry in a way that slows absorption and emergence of information, lowering the level of attention and reducing the capacity to concentrate.

Depressed individuals have trouble remembering recent and sometimes past events. Other memory processes most impaired by depression include recall of positive words (that are incongruent with the subjects' mood), immediate recall and recognition of verbal stimuli. One day a depressed person's memory may work well, and the next day the person can't remember anything. Depressed people can't concentrate, and they feel confused and bewildered.

Some depressed patients may ramble, finding it hard to keep to one topic.

Studies have shown that depressed subjects can remember incidental information, but they are not so good at storing information that requires more focused attention. In a study testing the memory of 32 depressed patients, 32 normals and 32 diabetics (with a mean age of 66 to 68), Palo Alto Veterans Hospital researchers found that depressed patients tended to use more passive approaches to remembering. They did not use semantic clustering as often as did the other subjects. (Semantic clustering involves remembering similar words together.)

Especially among older subjects, there was a correlation between poorer performance on memory tests and the physical symptoms of depression (sleepiness, appetite loss, problems in getting started in the morning). Those who reported negative feelings during the memory test also tended to do more poorly.

Depression so closely mimics SENILE DEMENTIA (characterized by forgetfulness, confusion and behavioral changes) that it is often diagnosed as PSEUDODEMENTIA.

However, depression usually is caused by some sort of loss—a spouse, self-esteem, status, job or health. One report indicates that depression is so prevalent among those aged 65 and over that 13 percent need intervention. Still, although depressive illness is serious, it is no bigger a problem in later life than in earlier stages.

Depression, whether present alone or in combination with dementia, can be reversed with proper treatment, which usually includes some type of cognitive therapy. Therefore, a good diagnosis is important. Unfortunately, many physicians still don't know what signs to look for and, as a result, often diagnose senile dementia instead of depression. The difference between the two diagnoses are important: A depressed person will anguish over forgetfulness, whereas a senile person will try to hide it; a depressed person makes little effort to perform tasks, whereas a senile person will struggle to perform well.

Adler, Tina. "Psychologists Examine Aging, Cognitive Change." *APA Monitor* (November 1990): 4–5.

depth of processing   Mental processes and strategies such as IMAGE ASSOCIATION, visualization, verbal elaboration, review and summarization that are indispensable to the recording of a good memory trace. .

detail salience   How memorable a detail is. A salient detail is one that has a high probability of being mentioned spontaneously by witnesses.

When a person sees a complex event, not all the details are equally salient. Some things catch a person's attention more quickly than others: Colorful, extraordinary, novel and interesting scenes attract our attention and hold our interest. Both attention and interest are important in the encoding of memories. Boring, routine, common or insignificant circumstances are rarely remembered as specific incidents.

Interestingly, witness estimates of time, speed and distance are often inaccurate, and speed is especially difficult to estimate. In one study administered to air force personnel who knew beforehand that they would be questioned about the speed of a moving auto, estimates ranged from 10 to 50 miles an hour. The car actually had been going only 12 miles an hour. In estimates of time, most witnesses overestimate the amount of time an event took. (See also AGE AND EYEWITNESS ABILITY; MEMORY FOR EVENTS.)

DHEA   See DEHYDROEPIANDROSTERONE (DHEA).

diaries, notebooks   See EXTERNAL MEMORY AIDS.

diencephalic amnesia   A type of permanent, global AMNESIA caused by lesions in the DIENCEPHALON caused by accident or illness. It usually appears as a result of KORSAKOFF'S SYNDROME.

This type of memory loss selectively impairs some aspects of memory while leaving others alone. Patients will score normally on IQ tests but will not do nearly so well on clinical memory tests. They have particular problems in remembering new information, but they can understand sentences—they just can't repeat them after a certain period of time. Skills that were learned before the lesions appeared are unaffected.

Controversy continues as to whether this type of amnesia and MEDIAL TEMPORAL AMNESIA are separate syndromes or the same type of amnesic syndrome. (See also AMNESIAC SYNDROME.)

diencephalon   An area in the uppermost part of the brain stem that includes the THALAMUS; it connects via the FORNIX to the TEMPORAL LOBES. The diencephalon and the MEDIAL TEMPORAL LOBE are the two structures that are crucially concerned with memory. The diencephalon is one of the structures most commonly involved in KORSAKOFF'S SYNDROME, and tumors found on the third ventricle (a part of the diencephalon) usually cause memory disorders. In fact, AMNESIA following damage to the diencephalon (from disease, neurosurgery, head injury, stroke or the deprivation of oxygen) is quite common.

diet and memory   While much research linking diet and memory is still inconclusive, there have been some studies that suggest a link between certain foods and memory.

Since medieval times, memory experts believed a good diet could enhance memory performance, although it was not always understood what constituted a good "memory diet." For example, 15th-century nutritionists advised citizens to eat hearty food for a good memory—roasted fowl, apples, nuts and red wine. Today, scientists have a different perspective on the role that nutrition plays in health and memory.

Scientists do know, for example, that imbalances in the diet can cause problems; a child's ability to remember is affected by iron, mineral and vitamin deficiencies, food additives, too much sugar and too little protein. And deficiencies of almost any nutrient can cause impaired nervous system function. Imbalances in certain vitamins and minerals also appear to play a part in problems with memory.

Water is also important in maintaining memory systems, especially in the elderly. Lack of water in the body has a direct and profound effect on memory, and dehydration leads to confusion and thinking problems.

Although researchers don't know exactly how nutrition affects memory, they do know that essential nutrients are important for enhancing chemical processes (such as registering, retaining and remembering information). These essential nutrients include protein, carbohydrates, lecithin and vitamin B_1.

Still, experts aren't sure if some of these foods are better at boosting memory than others. As a result, physicians advise that the best memory insurance is to eat "a good, balanced diet": a variety of dairy products, bread and cereals, vegetable and fruit, seafood, poultry or meat. Without sufficient levels of thiamine, folate and vitamin B_{12}, the brain cannot function properly; as a result, you may have memory and concentration problems.

In addition, it's not a good idea to eat large amounts of food right before beginning a thinking task; loading up the stomach impairs performance and distracts the mind during the critical registration and remembering phase. For this reason, memory experts advise eating only a light meal before giving a speech, taking a test or attending class.

Some experts advocate the use of "memory nutrients" (CHOLINE, B-complex vitamins, iodine, manganese and folic acid),

although other researchers argue that studies have not yet proven their efficacy.

When foods rich in choline (liver, soybeans, lecithin, eggs and fish) were fed to subjects in one study, the diet sparked an increase in ACETYLCHOLINE, the brain neurotransmitter crucial to the memory process. When the subjects then took 10 grams of choline, they were able to recall a list of unrelated words more quickly than those who did not take choline. In other studies, Alzheimer's disease patients showed improved memories when treated with choline.

Vitamins   Texas researchers found that rats deprived of B_6 and copper showed evidence of deteriorating dendrites (branchlike extensions that carry electrical impulses from one brain cell to the next). Researchers speculate that a mild deficiency of these nutrients over the course of years could have the same devastating effects on humans.

When researchers in New Mexico tested a group of normal subjects 60 years old and older on memory and problem-solving ability, they found that those with the lowest vitamin B_{12} and C levels did poorly on the memory test. Those with the lowest levels of vitamins B_{12} and C, riboflavin and folate scored the worst on problem-solving tests. And common deficiencies of vitamins B_{12} and B_6 and folic acid in the elderly can impair some of the body's enzymes, which may be responsible for at least some of the memory impairment observed in older patients.

Zinc is another substance that seems to affect memory. When researchers studied more than 1,200 patients over age 55, the 220 senile people in the group had significantly lower zinc levels than those who were not senile.

Dieting   At the same time, decreasing the amount of nutrients to the brain by going on a diet may affect the memory, too. Experts warn that any diet providing fewer than 2,100 calories a day for an adult is likely to be deficient in some vitamin, mineral or trace element unless the diet is carefully monitored by a physician. When a person diets, the brain (like the rest of the organs in the body) must make up a shortage of dietary nutrients by drawing on its own reserves. When those reserves are depleted, the dieter can become nervous, easily upset, clumsy, and experience memory problems.

In fact, one recent Mayo clinic study found that healthy patients on a low-calorie diet for three months became quarrelsome, hostile and anxious, felt persecuted, had nightmares and panic attacks, experienced attention deficits and had memory problems.

Dean, Ward, Morgenthaler, John, and Fowkes, Steven. *Smart Drugs II: The Next Generation.* Menlo Park, Calif.: Health Freedom Publications, 1993.
Krassner, Michael. "Diet and Brain Function." *Nutrition Reviews Supplement* (May 1986): 12–15.
Minninger, Joan. *Total Recall.* Emmaus, Pa.: Rodale Press, 1984.
Ostrander, Sheila, and Schroeder, Lynn. *Supermemory.* New York: Carroll & Graf, 1991.
Prevention magazine editors. *Future Youth.* Emmaus, Pa.: Rodale Press, 1987.

digit span   A technique to measure MEMORY SPAN by noting the number of randomly arranged digits that a person can repeat in the correct order immediately after hearing or seeing them. Normal subjects can recall about seven digits (plus or minus two).

Dilantin (phenytoin)   This well-known treatment for epilepsy also is reputed to have a wide range of other pharmacologic effects beyond its anticonvulsant benefits. More than 8,000 studies have examined the drug in a wide variety of uses, reporting that it may improve intelligence, concentration and learning. Studies have suggested that, given twice daily, it can improve long-term memory and verbal performance in young and old alike. However, excess amounts of the drug have the opposite effect on memory, intelligence and reaction time.

In the United States, Dilantin's only approved use is to control various types of seizures, since it works by stabilizing electrical activity in cell membranes.

Dilman, V.M., and Dean, W. *The Neuroendocrine Theory of Aging and Degenerative Disease.* Pensacola, Fl.: Center for BioGerontology, 1992.
Finkel, M.M. "Phenytoin Revisited." *Journal of Clinical Therapeutics* 6, no. 5 (1984): 577–91.

dimethylaminoethanol (DMAE)   This naturally occurring nutrient found in some types of seafood (such as sardines) also is normally found in human brains in small amounts. According to some research, DMAE has been found to improve memory and learning, elevate mood and increase physical energy in studies of lab animals. It is said to be both a mild stimulant and a sleep enhancer.

DMAE is believed to work by speeding up the brain's production of ACETYLCHOLINE, which plays an important part in memory and maintaining memory ability in the elderly.

There are reports that overdoses of DMAE may cause insomnia, headache or muscle tension, but no serious adverse effects have been reported. It has been found, however, to deepen the depression phase in manic-depression patients.

DMAE is considered to be a nutritional supplement and can be found under a variety of trade names in health food stores in bulk powder, capsules or liquid form.

direct priming   When amnesic patients are shown a list of words and later tested on recall, they perform very poorly on "yes/no" direct recognition tests. But by providing a portion of each word that had been on the list, subjects are able to fill in the blanks and come up with the word. This effect is called *direct priming.*

Scientists believe that direct priming results from some temporary activation of information in semantic memory, which is not affected by AMNESIA. Scientists assume that everyone has an individual representation for every word we know, and exposure of a word in a learning list leads to that representation becoming more active. Therefore, it is more easily recalled than comparable words that have not been preexposed.

However, direct priming appears to be restricted to preexisting associations and has only limited value in a therapeutic setting.

dissociation An unconscious defense mechanism through which emotional significance and affect are separated and detached from an idea, situation or object. Dissociation may defer or postpone experience with some emotional impact, as in selective AMNESIA.

This splitting of the normally integrated functions of consciousness (especially identity and memory) is the defining characteristic of the DISSOCIATIVE DISORDERS, which include MULTIPLE PERSONALITY DISORDER, PSYCHOGENIC AMNESIA, psychogenic FUGUE, and depersonalization disorder.

Dissociation was first mentioned by French *alieniste* (psychiatrist) Jacques Joseph Moreau de Tours in 1845 in his book about ALTERED STATES OF CONSCIOUSNESS. The first psychological elaboration of the concept of dissociation was written in 1889 by Pierre Janet (1859–1947) in *L' Automatisme Psychologique*.

In this book, Janet describes a syndrome he calls *desegregation*, in which associated ideas split off from consciousness and exist in a parallel with the dominant stream of consciousness. Janet believed this was a pathological psychological process that occurred in HYPNOSIS, hysteria and instances of multiple personality.

The syndrome was further discussed in *Studies on Hysteria* (1895) by Sigmund Freud (1856–1939) and Joseph Breuer (1842–1925), who interpreted the famous case of ANNA O. Anna, who suffered from psychosomatic problems and dissociation, had been treated for two years by Breuer. But Breuer and Freud disagreed about the nature of Anna's *absences;* Breuer thought they represented a form of autohypnosis, while Freud interpreted Anna's symptoms as a defense mechanism.

Freud's theory won acceptance by clinicians over the years, although Breuer's autohypnotic explanation has won converts for its explanation of early childhood creation of multiple personality. (See also BREUER, JOSEF; FREUD, SIGMUND; JANET, PIERRE; MOREAU DE TOURS, JACQUES JOSEPH.)

Bliss, E.L. "A Reexamination of Freud's Basic Concepts from Studies of Multiple Personality Disorder." *Dissociation* 1 (1988): 36–40.
Noll, R. "Multiple Personality, Dissociation, and C.G. Jung's Complex Theory." *Journal of Analytical Psychology* 34 (1989): 353–70.

dissociative disorders A category of psychological disorders in which there is a sudden, temporary alteration in normally integrated function of consciousness, identity or motor behavior so that some part of one or more of these functions is lost. While the process of dissociation is common in everyday life (for example, when a person is concentrating intensely on a task and doesn't hear what is being said), in extreme cases the behavior can lead to serious problems.

The disorders were first grouped together in 1987 in the *Diagnostic and Statistical Manual of Mental Disorders*, 3rd edition, revised (DSM-III-R), with the primary symptom of DISSOCIATION. The amnesia found in these disorders is a repression of disturbing memories; once the memories are repressed, access to them is cut off temporarily. The disorders include PSYCHOGENIC AMNESIA, FUGUE, MULTIPLE PERSONALITY and depersonalization disorder.

The dissociative disorders may often be misdiagnosed for more serious disorders such as schizophrenia, but because patients do not exhibit a significant break with reality, they are not considered psychotic. The dissociative disorders also may be referred to as hysterical neuroses, dissociative type. (See also CHILD ABUSE, MEMORY OF.)

Putnam, F.W. "Dissociation as a Response to Extreme Trauma," in R. Kluft, ed., *Childhood Antecedents of Multiple Personality.* Washington, D.C.: American Psychiatric Press, 1985.

distortions, memory Memory can be affected by a person's interests or values so that an experience is remembered the way a person *wants* to remember it. In other words, memories can be changed to fit what we want them to be or how we think they ought to be.

This theory can be tested by asking someone to repeat as many as possible of the following words that are read aloud: dream, awake, tired, bed, night, rest, sound, slumber, snore. Most people will also recall the word "sleep," although that particular word does not appear on the list. People recall that word because most of the words on the list are related to sleep, and it seems as if that word *ought* to be on the list.

Distortion is of particular importance in the courtroom, where a leading question may cause a witness to "remember" something that did not exist. For example, asking "What color was the victim's sweater?" may cause a witness to remember a sweater that was not even worn. Statements that imply a conclusion may cause a person to remember the conclusion as if it had happened. Madison Avenue ad agencies often use this aspect of distortion to promote products without directly making false claims.

DMAE See DIMETHYLAMINOETHANOL.

domain-specific knowledge Information relating to a particular setting in which a patient currently experiences difficulty.

dopamine A chemical messenger in the brain and a member of the class of CATE-CHOLAMINES. Dopamine is a NEUROTRANS-MITTER that appears to play some role in a range of mental disorders, including schizophrenia. Drugs that mimic dopamine are used in the treatment of Parkinson's disease.

dopaminergic Activated or transmitted by DOPAMINE.

dreams and memory While all humans dream, the ability to remember dreams varies a great deal from one person to the next. Some people have such poor memories for their dreams that they insist they never dream. In fact, however, research has revealed that every human being dreams during regular periods of each night, as evidenced by rapid eye movement (REM) when the eyelids flicker and the entire body may move.

People can be taught to recall their dreams. The first step is actually retrieving the dream itself. This can be done by "setting" the mind before sleep by one saying gently and firmly, "I will remember my dream." This prompts the brain to give priority to the recall of the dream on awakening. It may take up to three weeks of such training before dreams can be remembered with regularity.

Studies suggest that older subjects dream less than younger people do and therefore have fewer dreams to report. This may be due in part to the decline of spontaneous mental imagery related to old age; however, the ability to form mental images is a skill that can be improved with practice at any age.

drugs and memory Any medication that causes drowsiness is capable of affecting memory. The best known of all memory-influencers is ethanol (the alcohol contained in beverages). It interferes with the capacity to learn and slows down mental functions that create defective recording and storing of information.

Other drugs that have an immediate effect on memory include barbiturates, bromides, benzodiazepines (including lorazepam and diazepam) and other sedatives, antidepressants, tranquilizers, analgesics, antihypertensives, insulin, beta blockers (especially those used to control glaucoma), methyldopa, Symmetrel, Inderal, cimetidine, SCO-POLAMINE, seasickness patches, digitalis preparations, antihistamines, antipsychotic drugs (especially haloperidol and Thorazine) and certain antiepileptic drugs. Combinations also can cause memory problems, such as the interaction between haloperidol and methyldopa.

Medications that alter perception and consciousness destroy brain cells; others (such as LSD, amphetamines and phencyclidine [PCP]) provoke psychoses that can become permanent.

Patients should always ask if the medications or combinations they are taking (and dosages) pose potential problems.

duplex theory   The idea that short-term and long-term memory are fundamentally different systems.

dyslexia and memory   A specific reading disability characterized by problems in coping with written symbols. The term "dyslexia" is not used to describe other kinds of reading problems resulting from other causes, such as brain damage, mental handicaps or speech or visual defects.

New research suggests that problems in encoding are the cause of a dyslexic person's problems with verbal memory. Other theories have pointed to a specific, sometimes inherited, neurological disorder, emotional disturbance, minor visual defects or a lack of attention. Recent research, however, using new clinical tests of many more memory measures has challenged the long-held view that verbal memory problems of dyslexic children are related to their attention span, memory strategy use or ability to retrieve memories. But the relationship between verbal memory and reading problems is still unclear.

In a Nova University study of 122 children eight to ten years old, the dyslexic subjects differed from normals only in their ability to encode words—to store the word in memory when they hear it. Both dyslexic

and normal children had the same attention spans.

While some researchers had believed that dyslexic subjects' memory problems are actually a retrieval problem (they encode the words, but then can't recall them), researchers found that both normal and dyslexic children improved at the same rate when given memory cues, indicating that retrieval is not a problem.

Symptoms   Some 90 percent of dyslexics are male; most of the time, their intelligence is normal but the attainment of reading skills lags far behind other abilities and overall IQ. Usually dyslexic children can read musical notes or numbers much more easily than letters. While many children in the first two elementary grades make common mistakes in reversing letters or words, dyslexic children continue to make these errors. Letters are transposed ("saw" for "was") and spelling errors are common. Writing from dictation may be hard, although most can copy sentences.

Treatment   Early diagnosis is critical in maintaining a child's self-esteem and to avoid any added frustrations. Specific remedial methods can help the child develop tricks to cope with the disorder, and praise for success is crucial. With the right support and training, dyslexics can usually overcome their problems.

Adler, Tina. "Encoding Is Achilles' Heel for Dyslexic Kids." *APA Monitor* (November 1990): 11.

dysmnesia/dysmnesic syndrome   General intellectual impairment secondary to defects of memory and orientation.

dysphasia   A disturbance in the ability to select the words with which to speak and write, comprehend and read. Dysphasia is caused by damage to regions of the brain concerned with speech and comprehension. (See also AGRAPHIA; ALEXIA; APHASIA; APRAXIA.)

E

Ebbinghaus, Hermann E. (1850–1909)

The father of the psychological study of memory, this German pioneer proposed three basic questions: How much information can we store, how fast can we acquire it and how long can we keep it? To this day, many psychology labs still use his basic method of testing memory for lists.

Ebbinghaus began the first modern systematic study of memory in 1879, using himself as his subject in research designed to test the above questions by first inventing a string of nonsense syllables (two consonants with a verb in between) and then reciting them in sequence to see how many repeats he needed before he could memorize them. Ebbinghaus assumed that memory involved the storage of items somewhere in the brain and that remembering required a person to reproduce the information using accurate recall. In his studies, Ebbinghaus refused to use any methods (he called them tricks) to make recall easier, hoping to study natural (not artificial) memory.

Ebbinghaus discovered that he learned at a constant rate, and the more often he repeated the syllables to himself, the better he could remember them. He also discovered that he could remember much better if he studied first thing in the morning than if he studied at 4 P.M., and he concluded that fatigue affected memory. Moreover, after mastering lists of these nonsense syllables, the number of syllables he could remember fell off in a predictable way. This enabled Ebbinghaus to fit a logarithmic curve to the retention as a function of time.

His studies led him to describe three possible ways we forget:

1. INTERFERENCE THEORY: Early memories basically get buried by later-memorized ones.
2. TRACE DECAY: Memories undergo changes over time that affect their nature.
3. Forgetting occurs when memories "fall apart" and crumble into parts, where separate components are lost.

Ebbinghaus's work led to the publication in 1885 of his classic book, *On Memory,* which opened up the study of memory as an experimental problem. In the book he charted the decay of memories and suggested that a great deal of information is forgotten immediately after it is acquired. If the information is remembered for as long as a day or two, he wrote, it is likely to be retained for a much longer period.

The basic style of learning that Ebbinghaus described could be called rote learning, or verbal list learning. Modern researchers understand, however, that what Ebbinghaus was really studying was rote learning *without arousal;* in other words, factual memory for events that have no emotional importance. And because rote learning without arousal is a poor way to construct memory, it is not surprising that Ebbinghaus and his colleagues concluded that memory doesn't work very well or endure for a very long time.

While Ebbinghaus developed his technique as a way of sidestepping problems in memory study, the technique limited his ability to understand memory. He believed that memory was simply a storage bin for objective items that were either retained or not—a point of view that eventually was challenged by psychologists who believed that subjective factors are also vital to memory systems. (See also BARTLETT, SIR FREDERIC C.)

Eccles, Sir John (1903–   )

The Australian research physiologist who shared the 1963 Nobel Prize for Physiology or Medicine for his discovery of the chemical means by which impulses are communicated or suppressed by nerve cells.

Eccles showed that the excitement of a nerve cell causes one kind of SYNAPSE to release a neurotransmitter into the neighboring cell that expands the pores in nerve membranes. (See NEUROTRANSMITTERS.) These expanded pores allow sodium ions to pass into the neighboring cell, reversing the polarity of electric charge, which is conducted from one cell to another as a nerve impulse.

The complexity of the brain has so impressed Eccles that he has called the mind the so-called ghost in the machine, an incorporeal essence in the body.

echoic memory The registration of sounds. This form of memory lasts up to four seconds. The long-term form of echoic memory is called AUDITORY MEMORY.

EEG See ELECTROENCEPHALOGRAM.

effortful processing Effortful encoding and retrieval of memory. This effortful processing uses a great deal of attentional capacity and therefore disrupts—and is disrupted by—the simultaneous performance of another attention-demanding task. Effortful processing probably always requires planning, therefore it is likely to be damaged by frontal cortex lesions that disrupt the ability to plan.

ego One of the three major divisions in the psychoanalyst's model of the psychic apparatus; the others are the id and the superego. The ego represents the sum of certain mental mechanisms, including memory, and specific defense mechanisms. It mediates between the demands of primitive instinct (the id) and of internalized parental and social prohibitions (the superego).

ego psychology The study of slowly changing functions known as psychic structures that usually shape, channel and organize mental activity into meaningful patterns—among which is MEMORY.

eidetic images Similar to the idea of "photographic memory," an eidetic ("identi-cal" or "duplicative") image is a very strong afterimage that allows a person to duplicate a picture mentally and describe it in detail after looking at it. Among children the ability to form eidetic images is rare (no more than 10 percent of children have the ability), and it is even rarer after adolescence. An eidetic image may be a MEMORY, FANTASY or dream.

An eidetic person not only can imagine an object that isn't there, but behaves as if it really can be seen, either with closed eyes or while looking at some surface that serves as a convenient background for the image. While a particular object can be recalled eidetically immediately after its disappearance or after a lapse of minutes, days or years, spontaneously appearing eidetic images also have been reported. Sometimes eidetic images and the objects they represent have different colors, forms, size, position and richness of detail, or the objects may be reproduced in almost photographic detail and fidelity.

Most experts suspect that eidetic imagery is not a different kind of visual memory, but just a greater skill in the ability to form visual images that everyone has to some degree.

While eidetic imagery is most likely the source of the concept of a photographic memory, there are differences in the two concepts. An eidetic image fades soon after one sees the original image and does not stay with a person over time. The image is subjective, and the details of greatest interest to the person are the ones most easily reproduced. Moreover, a person can't form an eidetic image in one second, as a camera can snap a photo; several seconds are required to scan the picture. Once the picture has faded away, eidetic images cannot be retrieved. Those who can form eidetic images don't seem to be able to use their special ability to improve long-term memory.

Phenomena corresponding to visual eidetic images are believed to exist in other sense fields as well, but research has not uncovered much about their nature, causes and significance.

eidetic memory See EIDETIC IMAGES; PHOTOGRAPHIC MEMORY.

elaboration The formation of a more richly encoded memory trace or ENGRAM that is more easily accessible because there are many different ways of contacting it in the process of retrieving a memory. Elaboration is an unconscious process of expansion and embellishment of detail, especially with reference to a symbol or representation in a dream. To consolidate a memory trace for long-term storage, a person needs to observe, analyze and judge.

electrical stimulation of the brain
Stimulating various areas of the cortex produces a range of responses from patients; however, only stimulation of the temporal lobes elicits meaningful, integrated experiences, including sound, movement and color, far more detailed, accurate and specific than normal recall.

Stimulating one side of the brain may bring back a certain song to one patient, the memory of a moment in a garden listening to a mother calling her child to another. Interestingly, stimulating the same point in the brain elicits the same memory every time. (See also EMOTION AND MEMORY; PENFIELD, WILDER.)

electroconvulsive therapy (ECT) and memory ECT therapy is a controversial therapy still used in psychiatric treatment to induce a seizure, most often in cases of severe depression; it also can cause a temporary memory loss. The question of whether ECT affects memory permanently is still debated.

In ECT therapy, patients are given an anesthetic and a muscle relaxant before two padded electrodes are applied to the temples. A controlled electric pulse is delivered to the electrodes until the patients experience a

brain seizure. Treatment usually consists of six to 12 seizures (two or three a week).

After the treatment, patients usually experience a period of confusion, which they do not remember afterward; there is usually also a brief period of AMNESIA covering the time right before the treatment. On regaining consciousness, patients who have received ECT are similar in many ways to those who have experienced posttraumatic amnesia. Typically, patients first regain their personal identity followed by the knowledge of where they are; orientation in time occurs last of all.

Tests of memory after ECT reveal a substantial memory impairment in addition to a clear ANTEROGRADE AMNESIA. However, after a number of treatments some patients say they experience a more serious memory loss, involving everyday forgetfulness, which usually disappears within a few weeks after treatment. Critics of ECT claim, however, that it produces more substantial effects on memory.

New research suggests that ECT administered to only one side of the head produces equally beneficial results to the more standard method without any accompanying memory loss.

The origins of ECT are thought to lie in the ancient Roman tradition of applying electric eels to the head as a cure for madness; mild electric shocks have been used since the late 1700s to treat illness. A machine using weak electric currents was used in Middlesex Hospital in England in 1767 to treat a range of illnesses, and at the same time London brain surgeon John Birch used a machine to shock the brain of depressed patients.

At about the same time, American inventor and patriot Benjamin Franklin was shocked into unconsciousness—and suffered a RETROGRADE AMNESIA—during one of his electricity experiments; he is said to have recommended electric shock for the treatment of mental illness.

However, the modern practice of electric shock treatment for the treatment of depression and mental illness is less than 65 years old. A Hungarian psychiatrist noted a number of studies reporting that schizophrenia and epilepsy did not occur in the same patient and wondered if an artificially induced seizure might cure schizophrenia. While the seizures were originally induced through the use of camphor and other drugs, Italian psychiatrist Ugo Cerletti and colleagues explored the possibility of using electric shock to achieve similar results. Cerletti's idea was considered an improvement over the drug-induced seizures, which were associated with toxic side effects.

The first patient to receive ECT to treat schizophrenia received it on April 15, 1938. Because it was simple and inexpensive, the use of ECT spread, and by the 1950s it was the primary method of treatment for schizophrenia and depression. The discovery of neuroleptic drugs led to a substantial decline in its use.

The controversy surrounding ECT is likely to continue for some time, and the question of whether ECT affects permanent memory remains unclear. Many studies that have examined long-term experience with ECT and controlled for influence of other factors indicate that ECT doesn't have any extensive effect on permanent memory function. All patients show some amount of retrograde amnesia for events immediately before ECT itself.

Some scientists believe that some patients may falsely conclude that their memory is impaired. In one study, scientists found significant differences between patients who reported memory problems and those who didn't. Those who complained tended to believe the ECT hadn't helped their depression, which could mean that their own assessment of memory might be the result of their continuing illness. Three years after treatment, this group insisted their memory problems, which they believed were of an amnesic type, remained—even though there was no objective proof of this. Researchers believe that these patients' initial experience

of true amnesia immediately following ECT might have caused them to question whether their memory function had really recovered.

Still, in elderly depressive patients ECT can worsen their decline in the presence of DEMENTIA, and ECT can be abused as a treatment. Even ECT proponents admit adverse reactions to the treatment are possible, although estimates of how great a risk exists vary.

Impastato, D.J. "The Story of the First Electroshock Treatment." *American Journal of Psychiatry* 116 (1960): 1113–14.

Salzman, C. "The Use of ECT in the Treatment of Schizophrenia." *American Journal of Psychiatry* 137 (1980): 1032–34.

electroencephalogram (EEG)   One of the first brain-monitoring techniques, EEGs chart the electrical activity of the brain through electrodes attached to the scalp. An EEG can uncover brain abnormalities because each brain region has its own characteristic pattern of electrophysiological activity. An EEG averages the electrical activity from a large area of the brain and is a valuable means of diagnosing epilepsy. However, the test is of limited use in locating specific areas of brain damage.

A more recent addition to the EEG arsenal is the quantitative EEG (qEEG). A quantitative EEG is different from an EEG in that the signals from the brain are played into a computer, digitized and stored. This type of EEG can measure the time delay between two regions of the cortex, for example, and the amount of time it takes for information to be transmitted from one region to another. (See also BRAIN SCANS; COMPUTERIZED TOMOGRAPHY (CT) SCAN; MAGNETIC RESONANCE IMAGING; POSITRON EMISSION TOMOGRAPHY.)

emotions and memory   Emotions play a complex negative and positive role in the formation of memory. Emotions are so powerful that they can seal a memory trace, protecting it from the passing years. It is for this reason that we remember most vividly what touches our heart and our spirit.

The idea that emotions and memory were intertwined has been a popular belief for centuries. Scientists as early as Sir Francis Bacon (1561–1626) believed that events associated with strong emotions (whether good or bad) were remembered more easily than those that aroused little emotion.

The idea appealed to Sigmund Freud, who blamed REPRESSION for the selective memory of some things. According to Freud, a person "forgets" (or represses) information or memories that would cause anxiety. Freud's ideas about repression usually were drawn from psychoanalytical interviews with the mentally ill, but he also believed that normal people repressed information.

Today scientists believe that emotions are essential for creating and filing memories away; in fact, both perception and recollection seem to require the aid of the limbic system (seat of the emotions). If the limbic area is damaged, thereby interfering with emotion and memory, the patient experiences confusion, automatism and AMNESIA. Of course, the activation of the limbic system alone is not enough to give a true sensation of memory.

Interestingly, some studies suggest that emotion exerts state-dependent effects on retrieval. That is, a person's mood experienced at the time of an event becomes a part of that memory of the event, and retrieving that memory is easier if the person's mood when trying to remember is similar to that associated with events he or she is trying to recall. In the study, scientists read stories to hypnotized subjects about a sad character and a happy character when half the subjects were in a happy mood and half in a sad mood. They found that most subjects remembered more facts about the character that was consistent with their mood while listening to the story. (See also FREUD, SIGMUND; HEDONIC SELECTIVITY; RESPONSE BIAS.)

encephalitis and memory   Encephalitis (inflammation of the brain) is an often-fatal viral disease that damages the brain on both sides, especially the MEDIAL TEMPORAL LOBE and the orbital frontal lobe, and often causes a form of AMNESIA resulting from brain damage. Encephalitis may be caused by several different viruses, but the herpes simplex virus is the most common cause.

The amnesia in patients with this disorder is probably caused by the destruction of the HIPPOCAMPUS and AMYGDALA, whereas the poor recall for previously well-established memories that these patients have been reported to show may be caused by destruction of the temporal association neocortex. Some patients also may suffer damage to the frontal lobes and in extreme cases show symptoms of the KLUVER-BUCY SYNDROME, which causes a range of symptoms including amnesia, visual AGNOSIA and altered sexual behavior.

Another cause of postencephalic amnesia is a virus transmitted to humans by mosquitoes, which causes an illness called St. Louis encephalitis. In addition, an increasing number of cases are caused by infection with HIV (human immunodeficiency virus), the organism responsible for AIDS.

A form of brain inflammation called acute inclusion body encephalitis can cause a severe and persistent memory defect that resembles KORSAKOFF'S SYNDROME, except that the patient usually recognizes the memory problems and does not lie about the condition.

encoding   The process by which information is translated into electrical impulses in the brain. In order for a new memory trace (engram) to be formed, information must be translated into this code.

There are two main kinds of encoding—maintenance and elaborative encoding. *Maintenance encoding* consists of repeating word chunks over and over, which is good for recognition but usually is not enough for recall. *Elaborative encoding* may take several forms:

- Reorganizing chunks by classifying and categorizing them so that they can be associated more easily with ideas already held in long-term memory
- Associating chunks with images
- Changing chunks for easier repetition (for example, changing them into rhymes)
- Noting distinctive features of a chunk
- Rehearsing and self-testing

Encoding can be understood best by looking at how a person remembers words—visually, acoustically or semantically (having to do with meaning). Because of the multifaceted nature of words, there is some flexibility in how they can be represented in memory. If a person wanted to memorize the word "chair," for example, the brain could devise a code based on visual, acoustic or semantic properties (or a combination of any or all three).

encoding deficit theories   There are two general types of theories regarding encoding deficits: The problem is either a failure of effortful processing or a failure of automatic processing. Proponents of the first theory believe that AMNESIA resulting from "effortful processing" failures is caused by a failure to pay adequate attention to the meaningful aspects of stimuli and that amnesics encode at a shallow level.

encoding specificity   A theory stating that memory retrieval is enhanced when the original encoding situation is reinstated at the time of recall. Therefore, if the recall (or test situation) is similar to the situation present during the original learning, more information will be retrieved. (See also PQRST METHOD.)

engram   Also known as a memory trace, an engram is the physical basis of memory, a unit of information encoded as a pattern of lowered resistance to electrical impulses or an increased readiness to respond to NEUROTRANSMITTERS. Engrams are presumed to persist in a network of nerve cells as the result of the consolidation of memory.

Memories seem to be encoded in the brain's cells (neurons), which convert chemical signals to electrical signals and then back to chemical signals again. Each neuron receives electrical impulses through dendrites, whose tiny branches direct signals into the body of the cell. When some of the arriving signals stimulate the neuron, others inhibit it; if there are enough stimulating signals, the neuron fires, sending its own pulse down its axon, which connects by a synapse into the dendrites of other cells.

Electrical pulses carry information inside a neuron; once the signal reaches the end of the axon, neurotransmitters carry it across the synaptic gap. On the other side of the synapse is another dendrite, containing "receptors," which recognize the neurotransmitters. If enough signals are registered, the second cell fires. A single neuron can receive signals from thousands of other neurons, and its axon can branch repeatedly, sending signals to thousands more.

While researchers have long understood the mechanism of neurons, only recently have they begun to understand how these cells might be able to store memories. Most agree that when a person experiences a new event (such as meeting a new person), a unique pattern of neurons (an engram) is activated in some way, and within the entire configuration of brain cells, certain ones light up.

In order to store this memory of the new person, there must be a way to save the memory—to forge connections between neurons to create a new circuit that acts as a symbol of something in the outside world. By reactivating the circuit, the brain can retrieve the memory—a replica of the original perception.

We would recognize the person again when we encountered something that evoked a neural pattern similar to one that was already stored in the brain. Seeing a picture of that person in a photo album might cause the lighting up of a pattern of neurons that resembled the patterns joined together during the initial introduction. The brain would detect the similarity and there would be a pleasant shock of recognition.

Unlike the wiring in appliances at home, the brain's circuits are not permanent but malleable; as knowledge is acquired, circuits break up and form new connections, constantly rewiring themselves and influencing our representations of the world. Scientists believe that ideas are formed in the same way. The neural circuit forming the concept of "table," for example, would preserve the overlapping features of each of the many different types of tables stored in memory.

For a memory as complex as a person's wedding day, the engram would not be stored in one tiny place in the brain, but would be encoded within the vast weblike structure of neurons sprawling throughout the brain.

Engrams are formed on tasks we must perform over and over again, such as threading a needle; to thread the needle, the person must activate the appropriate engram. The motor area of the brain then reads this engram, and the person threads the needle. When someone has trouble getting the thread through the eye, sensory signals from the fingers don't match the information stored in the engram; this triggers the brain to send out more signals so that the sensory signals sent back by the fingers now match the engram. This is how we store the ability to perform skills precisely over and over. Engrams are not constructed quickly; the more complex the activity, the more time and rehearsal it takes to form a reliable engram.

Not all memories are stored in the same way, so that not all memories are remembered equally well. Certain memories have left stronger or weaker traces, depending on how they were used. What remains in long-term memory has been used many times,

recalled and stored differently with multiple references that allow the trace to be systematically integrated.

Every time a memory is recalled, it appears in a different context and is altered by the new recall; some elements have been expanded at the expense of others. The more time that has elapsed, the greater the chance that the memory trace has been manipulated.

Scientists weren't sure whether an original memory trace is overwritten or displaced, whether a new memory blends old and new attributes or whether the original memory and a memory of the new postevent information both exist at the same time. Recent research at Rutgers University has found that original memories can be overwritten, but only if new information is presented immediately afterward. Given the specificity of early memories and the strong contextual constraints on their retrieval, scientists think that early memories of unique events that were protected from modification are quite likely to be accurate reflections of events as the child originally perceived them.

From the time of Plato up to the 19th century, scientists believed that memories were stored permanently in the mind. In fact, for many years scientists thought that engrams were stored in a specific place in the brain. Neurological researcher Karl Lashley was searching for this specific area when he began a series of experiments in the 1920s. He trained rats to run mazes, cut out snippets of their brain tissue and then set the rats loose in the mazes again. After operating on hordes of rats, Lashley could not find one single place in the brain where the memory of the maze existed.

Not surprisingly, the more bits of brain he cut away, the more problems the rats had running a maze—but it didn't seem to matter *what* portion of the brain he cut out. Eventually Lashley gave up trying to map the location of memory in the brain, believing that memory existed everywhere, disseminating like smoke throughout the folds and fissures of the brain.

By the 1950s, neuroscientists turned to new metaphors in their search for an understanding of memory. Using laser beams, scientists created eerie three-dimensional photographs called holograms that, when cut apart, retained the entire image in each fragment. Neurologists began to wonder whether this might be the way the brain retained memories, with each tiny neuron containing the entire memory of the animal.

Into this ideological fray stepped Canadian surgeon Wilder Penfield, who stumbled upon evidence during open brain surgery that seemed to show that engrams could be activated and replayed like records on a stereo. What Penfield found amazing was that when he touched an electrode in a specific spot, the patient would instantly become aware of everything that was in his memory during an earlier time. Sometimes these memories were visual, sometimes aural—but the memory stopped when the electrode was removed and replayed if the electrode was replaced without delay. Some scientists argued that what Penfield was activating were not memories at all but hallucinations.

As the computer rose to popularity at the end of the 20th century, the idea that memories could be stored as engrams in specific locations became popular once more, since this is the way computers store memory. Other researchers began to wonder if—based on the double helix structure of DNA—memory might be stored within molecules in the brain. If molecules could encode genetic information, these scientists argued, it seemed logical that they could record memories in the same fashion. Scientists began studying the nucleic acids adenine, cytosine, thymine and guanine, molecules that carry the blueprint for making enzymes and proteins. Other scientists argued that memories might lie not in nucleic acids but in amino acids that make up protein chains.

Today scientists believe that engrams (memory traces) are encoded in the neurons throughout the brain, a theory that encompasses both Lashley's and Penfield's ideas. And like any circuit, touching one part of it with an electrode could produce the entire memory. (See also NEURONS AND MEMORY; PENFIELD, WILDER.)

Johnson, George. *In the Palaces of Memory: How We Build the Worlds Inside Our Heads.* New York: Alfred Knopf, 1991.

Myers, N.A., Clifton, R.K., and Clarkson, M.G. "When They Were Very Young: Almost-threes Remember Two Years Ago." *Infant Behavior and Development* 10 (1987): 123–32.

Rovee-Collier, Carolyn. "The Capacity for Long-Term Memory in Infancy." *Current Directions in Psychological Science* 2 (August 1993): 130–35.

enzymes and memory   All brain function depends on chemical messages transmitted from cell to cell by a carrier (neurotransmitter), and brain enzymes are critically important parts of this message network. Enzymes are organic compounds that interact with other substances to form a new chemical, either by synthesizing or degrading it.

For example, choline acetyltransferase is a brain enzyme that is important in the production of ACETYLCHOLINE, a neurotransmitter involved in learning and memory. Scientists have found low levels of this neurotransmitter in the areas of the brain of Alzheimer's disease patients where plaques and tangles are located. The enzyme is involved in the passage of nerve signals. (See also NEURONAL PLASTICITY.)

epilepsy   A disorder marked by recurrent seizures or temporary alteration in one or more brain functions. Temporal lobe epilepsy, which is a type of partial seizure of the brain, may result in uncontrollable flashbacks to distant memories.

Surgery to remove temporal lobe tissue that produces symptoms of epilepsy may cause a degree of memory defect. Operations on the dominant temporal lobe often interfere with the ability to learn verbal information by hearing or reading and may last for as long as three years after surgery.

In a series of operations during the mid-1950s, surgeons removed the medial temporal lobe in ten epileptic patients in order to lessen seizures. While the operations were successful, eight of the ten suffered pronounced memory deficits. The most famous of these patients was known as HM, whose AMNESIC SYNDROME is considered to be among the purest ever studied. After the operation, HM was unable to remember anything other than a handful of events since the time of his operation and was described as living in the "eternal present."

The study revealed that amnesia was present only in those who had lost both the hippocampus and the amygdala; removal of the amygdala alone did not produce amnesia.

epinephrine   Also known as adrenaline, this naturally occurring hormone may be a primary piece of the puzzle involved in locking memories in place. Produced synthetically as a drug since 1900, it is released into the bloodstream by the adrenal gland in response to signals from the autonomic nervous system triggered by stress, exercise or fear. Epinephrine increases the speed and force of the heart, allowing it to do more work, and seems to be responsible for imprinting memories indelibly in the long-term memory. In other words, people seem to remember better when their bodies are flooded with adrenaline. Some scientists suggest that hormones such as epinephrine may act as a "fixative" to lock memories of stimulating or shocking events in the brain. This could allow the brain to discard unimportant information while maintaining the important impressions we experience. On the other hand, some memories are so unpleasant that although they are retained in long-term memory, they are not available to the conscious mind. It is believed that these memories are so potentially harmful to the psyche that the brain actually guards against their recall.

Additional research also suggests that adrenaline plays an important role in regulating memory storage; it enhances memory for many different kinds of tasks, including those that train animals using rewards as well as punishment.

Some researchers have discovered that rats not capable of producing epinephrine have a poorer recall ability than their normal rat relatives. And rats injected with additional epinephrine after a learning task appear to remember it better.

Some studies also suggest that injecting epinephrine into older rats after they had learned how to run a maze improved their performance in maze running, leading to the conclusion that older people with memory problems may be deficient in epinephrine.

Epinephrine may act directly on the brain, or it may alter brain chemistry that allows another substance to travel to the brain and "fix" the memory.

However, although epinephrine appears to regulate memory storage, it is clear that the hormone itself does not pass from blood into brain cells—at least not in amounts large enough to measure. Instead, research suggests that epinephrine's action outside the brain might be responsible for modulating memory storage. Findings indicate that epinephrine release results in an increase in plasma levels of glucose, which also has been implicated in memory improvement. It appears, then, that epinephrine release may in turn initiate the release of glucose, which crosses the blood-brain barrier and affects memory storage.

Unfortunately, because epinephrine has a variety of unpleasant side effects on the heart and other body systems—especially in older patients—more research needs to be completed before it can be used as some sort of "memory enhancement" drug.

"How the Brain Works." *Newsweek*, February 7, 1983.

episodic memory Memories for individual episodes in someone's personal life, such as the senior prom or a first date.

According to psychologist Endel Tulving, episodic memory is one of the five major human memory systems for which reasonable evidence is now available. (The others are semantic, procedural, perceptual representation and short-term memory.) Several of these systems, according to Tulving, usually interact to perform everyday tasks. It is episodic memory that enables a person to remember personal experiences, to be consciously aware of an earlier experience in a certain situation at a certain time.

Tulving believes that episodic memory has evolved out of semantic memory, the memory system that registers and stores knowledge about the world in the broadest sense and makes it available for retrieval. Episodic memory cannot operate independently of semantic memory, although it is not necessary for encoding and storing information into semantic memory.

Tulving, Endel. *Elements of Episodic Memory.* Oxford: Clarendon Press, 1983.
———. "How Many Memory Systems Are There?" *American Psychologist* 40 (1985): 385–98.

event factors Factors that can reduce a witness's ability to report facts accurately. Event factors include how long and how often an event was viewed, salience and type of details and violence.

Exposure Time The less time a witness has to look at something, the less accurate the perception. When an event occurs over a long period of time, a witness should be better able to recall it.

Frequency Also, the number of times a witness has to observe particular details, the better memory he or she will have of those details.

Detail Salience When a person sees a complex event, not all the details are equally salient, or memorable. Some things (color,

novelty, interest) catch a person's attention more quickly than others; interesting scenes attract our attention and hold our interest. And both attention and interest are important in the encoding of memories.

On the other hand, boring, routine, common or insignificant circumstances are rarely remembered as specific incidents.

Detail Type It's important to remember that details (a person's height, weight, speed, conversational details, colors) are not all remembered equally. The estimates of time, speed and distance—especially speed—are often inaccurate. And initial inaccuracies in these details can guarantee that they also will be recalled incorrectly. Interestingly, while most people have great trouble estimating how long an event takes, their mistakes are almost always *overestimates*.

Violence Research has found that testimony about an emotionally volatile incident may be more likely to be incorrect than testimony about a less emotional incident. It is suspected that viewing a violent scene is so emotionally stressful that an eyewitness's ability to recall the events accurately is negatively influenced. (See also AGE AND EYEWITNESS ABILITY; CROSS-RACIAL WITNESS IDENTIFICATION; EYEWITNESS TESTIMONY; GENDER AND EYEWITNESS ABILITY.)

event memory The limitless capacity for images of past events, centered in the HIPPOCAMPUS and the cortex of the frontal lobes.

exercise and memory Aerobic exercise may help maintain short-term memory, particularly as it applies to general memory and verbal memory tests. This type of memory is particularly important in recalling names, directions and telephone numbers, or pairing a name with a face.

While scientists are not yet sure why aerobic exercise seems to help, researchers believe it may be due to increased oxygen efficiency to the brain or a rise in GLUCOSE metabolism. In one study, a group of 30 volunteers took an in-pool aerobics program or simply socialized or did nothing for nine weeks. In the workout group, the three-times-a-week sessions included water aerobics and some resistance training exercises. After the nine weeks, general memory tests were given to all groups. The results of this study suggest that those who become actively involved in an aerobic exercise program may be able to improve general short-term memory.

In another study, Utah researchers studied out-of-shape subjects aged 55 to 70, putting them on a four-month program of brisk walking. All participants increased their short-term memory, ability to reason and reaction time.

Other good aerobic exercises are cycling, swimming, jogging and racquet sports. For best results, these activities should be done three times a week for 30 minutes each.

explicit memory
Another name for intentional recollection, this is one of two types of memory—the other is its opposite, IMPLICIT MEMORY.

Research studies indicate that explicit memory declines as a person ages, in contrast to implicit memory, which may not. Explicit memory differs most importantly from implicit memory in the way memories are retrieved. A person uses explicit memory when struggling to recall information, such as a person's name. Implicit memory is being used if a person's name "pops into the head" effortlessly and automatically.

The two terms were invented in 1985 by psychologists Peter Graf and Daniel Schacter of the University of Arizona, although researchers recognized that two memory systems existed five years earlier. Traditionally, memory experts have tested only explicit memory by giving subjects lists of items to recall intentionally during a study period before a test. (A test of implicit memory would require subjects to respond to questions that don't require any sort of intentional recall, but only to respond with whatever comes to mind.)

Interestingly, techniques that improve explicit memory do not improve the implicit system, and vice versa. Studies also show that amnesic patients who have serious problems with explicit memory do not show problems with implicit memory.

Researchers suspect there are two separate biological systems for implicit and explicit memory and that the implicit memory system develops first; the explicit memory system is then built onto the implicit system and, being more vulnerable, suffers from life stress.

Adler, Tina. "Implicit Memory Seems to Age Well." *APA Monitor* (February 1990): 8.

external memory aids
A variety of techniques to help a person remember, such as notebooks, signs, electronic devices and the like.

Diaries and daily timetables are very helpful to those with memory problems, since they can store information about what patients have to do at certain times. These types of aids can help patients remember appointments, recall routines and reduce daily life activity problems. *Lists and plans* can be displayed prominently so that patients can have easy access to general information.

For those patients with both retrograde and ANTEROGRADE AMNESIA, *photos and memorabilia* can be displayed to help jog memory.

To be most effective, external memory aids must be given as close as possible to the time at which a desired act is required; it is not helpful to remind someone with memory problems in the morning of a task that must be done after dinner. The aids also must be active rather than passive—they must alert the patient to the fact that something needs to be done. And they should specify as clearly as possible what needs to be done. Therefore, the best external memory aid is a timer that can be programmed to display specific messages at set times or a simple timing device with a timetable or diary. All the patient needs to know is to check the timetable when the alarm goes off. (See also RETROGRADE AMNESIA.)

extrinsic context   Also called independent context, this term comprises both background and format awareness; it does not affect the meaningful interpretation of target information. It is the opposite of INTRINSIC CONTEXT, which is recently perceived.

Priming can occur with items that already exist in well-established memories and with items not presented before. There is some evidence that both forms of priming may be preserved in organic AMNESIA.

eyewitness testimony   If 100 people saw the same auto accident, no two reports would be identical. People who are generally anxious, neurotic or preoccupied tend to make slightly worse eyewitnesses than those who generally are not, since high arousal apparently causes witnesses to concentrate on certain details and neglect others.

According to psychologist Elizabeth Loftus, witness accuracy may be affected by stress, arousal and attention. Other factors also may influence whether an eyewitness can accurately report an occurrence: sex, age, amount of general anxiety or happiness and amount of training.

When a witness sees a serious crime or traffic accident, a range of errors can interfere with accurate recall at different stages of the event. During the actual event, the witness is affected by the amount of time the event lasted and how much stress he or she experienced. Both factors can dramatically affect a witness's ability to perceive the events accurately.

People who are highly anxious and preoccupied tend to do worse on eyewitness tasks and aren't able to identify faces as well as those who aren't as anxious. This is because high-anxiety subjects don't use as much of the information as they could be using when they initially look at a face or a scene. Those who are experiencing great life stress also have a slight tendency to perform more poorly on a test of eyewitness ability. Neurotic individuals also fared worse on tests of eyewitness ability.

The time between a complex experience such as witnessing a crime and the recollection of that event is crucial to accurately remembering facts. It is well established that witnesses are less accurate and complete in their descriptions of an event after a long interval than after a short one. Classic research in this area was performed by Hermann Ebbinghaus, who tested how well he could remember a list of nonsense syllables after an elapse of time and then how well he could relearn them. His results, which he plotted on the famous FORGETTING CURVE, proved that people forget very rapidly after an event, but that forgetting becomes more and more gradual as time goes by.

Other researchers have shown that after a year, memory will be less accurate than after a month, and after a month it will be less accurate than after a week. But it is not just time that begins to erase information held in memory, it's what goes on during that time. For example, a witness sees a car accident, but later reads in the paper that the driver had been abusing drugs. Research suggests that such new information can dramatically affect the memory of the original event, changing a witness's memory and absorbing itself into a previously acquired memory.

When witnesses see an event and later hear information that conflicts with the original memory, many will compromise, consciously or unconsciously, what they have seen with what they have heard after the fact—particularly in estimating size or remembering color.

On the other hand, it is possible to introduce nonexistent objects into a witness's recall; casually mentioning a nonexistent object during the course of questioning can increase the likelihood that a person later will report having seen that nonexistent object. It's also possible to "remember" events from the past that never happened at all.

Psychologist Jean Piaget describes his vivid childhood memory from the age of two, when his nurse saved him from abduction by kidnappers. He remembered everything, from the scratches on his nurse's face to the size of the crowd and the appearance of the policeman. However, at the age of 15 his nurse (who had since joined the Salvation Army) confessed to having made up the entire story, and returned the watch she had been given as a reward. Apparently the young Piaget had heard discussions of this event as a child and projected the story into his past in the form of a visual memory.

Sex and Eyewitness Ability Other research has found that both men and women pay more attention to items that catch their interest, and therefore store more or better information in memory about those items, according to Loftus. In a study of 50 subjects who were tested after looking at 24 slides of a wallet-snatching incident, women were only slightly more accurate overall. But women were far more accurate than men on questions dealing with women's clothing or actions, and men were far more accurate on questions concerning the thief's appearance and the surroundings.

Age and Witness Ability In general, recall and recognition ability improves up to about age 15 or 20, and a decline may begin to occur about age 60. In numerous cross-sectional studies comparing eyewitness ability of children of different ages, older children outperformed younger ones in most. Often this increased ability is due to the fact that older children make many fewer false identifications, which may be because older children are less likely to guess when they aren't certain. However, it also could represent a genuine improvement in the ability to discriminate what was seen from what was not.

However, eyewitness accuracy does not continue to improve forever. Eyewitnesses over age 60 perform more poorly than do somewhat younger people, and many tasks show some decrease in performance between ages 40 and 60. But although some tasks, such as memory for details, may weaken slightly with age, other cognitive skills are maintained as people age. In addition, there are great individual differences among people. Therefore, while performance on some tasks may decline somewhat, performance on others—memory for logical relationships or the ability to make complex inferences, for example—doesn't deteriorate.

In addition, age may affect whether a witness is susceptible to potential biases and misleading information. Researchers always have believed children were both highly suggestible and particularly inaccurate.

Training While a witness's prior knowledge and expectations can influence perception and memory, researchers found there were no significant differences between the number of true detections of people and actions between the police and civilians. (See also AGE AND EYEWITNESS ABILITY; CROSS-RACIAL WITNESS IDENTIFICATION; GENDER AND EYEWITNESS ABILITY.)

F

face-name association method A type of memory system relying on visual imagery for success. The technique includes four stages. First, the subject is asked to select a distinctive feature from the face of the person to be remembered (such as flaming red-orange hair) and, second, to transform the person's name into one or two common nouns (change "Carol" into "carrot"). Third, the distinctive feature and the transformed name must be linked in some way (imagine an orange carrot), and then recall the name. Research subjects with normal memories who followed all the steps in the procedure remembered names better than did those who only selected the distinctive feature or transformed the name into a noun.

familiarity   The more a person is familiar with a topic, the easier it is to learn, remember and understand new information about it. The reason is that if a person already knows something about a subject, the new information will be more meaningful and there will be something with which to associate the new information.

Familiarity also works by the concept of *exposure;* exposure to information may result in partial learning even if a person does not intend to learn it. Therefore, young children whose parents read to them may later learn to read more easily.

fantasy   An imagined sequence of events or mental images (such as daydreams) that serve to express unconscious conflicts, to gratify unconscious wishes or to prepare for anticipated future events.

"fat lady" syndrome   A phenomenon involving the ability of overweight anesthetized patients to be aware, on some level, of disparaging remarks made about their weight to the detriment of their recovery.

In several cases, unkind remarks made during surgery of obese women appeared to be linked to unexplained heart attacks shortly after surgery. At least one lawsuit was settled out of court regarding comments about a "beached whale" by surgeons around an anesthetized obese woman. In this case, the woman suffered a range of autonomic and vegetative disorders for several days until she told her nurse that the surgeon "called me a beached whale." The operating room nurse confirmed the insult. (See also ANESTHESIA, MEMORY WHILE UNDER.)

feeling of knowing   A subject's ability to predict whether an unrecalled item will be recognized later.

fipexide   A cerebroactive drug that has been shown in some studies to improve short-term memory. The drug appears to mildly enhance the release of DOPAMINE, the neurotransmitter critical to fine motor coordination, motivation, emotions and immune function. (See NEUROTRANSMITTERS.)

In laboratory mice studies, the drug appears to consolidate new memories and improve recall. Unlike other nootropic drugs, however, fipexide must be given both before learning new material and during the recall period in order to show an improved recall.

In one double-blind study of 40 elderly patients with severe cognitive problems, fipexide improved cognition and performance, short-term memory and attention. Average improvement in cognition was estimated to be 60 percent.

Bompani, R., and Scali, G. "Fipexide, An Effective Cognition Activator in the Elderly: A Placebo-controlled, Double-blind Clinical Trial." *Current Medical Research and Opinion* 10, no. 2 (1986): 99–106.

Sera, G., et al. "Effect of Fipexide on Passive Avoidance Behavior in Rats." *Pharmacological Research* 21, no. 5 (1989): 603–8.

first-letter cueing   The use of the first letter of a word as a cue to remembering the word itself. This cueing usually employs acronyms—making a word out of the first letters of the words to be remembered. For example, it's possible to remember the Great Lakes by the acronym "HOMES" (*H*uron, *O*ntario, *M*ichigan, *E*rie, *S*uperior). Another related type of first-letter cueing is the ACROSTIC, in which the first letter in a series of words, lines or verses form a word or phrase. For example, the notes on the lines in the treble clef can be remembered by this acrostic: Every Good Boy Does Fine (EGBDF).

Because the system is so effective, most organizations and governmental bodies make use of first-letter cueing: NATO (North Atlantic Treaty Organization) or AA (Alcoholics Anonymous).

The only problem with acronyms or acrostics lies in the propensity to forget which strategy has been devised. Therefore, it's a good idea to make the association remind you of the information to be remembered. Imagine HOMES floating on the Great Lakes; when you want to think of the names of all the lakes, the image of HOMES will return to you and with it, the first letter of each lake's name.

First-letter cueing also has been used to help brain-injured patients remember names. In one case, researchers used it to teach a patient with KORSAKOFF'S SYNDROME the names of two hospital staffers. Before this try, the patient had not been able to learn one person's name in five years. The patient was told: "This person's name is John Smith. Try to remember the initials JS." The next time they met, John Smith was introduced as "John S.," and the patient was asked to remember the rest of the last name. Subsequently, each time they met the verbal cues were reduced, and the patient learned two names using this method within two weeks. (See also MEMORY FOR NAMES.)

first-letter mnemonic See ACROSTIC.

flashbacks during surgery A phenomenon of spontaneous recall of distant memories during neurosurgery, when a probe touches certain parts of the brain thought to be associated with memory storage.

The phenomenon was discovered by Wilder Penfield during neurosurgery on a conscious patient in 1933; when he electrically stimulated the brain's surface, the flashback occurred.

"The astonishing aspect of this phenomenon," Penfield wrote, "is that suddenly [the patient] is aware of all that was in his mind during an earlier strip of time. It is the stream of a former consciousness flowing again."

The flashbacks—which are profoundly vivid—cease as soon as the probe is removed from the brain, but they may be repeated many times if the electrode is replaced without too long a delay. Apparently the recall is random, since the retrieved memories are usually neither significant nor

important. The patient describes the experience as being like a dream, or "seeing things." Interestingly, these "memories" are often of things the patient was not likely to have witnessed; for example, one woman saw herself during birth, feeling as if she were reliving the experience of being born, and another woman saw herself in a place where she had never been.

Of the 520 patients who received electrical stimulation of the temporal lobes (the area of the brain in which Penfield believed these memories were stored), only 40 produced "experiential responses." Later studies showed that these responses can occur only when the limbic structures, which are thought to be responsible for emotion, have been activated. If these limbic structures are not activated, then the experiential phenomena do not occur.

Other psychologists, however, disagreed with Penfield that the patients were recalling true memories, pointing out that the memories could result from reconstruction of fragments of past experience. Emotions link the ambiguous fragments of "memory" into more coherent wholes that can be related to the immediate setting, later scientists realized. The brain contains only patterns of activity, not symbols, and these patterns acquire different meanings in different contexts.

Pettinati, Helen. *Hypnosis and Memory*. New York: Guilford Press, 1988.

flashbulb memory A memory formed in relation to dramatic or emotionally upsetting events. The memory is sharply etched in the mind because it involves a sudden powerful emotion: shock, anger, disbelief, outrage, fury. Scientists believe that these flashbulb memories are almost certainly encoded in the brain in a different way from regular, everyday memories. Remembering the day President John F. Kennedy was shot stands out in the memory, whereas remembering the day before can be recalled only in bits and pieces, if at all. The more muted the emotion, the less powerful and enduring the memory.

fluid imbalances and memory Too much or too little water will disturb brain function, because water contains electrolytes (potassium, sodium, chloride, CALCIUM and MAGNESIUM) crucial to memory. Especially during hot weather, aging patients are particularly at risk for electrolyte-induced memory loss. The careful administration of water can have dramatic improvements on the memory loss in these patients. (See also PHYSIOLOGICAL CAUSES OF MEMORY LOSS.)

folic acid and memory New reviews of scientific evidence suggest that low levels of folic acid (a B vitamin) are closely tied to psychiatric symptoms in the elderly; one study has found that elderly patients with mental disorders (especially DEMENTIA) were three times more apt to have low folic acid than others their age. Studies also suggest that among healthy aged people, those with low folic acid intake scored lower on memory and abstract thinking ability. Surprisingly, even borderline deficiencies can be harmful to the mental state, according to E.H. Reynolds, M.D., of Kings College School of Medicine in London.

Folic acid is a vitamin essential to the production of red blood cells by the bone marrow and is contained in a wide variety of food, particularly liver and raw vegetables, legumes, nuts, avocados, cereals, spinach and leafy greens. Scientists have also found that low daily doses of folic acid supplements (200 micrograms, found in ¾ cup of cooked spinach) may lift mood and relieve depression. Normally, a well-balanced diet provides adequate amounts of folic acid. Low-dose supplements (200–500 micrograms) seem safe, experts say, but high doses require medical supervision.

Folic acid is particularly important during pregnancy, since the vitamin plays an important part in fetal growth, especially the development of the nervous system and the formation of blood cells. Its lack during pregnancy has been linked to neural tube defects; during pregnancy, some women may need folic acid tablets to supplement their diet. Folic acid deficiency also has been linked to megaloblastic anemia, fatigue and pallor.

forensic hypnosis While experts concede that HYPNOSIS has positive uses, accepting hypnosis in the courts as virtually foolproof is dangerous. Research has shown that the brain is not some sort of 24-hour video camera on which anything that is recorded can be recalled automatically under hypnosis. In fact, witnesses can "remember" information that may be totally inaccurate, and—because of a jury's misperception of hypnosis—this testimony can carry great weight with the court. Juries can convict a person on the strength of a memory that could have been influenced by the questioning techniques of the hypnotist or by a mental quirk in the subject.

When a person wants to remember something, the memory is not plucked intact out of a "memory store" but is constructed from stored available bits of information. Gaps in the information are filled in unconsciously by inference, and when these fragments are joined together, they form memory.

But memories are often faulty. The person may not have perceived the information correctly in the first place, or the data could have been lost or disturbed. Even if the information had been perceived and stored correctly, it could be forgotten upon questioning. And the longer the time between the event and its recollection, the less accurate it will be.

It's not just the length of time that is important during this retention interval, but what occurs during that period of time—conversations the subject hears, other information uncovered, and hypnosis itself, which can supply new information or supplant information already stored by the subject.

Witnesses who are not certain about what they saw can, when hypnotized, recall the events as if they were actually there. They may relive the crime as if it were a scene on TV and become convinced that they saw and heard relevant facts—and then testify in court based not on true recollection but on their response to explicit and implicit suggestions during hypnosis.

Hypnotists try not to ask "leading questions"—but whether a question is leading or not is known only if the hypnotist knows the truth, and if the hypnotist did know the truth, hypnotizing the witness would be irrelevant. For instance, it is very easy for a hypnotist to translate the belief that the witness may have seen something into the memories of a responsive hypnotic subject.

Hypnotic intervention might actually alter memory itself, since some experts believe a memory must be evoked before it can be changed. Since the hypnotic process causes activation of memory, this process may make these memories especially subject to change.

Once a memory has been altered, there may be no practical means of distinguishing between the portions that are derived from the witness's sensory experiences and the parts that come from somewhere else.

Hypnotic intervention may help in those situations where original memories remain intact, but for memories that undergo transformation due to postevent suggestion, no technique results in successful retrieval.

In a legal context, hypnosis may interfere with the constitutional right of confrontation by making a previously uncertain witness certain, according to hypnosis expert Martin Orne. After being hypnotized, witnesses are no longer the same witnesses as they were before, especially since they now may be profoundly resistant to cross-examination. (See also MEMORY FOR EVENTS.)

forebrain   One of three major subdivisions of the brain, including both the cerebral hemispheres and the thalamus and hypothalamus.

forgetting   When the memory for a past event has not been called up for days or months, the memory itself begins to fade. Some researchers suggest that passing time actually alters the physiological basis of memory, gradually clouding and eroding the neural engram (the memory trace in the brain). Currently, no neurochemical basis of memory has been found to account for this chemical description of forgetting.

Behavioral theories suggest that forgetting may be based on the phenomena of interference: RETROACTIVE INHIBITION would mean that new learning interferes with the old memories; in PROACTIVE INHIBITION, memories interfere with the retention of information. (See INTERFERENCE THEORY.)

forgetting, theories of   There are many different explanations for why information may be "forgotten." FORGETTING is part of the memory mechanism, because it allows concentration on one subject at a time. At some point the brain must sift, choose and eliminate some memories or else it would face a daunting overabundance of memories. This sifting, whether conscious or not, often occurs amid the tapestry of emotion. "We forget," said the poet Matthew Arnold, "because we must, not because we will." People forget traumatic memories of abuse, war, assault and great pain, such as childbirth.

Errors may occur during any of the three stages of remembering (recording, retaining or retrieving), but to remember, a person must correctly execute all three stages. This is why it's easier to forget than to remember.

In one study that looked at people who tended to have problems with forgetting, it was discovered that both children and adults shared common problems that explained their reduced memory performance. They tended to have shorter attention spans and a lack of awareness, they weren't spontaneously organized and they had difficulty focusing and selecting the most important elements of any information. They were passive, did not visualize well and did not set goals.

At least five main reasons can explain why we forget something: DECAY, REPRESSION, distortion, interference and cue dependency. No single explanation can account for all instances of forgetting.

Decay Decay is one of many theories of forgetting that suggests memories leave a physical trace in the brain that gradually fades away with time after a period of non-use. Decay is believed to affect short-term memory almost exclusively.

Repression Forgetting occurs because unpleasant memories are intentionally forgotten, or repressed.

Memory Distortions Memory can be affected by a person's interests or values so that an experience is remembered the way a person wants to remember it. In other words, memories can be changed, or distorted, to fit what we want them to be or how we think they ought to be.

Interference Theory The interference theory holds that forgetting may be affected more by what happens after something is learned—such as interference by other learning—than by how much time passes. It does not imply, however, that there is a limited memory capacity that pushes old information out when new data are learned. Rather, what we learn, not how much we learn, determines forgetting by interference.

Cue Dependency Memories are cue dependent when they do not fade away or are displaced by other information; instead, the right cue must be used to retrieve the memories.

Research suggests that most forgetting occurs because we haven't used the right cue and that much other forgetting is caused by interference. In addition, studies suggest that most forgetting occurs right after the information has been learned; as time passes, the rate of forgetting slows and levels off. But material that has been learned thoroughly,

or that is very important to an individual, can be remembered throughout a lifetime.

Researchers also discovered that "slow" learners don't forget any quicker than fast learners. If a slow learner is given enough time to learn something, the rate of forgetting is about the same as for a fast learner, because when it comes to forgetting, how well a person learns something is more important than how fast the information was learned. And while young people generally learn faster than the elderly, once the information has been learned, forgetting rates are about the same for both age groups.

This fact holds important implications for students. If both a fast and a slow learner are given only one hour to study a subject, the fast learner will likely perform better on a subsequent test of the material. But if the slow learner is given an extra hour or two to master the subject, that student can do just as well on the test. (See also CUE-DEPENDENT FORGETTING; DISTORTIONS, MEMORY; INTERFERENCE THEORY.)

forgetting curve A graph of forgetting rates drawn by Hermann Ebbinghaus in 1885 showing that we forget very rapidly immediately after an event, but forgetting becomes more and more gradual as time passes. Ebbinghaus's classic experiment is the most often cited study that reveals the loss of retention with an elapse of time.

In his study, Ebbinghaus tested how well he could remember a list of nonsense syllables after a lapse of time and then how well he could relearn them. He plotted his results on his forgetting curve. (See also EBBINGHAUS, HERMANN E.; EYEWITNESS TESTIMONY; MEMORY FOR EVENTS.)

fornix One of four areas of the brain associated with memory, the fornix is the bridge between the temporal lobes and the diencephalon. Some researchers believe that AMNESIA is a result of a disconnection between the fornix and MAMMILLARY BODIES. (See also LOCALIZATION OF MEMORY.)

Freeman, Walter (1895–1972) The inventor of the LOBOTOMY and a prominent neurologist, Freeman was a scion of a well-known Philadelphia medical family who had worked for many years at St. Elizabeth's Hospital in Washington, D.C. At a conference in London in 1935, Freeman met Portuguese neurologist Antonio Egas Moniz, who had been conducting psychosurgical experiments with animals and who soon began operating on humans with a procedure called LEUCOTOMY.

After studying Moniz's book on the procedure, Freeman and his partner, James Watts, performed the first American leucotomy on a depressed patient in 1936. Impatient with the procedure and convinced he could perform it faster with a minimum of preparation, Freeman adapted the technique that he began calling lobotomy. Instead of opening the skull, he inserted an ice pick through the eye socket directly into the frontal lobe. This allowed him to operate more quickly on far more patients, on an outpatient basis. By 1946 Freeman started performing the lobotomies "assembly-line style," operating on ten patients a day in his office.

Based on 80 lobotomies, Freeman and Watts published their textbook *Psychosurgery* in 1942. Before the procedure eventually faded into disrepute as dangerous and inhumane, more than 40,000 lobotomies had been performed in the United States through the 1950s.

As public sentiment turned against lobotomies and the development of psychoactive drugs made them unnecessary, Freeman left Washington in 1954 and abandoned his assembly-line lobotomies. He performed his last lobotomy at the age of 72 in Berkeley.

Freeman, W., and Watts, J. *Psychosurgery.* Springfield, Ill.: Charles C Thomas, 1942 (2nd ed., 1950).

free recall The production of material from memory without the aid of specific cues.

freezing effect A high degree of persistence of a memory. Early comments are frozen into place in the memory and later reappear often when the witness recalls the experience. For example, when a person is asked to recall some prelearned information, statements that appear in an early recollection tend to reappear later. Therefore, when a witness reports that a bank robber carried a gun, this detail would probably appear in later recollections regardless of whether it was true or not.

The freezing effect may occur because after an event takes place but before a witness recalls that event (called the retention interval), details about the event aren't just lying in memory waiting to be recalled. Instead, the details are prone to influences, such as personal thoughts or external information. (See also AGE AND EYEWITNESS ABILITY; CROSS-RACIAL WITNESS IDENTIFICATION; EVENT FACTORS; EYEWITNESS TESTIMONY; GENDER AND EYEWITNESS ABILITY.)

Freud, Sigmund (1856–1939) A Viennese specialist in nerve and brain diseases who is best known for the creation of psychoanalysis and his theories on sexuality. Freud also was fascinated with the idea of memory, including the baffling questions of how—and why—we forget. It was Freud who compared memory to a magic slate: the clear celluloid receives the imprint of short-term memories, soon to be wiped clean, and the waxy cardboard underneath becomes etched with the lasting impressions.

Freud accepted the belief popularized by his contemporary, psychologist Hermann Ebbinghaus, that the brain files away all memories, but his angle of approach was wildly different. Freud studied memory not from the position of what we remember or how we remember, but on how little we remember—and why. He believed that any failure of recall had a specific cause, and since people forget things every day, he had plenty of material with which to work. For example, Freud found it implausible that childhood, filled with the richness of new experience, pleasure and pain, should be so totally forgotten.

He argued that recalled experiences and ideas were related to other symbolically and emotionally important thoughts and feelings and that much of what a person forgets is simply repression. He believed that the lack of memories of early childhood (usually before age four in most people) was caused by repression of infantile sexuality, which peaks in the third and fourth years of life. This repression is caused by the "psychic forces of loathing, shame, and moral and aesthetic ideal demands," he said. His basic theory describes both the unconscious and conscious mind, noting that the unconscious mind can have a great effect on a person's conscious actions. We remember something, he postulated, because it is meaningful to us and significant, although that significance may be hidden.

Freud believed it was conflict, followed by repression, that made the problem of deciphering early memories so difficult. Because he thought there is nothing accidental or arbitrary about the things we forget, he believed that everyday absentmindedness could be divided into "forgetfulness" and "false recollection" (also called a "Freudian slip," or substituting one word for another). The process that should have produced the actual memory was interrupted and the memory was "displaced" by another.

And displacement isn't simply a quirk, he argued—it followed a routine as logical as summoning up the actual memory. For example, he analyzed a number of his own "Freudian slips" in his book *The Psychopathology of Everyday Life*. When he couldn't remember the name of Rosenheim, a major railway station (translation: Rose's home), he decided that the name was lost in his memory because he had just come from visiting the home of his sister, Rose, and the name was taken away by his "family complex." He concluded that forgotten names were associated—sometimes very indirectly—with painful and unpleasant memories. In other words, we eliminate from the conscious mind everything that makes us anxious, which, he believed, explained the loss of memories during the first four years of life.

Goleman, Daniel. "In Memory, People Re-Create Their Lives to Suit Their Images of the Present." *New York Times*, June 23, 1987.
Pettinati, Helen. *Hypnosis and Memory*. New York: Guilford Press, 1988.

frontal lobe   The area just forward of the central fissure of the brain. One of the functions of the frontal lobe is concerned with intellectual functioning, including thought processes, behavior and memory.

frontal lobe lesions and memory   The frontal lobe of the brain deals with intellectual functioning, including thought processes, behavior and memory. Abnormalities, or lesions, in this area of the brain can cause a wide variety of memory problems, especially if the damage is bilateral (affecting both lobes).

Some patients with frontal lobe lesions experience a problem in learning complex material. Some researchers have reported that patients with lesions of the lateral frontal zones can't form stable intentions to memorize new material and therefore can learn new information only in a passive way. For example, such subjects could pick up four or five words on a list but could not learn the rest. In addition, other researchers note that similarly affected patients can't learn weakly associated word pairs very well (such as horse—tree).

It is also believed that frontal lobe lesions may disrupt recall more than recognition, although this view is not universally accepted. Patients with lesions of the frontal lobe usually can recognize recently presented material, even though their recall may be severely disrupted. Even though some patients with these lesions do badly in both recall and recognition, there is evidence that they are likely to do worse on recall.

Third, patients with bilateral frontal lobe lesions (but not unilateral) show a disturbance in metamemory—the knowledge of one's own memory and memory strategies. This supports other researchers' idea that frontal lobe lesions impair patients' ability to monitor their own effectiveness. This inability to monitor the effectiveness of plans and actions may also underlie another group of retrieval disorders that may be caused in part by frontal lobe lesions. The best known of these is CONFABULATION, the recall of incorrect information in response to standard questions, usually to cover up a memory deficit. Researchers have discovered that the degree of confabulation is not related to the extent of memory disturbance but is related to the inability to self-correct.

Frontal lobe lesions also have been linked to reduplicative paramnesia, in which a patient insists that two places (such as his home) exist with identical properties when only one such place exists. Reduplicative paramnesia is linked to CAPGRAS SYNDROME, in which the reduplication concerns close relatives, so that a wife may insist her husband is a "double" and not her true spouse. While the precise cause of the reduplicative disorders is not known, they have been linked to massive frontal lobe lesions. Another group of frontal lobe lesion effects relates to a patient's sensitivity to high levels of interference during learning. (See also AGNOSIA.)

fugue A period during which a person forgets his or her identity and often wanders away from home or office for several hours, days or even weeks. The belief that psychogenic disorders may be a way of avoiding depression or suicide is expressed in the term "fugue," which is derived from the Latin *fugere* (to "run away" or "flee"). Causes include DISSOCIATIVE DISORDERS, depression, HEAD INJURY and DEMENTIA. In addition, psychomotor or temporal lobe epileptics who suffer from complex, partial seizures may experience long periods of aimless wandering, or PORIOMANIA.

Other cases of fugue are clearly psychogenic in nature. Some researchers believe that the tendency to wander away from home while experiencing an attack of AMNESIA often occurs together with other symptoms, including a history of a broken home, periodic depression and predisposition to states of altered consciousness. On the other hand, psychoanalysts see the fugue state as a symbolic escape from severe emotional conflict.

In fugues of long duration, behavior may appear normal but certain symptoms, such as hallucinations, feeling unreal or unstable moods, may coexist.

One of the most celebrated cases of fugue involved the Reverend Ansell Bourne, a patient of psychologist William James, who wandered away from home for two months. During this time, the patient acquired a new identity and—once he returned home—claimed no memory of the entire two months he had been away. His memory for this time period finally surfaced after he underwent HYPNOSIS. (See also FREUD, SIGMUND; HYSTERICAL AMNESIA.)

functional amnesia See PSYCHOGENIC AMNESIA.

fuzzy trace theory The idea that human cognition is primarily a system in which inferences are drawn by processing vague, gistlike representations (fuzzy traces) and that stored information is recalled by reconstructively processing these representations.

The theory, developed by psychologist C. J. Brainerd of the University of Arizona, is an experimental concept of intuition. The term "fuzzy trace" was borrowed from mathematics, where it also emphasizes creativity and imagination. This theory is an alternative to the two most comprehensive theoretical approaches in the field: Swiss psychologist Jean Piaget's belief that a child's mind evolves through a series of set stages to adulthood and the theory of information processing.

G

Ganser's syndrome A rare "factitious disorder" that occurs as a response to severe stress in which a person tries (consciously or unconsciously) to mislead others regarding his or her mental state. Its symptoms also include AMNESIA and clouded consciousness.

Called prison psychosis, it was found almost always among prisoners and was first described by German psychiatrist Sigbert J. M. Ganser (1853–1931). However, most cases have been among those who are not confined.

The hallmark of Ganser's syndrome is that the sufferer often displays symptoms that simulate psychosis (episodes of intense agitation or stupor) and often gives approximate answers—that is, $4 + 2 = 7$. The choice of an answer near the correct one suggests that the person does know the correct answer. Other symptoms reveal that patients with Ganser's syndrome also experience a clouded consciousness, hallucinations, delusions and periods of amnesia for the intervals when the symptoms were present.

In his 1897 lecture on this hysterical state, Ganser noted the "inability" of the prisoners to answer the simplest question correctly even though it was obvious by their answers that they understood the question. Further, their answers showed that they lacked a great deal of knowledge that they once clearly had—or still have. He believed these patients were not malingerers; rather, their answers were a true symptom of mental disorder of a hysterical origin. Today Ganser's syndrome is most often considered either a true psychotic disorder or simple malingering, but it

is classified among the nonspecific dissociative disorders under that category in the *Diagnostic and Statistic Manual of Mental Disorders*, 3rd ed., revised (DSM-III-R).

While this syndrome is sometimes referred to by the German word *Vorbeirden* ("to talk past the point"), Ganser never used this term himself.

gender and eyewitness ability While men and women in general are about equally reliable as witnesses, both men and women pay more attention to items that catch their interest and therefore store more or better information in memory about those items.

In a study of 50 subjects who were tested after looking at 24 slides of a wallet-snatching incident, women were only slightly more accurate overall. But women were far more accurate than men on questions dealing with women's clothing or actions, and men were far more accurate on questions concerning the thief's appearance and the surroundings.

In another study of 200 men and women who saw slides of a man and a woman who witness a fight, women were more accurate and less suggestible on the female-oriented questions and less accurate and more suggestible on the male-oriented items. Men were more accurate and less suggestible on the male-oriented questions and less accurate and more suggestible on the female-oriented questions. According to researchers, this indicates that men and women tend to be accurate on different types of items, perhaps because they differ in their interest in particular items and differ in the amount of attention they pay to those items.

Other researchers note that people are more readily influenced to the extent that they lack information about a topic or think of it as trivial or unimportant. (See also AGE AND EYEWITNESS ABILITY; CROSS-RACIAL WITNESS IDENTIFICATION; EYEWITNESS ABILITY.)

Loftus, Elizabeth. *Eyewitness Testimony.* Cambridge: Harvard University Press, 1979.

generalized amnesia A type of PSY-CHOGENIC AMNESIA in which a patient cannot recall anything of his or her entire life. (See also HYSTERICAL AMNESIA.)

generation-recognition theory The theory that retrieval of information involves an initial search stage in which possible "targets" are generated; each of these possible targets is then subjected to a recognition process to determine whether it is the information needed.

Both stages must be implemented for recall to take place, whereas for recognition only the second stage is required. Recall is therefore less reliable, because there are two stages at which problems can occur.

Ginkgo biloba The oldest known species of tree, also known as the maidenhair tree, this alleged memory-enhancing tree dates back 300 million years and is the only living representative of the order Ginkgoales. Called a living fossil because it does not exist in the wild, it has been planted since ancient times in China and Japanese temple gardens and is now used throughout the world as an ornamental tree.

Used for millennia in China as a valuable medicine, today it is used throughout Europe for the same purpose. Leaves from the ginkgo tree are said to improve short-term memory loss and may be of some benefit to Alzheimer's disease patients.

The leaves work by boosting blood flow throughout the body and the brain, increasing the production of adenosine triphosphate (ATP) and streamlining the brain's ability to metabolize GLUCOSE. They also prevent platelet clumping in arteries, improving nerve signal transmission and serving as a powerful antioxidant.

Some studies have found ginkgo to improve cognitive function in Alzheimer's disease patients, although another study could not substantiate such a link. Research suggests that ginkgo leaves are most effective for those patients with reduced blood flow to the brain. While most research has been performed with a ginkgo biloba extract (with a 24 percent flavonoid concentration), many ginkgo products on the market are not as strong. *Ginkgo biloba* leaf and extracts are available in vitamin and health food stores.

Petkov, V. "Effects of Standardized Ginseng Extract on Learning, Memory and Physical Capabilities." *American Journal of Chinese Medicine* 15, no. 1 (1987): 19–29.

ginseng This herb and its root of the family Araliaceae (*Panax quinquefolium* and *Panax schinseng*) have been used for centuries by Chinese healers as a way to increase resistance to stress. The herb is said to improve memory, brain function, concentration and learning.

Ginseng is a powerful building block of Chinese medicine that has numerous beneficial properties. Indeed, the generic name *panax* is derived from the same Greek word as "panacea," an indication of the many uses the Chinese have found for this herb. The action of ginseng is said to be linked to its saponins, a group of chemicals that influence the metabolism of neurotransmitters such as serotonin and ACETYLCHOLINE, which are important for memory function. Ginseng also appears to interfere with the activation of the adrenal cortex, the seat of stress. In addition, saponins increase the activity of lymphocytes, which would enhance immune function.

Panax quinquefolium is the North American ginseng, which is found in woodlands from Quebec to the Gulf coast. The plant also is cultivated for its root in the United States.

Chinese medical experts caution that people with high blood pressure should not use ginseng. Also, it should be used only as an occasional "tonic," not on a daily basis. Most health food stores carry several varieties of ginseng; the amount of active ingredients found in different preparations varies greatly.

global aphasia　A total or near-total inability to speak, write or understand spoken or written words. Global aphasia usually is caused by widespread damage to the dominant cerebral hemisphere.

glucose　A simple sugar carbohydrate, the body's chief source of energy, which also seems to play an important role in declarative memory (memory for events and things). In recent studies at the University of Virginia, scientists found that increasing the level of glucose circulating in the blood improved a person's ability to store memories while not affecting other cognitive functions.

Despite wide variations in carbohydrate intake, the concentration of glucose in the blood (the blood sugar level) is usually kept within narrow limits through the action of hormones including insulin, glucagon, epinephrine, corticosteroids and growth hormone.

Animal studies suggest that raising blood glucose levels helps some brain cells transmit ACETYLCHOLINE, a chemical messenger involved in memory. It is believed that acetylcholine becomes less available to the brain as people age.

In one study, researchers found that after drinking glucose-sweetened lemonade, elderly subjects performed better on certain memory tests by 30 to 40 percent. The glucose reversed most of the age-related deficits, according to psychologist Paul Gold and colleagues. Subjects performed better on tests of declarative memory (memory for events and things), the type of memory most often impaired in the elderly. Gold also discovered that those subjects whose bodies did not process glucose well performed less well on the declarative memory tests.

Results suggest that glucose seems to enhance memory storage for at least 24 hours. Glucose also improves sleep—another problem the elderly face. In related research, scientists found that in animal studies, those who have memory deficits also have sleep

problems. Perhaps the same neural system is influencing memory storage and sleep.

Other scientists at McGill University have noted that glucose levels are monitored by the liver, which sends signals to the brain by the autonomic nervous system. When nerves from the celiac ganglion (the structure through which most of the nerves connect the liver to the brain) were cut, memory improvement following glucose did not occur.

In the late 1980s memory researchers found that epinephrine and glucose are partly responsible for signaling the brain that "here's something important to remember." The first step in storing a memory is the release of epinephrine, which then triggers the release of glucose into the blood, which may act on the central nervous system and enhance memory storage. Older people may begin to have memory problems because the neuroendocrine responses responsible for the demand to "store this memory" are wearing out.

Recent findings also suggest that glucose increases the effects of the memory-enhancing cholinergic agonists (drugs that increase the function of acetylcholine systems). Studies also show that glucose interferes with the effects of cholinergic antagonists (drugs that impair memory storage).

Glucose may regulate a system in the brain that handles the inhibition of cholinergic functions. Scientists do not know yet what parts of the brain are affected by the glucose.

Despite its possible memory benefits, frequent glucose consumption may not be a healthy way to boost memory for elderly patients, however, since high glucose levels increase the risk of developing health problems such as diabetes.

Adler, Tina. "Ability to Store Memories Linked to Glucose Levels." *APA Monitor* (September 1990): 5–6.

glutamate　A common nerve cell stimulator found in every cell in the body, this amino acid also plays a central role in the workings of the brain and memory. Glutamate is important in the proper function of the hippocampus, among other brain areas, and an imbalance will cause epileptic seizures, memory disorders or both.

Glutamate is the best known of a group of excitatory amino acids that plays an important part in initiating and transmitting signals in the brain. Almost half of the brain's neurons use glutamate as a primary transmitter.

Normally glutamate is bound tightly in the cells, and only tiny amounts are allowed into the spaces between brain cells at any one time. But new research suggests that abnormal glutamate activity also may be responsible for brain damage following lack of oxygen from injury, stroke or seizure. When the brain is deprived of oxygen and some of the cells that store glutamate shut down, glutamate comes flooding out; in such high levels, it kills brain cells. Just five minutes of excess glutamate is enough to kill cells.

Blakeslee, Sandra. "Pervasive Chemical, Crucial to the Body, Is Indicted as an Agent in Brain Damage." *New York Times*, November 29, 1988.
Ezzell, Carol. "Watching the Remembering Brain at Work." *Science News*, November 23, 1991.

H

habituation   A decrease in the intensity of a behavioral response because a stimulus has been presented so often that it is no longer consciously noticed. Perhaps the most common form of learning, habituation enables humans and other animals to ignore unimportant stimuli and focus on those that are rewarding or important for survival.

Memory experts believe that habituation is the very first learning process found in infants, who learn, for example, to ignore harmless household noises. (See also POTENTIATION.)

Morimoto, Bruce, and Koshland, Daniel K., Jr. "Short-term and Long-term Memory in Single Cells." *Federation of American Societies for Experimental Biology Journal* 5 (April 1991): 2061.

hallucinations   Perceptions that occur in the absence of an actual stimulus. They are different from illusions, in which a real stimulus has simply been misinterpreted (thinking that a ticking clock is a bomb). There are several different types of hallucinations; the most common are auditory hallucinations (hearing voices), which make up the primary symptom of schizophrenia, but are also found in manic-depressive illness and certain other brain disorders. Hallucinations involving smell may be caused by temporal lobe epilepsy. Visual hallucinations occur most often during DELIRIUM brought on by illness or alcohol withdrawal. Hallucinations also may be caused by certain types of drugs.

head injury   Even the mildest bump on the head can damage the brain by causing a subdural hematoma, especially in those who are taking corticosteroids or who have rheumatoid arthritis or osteoporosis. In fact, research suggests that 60 percent of patients who sustain a mild brain injury are still having symptoms after three months. These patients often develop bizarre symptoms (called postconcussion syndrome) including memory loss following even the slightest bang on the head.

The fact that head injury can have effects throughout the body has been known for at least 3,000 years; the Edwin Smith Surgical Papyrus, written between 2,500 and 3,000 years ago, contains information about eight cases of head injuries affecting other parts of the body. In reports in the 1800s, physicians also knew that memory impairment often followed closed head injuries.

Mild head injury symptoms can result in a puzzling interplay of behavioral cognitive and emotional complaints that make the problems difficult to diagnose.

Symptoms following head injury may be caused by direct physical damage to the brain as well as secondary factors (lack of oxygen, swelling and vascular disturbance). A penetrating injury also may cause a brain infection. The type of accident determines the kind of injury the brain receives in a closed head injury; injuries very depending on whether the head was unrestrained upon impact and the direction, force and velocity of the blow. If the head was restrained upon impact, the maximum damage will be found at the impact site; a moving head will cause a "contrecoup" injury where damage will be on the side opposite the point of impact.

Both kinds of injuries cause swirling movements throughout the brain, tearing nerve fibers and causing widespread vascular damage. There may be bleeding in the cerebrum or subarachnoid space leading to hematomas, or brain swelling may raise intracranial pressure, blocking oxygen to the brain.

Both direct and diffuse effects may cause memory deficits after a head injury; the temporal lobes are particularly vulnerable to this type of trauma. In most cases, however, permanent severe memory loss with intact functioning in other areas does not occur. Severe diffuse damage may lead to posttraumatic dementia with general intellectual impairment.

After a head injury, patients suffer from a period of impaired consciousness followed by a period of confusion and impaired memory known as POSTTRAUMATIC AMNESIA (PTA), with confusion, disorientation, RETROGRADE AMNESIA and impairment in the ability to store and retrieve new information. For some reason, the physical and emotional shock of the accident interrupts the transfer of all information that happened to be in the short-term memory just before the accident; this is why some people can remember information several days before and after the accident, but not information right before it occurred. The length of both the unconsciousness and PTA have been linked with how well a person recovers after head injury.

Temporary retrograde amnesia following head injury often begins with a memory loss for a period of weeks, months or years prior to the injury, but it will diminish as recovery proceeds. Permanent retrograde amnesia, however, may extend for just a few seconds or minutes before the accident; in very severe head injuries, however, the permanent retrograde amnesia may also cover weeks or months before the accident.

Until recently, diagnostic tools were not sensitive enough to detect the subtle structural changes that can occur and sometimes persist after mild head injury. Many patients are plagued by symptoms, including headache, dizziness, confusion and memory loss, which may continue for months. Typically, computerized tomography (CT) scans of this group of patients reveal no damage. But studies involving magnetic resonance imaging (MRI) and brain electrophysiology indicate that contusions and diffuse axonal injuries associated with mild head injury are likely to affect those parts of the brain that relate to functions such as memory, concentration, information processing and problem solving.

In fact, a 1981 study of 424 patients diagnosed with mild head injury showed that many had recurrent problems with deviant behavior, headaches, dizziness and cognitive problems; only 17 percent were symptom-free three months after the accident. A third study in 1989 reached the same conclusions.

Only 12 percent of patients with mild head injury are hospitalized overnight, and instructions they receive upon leaving the emergency room usually do not address behavioral, cognitive and emotional symptoms that can occur after such an injury.

Diagnostic Tests
CT Scans While CT scans are widely available in emergency rooms to help in

the diagnosis of neural hematomas, many experts believe these scans may not pick up the subtle damage following a mild head injury.

MRI   Many researchers believe MRI is more sensitive in diagnosing many brain lesions beyond a basic hematoma. For example, MRI is more sensitive in detecting the diffuse axonal or shearing injury and contusions often seen in mild head injury.

Quantitative EEG (qEEG)   In many patients, neither CT scans nor MRI can detect the microscopic damage to white matter that occurs when fibers are stretched in a mild, diffuse axonal injury. In this type of mild injury, the axons lose some of their covering and become less efficient, but MRI detects only more severe injury and actual axonal degeneration. Mild injury to the white matter reduces the quality of communication between different parts of the cerebral cortex. A quantitative EEG is different from a regular electroencephalogram in that the signals from the brain are played into a computer, digitized and stored. EEGs can measure the time delay between two regions of the cortex and the amount of time it takes for information to be transmitted from one region to another.

Evoked Potentials   The electrophysical technique of measuring evoked potentials (EPs) generally is not useful in patients with less serious mild head injury. EPs are not sensitive enough to document any physiologic abnormalities, although a patient may be having symptoms. If testing is done within a day or two of injury, an EP may pick up some abnormalities in brain stem auditory evoked potentials.

Neuropsychological   Testing   Neuropsychological tests may show positive results when imaging tests and neurologic exams are negative. In some patients with persistent symptoms following mild head injury, neuropsychological tests are part of a comprehensive assessment. The tests also can provide information when litigation is an issue.

Future Tests   PET (positron emission tomography), which evaluates cerebral blood flow and brain metabolism, may provide useful information on functional pathology. Single photon emission computed tomography (SPECT) is less expensive than PET and might provide data on cerebral blood flow after mild head injury.

Patients who do experience symptoms are advised to seek out the care of a specialist in mild head injury. Experts caution that there is a great chance that patient complaints will be ignored by most family physicians. Patients with continuing symptoms after a mild head injury are advised to call a local head injury foundation, which can refer them to the most suitable nearby practitioner. (See also CONTRECOUP EFFECTS.)

Evans, C.D., ed. *Rehabilitation after Severe Head Injury*. Edinburgh: Churchill Livingstone, 1981.

Howard, Rosanne. "Mild Head Injury: Challenging Emergency Room Decisions." *Headlines* 3 (March/April 1992): 6–7.

Larkin, Marilyn. "Treating Head Pain Resulting from Subtle Brain Injury." *Headlines* 3 (March/April 1992): 14–16, 18.

"New Diagnostic Techniques for Mild Brain Injury." *Headlines* 3 (March/April 1992): 1.

Squire, L.R., and Cohen, N.J. "Remote Memory, Retrograde Amnesia and the Neuropsychology of Memory." In *Human Memory and Amnesia*. Hillsdale, N.J.: Erlbaum, 1982.

Hebb, Donald (1904–1985)

A Canadian neuroscientist who revived the idea that memories are stored as patterns of newly connected neurons. In his book *The Organization of Behavior* (1949), Hebb speculated that the new circuits might be made during a learning situation, when one neuron tends to fire another, strengthening the synapse between them.

Two neurons that tend to be active at the same time will form a new connection automatically; if they are already weakly connected, the synapse between them will be stronger, and if not, an entirely new synapse will be made. This has come to be called the HEBB SYNAPSE.

Hebb's theory also includes ideas about long-term potentiation (LTP), which explains how when an axon of one cell excites its neighbor cell repeatedly or consistently, some growth process or metabolic change takes place in both cells. This increased synaptic efficacy may last for weeks.

While today the idea does not seem unusual, in the early 1940s when Hebb came up with the notion, there was no evidence to believe that experience caused any kind of physiological change in the brain.

Hebb's rule If two neurons fire at the same time, they increase the strength of the connection between them. The rule is named for Canadian neuroscientist Donald Hebb, who explored the idea of long-term potentiation in his book *The Organization of Behavior* (1949). (See also HEBB, DONALD.)

Hebb synapse The name given to a synapse strengthened by a link formed when two connected neurons fire together. It also refers to a new synapse formed if there is no connection between firing cells.

The idea, formulated in 1949 by Canadian neuroscientist Donald Hebb, is part of his learning theory that explains how neurons are connected to form neural assemblies that are integrated into still larger structures called phase sequences. (See also HEBB, DONALD.)

hedontic selectivity The idea that unpleasant memories are harder to remember than pleasant ones. (See also FREUD, SIGMUND; REPRESSION.)

herpes simplex encephalitis A highly contagious and frequently fatal disease that leaves patients with extensive brain damage in the MEDIAL TEMPORAL LOBES, where it affects the HIPPOCAMPUS, AMYGDALA and uncus, causing a pronounced AMNESIC SYNDROME. In extreme cases, it causes the

KLUVER-BUCY SYNDROME, including AMNESIA, visual AGNOSIA and altered sexual behavior. (See also ENCEPHALITIS AND MEMORY.)

hippocampal formations A group of brain structures found on the surface of the temporal lobe, the parahippocampal gyrus lies near the middle of the brain; the one end of this gyrus curves around the hippocampal fissure, forming the uncus. The HIPPOCAMPUS lies in the inferior horn of the lateral ventricle. The best-documented link between the hippocampus and memory was discovered during treatment of HM, an epileptic whose temporal lobes were destroyed to alleviate his seizures. After surgery, he was unable to learn any new information and showed symptoms of a classic AMNESIC SYNDROME.

In eight other cases, patients who had received the same operation developed the same type of amnesic syndrome when the hippocampus was damaged; when the hippocampus was spared, no memory problems developed.

From these data, scientists realized that an intact hippocampus is essential for normal memory function. Further research has suggested that removing the left temporal lobe causes verbal memory deficits and removing of the right lobe impairs nonverbal memory (such as remembering mazes, patterns or faces). However, memory problems following damage to the hippocampal structures do not occur only after surgery; injury due to a stroke also can cause a profound short-term memory problem.

hippocampus Called the gatekeeper of memory, the hippocampus is a ridge along a fissure of the brain that is crucial to learning and memory. Part of the LIMBIC SYSTEM, the hippocampus is one of the most ancient parts of the brain and is named for its curving shape, which reminded early neuroscientists of a seahorse. A paired organ found on each side of the brain, it directly links nerve fibers involved in sense (touch, vision, sound and smell) as well as the limbic system.

Many researchers believe that the hippocampus links the separate parts of a memory as it is formed, enabling all to be evoked when the memory is recalled. The hippocampus, whose role in memory storage may be time-limited, receives nerve cell input from the cortex and appears to consolidate information for storage as permanent memory in another brain region (probably also the cortex). It seems to be particularly important in learning and remembering spatial information.

In order to store a memory, the nerve messages reaching the hippocampus from a perception must be passed back through the medial temporal lobe and out onto the relevant regions of the neocortex; the specific memory then can be recalled from its various storage sites through the links made by the hippocampus.

The hippocampus can recall a memory by using a single moment or sensation to trip off the recall of others. Repeated recall gradually strengthens the connections between the various elements of each perception, boosting their strength each time the memory is called upon. Only after months or years of recall is a memory laid down permanently in storage, where one detail may call up the others without the help of the hippocampus.

The hippocampus is intimately related to memory because of its response to repetitive stimulation; its synapses change according to previous experience, which may form the structural basis of memory itself. But because research shows that a person with a damaged hippocampus can still retain long-term memory, it is not likely that the hippocampus is the primary storehouse for this type of memory.

Specifically, a damaged hippocampus interferes with the ability to form new memory, but only one specific type of memory is affected—the conscious memory or recall of facts and events. Unconscious memory, including the ability to learn both mental and physical skills, remains intact. Nor is there damage to the memory used in immediate recall (that is, matters to which a person is paying current attention).

The actual role in memory played by the hippocampus is still not completely understood, although its contribution is only temporary. Scientists suggest that the actual memories involved in integrating stimuli may be in the neocortex all along, and the hippocampus—together with the amygdala—may simply play a role in their storage and retrieval. Scientists theorize that memory gateposts such as the nucleus basalis keep the brain free of inconsequential bits of information by allowing only certain impressions into the cortex.

In addition, while the hippocampus does not play a vital role in storing older memories, it is profoundly important in the short-term memory of contextual information (such as the series of clues a person would recall when trying to find a parked car in a crowded lot, for example). It is also important in converting new sensory information into a form that can be preserved elsewhere in the brain.

In recent studies at the University of California at Los Angeles, researchers discovered that the hippocampus is involved in learning that requires integrating various stimuli (such as the look, feel and smell of a test cage, or the different views of a car in a parking lot). But the hippocampus is *not* involved in learning a single stimulus.

Other research into the action of the hippocampus has found that people use different areas of their brains to perform different types of memory tasks. Using PET (positron emission tomography) scans, researchers monitored changes in blood flow in volunteers' brains as they provided endings to words flashed before them. Areas of increased blood flow revealed the brain regions used during the various tasks.

When subjects drew upon memories of

previous lists to complete the fragment "mot-," the right sides of their hippocampi flooded with blood. This means that subjects were using this part of the brain to remember the word, even though researchers always had attributed such verbal processing to the left brain. If the subjects did not search their brains for a word they had already seen and instead gave the first word that came to them, blood flow did *not* increase to either side of the hippocampus. Sometimes subjects spontaneously recalled words from the lists even if they didn't remember having seen the words before. Psychologists call this phenomenon priming, and it prompted increased blood flow to the visual cortex.

Still other studies suggest the hippocampal time limitations; monkeys that learned to recognize objects 16, 12, eight, four and two weeks before surgery damaged their hippocampus forgot what they had learned two to four weeks before the damage, but they recalled early learning better. Normal monkeys remembered more recent learning better than older memories.

Both the neurotransmitters GLUTAMATE (a nerve cell stimulator) and GABA (gamma aminobutyric acid, implicated in anxiety disorders) are important in the proper function of the hippocampus; an imbalance in either of these transmitters will cause epileptic seizures, memory disorders or both. (Patients with epilepsy usually demonstrate memory problems as well.)

The most common cause of damage to the hippocampus is anoxia (loss of oxygen) to the brain during a difficult birth and delivery; most patients with idiopathic epilepsy suffered from anoxia at birth that damaged the hippocampus. One reason why memories may be so vulnerable to the loss of oxygen is that hippocampus cells are the quickest to die when oxygen to the brain is cut off. (See also HIPPOCAMPAL FORMATIONS; HM.)

Bower, Bruce. "Monitoring Memories Moving in the Brain." *Science News,* May 2, 1992.
Ezzell, Carol. "Watching the Remembering Brain at Work." *Science News,* November 23, 1991.
Hilts, Philip. "A Brain Unit Seen as Index for Recalling Memories." *New York Times,* September 24, 1991.
Maugh, Thomas H. "Researchers Observe Brain's Memory-Forming Process." *Philadelphia Inquirer,* November 12, 1991.
"Photos Show Mind Recalling a Word." *New York Times,* November 11, 1992.
Skinner, Karen. "The Chemistry of Learning and Memory." *Chemical and Engineering News* (vol. 69), October 7, 1991.

history of memory   The first sophisticated ideas about memories have been attributed to the Greeks 600 years before the birth of Christ. They were the first people to develop a physical instead of spiritual basis for memory. The Greeks developed both scientific concepts and a language structure to help describe their beliefs about memory.

Parmenides has left us the first description of memory, which he explained as a mixture of dark and light, heat and cold. He believed that the memory would be perfect as long as the given mixture was not stirred up; as soon as the mixture was altered, the memory was lost. One hundred years later Diogenes of Appollonia suggested that memory produced an equal distribution of air in the body and that forgetting occurred when the equilibrium was disturbed.

In the fourth century B.C. Plato introduced his theory, known as the Wax Tablet Hypothesis, which held that the mind was like a clean slate that accepted impressions in the same way that wax can be marked by pointed object scratching its surface. Once an impression was made on the mind's surface, Plato thought, it remained there until the impression wore away with time— which was the definition of forgetting. While some people still adhere to this philosophy today, most believe that remembering and forgetting are two very different processes.

Plato's theory was subsequently modified by Zeno the Stoic, who believed that the memories were actually written impressions on the wax tablet.

Like many people of their time, Zeno and Plato did not believe that memory was found in any particular part of the body.

Later in the fourth century B.C. Aristotle developed a more scientific explanation to explain the phenomenon of memory. He believed that earlier theories did not adequately explain the physical experience of remembering or forgetting. Because Aristotle knew that the heart's main function involved blood, he located in that organ most of the important functions that we know now actually take place in the brain. He believed that memory was based on the movement of blood and that forgetting was caused by the gradual slowing of blood being pumped throughout the body. Aristotle also introduced the concept of the association of ideas, one of the most important underlying concepts in memory today.

In the third century B.C., Herophilus developed his theory of vital and animal spirits. In his view, the vital (or "higher-order") spirits produced the lower-order animal spirits, including the memory, the brain and the nervous system. Indeed, Herophilus believed that man was superior to animals because of the larger number of creases in the brain, but he could not explain his belief; the real importance of the cortex was not discovered for another 2,000 years.

Surprisingly, the Romans did not contribute much that was new in the area of the physical basis of memory. Both Cicero (106 B.C.–43 B.C.) and Quintilian (c.35–c.96) accepted the Wax Tablet Hypothesis. They were the first to develop both the LINK SYSTEM and the room system of memory.

In the second century A.D. the Greek physician Galen made great inroads into the description of the nervous system. Like the Greek physicians before him, Galen believed that memory was part of the lower animal spirits and that memory was found in the sides of the brain. He believed that air mixed with vital spirits in the brain, producing animal spirits that were pushed down through the nervous system.

Galen's ideas were accepted by the Catholic Church. Part of religious doctrine was that memory was a function of the soul and that the soul was located in the brain. Because of the great power of the church, almost no new beliefs in the area of memory were developed until the 17th century. Even thinkers such as Descartes (1596–1650) accepted the church's philosophy, although he adapted it slightly to state that the pineal gland sent animal spirits on special courses through the brain to the seat of memory. The more straightforward the course, the more easily it could open when animal spirits traveled along the passageways. This explained how memory could be improved.

It was not until the 18th century that new thinking on memory began to spread throughout the scientific community. David Hartley, influenced by the Newtonian ideas on vibratory particles, developed a vibratory theory of memory. He suggested that memory vibrations in the brain began before birth and that new sensations modified existing vibrations. After experiencing new sensations, vibrations returned to normal, but if the same sensation reappeared, the vibrations took longer to return to normal. Eventually the vibrations would remain in this new state, forming a memory trace.

During this same century other scientists began to be influenced by developments in related scientific fields. As a result, new theories of brain function looked at electrical forces and flexible nerve fibers as possible connections to memory.

With the scientific advances of the 19th century came the final denunciation of the more primitive Greek ideas of memory. Czech physiologist Georg Prochaska proved that the old theory of animal spirits had no scientific basis. While Prochaska admitted that it was then impossible to locate memory in a particular part of the brain, French physiologist Pierre Flourens explained that memory was in fact found in every part of the brain. Because the brain functioned as a whole, it could not be broken down into simpler parts.

hologram theory of memory A theory of memory, based on the same concept as holographic photography, that suggests that every part of the brain may hold every memory. In holographic photography, a holographic photographic plate is a piece of glass that produces a three-dimensional photograph when two laser beams are passed through it at the right angle. But when this photographic plate is smashed, any one piece will still produce the same photograph when two lasers shine through it. In other words, every part of the holographic photographic plate contains a record of the entire picture.

Some scientists believe that the brain may act in much the same way; that is, that each of the brain's cells may record each of our experiences, operating as a sort of individual minibrain. They believe this theory explains the perfect memories in dreams, surprise random recall, cortex stimulation memories and much of the near-death experiences. (See also PENFIELD, WILDER.)

HM (1928–) The most famous amnesic in medical history, whose surgery to cure a severe case of epilepsy resulted in a total inability to record new memories. Studies of his memory loss over the years has revealed that memory is not one overarching ability but comprises numerous separate abilities, each carried out in a specific area of the brain.

Selected items from short-term memory are transferred to long-term memory in a process as yet little understood. But the terrible error in HM's surgery has shown that two parts of the limbic system—the amygdala and the hippocampus—are essential to the process. During the operation, surgeons removed parts of the temporal lobes, including the hippocampus and amygdala, from the left and right hemispheres of his brain.

After the surgery, HM had a fairly good memory of his life up to the surgery, and he does have some short-term memory capability but almost no long-term memories after the operation, which took place almost 40 years ago. Everything vanishes from his mind, so that each day to him exists separate and apart from any other. He does not know where he lives, cannot recognize people he sees every day and rereads copies of old magazines that seem forever new to him.

Oddly, however, he retains a high IQ and can carry on an intelligent conversation, as long as it does not touch on anything that happened since the surgery. He also can learn new skills but has no memory of mastery. For example, he has been taught to solve puzzles, and though he improves with each trial he insists he has never seen that puzzle before. He can "mirror read" (that is, read upside down and backward), but he still has no memory of being taught this skill.

This case suggests that people have two separate memory networks—one for facts (declarative, or conscious memory) and one for skills (procedural, nondeclarative or unconscious memory).

HM is now 65 and has been living in a nursing home for many years. After the operation, he could not resume his job as an electrician's assistant, nor could he handle even the simplest of jobs. He particularly enjoys working on crossword puzzles, because progress in such an activity is never lost as the words are written down.

Hilts, Philip. "A Brain Unit Seen as Index for Recalling Memories." *New York Times*, September 24, 1991.

Huntington's disease An inherited disorder that causes abnormal involuntary movements (chorea) and progressive mental impairment, including memory loss. It is caused by the degeneration of the CAUDATE NUCLEUS in the BASAL GANGLIA (paired nerve cell clusters in the brain) and of the frontal association neocortex. This degeneration is responsible for the rapid, jerky, involuntary movements and dementia characteristic of the disease.

The genetic marker for Huntington's disease was identified on chromosome 4; researchers have recently found the gene itself. The origins of this brain atrophy are unknown, but some scientists believe the damage may be caused by a buildup of natural chemicals that flood the bundles of neurons within the forebrain, killing them and causing the progressive memory loss, angry rages and muscle spasms that mark the disease.

The two main chemicals believed responsible for the nerve cell degeneration are quinolinic acid and glutamate. In normal concentrations these chemicals play essential roles in the brain. (Quinolinic acid is a breakdown product of tryptophan and glutamate is a neurotransmitter and metabolic agent.) But too much of either chemical kills certain cells, and both bind to the receptor site for a chemical called N-methyl-D-aspartate (NMDA). Researchers have found that the brains of Huntington's disease patients had 93 percent fewer NMDA receptors; the cells with those receptors had died. In two other studies, researchers found decreased number of receptors for five other chemicals in the brains of Huntington's patients.

Symptoms Symptoms usually appear between the ages of 35 and 50, although in rare cases they appear during childhood. Huntington's is a genetic disorder with an autosomal pattern of inheritance; each child of an affected parent has a 50 percent chance of developing the condition. Huntington's is found in about five out of every 100,000 Americans.

The jerky movements usually affect the face, arms and trunk, causing random grimaces and twitches and general clumsiness. These changes usually occur first, followed in several years by dementia, beginning with personality and behavior changes, irritability, problems making decisions, memory loss and apathy. Language tends to remain normal for a much longer period than it does in other cortical dementias. Psychotic disorders may also become apparent, including both manic-depressive (bipolar) psychosis and schizophreniclike hallucinations.

Diagnosis/Treatment Today offspring of affected parents can take a test to discover, with 95 percent accuracy, whether they have inherited the abnormal gene responsible for the condition.

There is no known cure for Huntington's disease, but drugs such as chlorpromazine (Thorazine) can lessen the jerky movements. Most people with Huntington's disease live for about 15 years after the onset of symptoms, although some have lived as long as 30 years.

Researchers suggest that some cells may be more vulnerable to damage from glutamate and quinolinic acid because they contain more NMDA receptors. It is hoped that finding a way to block those receptors might slow, but not cure, the disease. Although there is no treatment available to stop the progression of the disease, the movement disorders and psychiatric symptoms can be controlled by drugs.

Beil, L. "Some Neurons Predisposed to Huntington's." *Science News*, August 29, 1988.
Wilson, Barbara. *Rehabilitation of Memory*. New York: Guilford Press, 1988.

Hydergine   This extract of ergot, a fungus that grows on rye, is a widely used treatment for all forms of senility in the United States and for a variety of other problems throughout the world.

Hydergine is said to increase memory, learning, recall and intelligence, inhibit free radicals, enhance brain cell metabolism and increase blood supply and oxygen to the brain. It also speeds the elimination of LIPO-FUSCIN in the brain. Some scientists believe that the drug may enhance memory by mimicking the effect of NERVE GROWTH FACTOR, a substance that stimulates dendrite growth in the brain, crucial to memory and learning.

Hydergine was the first drug that showed promise in use against Alzheimer's disease;

by 1979 at least 20 double-blind studies had produced statistically significant improvements in behavior and psychological tests of demented patients. Since then, one study failed to find improvement among Alzheimer's disease patients using the drug at doses of 3 milligrams (mg). Studies using 6-mg doses appeared to be more effective.

While in the United States the recommended dose in 3 mg per day, in Europe the recommended dose is 9 mg per day. Hydergine is available by prescription under a variety of trade names.

Branconnier, R. "The Efficacy of the Cerebral Metabolic Enhancers in the Treatment of Senile Dementia." *Psychopharmacology Bulletin* 19, no. 2 (1983): 212–20.

hypermnesia Enhancement of memory under hypnosis (and also in some pathological states). This memory enhancement was often described by medical writers in the 1800s, who believed that anyone could remember events better under hypnosis than in the waking state. But while it is true that some information sometimes can be recalled more accurately while in a hypnotic state, research has indicated that memorized information (such as poetry) can be remembered no better under hypnosis than when awake.

Some memory prodigies, such as the Russian mnemonist (memory artist) named "S," are capable of exceptional mnemonic feats; mathematicians and musicians also have revealed some astonishing abilities in memory in their particular fields. But even to this day, the anatomical or physiological basis of hypermnesia is, at best, only poorly understood.

hyperzine A A chemical found in a type of tea brewed with club moss *(Huperzia serrata)* that Chinese folk doctors have used for hundreds of years to improve memory. It is now being investigated as a possible treatment for ALZHEIMER'S DISEASE.

About seven years ago, researchers at the Shanghai Institute of Materia Medica isolated a natural compound in the tea that inhibits acetylcholinesterase. Acetylcholinesterase is an enzyme that breaks down ACETYLCHOLINE, a key chemical messenger in the brain involved in awareness and memory; an acetylcholinesterase inhibitor like hyperzine A interferes with this acetylcholine-harming chemical. Like the drug TACRINE (approved for the treatment of Alzheimer's disease), hyperzine A prevents acetylcholinesterase from breaking down acetylcholine, thus raising levels of acetylcholine in the brain and improving memory.

Ever since the Chinese isolated the compound, chemists at the Mayo Clinic in Jacksonville, Florida have been studying hyperzine A. Researchers say hyperzine A is a more effective, more specific agent than Tacrine; drug companies are seeking permission from the U.S. Food and Drug Administration to test the compound on humans.

hypnopedia Another name for sleep learning.

Hypnos The Greco-Roman god of sleep, Hypnos was the son of Nyx (Night) and brother of Thanatos (Death). Mythical stories variously locate him in the underworld, in the land of the Cimmerians or in a dark, misty cave on the island of Lemnos. The river of Lethe, (the river of forgetfulness and oblivion), flowed near Hypnos where he lay surrounded by his sons, the bringers of dreams. His sons included Morpheus (with dreams of men), Icelus (with dreams of animals) and Phantasus (with dreams of inanimate objects).

According to the *Iliad*, Hera asked Hypnos to put Zeus to sleep so she could help the Greeks in the war against Troy. As a reward Hypnos was given Pasithea, one of the Graces, to marry.

hypnosis A trancelike psychological state of altered awareness that is characterized by extreme suggestibility and certain physiological attributes. Hypnosis was once believed to be a form of sleep, but the encephalogram (electrical tracing of brain wave activity) of a hypnotized person does not show the brain wave patterns typical of sleep.

Under hypnosis, a person functions at a level of awareness other than the ordinary conscious state. This new level of awareness is characterized by receptiveness and responsiveness in which inner experiences are given as much significance as is normally given only to external reality. While hypnotized, a person can think, act and behave as well as—and usually better than—during ordinary awareness. This is probably because of the person's heightened attention and intensity and the freedom from the ordinary conscious tendency to pay attention to distracting events.

While many people believe that subjects under hypnosis can't lie and can recall information they are not even consciously aware of knowing, there is no objective scientific documentation that hypnotic memory is accurate, according to hypnotism expert Martin Orne, M.D. In fact, the brain is at best an incomplete storehouse of impressions widely influenced by interpretation prey to the unconscious biases of the hypnotist.

In the past, hypnotists uncritically accepted the memory details of a hypnotized subject without verification. But the richness of memory under hypnosis is no guarantee that it is accurate, and the corroboration of some memories does not mean that all memories are correct.

Still, HYPERMNESIA (an increase in memory capability) is an aspect of hypnotic behavior. While hypnotized, some people can remember vivid, long-forgotten and even deeply repressed experiences. They can recount them in detail and yet not remember them during normal consciousness. This hypermnesia is believed to be due to a willingness to make the effort to remember and a freedom from inhibitions.

The phenomenon of hypnosis has been discovered and rediscovered throughout the ages. Both the early Egyptians and the Greeks had "healing temples" where procedures similar to hypnosis took place. During the time of Alexander the Great (356 B.C.–323 B.C.), there were about 300 temples dedicated to the god of medicine, Askelepios. One of the practices in these temples included a type of sleep therapy called incubation in which a priest (in the guise of a god) talked to the patient during a form of half sleep. It is said that such treatments cured blindness, speech problems and paralysis.

Because it is so easy to hypnotize a person, scientists assume the technique has been used throughout history. But the modern use of hypnotism began during the 18th century with the study of animal magnetism by Austrian physician Franz Anton Mesmer.

While still a student at the University of Vienna in 1766, Mesmer discovered the work of the Renaissance mystic physician Paracelsus. He tried to uncover a link between astrology and human health as a result of planetary forces transmitted through a subtle invisible fluid. By 1775 Mesmer began to teach that a person may transmit universal forces to others in the form of "animal magnetism." He based his therapeutic sessions on those beliefs. During these sessions, several people sat around a vat of dilute sulfuric acid while holding hands or iron bars that stuck out of the solution. Eventually Mesmer's beliefs became increasingly unpopular with other physicians, and he was forced to leave Austria for Paris and then London. Still, those he had taught continued to practice his techniques.

Among his former students was the Marquis de Puysegur of Buzancy, who treated a young peasant able to go into a state that would be today described as a hypnotic trance. Because it was similar to sleep but more like sleepwalking, Puysegur called the state artificial somnambulism; the term later became associated with a highly hypnotizable person. Despite the peasant's alertness during the trance, when he awoke he had no recollection of what had happened. Puysegur had discovered POSTHYPNOTIC AMNESIA.

After Mesmer died in 1815, his followers were called "mesmerists" and their technique was known as MESMERISM. One of his followers, Abbé Faria, renamed somnambulism "lucid sleep" and criticized Mesmer's theory that some sort of fluid was transferred from the operator to the patient. He was one of the first to understand that the ability of a person to enter lucid sleep depended more on the patient than on the mesmerist.

Meanwhile, British physicians were beginning to consider the possibility of using mesmerism as an anesthetic during surgery; the English surgeon John Elliotson, who invented the stethoscope, was such a strong proponent of the practice that he resigned from his professorship at the University of London when he was required to stop using mesmerism.

At about the same time, James Braid (1795–1860) began practicing in Manchester. He became known as the father of modern hypnotism because of the methods he used and because he renamed mesmerism "hypnosis," after Hypnos, the Greek god of sleep; he also coined the term "hypnotic." Celebrated Parisian physician Jean-Martin Charcot gave public demonstrations, and Sigmund Freud was impressed by the therapeutic potential of hypnosis. On his return to Vienna, Freud began to use hypnosis in his early treatment of hysteria and to help neurotics forget disturbing events. But as Freud began to develop the system of psychoanalysis, his difficulty in hypnotizing some patients combined with some theoretical problems convinced him to discard hypnosis in favor of free association.

Despite Freud's rejection of hypnosis as a treatment option, the technique was used during both World Wars I and II to treat combat neuroses. In the United States during the 1930s, psychologist Clark Hull brought the study of hypnosis into the laboratory, concluding that it was best understood as a form of hypersuggestibility. By the mid-1950s both British and American physicians had formally approved its use for medical purposes.

Modern Outlook While early practitioners understood that hypnosis was not a reliable way to recall information or improve the memory, modern supporters promoted its use by police around the world. In fact, however, there is no such thing as a "tape recorder" in the brain that can spill out previously recorded facts under hypnosis. Because a hypnotized person is never free from susceptibility, the hypnotist cannot avoid planting suggestions.

Studies by expert Elizabeth Loftus and others have shown that the human memory is fragile; it can be supplemented, restructured or even altered completely by input after the event. It is susceptible to the power of a single word.

As many as 80 percent of Loftus's hypnotized subjects have shown by their answers that their recollections were influenced by misinformation or leading questions. Once the alteration has occurred, Loftus has found it is very difficult—if not impossible—for a witness to retrieve the original memory.

To illustrate the inaccuracy of the hypnotic state, subjects watched a film of an accident and immediately afterward were asked a series of questions, some of which included misleading information. Subjects were asked, "How fast was the white sports car going when it passed the barn while traveling along the country road?" But no barn existed. Those who were asked the leading questions under hypnosis were more likely to "recall" seeing a barn later than those subjects who were not asked the leading questions.

Some researchers have argued that hypnosis is actually a form of "compliance" and that hypnotized subjects abdicate responsibility for their actions because they assume they are under the "control" of the hypnotist. When asked to recall information under hypnosis, their readiness to recall more information results in inaccurate statements (especially after leading questions). Proponents of the compliance theory say that it is even possible to plant false memories in hypnotized subjects. In one study, 13 of 27 hypnotized subjects stated they heard loud noises during their trace when these noises had simply been suggested by the hypnotist.

Hypnosis supporters claim that laboratory simulations of hypnosis are not valid, since they don't mimic the real situations in which hypnosis is used. But according to psychiatrist Martin Orne and psychologist Ernest Hilgard, people can lie under hypnosis, and an examiner is no better able to detect a hypnotic lie than any other kind. In addition, a willing hypnotic subject is more pliable than he or she would normally be, more eager to please the questioner. Knowing even a few details of an event may provide the subject with enough to create a highly detailed "memory" of what transpired whether he or she was there or not.

Process   It is not possible to hypnotize someone who does not want to be hypnotized, so the first requirement for the technique to work is a willingness on the part of the subject. In fact, responsiveness is greatest when the subject believes that he or she can be hypnotized, that the hypnotist is competent and trustworthy and that the trance will be safe and appropriate.

The person sits in a comfortable chair in a quiet, dimly lit room for maximum relaxation and is usually asked to fix attention on a particular object while the therapist repeats phrases quietly that would be accepted by any subject, such as "Be still and listen to my voice," or "Relax." At this point, neither the subject nor the hypnotist can easily tell whether the subject's behavior constitutes a hypnotic response or mere cooperation. Gradually suggestions are given that demand increasing distortion of perception or memory ("You find it harder and harder to open your eyes").

As the subject becomes more relaxed, he or she eventually loses touch with the environment and hears only the therapist's voice; at the end of the session, the subject "wakes up" when told to do so. The resulting hypnotic trance differs from one subject to another and from one trance to another, depending on the reason for the hypnosis. However, all trance behavior is characterized by a simplicity, directness and literalness of understanding and emotional response. With training, it is also possible to practice "autohypnosis" (self-hypnosis) by relaxing, repeating certain phrases or visualizing relaxing scenes.

Some people are more hypnotizable than others, although most people can be hypnotized to some degree. In general, the more intensely imaginative and the more easily a person can visualize, the more hypnotizable that person will be. The ability seems to be related to early childhood experiences and may be inherited in part.

While hypnotized subjects appear to wait passively to be directed what to do by the therapist and are very suggestible, they do not obey commands to behave in a manner they would normally believe to be dangerous or improper. Attention is usually highly selective, so only one person can be heard at a time. It is possible to suggest to a subject to forget everything that happened during hypnosis or to remember or repeat behavior learned while hypnotized (posthypnotic suggestion).

Some psychoanalysts use hypnosis as a way to help patients remember and deal with disturbing events or feelings they have repressed. Others use hypnosis to help patients relax, especially those who suffer from anxiety, panic attacks or phobias, or to prepare patients for anesthesia. It is particularly helpful in childbirth because it can reduce the mother's discomfort without affecting the child. Hypnosis also is valuable in managing otherwise intractable pain. It is sometimes successful in treating addictive habits, such as overeating or smoking cigarettes, and patients can be trained while under hypnosis to control blood pressure, headache and functional disorders. (See also AGE REGRESSION, HYPNOTIC; HYPNOTIC DRUGS; HYPNOTIZABILITY; MESMER, FRANZ ANTON; MESMERISM; SODIUM AMYTAL.)

hypnotic age regression   See AGE REGRESSION, HYPNOTIC.

hypnotic drugs   Drugs that induce sleep, such as antianxiety drugs or BARBITURATES. (See also SODIUM AMYTAL.)

hypnotizability   The ability of a person to be hypnotized; this is a relatively enduring attribute. Most people are capable of experiencing at least some of the effects of HYPNOSIS when it is performed correctly.

Hypnotizability is related to the amount of trust in the hypnotist, the patient's motivation to cooperate and his or her preconceptions about hypnosis and its effects. (See also AGE REGRESSION, HYPNOTIC; BARBITURATES; HYPNOTIC DRUGS; SODIUM AMYTAL.)

hypoglycemia and memory   Because brain cells require an adequate amount of sugar to maintain metabolic activity, hypoglycemia (a drop in the blood sugar level) can lead to memory problems. Insulin (a hormone secreted by the pancreas) is of great importance in helping maintain the blood sugar level at normal levels; too little insulin and the level will rise; too much and the level will fall. Diabetics are at particular risk for memory problems resulting from low blood sugar; excess amounts of insulin can cause blood sugar to plummet, triggering a seizure.

Even a slight decrease in blood sugar, however, can alter brain function and trigger memory problems in almost anyone. It's not just diabetics who can get too much insulin—stress or nerves can activate the production of this hormone, as can eating too much sugar. One way to avoid excess insulin is to eat another food (such as peanut butter) with high-sugar meals to help slow the stomach's

emptying and to help the body absorb sugar. (See also GLUCOSE.)

hypothyroidism   Underactivity of the thyroid gland. Severe hypothyroidism can cause a depression and DEMENTIA because of a drop in metabolic activity; borderline hypothyroidism (subclinical hypothyroidism) can cause memory disturbance, poor concentration and mental confusion.

Patients with a severe lack of thyroid hormone may appear unclean and disheveled, and overdrugged. There may be generalized tiredness, muscle weakness, cramps, a slow heart rate, dry flaky skin, hair loss and a deep, husky voice, thickened skin, weight gain and goiter. The severity of the symptoms depends on the degree of thyroid deficiency. Mild deficiency may cause no symptoms; severe deficiency may produce all of the symptoms. Those with the borderline problem also may experience cold hands and feet, menstrual problems, dry skin, thin hair and low energy levels.

A simple test for hypothyroidism is to take the temperature immediately upon awakening (while still in bed); temperature below 97.8 degrees F. may indicate hypothyroidism. It also can be diagnosed by measuring the level of thyroid hormones in the blood.

Treatment includes replacement therapy with the thyroid hormone thyroxine; in most cases, hormone therapy must be continued for life. Once replacement therapy has begun, most or all of the symptoms with this disorder can be reversed; however, treatment may not cure goiter, which may require surgery.

hysterical amnesia   A type of psychogenic amnesia that involves disruption of episodic memory, hysterical amnesia is quite different from loss of memory associated with injury or disease. Unlike organic-based AMNESIA, this type of forgetfulness is sharply restricted to specific emotionally important groups of memories. In general, it can be understood in relationship to a patient's needs or conflicts, such as the need to escape a particularly distressing argument.

In addition, hysterical amnesia may extend to basic knowledge learned in school (such as arithmetic), which is never seen in organic amnesia unless there is an accompanying aphasia or dementia. Hysterical amnesia almost always can be treated successfully by procedures such as HYPNOSIS.

A normal, mentally healthy person is assumed to be integrated within a unified personality. But under traumatic conditions, memories can become detached from personal identity, making recall impossible. Modern accounts of hysterical amnesia have been heavily influenced by Sigmund Freud, who attributed it to a need to repress information injurious to the ego. According to this theory, the memory produces a defense reaction for the individual's own good. This explains why hysterical amnesia occurs only in the wake of trauma and is consistent with the high incidence of depression and other psychiatric disorders in those who subsequently develop psychogenic memory problems. (See also FREUD, SIGMUND; FUGUE.)

I

iconic memory   The registration of visual stimuli. This type of memory lasts only for a few milliseconds. Its name comes from the word "icon," meaning an image or representation.

idebenone   An important antioxidant, idebenone protects experimental animals against memory loss caused by hypoxia (loss of oxygen) and low serotonin levels. It also can reduce the damage caused by strokes in animals. It has been widely studied in Japan, where it is available by prescription.

idiot savants   See AUTISTIC SAVANTS.

image association   The conscious pairing of two mental images so that the sight or recall of one will trigger recall of the other.

imagery   Mental pictures. Imagery is a very powerful aid to memory.

imagery process and memory   The imagery process is a way which the brain records visual memory (pictures, scenes or faces), as opposed to VERBAL PROCESS (words, numbers and names).

The visual imagery process is best suited to remembering concrete occurrences and objects, whereas the verbal process is better at representing abstract verbal information. Researchers believe that the two types of processing involve different brain systems and that concrete nouns are processed differently from abstract nouns.

It seems as if concrete words and images may be processed by the visual system and abstract words by the verbal system—and each system operates in separate locations in the brain. The right half of the brain seems to be the predominant place for the visual imagery process, and the left hemisphere is the predominant location for the verbal process.

Visual information travels first from the retina to a region deep within the brain, then on to another area at the rear of the brain. There, information about patterns and object identification travels to the temporal region just above the ears and spatial information is directed to the region at the back of the top of the head (parietal region).

Nerve cells in different parts of the brain fire at the same time in a rhythmic pattern when responding to visual stimuli appearing to come from the same object. This suggests that the combination of a thought or image in the brain may require simultaneous firings of neurons, called binding.

In addition, visual and verbal memory processes operate at different speeds; for example, it may take only four seconds to recite the alphabet, but it takes about 13 seconds to generate visual images of the alphabet.

Visual images also are remembered better than verbal images. Many studies have discovered that pictures of objects are remembered better than the names or verbal descriptions of those objects. In another study, subjects were shown 2,560 pictures over several days and then later shown 280 pairs of pictures. One of each pair was a picture the person had seen before. Ninety percent of the time the subjects could identify the pictures they had seen before correctly. Other research has duplicated these findings using an incredible 10,000 pictures. And pictures were remembered with great accuracy up to three months after they were seen just once.

immediate memory   See SHORT-TERM MEMORY.

immediate perceptual memory   A type of reflex memory in which an impression is replaced immediately by a new memory (such as in typing or reading words in a book). Because these memories don't need to be combined or stored, they are used right away.

implicit memory   Another name for spontaneous, tacit or unintentional memory. Researchers believe humans have two types of memory, implicit and EXPLICIT MEMORY (intentional recollection).

Implicit memory differs most importantly from explicit memory in how the memories are retrieved. The effortless and automatic recall of a person's name is an example of implicit memory. Struggling to recall the name uses explicit memory.

The two terms were invented in 1985 by psychologists Peter Graf and Daniel Schacter of the University of Arizona. However, not all researchers agree on the proper term for implicit memory; others prefer "in-

direct measures of memory" or "retention without awareness."

Traditionally, memory experts have tested only explicit memory by giving subjects lists of items to recall intentionally during a study period before the test. A test of implicit memory would require subjects to respond to questions that don't require any sort of intentional recall with whatever comes to mind.

While explicit memory may indeed decline as a person ages, implicit memory may not. For example, when subjects are asked to identify words presented only briefly to them, both older and younger subjects improved the same amount during the study period before the test. Implicit memory doesn't fail as people age because the type of thinking it requires is more automatic. It uses reintegrative processing, in which seeing a part of a word that one remembers triggers the brain to reintegrate the whole memory.

Researchers suspect there are two separate biological systems for implicit and explicit memory, and that the implicit memory system develops earlier. The explicit memory system is then built onto the implicit system and suffers more from life stresses because it is more delicate.

In some form, implicit memory is already in place during the early preschool years. Some researchers believe this type of memory system may be involved in helping an infant recognize its mother's voice, although no tests have been developed to test implicit memory in infants.

Researchers first recognized there were two memory systems in 1980, and have since shown that the techniques that improve explicit memory do not improve the implicit system—and vice versa. Studies also showed that amnesic patients who have serious problems with explicit memory do not show problems with implicit memory.

Adler, Tina. "Implicit Memory Seems to Age Well." *APA Monitor* (February 1990): 8.

imprinting   A process similar to rapid learning or behavioral patterning that occurs at critical points in very early stages of development in animals. The extent to which imprinting occurs in humans has not been established.

incidental learning   A technique that involves presenting subjects with a series of items and requiring them to make a decision about each one. By manipulating the type of decision that needs to be made, the examiner can create various orienting tasks, each of which addresses a different level of mental processing.

Such orienting tasks can include: Is the word in small letters? (orthographic). Does it rhyme with "bolt"? (phonological). Does it canter around? (semantic). All of these would stimulate a "yes" for the word "colt."

With incidental learning, subjects don't expect their memory is being tested, so the retention pattern can be attributed to the processing evoked by the orienting task, not by an attempt at memorization.

indomethacin   An anti-inflammatory drug used to treat arthritis that shows promise for slowing the advance of ALZHEIMER'S DISEASE. One recent six-month study of 44 people at the Sun Health Research Institute treated patients mildly to moderately affected with Alzheimer's disease. The degenerative disease, which afflicts about four million elderly Americans, kills 100,000 a year and wipes out memory.

In the study, 24 patients were given indomethacin in doses equivalent to about 15 aspirin tablets daily; 20 others were given placebos. After six months, the control group showed an average 8.4 percent memory loss. The patients taking indomethacin showed no memory loss but rather an average improvement of 1.3 percent on the memory tests.

Experts caution that indomethacin, like other anti-inflammatory drugs, also may cause ulcers and other stomach problems.

infantile amnesia   The term used to describe the almost universal phenomenon of memory loss for events before age three and a half—except for memories of sibling birth or hospitalization. The reason why is not yet understood.

Psychoanalyst Sigmund Freud wrote in 1919 that this type of childhood AMNESIA was caused by the REPRESSION of infantile sexuality, but later researchers suggested that infants construct a record of their experience that is organized differently from the record of later experiences; this would mean that adults could no longer access information acquired during early childhood.

Many modern memory researchers say infantile amnesia is due to the lack of early development of various mental abilities (such as language) used to cue memory. Scientists argue that these developmental changes in memory are linked with specific maturational changes in the brain; they also propose that the hippocampus is the key region undergoing this change.

Studies have shown that babies can recognize people and places they have been to before, but their memories aren't permanent. When something is out of sight, they have no idea that it still exists. Not until nine months of age will an infant look under a pillow to find a toy that she has seen someone hide there. When the toy disappeared—even though she saw where it went—her memory of the toy also disappeared. Some researchers believe this is a kind of error very similar to those made by adult amnesics. Other researchers believe that memories do exist but are difficult to retrieve because they were stored before an infant could talk, when the baby relies more on its senses.

However, new research by Emory University psychologists JoNell Adair Usher and Ulric Neisser found that going to the hospital or the birth of a sibling are memorable events that can be remembered as early as age two. Other events, even those as important as a death in the family or a move, are not recalled in adulthood unless they occur at a somewhat later age.

Usher and Neisser found that these early memories do prove accurate, although repeated exposure to family stories and photographs about the experience may worsen memory of the actual event. The researchers studied 222 college students, each of whom experienced at least one of the four events mentioned above at ages one, two, three, four or five. Subjects answered questions about the events that were later reviewed by their mothers for accuracy. About 60 percent of those who were two at the time of a birth or hospitalization answered three or more questions about those events, as did more than 75 percent of those who were three at the time. But only a few of those who were one could answer at least three questions. Interestingly, only about 10 percent of those who were two at the time of a move or a death could answer more than three questions, and no one-year-olds could remember these events.

Volunteers who were three or younger at the time of one of the events recalled less if they had access to family stories or photographs; perhaps, researchers say, because this information replaced their few memories of the actual events. Neisser and Usher note that brain mechanisms that handle personal memories may not reach maturity until after age four, but by age two events that prove especially meaningful to a child may make an impression in memory.

The first memories that a person can remember may have important implications for later psychological development, since a person's earliest memories also may reveal information about overall psychological makeup, according to Alfred Adler, one of Freud's early disciples. Other memory researchers believe that earliest memories are not true memories at all, but retrospective inventions or selections that reveal some psychological truth about a person's life. In fact, studies show that a person's earliest memories sometimes change as psychother-

apy progresses and interpersonal conflicts are resolved.

Relationships reflected in these early memories often repeat themselves throughout a person's life, according to a University of Missouri at St. Louis study. This research revealed that college students who had reached the fullest psychological maturity (such as achieved commitments after a period of doubt and searching) tended to have early memories reflecting striving and mastery. But those who had adopted parental values without independently seeking an identity had highly dependent early memories revolving around a need for nurturance, safety and compliance with authority.

When a person does remember something from childhood, it is usually in response to a strong sensory cue—the smell of a particular kind of tobacco, the sound of a train whistle, a visit to an old school. Of all the senses, smell is most strongly linked to memory, probably because of its link with the brain's limbic system—the seat of emotions. Psychologist Jean Piaget described his vivid childhood memory from the age of two, when his nurse saved him from abduction by kidnappers. He remembered everything from the scratches on his nurse's face to the size of the crowd and the appearance of the policeman. However, when he was 15 his nurse (who had since joined the Salvation Army) confessed to having made up the entire story, and returned the watch she had been given as a reward. Apparently the young Piaget had heard discussions of this event as a child and projected the story into his past in the form of a visual memory.

New phases in development, such as becoming a parent, also may trigger a flood of memories, psychologists say. (See MEMORY IN INFANCY.)

Bower, Bruce. "Some Lasting Memories Emerge at Age 2." *Science News* 143 (June 12, 1993): 372.

infarction   See CEREBRAL VASCULAR ACCIDENTS (CVAS).

insight   By measuring the differences between assessments of an AMNESIA patient's condition by the patient and by relatives, the results can indicate the level of insight patients have about their memory. This is of considerable importance in determining the potential for rehabilitation.

interactional chaining   A mnemonic strategy in which an item to be remembered is visualized as linked in some way with the next item; sometimes called linking.

interference theory   The idea that forgetting may be affected more by what happens after something is learned—such as interference by other learning—than by how much time passes. This idea does not imply, however, that there is a limited memory capacity that pushes old information out when new data are learned. Rather, what we learn, not how much we learn, determines forgetting by interference.

In *proactive inhibition,* information learned in the past may interfere with the memory for something leaned recently; it is called proactive because the interference comes in a forward direction (earlier learned information affects memory for newer material).

On the other hand, *retroactive inhibition* occurs in the opposite direction, when material learned recently interferes with data learned in the past.

internal memory aids   Mental methods to help improve memory. These aids can include any of a range of mnemonic devices or rehearsal strategies. (See also EXTERNAL MEMORY AIDS; MNEMONICS.)

intrinsic context   The kind of context that affects the interpretation of target information. For example, seeing the word "tear" in the intrinsic context of the word "down" will affect the semantic interpretation of the first word. It is believed that intrinsic context is processed effortfully and that its encoding

and retrieval depend on the planning functions of the frontal association neocortex.

Intrinsic context is contrasted with EXTRINSIC CONTEXT, or independent context, in which the context does not affect the meaningful interpretation of corresponding target information.

ischemic amnesia   Forgetting related to the temporary reduction in blood supply (ischemia) to regions of the brain concerned with memory function. Amnesia due to ischemic causes is believed to underlie TRANSIENT GLOBAL AMNESIA, a form of amnesia that occurs in brief episodes and then fades away. It features a sudden onset of ANTEROGRADE AMNESIA and RETROGRADE AMNESIA for more recent events and a disorientation in time. However, there is no loss of personal identity and no impairment in any other psychological function.

J

jamais vu   The opposite of DÉJÀ VU, this is a phenomenon where a person reports that a situation or scene that was experienced before does not have the quality of familiarity. "I knew it was my car, but I felt as if I'd never seen it before."

Jamais vu is less common than déjà vu, and it may be attributable to very different mechanisms, although both are anomalies of recognition. Jamais vu is related to PSEUDOPRESENTIMENT, in which a person feels not that he or she has previously witnessed the event but that he or she has previously foretold it.

James, William (1842–1910)   A U.S. philosopher and psychologist of the late 19th century who was a leader of the psychological movement of functionalism and well known for his attempts at improving his memory. He concluded that it is possible to improve memory not so much by how much practice a person does, but by how the person learns—that is, by improving the way facts are memorized.

James was the eldest son of a witty philosopher named Henry James and the brother of the distinguished novelist Henry James, one of the most influential fiction theorists of the English-speaking world. A student of widely divergent interests, William studied medicine at Harvard University, physics and physiology with Hermann von Helmholtz in Germany and pathology and experimental medicine with others. He also read widely in psychology and philosophy until suffering a nervous breakdown and coming close to suicide. While recovering in his father's house, he received his M.D. from Harvard but was unable to practice and suffered from phobic panic until 1872. Appointed an instructor in physiology at Harvard College in that year, he began to teach physiological psychology, a revolutionary approach at a time when interest in the mind was primarily theological in nature.

In 1878 he began a ten-year project to write *The Principles of Psychology*—a definitive, monumental work in two huge volumes from which a textbook of the same name was condensed two years later. The work blended mental science and the biological disciplines, treating thinking and knowledge as part of the struggle to live, and was recognized immediately as an innovative landmark in the field. In the book James dwelt on attention and the mind, briefly describing the digit-sound equivalents in the phonetic memory system. He believed that it was possible to improve memory by improving the way facts are memorized.

One of the most celebrated cases of FUGUE was experienced by one of James's subjects, the Reverend Ansell Bourne, who wandered away from home for two months, acquired a new identity and retained no memory of the time once he returned home. His memory for the period did not surface until he underwent hypnosis.

James next turned his attention to free observation and reflection on philosophy and religion. A proponent of pragmatism, he published *A Pluralistic Universe* and *The Meaning of Truth* in 1909, and died one year later in New Hampshire.

Janet, Pierre (1859–1947)   A French psychiatrist and philosopher, one of the most famous figures in psychology, who explored the realm of the unconscious mind. A professor of philosophy at the Liceum of Le Havre in 1881 at age 22, he volunteered to work at the local asylum, where he conducted research.

He included his studies of the highly hypnotizable hysterical female patients there in his book *L'Automatisme Psychologique (Psychological Automatisms)* (1889). There he described systems of associated ideas that have been split off from consciousness and exist in a parallel life along with the dominant stream of consciousness. Calling this desegregation (or dissociation), he noted that the gaps between the parallel streams of consciousness gradually widen, and secondary existences are created. He believed this pathological process could be found in hysteria, HYPNOSIS and MULTIPLE PERSONALITY DISORDER.

Janet invented the term "*abaissement du niveau mental*" (lowering the level of consciousness, or ALTERED STATES OF CONSCIOUSNESS) to describe the weakening control of consciousness prior to dissociation. While Janet believed this altered state of consciousness was found not just in dissociation but also in multiple personality, trances and automatic writing, Swiss psychoanalyst Carl Jung adopted the term to describe schizophrenia. Jung believed that Janet's *abaissement* was the root of schizophrenia. Jung became a student of Janet in 1902 in Paris and was influenced by Janet throughout his life.

While Janet wrote widely in French, very few of his works have been translated in English.

K

keywords A type of mnemonic using a combination of two techniques—substitute words and visual associations—to categorize and remember information. (See MNEMONICS.) Its invention is generally credited to psychologist Richard Atkinson, who described the system in 1975, but the technique was developed and used by others (especially in learning foreign languages) before that time.

The first step in the keyword mnemonic is to construct a concrete keyword to represent the foreign word to be learned. For example, the French word for "chicken" is *poulet* (pooh-lay), which could be represented by the sound-a-like keyword "lay." The second step is to associate a visual image connecting the keyword "lay" with its English meaning—picture a chicken laying eggs. To recall the meaning of the French word *poulet*, you first retrieve the keyword "lay" and then the stored image linking it to a chicken follows. Research indicates that the keyword mnemonic can be effective in learning foreign vocabulary.

kinase C See PROTEIN KINASE C.

kinesthetic memory Remembering with the muscles. Kinesthetic memory is essential to everyday functioning and a valuable reinforcer of verbal and visual memory. Playing tennis, running down stairs, riding a bike or playing the trumpet all are the result of kinesthetic memories.

If it's easier for someone to find an object than describe where it is, that person is remembering kinesthetically. Most people remember kinesthetic skills better and longer than verbal or visual skills. Even if someone hasn't ridden a bicycle for 50 years, as soon as that person gets back on the bicycle, the memory of how to pedal and balance the bike will return.

Kinesthetic memory also can reinforce visual and verbal memory. In addition, some experts believe it is responsible for DÉJÀ VU. For example, if a person has felt strong emotions in a particular position, the person may reexperience that sensation in the same position later.

One way to use kinesthetic memory to aid visual and verbal memory is to "take a picture" of something to be remembered. A person who always forgets the location of the car keys would be able to use kinesthetic memory to find them more easily by pretending to take a photograph of the keys as they lie on the counter. At the same time, the person should say "My keys are on the kitchen counter" out loud; this results in an aural and visual image of the keys' location, in addition to a kinesthetic memory cue of taking a photo of the keys.

Kinesthetic memory can also be used to nudge verbal or visual memory by repeating physical actions. A person who wants to remember something should resume the position he or she was in during that experience.

Klüver, Heinrich (1897–1979) A German-born American psychologist/ neurologist who made many contributions to the understanding of the relationships between behavior and the brain, including studies of photographic visual memory in children and neural mechanisms involved in perception.

While a professor at the University of Chicago, Kluver wrote *Behavior Mechanisms in Monkeys* (1933), a book that profoundly influenced neurological and behavioral research. He gave his name to the KLUVER-BUCY SYNDROME, a phenomenon including amnesia, visual agnosia and altered sexual behavior after removal of the temporal lobes or herpes simplex encephalitis. Late in his career, he concentrated on neurochemistry, especially the study of free porphyrins in the brain.

Kluver-Bucy syndrome   A syndrome in which patients exhibit a range of symptoms including AMNESIA, visual AGNOSIA and altered sexual behavior. It usually appears as a result of HERPES SIMPLEX ENCEPHALITIS, a highly contagious and often fatal disease that causes extensive brain damage.

Kluver-Bucy syndrome also refers to the behavioral and physiological effects following the removal of the temporal lobes (comprising most of the lower cerebrum) from monkey brains.

knew-it-all-along effect   An effect that occurs when people given new facts that contradict their previous knowledge, seem unable to remember what they originally believed and claim to have known the new fact all along. Apparently the new knowledge is assimilated immediately with the earlier knowledge and any inconsistencies are eliminated to produce the updated version.

This type of updating mechanism may be an efficient kind of information storage system, although it is a limitation of meta-memory. While people are fairly accurate at knowing what they know, they are far less accurate at knowing what they used to know.

Three different processes make it necessary to update information: Contradiction, change and the accumulation of counterexamples. In contradiction, one person may believe the capital of Pennsylvania is Philadelphia, but if another authoritative source says that the correct capital is Harrisburg, the person probably will discard the original belief. Information also needs to be updated when data change—for example, a new road is built and a new route then becomes the better choice. In this case, the old information is not so much wrong as simply obsolete. Finally, in the accumulation of counterexamples, the belief that drinking a glass of wine daily is healthful because it's good for the heart needs to be changed if subsequent research shows that it also causes breast cancer.

Korsakoff, Sergey Sergeyevich (1853–1900)   A Russian psychiatrist who first described the syndrome that bears his name in 1887, when he described a disorder (he called it cerebropathia psychica toxemica) among alcoholics with severe AMNESIA. The founder of psychiatry in Russia, Korsakoff is believed to have been the first to recognize that amnesia does not necessarily have to be associated with DEMENTIA, and he noted a severe but specific amnesia for recent and current events among alcoholics with no deficit in intelligence or judgment.

Now called KORSAKOFF'S SYNDROME, the problem is found in a number of brain disorders in addition to alcoholism and appears to be caused by relatively localized brain damage. (See also ALCOHOL AND MEMORY; WERNICKE-KORSAKOFF SYNDROME.)

Korsakoff's syndrome   Also known as Korsakoff's psychosis, this condition is the second stage in WERNICKE-KORSAKOFF SYNDROME, which is believed to be caused by the interaction of chronic alcohol abuse and a thiamine deficiency brought on by the poor diet typical of chronic alcoholics.

The syndrome is called alcohol amnestic disorder in the third revised edition of the *Diagnostic and Statistical Manual of Mental Disorders* (DSM-III-R). It is a chronic disease and causes an impairment that may be so severe it requires lifelong custodial care. Korsakoff's syndrome also is found in a number of brain disorders besides alcoholism and appears to be caused by localized brain damage.

Experiments show that animals deprived of thiamine begin to develop the symptoms of Wernicke's encephalopathy; administration of thiamine cures the problem. However, if Wernicke's encephalopathy is untreated, patients go on to develop Korsakoff's syndrome, including severe amnesia, apathy and disorientation. Recent memories are affected and often patients cannot remember what they did even a few moments before; they make up stories to cover up their memory loss (called CONFABULA-TION).

GROSS MEMORY DEFECTS ARE THE PRIMARY SIGN OF KORSAKOFF'S SYNDROME; SOMETIMES IMPAIRMENT IS SO PROFOUND THAT A PERSON IS CONSCIOUS ONLY OF EACH MOMENT AS IT PASSES WITHOUT STORING ANY NEW MEMORIES AT ALL. WHILE THIS MOST SEVERE FORM OF WERNICKE-KORSAKOFF SYNDROME IS RARE, MANY KORSAKOFF'S PATIENTS CAN STORE MEMORIES FOR JUST A BRIEF PERIOD OF TIME.

IN ADDITION, MOST SUBJECTS EXPERIENCE A RETROGRADE AMNESIA ranging from a week to as much as 20 years prior to onset of their condition except for clumps of isolated memories. Many patients are not oriented in place or time, often believe they are younger than they are and often lie; they often deny memory problems and in fact usually exhibit normal personality otherwise.

While Korsakoff's syndrome may appear only in an acute phase, it is generally a chronic problem; even when patients do improve, there are often lingering recent memory problems. No matter how volatile patients might have been before the onset of the disorder, afterward these patients tend to be malleable, extremely passive and emotionally flat.

While Korsakoff's patients share many similar characteristics with those suffering from other amnesic disorders, there are differences. Unlike confusional states, patients with Korsakoff's syndrome have normal consciousness and perception. Unlike patients with dementia, those with Korsakoff's syndrome test normally on IQ exams but experience striking personality changes. Retrograde amnesia also has been reported more extensively among Korsakoff's patients than in those who have had temporal lobectomies. And SHORT-TERM MEMORY problems exist in Korsakoff's patients, but not in other amnesics.

In one study, Korsakoff's patients were able to acquire and retain mirror-reading skills while Huntington's disease patients found this very difficult; on the other hand, patients with Huntington's disease were able to complete recognition tasks that Korsakoff's patients found impossible.

But Korsakoff's patients also differ among themselves. Research suggests that Korsakoff's patients vary a great deal both in the nature of and extent of their cognitive deficits; indeed, different cerebral structures may be involved in different patients. (See also ALCOHOL AND MEMORY; FIRST-LETTER CUEING; KORSAKOFF, SERGEY SERGEYEVICH; LOCALIZATION OF MEMORY; MEMORY FOR NAMES.)

L

lag effect The recall of items given spaced repetition increases as the interval between repetition increases. It is related to the SPACING EFFECT, in which recall of items repeated immediately is far worse than of items given spaced repetitions.

Lashley, Karl (1890–1958) A pioneering psychologist and brain researcher who conducted extensive investigations from the 1920s through the 1950s into brain mass and learning. This memory expert devoted the greater part of his career to the search for the part of the brain that stores engrams (memory traces). In his search for the location of memory, he assumed that memory can be found in one place.

Lashley believed that if learning involves the construction of specific connections between behavior and events, and if memory is the impact of that connection on behavior, then that connection ought to be found in a specific location in the cerebral cortex. To test his assumption, he trained rats to run mazes, cut out snippets of their brain tissue, and then set the rats loose in the mazes again. But after operating on hordes of rats, Lashley could not find one single place in the brain where the memory of the maze existed.

Not surprisingly, the more bits of brain he cut away, the more problems the rats had running the maze—but it didn't seem to matter *what* portion of the brain he cut out. Eventually Lashley gave up trying to map the location of memory in the brain, believing that memory existed everywhere, disseminating like smoke throughout the folds and fissures of the brain.

He served as professor at the University of Chicago (1929–35) and at Harvard University (1933–35); he also served as director of the Yerkes Laboratories of Primate Biology in Orange Park, Florida, from 1942. (See also ENGRAM.)

law of disuse A theory popular during the early 1900s that memories naturally deteriorate over time. It remained popular until the 1930s, when critics noted that in many situations disuse had no effect on retention and that even if disuse does lead to forgetting, it doesn't mean it explains forgetting.

In other words, if a memory fades it is not time that has caused the forgetting, but something that happens in the brain during that time—any more than the fact that a rusty nail gets rustier because of time, not oxidation.

L-dopa See LEVODOPA.

lecithin Called nature's nerve food, this is the major dietary source of CHOLINE, the brain chemical implicated as a possible aid to improving memory. Repeated studies of administering lecithin to treat the memory problems of Alzheimer's disease patients have resulted in conflicting evidence, although the majority found it was not helpful. Other studies suggest it might be useful in heading off some deterioration in the early stages of the disease.

Lecithin raises the body's choline level and, as a result, the levels of acetylcholine in the brain, all of which may boost memory function. Foods rich in lecithin include eggs, salmon and lean beef. While some research-

ers dismiss the idea that eating these foods can improve memory significantly, other scientists note at least that a "normal" level of lecithin in the diet may not be enough as people age.

Although lecithin is available in supplemental form, many researchers do not believe it can offer significant memory improvement. Still, according to the Food and Drug Administration, lecithin is not toxic and has no side effects. It is found in the cells of all animals and plants and helps build the insulation around nerves called the myelin sheath.

Ostrander, Sheila, and Schroeder, Lynn. *Super-Memory*. Emmaus, PA: Rodale Press, 1991.

Lethe The river of death in Greek mythology, which destroys memory. The idea that forgetting the true order and origin of things is equal to death is a common theme in Greek mythology.

In Orphism, an ancient Greek mystical religious movement, a spring of memory (MNEMOSYNE) a spring of oblivion (lethe) were located near Lebadeia at the oracle of Trophonius, which was thought to be an entrance to the lower world. Lethe was also a Greek goddess, the personification of oblivion and the daughter of Eris (strife). (See also MEMORY IN MYTH MNEMOSYNE.)

leucotomy The shortened name for frontal leucotomy, this is a surgical procedure invented in 1935 by Portuguese neurologist Antonio Egas Moniz in which the surgeon severs nerve tracts connecting the frontal association cortex with deeper structures.

The term is derived from two Greek words meaning "white" and "to cut." In the operation, the skull of a person is opened and the white fibers connecting the frontal lobe to the rest of the brain are cut. Moniz developed the idea after hearing of experimental lobectomies (removal of the entire frontal lobe) with chimpanzees first performed at the Yale primate research lab in 1934. When the report was presented at an international conference in London in 1935, Moniz suggested that the procedure be tried on humans. The horrified response of his colleagues convinced him to modify his views, and he devised the less severe procedure of leucotomy upon his return to Portugal. He performed the first leucotomy there on a chronically depressed woman from a local mental hospital.

The first United States leucotomy was performed in 1936 in Washington, D.C. by American neurologists Walter Freeman and James Watts. That year Freeman began calling the procedure a lobotomy, a term that was first used in a published article in 1937.

Because the term "leucotomy" referred specifically to severing specific fibers, "lobotomy" was preferred as a more general term for any psychosurgical procedure that involved cutting the nerve fibers of a lobe in the brain.

A leucotomy involved opening the skull and major brain surgery. Freeman developed a less invasive transorbital lobotomy, involving the penetration of an ice picklike instrument into the eye socket, behind the eye and into the brain. A few quick strokes of the pick could damage enough brain tissue to tranquilize the patient.

Freeman first used this technique on an outpatient basis in his Washington, D.C. office against the advice of his associate, James Watts, who refused to cooperate with him. On his first patients, Freeman used an actual ice pick from his own kitchen; the utensil is now part of the collection of the James W. Watts and Himmelfarb Health Sciences Library of George Washington University in Washington, D.C.

levels-of-processing The assumption that deeper processing levels while learning will lead to better retention and, hence, better recall of information. This theory was developed in response to frustration with the MULTISTORE MODEL of memory.

Supporters suggest that three levels of processing are conceived for words: ortho-

graphic, phonological and semantic (the deepest level). Processing of new information is controlled by a "central processor" that represents the locus of conscious mental activity. (See also PQRST METHOD.)

levodopa Also known as L-dopa, this drug is used in the treatment of PARKINSON'S DISEASE, a neurological disorder caused by a deficiency of the chemical dopamine in the brain. L-dopa is absorbed into the brain, where it is converted into dopamine.

limbic system A network of ring-shaped structures in the center of the brain's neocortex associated with control of emotion and behavior, especially perception, motivation, gratification, memory and thought. The extensive limbic system consists of a number of connected clusters of nerve cells that seem crucial for learning and short-term memory. It includes a range of substructures including the HIPPOCAMPUS, cingulate gyrus and AMYGDALA.

The most common symptoms of damage to this area of the brain include abnormalities of the emotions, including inappropriate crying or laughing, easily provoked rage, unwarranted fear, anxiety and depression and excessive sexual interest. (See also EMOTION AND MEMORY.)

linking See INTERACTIONAL CHAINING.

link system The most basic of all the memory systems, used for memorizing short lists of items, such as shopping lists in which each item is linked to or associated with the next.

lipofuscin The material of which "age spots" are made. Buildup of lipofuscin has been linked to decreased learning ability.

lithium carbonate The most common medication used in the treatment of bipolar disorder (manic-depressive illness) and to diminish and prevent manic symptoms. Lithium helps prevent mood swings in mania and reduces their frequency and severity. Side effects of long-term treatment (which is often required) include memory problems. Regular blood tests are carried out to monitor the level of lithium in the body. Too much tea and coffee increases the risk of adverse effects.

lobotomy A psychosurgical procedure that involves cutting the nerve fibers of the lobe of the brain; used in the 1940s and 1950s as a way to permanently tranquilize difficult psychiatric patients by destroying their brain. The term was first used by American neurologist Walter Freeman to replace LEUCOTOMY, a more specific term referring to cutting certain white fibers in the brain.

A leucotomy involved opening the skull and major brain surgery. Freeman developed a less invasive transorbital lobotomy involving the penetration of an ice picklike instrument into the eye socket, behind the eye and into the brain. A few quick strokes of the pick damaged enough brain tissue to tranquilize the patient.

Freeman first used this technique on an outpatient basis in his Washington, D.C. office against the advice of his associate, James Watts, who refused to cooperate with him. The development of this transorbital lobotomy technique led to the brain damage of thousands of institutionalized psychiatric patients in the 1940s and 1950s.

Another version of the lobotomy, called a topectomy, involved a more localized procedure than the traditional ice pick method.

localization of memory The theory that memory can be found in one specific part of the brain. In fact, researchers have discovered that memory is not localized in one particular area or specific cell but is somehow distributed throughout the brain. Thus, when a researcher teaches a rat how to run a maze and then cuts out part of that rat's brain to see if the rat can remember how to run the maze, it doesn't matter which part of the brain is cut out as much as how much of the brain is removed. When an animal learns a specific task, scientists discovered, it learns the task with all of its cerebral cortex. If part of that cortex is removed, the rat's performance is affected in relation to how much of the cortex is missing.

Four areas of the brain are most often reported as being involved in memory function—the hippocampal formations within the TEMPORAL LOBES, FORNIX, MAMMILLARY BODIES and THALAMUS. Some researchers believe that a continuous pathway of connections can be found in the brain, forming one of the inner circuits of the limbic system (parahippocampal gyrus—hippocampus—fornix—mammillary bodies—mammillothalamic tract—anterior thalamic nuclei—cingulate gyrus—parahippocampal gyrus).

Hippocampal Formations Found on the surface of the temporal lobe, the parahippocampal gyrus lies near the middle of the brain; the one end of this gyrus curves around the hippocampal fissure, forming the uncus. The hippocampus lies in the inferior horn of the lateral ventricle. It was in the hippocampal area that the best-documented link to memory was discovered in the case of HM, an epileptic whose temporal lobes were destroyed to alleviate his seizures. After surgery, he was unable to learn any new information and showed symptoms of a classic amnesic syndrome. In eight other cases, patients who had undergone the same operation developed the same type of amnesic syndrome when the hippocampus was damaged; when the hippocampus was spared, no memory problems existed. From these data, scientists realized that an intact hippocampus is essential for normal memory function. Further research has suggested that removing the left temporal lobe causes verbal memory deficits and removing the right lobe impairs nonverbal memory (such as remembering mazes, patterns or faces).

However, memory problems following damage to the hippocampal structures does not occur only after surgery; injury following a stroke can also cause a profound short-term memory problem.

Fornix The tails of the fornix join together to become the body of the fornix, which divides again before connecting with the mammillary bodies. The fornix is the bridge between the temporal lobes and the diencephalon, and may be the focus of some forms of AMNESIA caused by disconnection among these structures. Still, research suggests that lesions in the fornix do not seem to produce such severe memory deficits as those that occur with hippocampal lesions. In fact, one study suggests that out of 50 cases of fornix damage, only three also reported memory loss.

Mammillary Bodies These bodies are part of the uppermost portion of the brain stem, the diencephalon. The top surface of the diencephalon forms the floor on which the mammillary bodies lie. In contrast to the fornix, the mammillary bodies do seem to be profoundly important to memory function and are commonly reported involved in Korsakoff's syndrome. Memory disorders also have been linked to those with surgical lesions in the mammillary body area or tumors. While not the only brain structure involved in memory (memory loss can occur even in patients with intact mammillary bodies), they do appear to be crucial to memory.

Thalamus One of the main parts of the diencephalon, the thalamus is involved in many cases of memory disorder in Wernicke-Korsakoff syndrome patients. One of the best-known cases of thalamic damage and memory problems is N.A., a man who was stabbed in the thalamic region at age 22. Cases of thalamic tumors have been reported that lead to a rapidly developing dementia.

localized amnesia A type of PSYCHOGENIC AMNESIA in which there is a failure to recall all events during a certain period of time, usually the first few hours after a profoundly disturbing event. (See also HYSTERICAL AMNESIA.)

loci, method of The most ancient mnemonic strategy known, dating back to about 500 B.C., in which items to be remembered are mentally placed in an imaginary place; to recall the item, a person simply recalls the location. It was the most popular system until about the middle of the 1600s, when other strategies (such as the phonetic and peg systems) were introduced.

To use the system, a person starts with a well-known place, such as the home, where a series of locations are visualized in a consistent order. An easy way to do this is to start at the front door and enter the living room (location B), go from there to the dining room (location C) into the kitchen, and so on. For more clues to help recall information, a person can subdivide the space in a particular room. (In the living room, the sofa would be visualized as a location, the mantel as another, the chair as another.) The person must hold these familiar locations clearly in the mind's eye, making sure a set of locations that are always seen in the same order has been established.

Then, to associate new information in the order it must be remembered, the person places the information in a particular location in the house. For example, to remember a shopping list filled with items that must be bought, one can first visualize the front door with shopping lists stuck over it (to remind one to take the list). Then, in the living room, one might see a cabbage sitting on the mantel, a tomato perched on the piano and a banana balancing on the table. For the system to work, the person must visualize vividly the locations and the items that have been connected with them.

Once at the store, one simply opens the front door, enters the living room, and mentally works one's way around the room. When the mantel is "seen," the cabbage will be remembered; when the piano is "seen," the tomato will spring to mind.

The word "loci" is the plural form of the word "locus," which means "place or location"—appropriate, since the system is based on memorizing a place or a location. According to CICERO, it was developed by a poet named SIMONIDES OF CEOS, who was the only survivor of a building collapse during a dinner at which he had been speaking. Simonides was able to identify the dead, who were crushed beyond recognition, by his recollection of where the guests had been sitting at the table. Because he was able to remember everyone's name through where they had been sitting, Simonides realized that a person's memory probably could be improved by associating mental images of items to be remembered with mental images of locations for those items.

The loci system was used as a memory tool by both Greek and Roman orators, who took advantage of the technique to speak without notes.

Gose, Kathleen, and Levi, Gloria. *Dealing with Memory Changes As You Grow Older.* New York: Bantam Books, 1988.
Yates, Frances. *The Art of Memory.* Chicago: University of Chicago Press, 1966.

Locke, John (1632–1704)   An English philosopher who studied memory and its laws, putting forward the philosophy of AS-SOCIATIONISM. The basic idea of associationism, which is still influential today, is that very complex ideas can be built up from very simple ones. The association of ideas was first coined by Locke in his *An Essay Concerning Human Understanding* (1690).

long-term memory   A type of memory consisting of many layers (or processes) of memory that lasts indefinitely. In long-term memory, a person stores an indefinite number of chunks in interconnected semantic networks. Long-term memory is very active in consolidation and association.

What a person chooses to store in long-term memory is probably closely tied to the emotions, and in fact the limbic system, which mediates emotion in the brain, is highly involved in memory function. Because humans generally seek pleasure and shun pain, we tend to repeat something that is rewarding (remember it) and avoid what is painful (forget it).

The amount of information each of us possesses is amazing, according to psychologist and memory expert Elizabeth Loftus. She notes that long-term memory records as many as 1 quadrillion separate bits of information; hypnosis and certain drugs are able to uncover stored information from early childhood, which can demonstrate how deeply information can be recorded. And on repeated recall tries, people usually can remember more material than they did on the first attempt. In addition, this ability to recall long-ago memories from childhood while under the influence of certain drugs or hypnosis illustrates the huge capacity, and permanent nature, of long-term memory.

Many researchers divide long-term memory into three types—procedural, semantic and episodic memory. Procedural memory is the ability to remember how to do something (such as ride a bike or write a letter). Semantic memory involves remembering factual information, such as the capital of North Dakota or multiplication tables, with no connection to where or when we learned the information. Episodic memory involves remembering personal events, such as a first kiss or where one learned how to ride horseback.

Long-term memory differs from short-term memory in more than the length of time that a memory is able to be retrieved. The nerve changes involved in long-term memory may be different; the process is not easily disrupted and its capacity is virtually unlimited. Retrieval from short-term memory is automatic, whereas retrieval in long-term memory is not easy or always automatic.

The evidence of the physiological difference between short- and long-term memory is bolstered by the fact that some diseases or drugs may affect one type of memory while leaving the other type intact. For example, one patient with a defective short-term memory (he could not remember more than two digits at a time) had a normal long-term memory—his retention of everyday events was not diminished. And the famous research subject HM, whose long-term memory was lost when his frontal lobes were destroyed, still retained old memories recorded in long-term memory. His short-term memory was also intact; he just couldn't form any new long-lasting memories. In other words, he could not transfer any information from his short-term memory into long-term memory.

Information reaches long-term memory by going through short-term memory; therefore, the amount of information that is remembered depends on the ability of the short-term memory to code information into long-term memory.

long-term potentiation The phenomenon in which an axon (presynaptic end) of a cell excites its neighboring cell often enough or consistently enough so that some growth process or metabolic process takes place in or on both cells that improves both cells' efficacy.

This phenomenon has prompted a search for conditions in which the opposite may be true, and synapses decrease in efficacy with use. This so-called anti-Hebbian phenomenon is called long-term depression, or LTD. Scientists have reported initial success in achieving LTD in rat studies using drugs to enhance the ability for cells to depolarize. With a constant level of excitatory input, LTD occurs when the magnitude of depolarization in the receiving cells falls within a certain range. This means that whether a synapse strengthens or weakens during synaptic activity could depend on the balance of influences that make it easier or more difficult for the receiving cell to depolarize. LTD also may play a part in habituation, in which response to a repeated stimulus decreases a cell's sensitivity instead of making it more sensitive. (See also HEBB, DONALD.)

LTP See LONG-TERM POTENTIATION.

Lullism An art of memory that evolved from a philosophical tradition of Augustinian Platonism rather than the study of rhetoric as classical art of memory.

Developed by Ramon Lull in the 13th century, the extraordinarily complex system depended on religious and philosophical ideas instead of graphic images. Lull began his memory system with the Nine Names for God: Goodness, Greatness, Eternity, Power, Wisdom, Will, Virtue, Truth and Glory. Each of these Names could be used on nine different levels ("steps to the House of Wisdom")—the Virtues and the Arts and Sciences; the Four Basic Elements: Earth, Air, Fire and Water; Plants; Animals; Imagination; Man; Stars; Angels; God.

In addition, Lull introduced movement into memory; the figures of his art revolve, and its concepts are set out on the revolving figures in letter notation. One of the figures consists of concentric circles marked with the letter notations standing for concepts. When the wheels revolve, combinations of the concepts are obtained.

For Lull, the aim of his art was conversion; he believed if he could persuade Jews and Muslims to practice his art of memory, they would become converted to Christianity. The art was based on religious conceptions common to all the three great religions and on the elemental structure of the world of nature accepted by scientists of the time.

Lull's verbal mnemonics The first verbal mnemonic system to be widely used, this extremely complex method was developed by Ramon Lull during the 13th century. Lull's system depended on religious and philosophical ideas instead of graphic images. He began his system with the Nine Names for God: Goodness, Greatness, Eternity, Power, Wisdom, Will, Virtue, Truth and Glory. Each of these Names could be used on nine different levels ("steps to the House of Wisdom")—the Virtues and the

Arts and Sciences; the Four Basic Elements: Earth, Air, Fire and Water; Plants; Animals; Imagination; Man; Stars; Angels; God. (See also LULLISM.)

lung disease and memory   Chronic obstructive lung disease (such as emphysema) can lessen the amount of oxygen available to brain cells, interfering with memory processes.

lupus erythematosus   A chronic episodic disease causing inflammation of connective tissue. The more serious type (systemic lupus erythematosus, or SLE) is potentially fatal and affects many systems of the body, including the joints and kidneys. At least 30 percent of SLE patients report psychosis and dementia.

If only symptoms are neurological—memory loss, problems in finding the right word, periods of delirium and confusion—the disease can be controlled with cortisone injections. SLE may cause hair loss and a characteristic red blotchy butterfly-shaped rash over the cheeks and bridge of the nose. There is no scarring and the hair grows back between attacks. Most patients feel sick, malaise, fatigue, fever, appetite loss, nausea, and joint pain and lose weight. Nonsteroidal anti-inflammatory drugs help alleviate joint pain and antimalarial drugs treat the skin rash.

Lupus is an autoimmune disorder in which the body's immune system begins to attack the connective tissue as if it were a foreign body, causing inflammation. Affecting nine times as many women as men, the disease is higher in certain ethnic groups, such as blacks in the United States. In high-risk groups, the incidence may be as high as one in 250 women, usually of child-bearing age. It is probably inherited, and hormonal factors may play a part, although sometimes an agent (such as a viral infection) triggers the immune response. In addition, certain drugs also can induce some of the symptoms, especially in older people. Drugs most often

associated with SLE are hydralazine, isoniazid and procainamide.

To diagnose lupus, blood is tested to determine if it contains a particular protein common in the blood of lupus patients. Treatment tries to reduce inflammation and ease symptoms, although there is no cure. Corticosteroid drugs may be prescribed for neurological symptoms.

Today the outlook for many SLE patients has improved, and most survive at least ten years after diagnosis of the disease. This improvement may be due to early diagnosis and more effective treatment of kidney problems.

Luria, Aleksandr R. (1902–1977) One of Russia's greatest neuropsychologists, Luria was fascinated with memory. In 1968, he wrote *The Mind of a Mnemonist*, which is recognized as a brilliant glimpse into the mechanisms of memory.

Luria wrote the book with his patient, identified only as S (for Shereshevsky, his family name), a Russian newspaperman with a phenomenal memory that apparently had no limit. S was born just before the turn of the century and was sent to Luria when his editor learned that S never bothered to take notes because he never forgot anything.

When Luria gave S the standard memory span tests (randomized lists of words to recall), he found that the man's memory did not stop at even 14 words—it appeared limitless. Time seemed not to affect S's recall; 16 years after the tests, Luria asked S to repeat a list and the man did so without a mistake.

Luria, blessed with a keen eye that allowed him to note the discrepancies between theory and experience, realized that S contradicted the common assumptions about memory storage. In the 1920s, it was assumed that memories were filed away in some tiny little file cabinet in the brain and that it took time to assimilate those memories. Hermann Ebbinghaus and his colleagues insisted that memory was constrained by the small number of items it could absorb during any one experience—but here was S, who seemed to have an unlimited ability to learn details.

Luria studied S for nearly 30 years and finally concluded that factors governing perception and attention, not storage, explained S's phenomenal ability to recall. And it is perception and attention that are the foundation of factual memory.

It was clear that S went about the task of memorizing differently from most people; if given a series of numbers, he said he could "see" the figures in his mind—so it didn't matter to him whether he was asked to remember the numbers front to back or vice versa. He could even skip around and report every second or third number.

S used a form of multisensory perception; if Luria asked S to recall a list recited many years ago, S would first recall that, at that time, Luria was wearing a gray shirt, and then he would recall the list that Luria had recited to him. He could describe the person perfectly, because he could see the person before him in almost hallucinatory detail.

Still, this was not really a help to S; his memory lacked one important feature—the ability to convert encounters with the particular into instances of the general. Because he relied on factual memory, he was unable to generalize—he couldn't see the forest because he was able only to count the trees. This occurs because generalized memory is really the result of an imperfect memory for the particulars—which S didn't have. In generalized knowledge, a person depends on having several similar experiences to which he or she didn't pay enough attention to remember the details that set the experience apart. S's associations were so exact, he couldn't separate his experience from the original context.

His memory also failed him when he was called on to use logical means of recall instead of relying on his factual memory. When he learned a list that included names of birds and was then asked to repeat only the bird names, he could not do it because he was called upon to recall a word and interpret its meaning. The task was so distracting, he was unable to perform it.

This lack of ability to interpret also is revealed in his inability to make the mistakes that others do when recalling lists—that is, recall a synonym instead of the actual word or cluster words by category. While the absence of these errors may seem like perfect memory, in fact he did not make these mistakes because he had no capacity for interpreting an experience and recalling through grammatical associations.

His memory also made him curiously unaware of the world around him. When he met Luria at the age of 30, S was astounded to learn that others didn't have perfect recall as he had. Yet he had grown up in a city, been educated at school and must have witnessed people making mistakes of memory all around him—though he never realized their imperfect memory.

He also had problems with memory chunks. While most people can recognize others even if they change subtly—get a new dress, grow a mustache or change a haircut—S could not. If someone showed up who had shaved off a beard, instead of remarking "Oh, you've shaved off your beard!" S was likely to ask "Have we met?"

Finally, the richness of his internal perceptions effectively excluded him from appreciating the external world: If he wanted something to happen, he had only to imagine it in his mind and for him, it became so.

S was synesthetic all his life—that is, he experienced sensations of color and taste in response to the sound of words, which distracted him from external reality. He would spend so much time experiencing the sensations of a person's words (the sight, the sound and the taste) that he often failed to attend and appreciate the content of the person's speech. If he heard a poet recite, he would concentrate on the sensory experiences of the words and miss totally the beauty and meaning of the poem itself.

While S did have an exceptional memory, he was only marginally effective in the activities of daily life. Luria noted that S was unusually passive, that he waited for great things to happen to him instead of doing something to achieve greatness.

Still, he did function; he had a wife and child, and he earned a living at various jobs until he obtained a job as a memorist on the stage.

M

magnesium and memory　At least one study has suggested that 1,000 mg. doses of magnesium may improve memory and alleviate other symptoms in patients with ALZHEIMER'S DISEASE and other dementias.

Magnesium is a metallic element vital for the transmission of nerve impulses. By competing with calcium for ion transport, magnesium may act similarly to calcium-channel blockers such as NIMODIPINE. Both magnesium and nimodipine dilate the blood vessels and are known to offset anxiety and seizures.

Several studies have noted that low levels of magnesium are one of the most common dietary deficiencies in the world, especially among older people. Deficiency usually occurs as a result of an intestinal disorder, severe kidney disease or alcoholism. There is some speculation that magnesium may be linked to the development of Alzheimer's disease.

Magnesium may be found in a range of products, including magnesium oxide powder, milk of magnesia (magnesium hydroxide) and magnesium carbonate, but exactly which form of magnesium is most easily absorbed is still debated among scientists. Dietary sources of magnesium include green leafy vegetables, nuts, whole grains, soybeans, milk and seafood.

Glick, L.J. "Use of Magnesium in the Management of Dementias." *Medical Science Research* 18 (1990): 831–33.

magnetic resonance imaging (MRI) Also known as nuclear magnetic resonance (NMR), this is a brain scanning technique that constructs cross-sectional images of the living human brain (among other structures and organs) by detecting molecular changes in neurons exposed to a strong magnetic field.

During the imaging process, the patient lies inside a hollow cylindrical magnet that emits short bursts of a powerful magnetic field. Because patients must lie very still during this procedure, children are sometimes given a general anesthetic. A scan usually takes about 30 minutes and can be done on an outpatient basis.

While the nuclei of the body's hydrogen atoms normally point in different directions, in a magnetic field they line up in parallel rows. If they are then knocked out of alignment by a strong pulse of radio waves, they produce a radio signal as they fall back into alignment.

Magnetic coils in the machine pick up these signals, which are then transformed by computer into an image according to the strength of the signal produced by different types of tissue. Tissue (such as fat) with a great deal of hydrogen produce a bright image, whereas tissue with little hydrogen (such as bone) look black.

MRI is particularly helpful in studying the brain and spinal cord, revealing tumors very clearly. MRI images are very similar to those produced by CT scan; however, MRI allows for far greater contrast between normal and abnormal tissue.

There are no risks or side effects associated with this technique, and because it does not use radiation the test can safely be repeated as often as necessary. However, a pacemaker, hearing aid or other electrical apparatus may be affected by the electrical field.

malnutrition Lack of adequate diet can lead to dementing brain disease if the deficiency includes lack of the B-complex vitamins (especially NIACIN, thiamine and B_{12}). This is one reason for the memory problems of serious alcohol abusers, who typically lack thiamine because they don't eat properly. In addition, a serious lack of dietary niacin can lead to pellagra, a symptom of which is memory loss. (Niacin is found in meats, poultry, fish and brewer's yeast.)

Vegetarians who don't get enough vitamin B_{12} (which is found in liver, kidney, meats, fish, eggs and dairy products) may experience symptoms of memory loss; recent research suggests that those with low-normal levels of B_{12} in their blood tend to experience depression and memory problems; a more serious lack of this vitamin can lead to spinal cord degeneration and associated brain diseases, including memory loss. (See also CHEMICALS AND MEMORY LOSS; KORSA-KOFF'S SYNDROME; PYROGLUTAMATE.)

mammillary bodies Part of the DIEN-CEPHALON, which is the uppermost portion of the brain stem; the top surface of the diencephalon forms the floor on which the mammillary bodies lie.

The mammillary bodies seem to be profoundly important to memory function and are the most commonly reported structures involved in the memory problems common in KORSAKOFF'S SYNDROME. In addition, those with surgical lesions or tumors in the mammillary body area also often have memory disorders.

While not the only brain structure involved in memory (memory loss can occur even in patients with intact mammillary bodies), the mammillary bodies do appear to be crucial to memory.

marijuana The Indian hemp plant *Cannabis sativa*. The dried leaves and flowering tops of marijuana have been implicated in a variety of memory problems—especially long-term memory loss—among habitual users.

Marijuana contains the active ingredient THC (tetrahydrocannabinol), which is also found in hashish *(Cannabis resin)*. The leaves usually are smoked, although they can be eaten in food, and they produce feelings of well-being and calmness lasting for about an hour. Large doses may result in panicky states, fear of death and illusions, although true psychosis rarely occurs. There is evidence that regular users can become physically dependent on the drug.

Marijuana's negative effects on memory have been recorded for some time; in 1845 French psychiatrist Jacques Joseph Moreau de Tours noted that hashish could gradually weaken the power to direct thoughts at will. More recent studies suggest that the most obvious problem with memory occurs within three hours of smoking, with a direct effect on the HIPPOCAMPUS, the memory center of the brain.

Some researchers suggest marijuana may affect the way a person processes and remembers different kinds of information. It appears to reduce the amount of ACETYL-CHOLINE necessary for cell communication, resulting in problems in retrieving words and making it difficult to recall numbers; the ability to store new memories also seems to be affected. Some scientists believe the chronic use of marijuana may cause the same kinds of memory effects as those experienced in patients suffering from brain infections, KORSAKOFF'S SYNDROME and ALZHEIMER'S DISEASE.

Other studies suggest marijuana may interfere with memory because it increases the number of intrusive thoughts (ideas that pass through the mind while the subject is trying to concentrate on something else).

meaningfulness effect The more meaningful the data, the easier they are to learn; if information doesn't make sense, it will be hard for a person to memorize it. The opposite of meaningful learning is ROTE

LEARNING, in which information is remembered by repeating over and over without making any of the details meaningful.

Since information should be meaningful to be remembered, it follows that nonsense syllables are not remembered as easily as words, that abstract terms are not as easy to remember as concrete words and that words in random order are harder to recall than words grouped in a meaningful way.

In one study of meaningfulness, subjects memorized 200 words of poetry, 200 nonsense syllables and a 200-word prose passage. The poetry took ten minutes to learn, the prose less than 30 minutes, and the nonsense syllables took 1½ hours. Therefore to memorize information, the more meaningful the material is, or can be made by organization into meaningful units or into a pattern, the better.

medial temporal amnesia　A type of amnesia caused by a bilateral lesion in the HIPPOCAMPUS, either alone or in combination with AMYGDALA damage. When only one side of the hippocampus is damaged, the most common outcome is a specific memory deficit: damage to the left hemisphere impairs the retention of verbal information, whereas right-hemisphere damage affects nonverbal memory. (See also HM; MEDIAL TEMPORAL LOBE.)

medial temporal lobe　An area of the brain important in memory formation. Direct evidence of the importance of this area of the brain comes in the wake of neurosurgery to remove parts of the temporal lobe as a treatment for epilepsy.

In a series of operations during the mid-1950s, surgeons removed the medial temporal lobe in ten epileptic patients in order to lessen seizures. While the operations were successful, eight of the ten suffered pronounced memory deficits. The most famous of these was known as HM, whose AMNESIC SYNDROME is considered to be among the purest ever studied. After the operation, HM was unable to remember anything other than moment-by-moment events since the time of his operation and has been described as living in the "eternal present." HM's case provided valuable information about the primary importance of the hippocampus in memory; amnesia was present only in those who had lost both the hippocampus and the amygdala, and removal of the amygdala alone did not produce amnesia.

memorist　A person skilled in ARTIFICIAL MEMORY or trained in one of a wide variety of memory strategies. (See also LOCI; METHOD OF MNEMONIC STRATEGIES.)

memory　Traditionally understood as the storage and retrieval of information, memory is really not so much a retrieval as an active construction. While people often talk about their "memory" as if it was a thing, such as a bad heart or a good head of hair, in fact memory does not exist in the way an object exists. Rather, it is an abstraction that refers to a process—remembering. If we say we know something, we are speaking metaphorically—we are judging that we can construct the answer. Our memories do not spring fully formed from little trunks stored in our heads, but instead represent an incredibly complex constructive power that we each possess.

Furthermore, memory cannot at present be found in any one place, but is believed to function at the level of synapses scattered in a weblike pattern throughout the brain. In fact, there is no firm distinction between how we remember and how we think. Scientists don't fully understand completely how a person remembers or what occurs when we recall something. The search for how the brain organizes memories and where those memories are acquired and stored has been an enduring quest among brain researchers. In order to study memory, traditional researchers have used drugs or surgery on animals to affect parts of the brain and then used behavioral tests to measure those effects.

Today, new imaging methods such as X-ray computerized tomography (CT scans) and magnetic resonance imaging (MRI) allows more precise views of these damaged animal brain sections. PET (positron emission tomography) scans have allowed scientists to study the human brain as it functions for clues to the relationship between brain structure and function.

Memory is a biological phenomenon with its root firmly in the senses. In fact, there are many different types of memories: visual, verbal, olfactory, tactile, kinesthetic and so on. The latest research suggests that all memory begins with perception.

For example, if a person's earliest memory is of nestling in the arms of her mother, her visual system identified the objects in space—this shape is a sweater, this shape is the mother's face, this is its color, this is its smell, this is how it feels—binding them into the experience of being held by the mother. Each of these separate sensations then travels to the HIPPOCAMPUS, which rapidly integrates the perceptions as they occur into a single, memorable experience. The hippocampus then consolidates information for storage as permanent memory in another brain region (probably the cortex).

While memory and perception can't be split, it is possible to speak of visual and verbal memory as two separate things. About 60 percent of Americans have primarily a "visual" memory, easily visualizing objects, places, faces and the pages of a newspaper. The others seem better at remembering sounds or words, and the associations they think of are often rhymes or puns.

While memory may begin with perception, many researchers believe its language is written with electricity. Nerve cells (called NEURONS) connect with other cells at junctions called SYNAPSES; they transmit electrical signals to each other by firing across this junction, which triggers the release of NEUROTRANSMITTERS (special signaling substances) that diffuse across the spaces between cells, attaching themselves to receptors on the neighboring nerve cell. The human brain contains about 10 billion of these nerve cells joined together by about 60 trillion synapses.

The backbone of memory could be the parts of the brain cells that receive electric impulses—the DENDRITES, the wisps at the tip of brain cells that connect to the next brain cell. It is suspected that when an electrical impulse reaches the brain cell (perhaps carrying the information of a seven-digit phone number), the impulse may compress the dendrite. When the dendrite springs back into its longish shape, the electrical pulse disappears—along with the phone number. This, then, could be the description of a short-term memory.

Most scientists today believe that memory occurs as a result of functional changes in these synapses or dendrites caused by the effects of external stimuli prompted by training or education. And while memory can be found throughout the brain, many scientists also believe that various specialized types of information are contained within specific areas of the brain. Perhaps the consolidation of information into a thought or image requires correlated nerve cell firings in different parts of the brain. Researchers have found that nerve cells in separate parts of the brain fire rhythmically and together when responding to visual stimuli that appear to come from the same object.

Researchers have generally agreed that anything that influences behavior leaves a trace (ENGRAM) somewhere in the nervous system. As long as these memory traces last, theoretically they can be restimulated, and the event or experience that established them will be remembered.

It could be that the hippocampus retrieves a memory using a single moment or sensation to trip off recall of the others: The smell of one's mother's perfume or the feel of a soft sweater brings with it the memory of *mother*. Each time the memory is called up, the hippocampus strengthens the connections between the various elements of each perception. It is only after years of such recall that a memory is laid down permanently in storage, where it can be called up without the aid of the hippocampus. The study of memory, then, tries to find out how to identify the conditions for the persistence of traces and how to restimulate them.

While people often think of memory as a single phenomenon, in fact there are two distinct mechanisms corresponding to different mental processes—voluntary and involuntary memory. The smell of one's grandmother's perfume may trigger an involuntary memory if the sensation comes by surprise or may appear as a voluntary memory if one chooses to search for it.

Types of Memory   Some researchers believe there are at least three different types of memory subsystems—sensory, short-term and long-term memory. (Other researchers believe long-term memory is made up of several different types of remembering.) While most people think of long-term memory when they say "memory," in fact these researchers believe information must pass through the first two systems before it can be stored in long-term memory.

Formation of a memory begins with registration of information during perception; the data are then filed in a short-term memory system that seems to be very limited in the amount of material it can store at one time. Unless it is constantly repeated, material in short-term memory is lost within minutes and is replaced by other material.

The next stage of memory formation is the transference of important material to long-term memory—called retaining—where the process of storage involves associations with words or meanings, with the visual imagery evoked by it or with other experiences, such as smell or sound. People tend to store material on subjects they already know something about because the information has more meaning. This is why a person with a normal memory may be able to remember in depth about one subject. In addition, people remember words that are related to something they already know because there is already a file in their memory related to that information.

The final stage of memory is retrieving (or recall), in which information stored on the unconscious level is brought up into the conscious mind at will. How reliable this material is, researchers believe, depends on how well it was encoded during stage 2.

While most people speak of having a "bad memory" or a "good memory," in fact most people are good at remembering some things and not so good at remembering others. When a person has trouble remembering something, it's generally not the fault of the entire memory system—just an inefficient component in the memory system.

For example, if a person wanted to remember where he had placed his keys, first he must have become aware of where he put them when he walked in the door. He registers (takes notice) of what he has done by paying attention to the action of putting his keys down on the hall table. This information is retained, ready to be retrieved at a later date. If the system is working properly, he can remember exactly where he left his keys. If he has forgotten where he put them, one of several things could have happened:

- He may not have registered clearly to start with.
- He may not have retained what he registered.
- He may not be able to retrieve the memory accurately.

Research indicates that older people have trouble with all three of these stages, but are especially troubled with registering and retrieving information. If people want to improve their memory, they must work on improving all three stages of that process.

Many factors go into how well a memory is formed, including how familiar the information is and how much attention has been paid. Good health also plays a major part in how well a person performs intentional memory tasks. When mental and physical conditions aren't at peak, the entire memory system functions at a slower pace. Attention (a key to memory performance) is diminished and long-term memory weakens. Ideas and images are not likely to be registered as strongly, and memory traces become fainter, making them harder to retrieve or file into long-term memory. In fact, patients who get sick often have significantly more memory problems than those who stay in good health, according to a survey of 1,000 subjects by the National Center of Health Statistics.

Techniques available for improving memory generally involve teaching association techniques that show people how to improve their coding systems. For example, a person might visualize a well-known street and then think of each building as representing a new fact. People with high IQs usually have good memories, although some people have exceptionally good memories that seem to be unrelated to their intellectual functioning. There are even some people with mental retardation who have profoundly intense memories for specific types of information—the so-called AUTISTIC SAVANTS.

Baddeley, Alan. *Your Memory: A User's Guide.* Emmaus, PA: Rodale Press, 1991.
Higbee, Kenneth. *Your Memory.* New York: Prentice-Hall, 1988.
Hilts, Philip. "A Brain Unit Seen as Index for Recalling Memories." *New York Times,* September 24, 1991.
Skinner, Karen. "The Chemistry of Learning and Memory." *Chemistry and Engineering News,* October 7, 1991.

memory and brain development
While scientists have long believed that basic language skills are a prerequisite for memory development, new research at Rutgers University suggests that infants as young as six months may be able to store information about their surroundings in a systematic way.

Researchers found that six-month-olds rely on specific aspects of their surroundings (such as the color or design of a crib liner) to retrieve memories of a simple learned task. This so-called place information seems to be the first level of retrieval for memories among infants and adults, according to researchers. Scientists tested how infants learned to move a mobile by kicking it, how long they remembered it and what changes in their environment affected their memories.

Six-month-olds remember how to move the mobile up to two weeks after training sessions, but only if the background design of their crib liner remains the same. Even three-month-olds learn that kicking sets the mobile in motion, and they retain this knowledge for up to five days. But a three-month-old who trains in the bedroom and gets tested in the kitchen, or who goes from crib training to testing in a lower portable crib, stares blankly at the previously encountered mobile. Apparently, researchers say, young infants learn what happens in what place long before they are able to move from one place to another or learn the spatial relations between those places.

Scientists theorize that the context information serves as an "attention gate"; the context during learning matches context at recall, and recognition of basic perceptual cues (such as color or form) permits attention to focus on memories for a learned task. This fact suggests that sensory receptors and the brain break information down into elementary perceptual units and then put them back together to form a coherent perception.

Bower, Bruce. "Infant Memory Shows the Power of Place." *Science News* 141, April 18, 1992.

memory, associative   See ASSOCIATION.

memory curve   See FORGETTING CURVE.

memory, disorders of   There are a wide range of specific impairments to memory that can occur from an astonishingly large number of causes, ranging from organic (brain dysfunction) to psychogenic (psychological).

The most common memory problems are specific memory dysfunctions involving language. While APHASIA is a general term for loss of language ability, experts classify the many different forms of aphasia. For example, a patient suffering with BROCA'S APHASIA has a very disturbed speech and some problems in comprehension; patients with WERNICKE'S (RECEPTIVE) APHASIA have fluent speech with a meaningless content.

ALEXIA refers to the loss of the ability to read, and AGRAPHIA is the loss of the ability to write; when these abilities are only partially dysfunctional, they are referred to as dyslexia and dysgraphia respectively. ACALCULIA is a problem in dealing with arithmetical concepts, and AMUSIA sufferers have lost the ability to understand music.

AGNOSIA refers to a patient's inability to recognize something despite no sign of sensory dysfunction; in visual agnosia, patients can't identify visual information although they can indicate recognition by other means (such as gestures). Agnosia is often limited to certain types of stimuli, such as objects or colors. Auditory agnosia (deficit in sound recognition) may take the form of pure word deafness (the inability to recognize spoken words even though the patient can read, write and speak) or cortical deafness (in which the patient can't discriminate sounds). In somatosensory agnosia, the patient can't recognize objects by shape or size.

PROSOPAGNOSIA is a selective impairment in recognizing faces and sometimes other classes of objects, such as species of dogs or makes of cars. In reduplicative paramnesia, patients can't recognize people and places they know well, but claim that doubles have replaced them. While some scientists believe the disorder is psychogenic, recent research suggests that sometimes there is an organic cause.

Disorders of memory can be caused by a problem at any of the three stages of memory: registration, long-term memory and recall. Most problems involve an inability to recall past events because of a failure at the retention or recall state. (See AMNESIA.) A person who can't store new memories suffers from ANTEROGRADE AMNESIA, while a pronounced loss of old memories is RETROGRADE AMNESIA. These two forms of amnesia may appear together or alone.

Sometimes, however, the problem occurs at the registration stage—for example, depressed people can't remember because their preoccupation with personal thoughts and feelings gets in the way.

Problems with memory is one of the most common symptoms of impaired brain function; these memory defects may be transitory (such as those after an epileptic seizure) or long term, such as after a severe HEAD INJURY.

In addition, memory problems may be the result of an organic problem in the brain. These could include Alzheimer's disease and the dementias, in which cognitive functions are progressively lost. In the early stages of Alzheimer's disease, there is usually a selective amnesia caused by degenerative processes in the parietemporal-occipital association neocortex, the cholinergic basal forebrain and the limbic system structures, such as the hippocampus and amygdala.

Organic amnesia (or global amnesia) is a memory disorder featuring very poor recall and recognition of recent information (anterograde amnesia) and very poor recall and recognition of information acquired before brain damage occurred (retrograde amnesia). It is caused by lesions in various brain regions, including the hippocampus and amygdala, by bursting aneurysms, and other problems.

Huntington's disease, an inherited disorder causing involuntary movements, also causes cognitive problems and memory deficits. Huntington's disease is caused by the increasing atrophy of the caudate nucleus in the basal ganglia and the frontal association neocortex.

Korsakoff's syndrome causes a form of organic amnesia resulting from chronic alcoholism, probably related to thiamine deficiency and poor diet. Parkinson's disease is a progressive motor disorder that also may include cognitive problems and poor memory arising from dysfunction of the frontal association neocortex.

Postencephalitic amnesia is caused by a viral infection of the temporal lobes of the brain; while the term covers various viruses, the herpes simplex virus is most commonly the cause. The amnesia in these cases is probably caused by destruction of the hippocampus and amygdala; the destruction of the temporal association neocortex probably causes retrograde amnesia.

Schizophrenia, the most common form of psychosis, affecting 1 percent of the population, also has been linked to memory disorders. However, it is unclear to what extent the memory problems depend on subtype of schizophrenia and to what extent they are the result of the effects of an inability to pay attention to external events.

Brain tumors are abnormal growths that destroy brain tissue and put pressure on nearby brain structures. Tumors that cause particular memory problems similar to Korsakoff's syndrome are often found on the floor of the third ventricle near the diencephalon. But memory deficits are likely to show up in a wide variety of brain tumors.

memory drugs See MEMORY EN-HANCEMENT.

memory enhancement Researchers believe that in the near future memory drugs will be on the market, not to make students more intelligent but to preserve the ability to remember and compensate for age-associated memory impairments. While drugs will almost certainly be used to help those with damaged brain functions improve memory, they may never do more than that.

Memory drugs might work in a variety of ways. They might help form an ENGRAM by

improving the efficiency of damaged neurons or by restoring a neuron's weakened capacity to emit a particular chemical, or by maintaining a neuron's ability to change in response to experiences.

Another way to improve factual memory might be to speed up the rate by which people associate experiences. The hippocampus somehow consolidates associations so that one experience reminds us of another. If we could speed up the rate at which the hippocampus works, we could improve memory. One hormone that may speed up the consolidation of associations is VASO-PRESSIN, which is secreted by the pituitary.

But while drugs may improve stimulation, memory still requires initial curiosity and attention. Arousal by itself does not guarantee attention; selectivity is what distinguishes human attention from an input device of a computer; our selections are based on emotional memory, and this selective attention allows us to concentrate on things that matter and ignore things that don't.

Potential memory enhancers include drugs, chemicals and natural substances including ACETYL-L-CARNITINE, ACTH (ADRENOCORTICOTROPIC HORMONE), ANIRACETAM, CENTROPHENOXINE, CHOLINE, DEHYDROEPIANDROSTERONE (DHEA), DILANTIN, DIMETHYLAMINOETHANOL (DMAE), EPINEPHRINE, FIPEXIDE, GINKGO BILOBA, GINSENG, HYDERGINE, IDEBENONE, NERVE GROWTH FACTOR, NIACIN, NIMODIPINE, ONDANSETRON, OXIRACETAM, PHENYLALANINE, PHYSOSTIGMINE, PIRACETAM, PRAMIRACETAM, PREGNENOLONE, PYROGLUTAMATE, TETRAHYDROAMINOACRIDINE (THA), VASOPRESSIN, VINCAMINE, VINPOCETINE, XANTHINOL NICOTINATE AND ZATOSETRON.

Acetyl-L-Carnitine This molecule, found naturally in the body, carries fats into the energy-producing part of the cell called mitochondria. Found in many common foods (including milk), long-term administration of ALC has preserved spatial memory in aged rats. Research suggests that it also may

may help protect the brain from the effects of aging. One study has found that ALC helps nourish certain brain receptors important for learning that tend to diminish with age.

ACTH (Adrenocorticotropic Hormone) A hormone that aids in memory retention and concentration. A combination of ACTH and melanocyte-stimulating hormone (MSH) has been studied as a possible "memory pill" helpful in treating some types of mental retardation, hyperactive children and adults with senile dementia; however, its use also has serious side effects.

Aniracetam One of the nootropic drugs that some studies suggest may be capable of improving cognitive performance on a number of intelligence and memory tests. Its chemical structure is similar to piracetam, a drug being investigated for the treatment of ALZHEIMER'S DISEASE.

Centrophenoxine This drug (trade name: Lucidril) is believed to improve various aspects of memory function by repairing synapses and removing lipofuscin deposits, the material of which "age spots" are made. Lipofuscin buildup in heart, skin and brain cells appears with age, and decreased deposits have been correlated with improved learning ability. In the bloodstream, centrophenoxine breaks down into dimethylaminoethanol, a naturally occurring nutrient found in seafood that is normally present in the brain in small amounts. Centrophenoxine can protect the brains of animals against lack of oxygen and may be of value in treating diseases in which tissue oxygenation is lowered (such as in dementia or stroke).

Choline This dietary substance is the forerunner of the brain compound ACETYLCHOLINE, considered important in the chemical basis of memory. Choline has been implicated as a possible aid to memory improvement because it increases the amount of acetylcholine in the brain. However, studies evaluating the ability of choline to boost memory performance in Alzheimer's disease patients have reached conflicting conclusions, although the majority found that giving choline was not helpful. Still others found that egg yolk (dietary source of choline) seemed beneficial in treating the memory problems of alcoholics and drug addicts.

Dehydroepiandrosterone (DHEA) This steroid hormone is produced in the adrenal gland from the metabolism of cholesterol and may be an important part of cognitive enhancement. DHEA may protect brain cells against Alzheimer's disease and other forms of senility, since nerve degeneration occurs most often when DHEA levels are low. Recent research suggests that adding DHEA to nerve cell tissue cultures could increase the number of neurons, their ability to establish contacts and their differentiation. DHEA also has been shown to improve long-term memory in mice.

Phenytoin (Trade Name: Dilantin) This well-known treatment for epilepsy also is reputed to improve intelligence, concentration and learning. Studies have suggested that, given twice daily, it can improve long-term memory and verbal performance in young and old alike. In the United States, Dilantin's only approved use is to control various types of seizures. Excess amounts of the drug has the opposite effect on memory, intelligence and reaction time.

Dimethylaminoethanol (DMAE) This naturally occurring nutrient found in some types of seafood (such as sardines, herring and anchovies) also is normally found in human brains in small amounts. According to some research, DMAE has been found to improve memory and learning, elevate mood and increase physical energy in studies of lab animals. It is said to be both a mild stimulant and a sleep enhancer. DMAE passes readily into the brain, where it is converted to acetylcholine, a neurotransmitter that is needed for clear thinking, memory, reflexes and positive mood. DMAE is considered to be a nutritional supplement and can be found under a variety of trade names in health food stores in bulk powder, capsules or liquid form.

Epinephrine This naturally occurring hormone (also known as adrenaline) and synthetic drug seems to be vital to locking memories in place; high levels of the hormone seem to be associated with better memory performance. Unfortunately, because of its unpleasant side effects on the heart and other parts of the body (especially in the elderly), more research needs to be done before epinephrine (or adrenaline) can be used as a memory enhancement drug.

Fipexide This cerebroactive drug has been shown in some studies to improve short-term memory and appears to enhance mildly the release of DOPAMINE, the neurotransmitter critical to fine motor coordination, motivation, emotions and immune function.

Ginkgo Biloba The oldest known species of tree (also known as the maidenhair), this alleged memory-enhancing herb has been used for millennia in China as a valuable medicine and memory enhancer. Ginkgo leaves are said to improve short-term memory loss and may be of some benefit to Alzheimer's disease patients. They boost blood flow throughout the body and the brain, increasing the production of adenosine triphosphate (ATP) and streamlining the brain's ability to metabolize glucose. *Ginkgo biloba* is most effective for those patients with reduced blood flow to the brain.

Ginseng This herb and its root is a substance and Chinese drug that some say may improve memory, brain function, concentration and learning. Its action is linked to a group of chemicals that influence the metabolism of neurotransmitters such as serotonin and ACETYLCHOLINE, important for memory function. It also appears to interfere with the activation of the adrenal cortex, the seat of stress.

Hydergine This extract of ergot, a fungus that grows on rye, is a widely used treatment for all forms of senility in the United States and for an ever wider range of other problems in other parts of the world.

Hydergine is an aid to memory, learning, recall and intelligence, it inhibits free radicals, enhances brain cell metabolism and increases blood supply and oxygen to the brain. It also speeds the elimination of LIPOFUSCIN in the brain. Some scientists believe that the drug may enhance memory by mimicking the effect of NERVE GROWTH FACTOR, a substance that stimulates dendrite growth in the brain, which is crucial to memory and learning.

Idebenone An important antioxidant, idebenone can reduce the danger caused by strokes in experimental animals and can improve brain metabolism. In animal studies, idebenone protects against memory problems caused by loss of oxygen, low levels of serotonin, etc.

Nerve Growth Factor This naturally occurring hormone stimulates the growth of neurites and may also improve learning capacity and memory. There are at least eight different varieties of nerve growth factors currently being studied, each with a different target cell in the body. Some studies are investigating the hormone's use in the treatment of Alzheimer's disease patients.

Unfortunately, nerve growth factor is not easily administered and must be pumped directly into the brain. Researchers hope new types of drug delivery systems (patches or nasal sprays) may simplify research and treatment.

Niacin Also called vitamin B_3, this vitamin has been shown in some studies to be a memory enhancer. In one double-blind study, normal healthy subjects improved their memory between 10 and 40 percent after taking 141 milligrams of niacin daily.

Nimodipine A possible "memory drug" that has been used successfully to treat stroke victims. The drug increases blood flow in the brain and blocks excess calcium in the part of the brain associated with memory and learning.

Ondansetron A drug that increases the release of acetylcholine, a neurotransmitter linked to improved learning and memory and involved in most types of memory impairment. By selectively blocking serotonin (a brain substance that inhibits the release of acetylcholine), the drug increases acetylcholine release and enhances memory and performance, according to some reports. Initial research suggests that ondansetron may improve memory in some healthy older adults with AGE-ASSOCIATED MEMORY IMPAIRMENT. One study found that improvements in immediate and delayed name-face recall still occurred after three months of ondansetron administration. Of 250 subjects with age-associated memory impairment, 12 weeks' treatment significantly improved the patients' memories as compared to controls, according to Glaxo, the British company that manufactures the drug. The extent of the improvement in memory function was about equivalent to the amount of memory that is lost every six years with aging.

Oxiracetam In a variety of studies, findings suggest this drug enhances vigilance and attention, with some effects on spontaneous memory and improvements in concentration. Oxiracetam is one of a class of nootropic drug called PYRROLIDONE DERIVATIVES, which also includes piracetam, pramiracetam, aniracetam and others. While the mechanism behind their memory-enhancing properties is unknown, most research suggests that the drugs affect the cholinergic system and the adrenal cortex in the brain. Oxiracetam currently is being investigated for the treatment of Alzheimer's disease at a number of centers around the country, but it is not currently available in the United States for other than experimental use.

Phenylalanine An amino acid from which the brain manufactures norepinephrine, which plays a major role in learning and memory. Phenylalanine is contained in cheese, milk, eggs and meats, and some research is investigating whether this substance might boost or sharpen memory.

Physostigmine An eyedrop treatment for glaucoma, this drug also produced a mild reversal in memory loss among Alzheimer's disease patients in at least one study. Scientists also discovered that physostigmine reverses the memory loss that usually follows scopolamine administration in normal subjects.

Piracetam A nootropic drug that appears to improve the learning ability of animals and protect against memory loss in the absence of oxygen by improving the transmission of impulses between neurons. Some studies also suggest that mixing piracetam with choline appears to boost the brain's metabolism and improve memory function. Outside the United States, the drug is used to treat alcoholism, stroke, vertigo, senile dementia, dyslexia and a wide variety of other health problems.

Pramiracetam A close relative of piracetam, this nootropic drug enhances the functioning of the cholinergic system, but is effective at much lower doses than piracetam. One study suggests that the administration of pramiracetam can boost intelligence and memory in Alzheimer's disease patients. The drug is not available in the United States.

Pregnenolone A simple steroid and potentially powerful memory enhancer, according to some recent studies. Administration of pregnenolone seemed to restore normal levels of memory hormones (such as acetylcholine), which decline during aging. The steroid also enhanced rats' ability to remember learned tasks. It is believed that pregnenolone might enhance memory because it serves as a raw material for the production of all steroid hormones used in storing information in memory. Concentrations of many of these steroids decline with age; by restoring these levels, pregnenolone may bring back memory abilities that had begun to erode.

Pyroglutamate (2-Oxo-Pyrrolidone Carboxylic Acid, or PCA) This amino acid is suspected to enhance cognition; it is also an important flavor enhancer found naturally in a wide variety of fruits and vegetables, dairy products and meat, and in large amounts in the brain, cerebrospinal fluid and blood. It is able to penetrate the blood-brain barrier, where some researchers believe it stimulates cognitive function, improving memory and learning in rats. At least one study has shown it is effective in alcohol-induced memory deficits in humans and in patients suffering from multi-infarct dementia. Administration of this amino acid increased attention and improved short- and long-term retrieval and long-term memory storage.

Tetrahydroaminoacridine (THA) Also known as tacrine or by its trade name, Cognex, this drug currently is being tested for use in the treatment of Alzheimer's disease and is expected to be approved for public use in the near future. In several studies, memory loss improved in those with the disease. It is believed that THA works by increasing the production of acetylcholine.

Vasopressin A chemical in the brain that may be involved in memory encoding, this substance also has been used to treat memory deficits of aging, senile dementia, Alzheimer's disease, KORSAKOFF'S SYNDROME and AMNESIA. It also is being studied as a possible memory enhancement drug.

Vincamine An extract of periwinkle, this drug is a vasodilator (widens blood vessels), increases blood flow and oxygen use in the brain and has been used with some benefit for the treatment of memory defects. In some studies, it has shown some memory improvement in Alzheimer's disease patients, and normalizes the brain wave patterns in elderly people with memory problems or with alcohol-induced organic brain syndrome. It also has been used to treat a variety of problems related to poor blood flow to the brain.

Vinpocetine This derivative of vincamine, a periwinkle extract, has fewer adverse effects and more benefits in memory enhancement, according to research. Marketed in Europe as Cavinton, the drug improves brain metabolism by improving blood flow and enhancing the use of glucose and oxygen. It is often used to treat memory prob-

lems and other cerebral circulation disorders, such as stroke, aphasia, apraxia, headache and so on. This drug is not sold in the United States.

Xanthinol Nicotinate This form of NIACIN passes into cells much more easily than niacin, where it increases the rate of glucose metabolism and improves blood flow to the brain.

In recent studies, it was found to improve performance of healthy elderly subjects in a variety of short- and long-term memory tasks. Like niacin, however, excess doses can cause flushing and a variety of other mild symptoms.

Zatosetron A drug that increases the release of acetylcholine by selectively blocking serotonin (a brain substance that inhibits the release of acetylcholine). Initial research suggests that zatosetron, like its cousin ondansetron, may improve memory in some healthy older adults with AGE-ASSOCIATED MEMORY IMPAIRMENT.

Bologa, L., Sharma, J., and Roberts, E. "Dehydroepiandrosterone and Its Sulfated Derivative Reduce Neuronal Death and Enhance Astrocytic Differentiation in Brain Cell Cultures." *Journal of Neuroscience Research* 17, no. 3 (1987): 225–34.

Dean, Ward, Morgenthaler, John, and Fowkes, Steven. *Smart Drugs II: The Next Generation.* Menlo Park, CA: Health Freedom Publications, 1993.

Flood, J.F., and Roberts, E. "Dehydroepiandrosterone Sulfate Improves Memory in Aging Mice." *Brain Research* 447, no. 2 (1988): 269–78.

Sunderland, T., et al. "Reduced Plasma Dehydroepiandrosterone Concentrations in Alzheimer's Disease." *Lancet* 2, no. 8675 (1989): 1335–36.

memory exercises Therapists sometimes use games such as Pelmanism, Mrs. Brown-went-to-town and Kim's game to reduce memory impairment. While research suggests that stimulation does not improve memory of severe global amnesiacs, it is not known whether this is true for those with less severe impairment. Some scientists believe that mental exercises may have some benefit for this group. Patients and relatives usually believe the exercises may help. Other research has suggested that neural regeneration may be enhanced by mental exercise.

memory for colors   Both strategy and instinct are useful in the recording of sensory information such as color. The best way to remember colors is to analyze them by studying a color chart to understand the scale of tones and values within each primary or secondary color. (For example, a red may have tinges of red or orange.) The more a color is analyzed, the better it will be recalled. It's also a good idea to associate colors with familiar objects such as "the green in my favorite dress" or with points of reference—"sky blue, salmon pink."

Intensely visualizing color will help develop visual memory so that colors can be recognized more accurately.

memory for crime   See AMNESIA AND CRIME.

memory for events   Failure of reality monitoring shows that people sometimes can't distinguish in memory between what they have really perceived and what they have only heard about or imagined. Memory for events tends to be incomplete; in everyday life situations, if an event is not very unusual, people probably won't pay much attention to it or may simply fail to see what is going on. However, if the event is dramatic, observers are more likely to pay attention—but if the event is at all frightening or emotional, stress can make their subsequent recall less reliable.

It is possible actually to alter a person's memory of a witnessed event, either through leading questions or subsequent misleading information. Once an alteration has occurred in a person's memory, resurrecting the original memory as it was first experienced is almost impossible.

The VACANT SLOT HYPOTHESIS holds that the original information was never stored, so that false information after the event was simply popped into a "vacant slot" in the memory representation. However, many leading experts in the field, including witness expert Elizabeth Loftus, reject this hypothesis on the grounds that 90 percent of subjects who are tested immediately after witnessing an event and aren't exposed to postevent information can correctly recall the event.

Those who believe the COEXISTENCE HYPOTHESIS state that both the original memory and the false postevent memory coexist, as two competing alternatives. When asked about the event, witnesses usually respond with the false version because it is the more recent memory and is therefore more accessible. This hypothesis suggests that even if a person produces a false memory, the original is recoverable.

The DEMAND CHARACTERISTICS HYPOTHESIS is similar to the coexistence hypothesis in that it also holds that both memories exist—but this theory argues that the memories are equally accessible. People produce the false memory because that is the one they think is what is demanded of them, not because it is more or less accessible. When Loftus tested this theory by asking subjects after witnessing an event to recall both the original and false memory versions, however, very few subjects could comply.

The SUBSTITUTION HYPOTHESIS explains that false information after an event replaces or transforms the original memory, which then is irretrievably lost. This theory, which is supported by Loftus's research, assumes a destructive updating mechanism in the brain; it assumes that subjects would have remembered the correct information if their knowledge hadn't been interfered with by false postevent information.

Finally, the RESPONSE BIAS hypothesis claims that misleading information after the event biases the response but has no effect on the original memory. This theory argues that in most experiments, people have forgotten the original information by the time it is tested, and when they respond with false data they are not remembering incorrectly but are simply choosing the wrong answer.

memory for faces   The memory of a face activates a region in the right part of the brain that specializes in spatial configurations. But recent research has found that the brain systems that learn and remember faces are found in a completely different place from those that learn and recall man-made objects. While the face memory is stored in the part of the brain responsible for spatial configurations, the memory of a blender, for example, activates areas that govern movement and touch.

Scientists believe the difference in remembering types of information lies in how the brain acquires knowledge. The theory says that memories are stored in the very same systems that are engaged with the interactions—in the case of the blender, the memory is found in the same part of the cortex that originally processed how the blender felt and how the hands operated it.

Other studies have shown that it's often easier to recognize someone's face than to remember the name that belongs to that face. This is because recognition requires a person to choose among a limited number of alternatives, but remembering requires a far more complex mental process; therefore, it is usually easier to recognize a person than re-member the person's name. The following quiz will illustrate the difference.

Recall
Who was president of the United States during the Civil War?

Recognition
Who was president of the United States during the Civil War?
   (a) Robert E. Lee
   (b) Abraham Lincoln
   (c) Ulysses S. Grant

"Mapping the Brain." Newsweek, April 20, 1992.

memory for languages   In order to maintain memory for language, a person must experience the language in written or verbal form; otherwise, active vocabulary will shrink, although passive understanding will be maintained. Recognition and recall of a language both depend on proficiency, exposure and practice.

The best way to do this is to listen to the radio or tapes, read books or newspapers and read at least once a week in the language to be maintained.

Although it is harder to learn a foreign language later in life, the more previous knowledge of the language, the more references there will be to facilitate new learning.

Vocabulary can be actively increased by putting the words in context and reviewing them often for several weeks.

memory for music   Even as a young child, Mozart could memorize and reproduce a piece of music after having heard it only once. Since he learned to read music and started composing at almost the same time, it is believed that he visualized the sounds on the musical staff as well as on the keyboard and mentally re-created the notes of the melody. He could play a piece immediately after hearing it, which crystallized the memory when the trace was freshest.

While few musicians can perform to the level of Mozart, they can mentally hear whole pieces of music, enabling them to rehearse anywhere—even far from their instruments.

Certain strategies can boost one's memory for sounds and music. One should concentrate on the sounds, analyze them and dwell on them. When hearing a piece of music, one should study in particular the transitions between movements, because they act as cues for what will follow. By rehearsing the links, the associations between musical elements will be strengthened.

memory for names   In everyday memory, remembering other people's names seems particularly problematic. In fact, poor memory for names appears to be quite common. While most people seldom forget the names of objects, names of individuals are often forgotten; it appears that memory for proper names appears to be different from memory for common nouns. Memory for names is a particularly difficult and embarrassing everyday problem for those who have suffered brain damage.

In fact, one study found that when subjects were given a brief history of a named individual and then asked to repeat this information, recall of first names and surnames was poorer than the recall of information about place names, occupations and hobbies. Furthermore, research suggests that last names tend to be harder to remember than other names, probably because they are less common. Recent studies have found that 13 percent of people age 18 to 44 have trouble sometimes or frequently remembering names, compared with 35 percent for ages 45 to 54, 48 percent for ages 55 to 64 and 51 percent at ages 75 and above.

Experts say that people forget a name because they haven't paid enough attention or rehearsed the name enough to register it, or they were tense, preoccupied or distracted as they heard the name. It is not clear, however, why proper names are organized differently from object names, or why they are particularly susceptible to age and stress. While it is true that names of new people we meet are hard to remember because we often aren't paying enough attention during the introduction, even well-known names elude us from time to time. Scientists suggest that our memory systems treat proper names more like the vocabulary of a foreign language than the words of our mother language.

Fortunately, research also has discovered several methods to help people with this problem, including external aids such as wearing name tags or keeping a notebook with photos and names of certain people likely to be encountered during the day. External aids have strengths and weaknesses, and there are several other options.

Rote learning is sometimes used to treat amnesia patients. In rote learning success and reinforcement is combined with a slowly increasing distribution of practice: The new name is presented followed by testing after a short time and then gradually increasing the interval of repeating the name and testing as learning proceeds. However, this method is rarely effective for severe amnesics.

There are two main groups of internal strategies, or "mnemonics"—verbal techniques (such as alphabetical searching and FIRST-LETTER CUEING) or the VISUAL IMAGERY METHOD.

Among the various memory strategies included in visual imagery, the FACE-NAME ASSOCIATION METHOD was designed specifically for learning names. Research has indicated that amnesic patients can learn some paired associations if they are based on a logical association (that is, if they rhyme or are phonetically similar). In research with Korsakoff's patients, subjects who were taught the face-name method (select a distinctive feature, transform the person's name into a noun, and then link the feature with the noun) were able to learn names.

A simpler type of visual imagery is simply to turn the name to be remembered into a picture, which is then drawn on a card. For example, Bill Smith could be drawn as a blacksmith with a long, rounded nose like a duck's bill. This type of system does not require mental imagery, and a person doesn't need to have any distinctive features.

However, research suggests that imagery is probably of limited value in a patient's day-to-day life. It works best when only the names of those who are regularly contacted are taught.

memory for numbers To remember a number, a person's eyes first register the individual numbers; once this visual sensory input enters the brain, the information is retained just long enough to be remembered briefly. Selected bits of information may enter long-term memory if the numbers are rehearsed or repeated over and over, or if there is a strong sensory or emotional component to the number.

Remembering numbers is probably one of the hardest memory chores—but it can be solved by using any of several memory strategies. For example, the number 8005552943 might be difficult to memorize, but by grouping the numbers, the task is much easier. Instead of the long series of 8005552943, by writing it as a telephone number, suddenly it becomes (800) 555–2943, a fairly simple number to maintain in short-term memory.

Other, more complicated techniques have been developed to memorize long strings of numbers, such as employing a simple phonetic alphabet with just ten pairs of digits and sounds to represent the numbers to be remembered.

Some researchers believe that short-term memory for numbers also can be improved through aerobic exercise. While researchers aren't sure why, they suspect it may be linked to the increase in oxygen efficiency or a rise in GLUCOSE metabolism. Good examples of aerobic activities include walking, cycling, swimming, jogging and racquet sports done three times weekly for 30 minutes at a time.

memory for objects In everyday life, memory for objects involves both object identification and object location. Humans identify and classify objects by relying on memory representations—to recognize what the objects are and to what category they belong. We must remember where objects are in our vicinity, not just what they are.

However, forgetting or misplacing objects happens everyday. We may forget an ob-ject's location because we are feeling absent-minded—it was put in an out-of-the-way place and we can't remember where that place is. Its loss might be attributed to being put in several different places lately, and we can't remember which place we put the object last (updating errors). Or the object may be lost because of a detection failure—it was put in its proper place, but it hasn't been detected there.

memory for odors Of all the senses, smell is most directly linked to memory because scent perceptions are recorded in the limbic system, which is considered to be the seat of emotions. In addition, smells are encoded exactly as they are without needing to be processed verbally in order to be retrieved.

Research has found that those born between 1900 and 1929 associate their childhood with fragrances of nature, including pine, hay, horses, sea air and meadows. Those born between 1930 and 1979 remember the smell of plastic, scented markers, airplane fuel, VapoRub, Sweet Tarts and Play-Doh.

Other research suggests that the happiness of a person's childhood influences which smell triggers childhood memories. The one in 12 subjects studied who reported having unhappy childhoods were most likely to remember somewhat unpleasant odors in connection with their youth, including mothballs, body odor, dog waste, sewer gas and bus fumes.

memory for places Information about location, orientation and direction is encoded in spatial memory, which is used to remember places and how to find our way, and to locate objects and remember to find things. In each case, the problem is to locate some thing (either oneself or an object) within a spatial layout.

In looking at individual differences in memory for places, such as the ability to read a map or find one's way in a strange environment, scientists testing students have discovered that those with "a good sense of direction" are those who can benefit from experience and acquire an accurate cognitive map. In addition, subjects with a good sense of direction also rated themselves as better at giving and following directions, remembering routes as a passenger, liking to read maps and finding new routes.

It is not clear whether a sense of direction is a particular ability that affects performance on a variety of spatial tasks, or whether a good sense of direction is a grouping of different abilities (such as good visualization, visuospatial memory, spatial reasoning, and so on) that reinforce each other.

In a study of the ability to use maps, researchers discovered large individual differences based on different acquisition strategies. Good learners allocated their attention, used visuospatial imagery to encode patterns and spatial relations, tested their own memory to find out how they were doing and focused on areas they hadn't learned. Poor learners tried to learn the whole map at once, used no imagery, relied on verbal rehearsal of named elements and did not evaluate their own memory. According to some researchers, maps are stored mentally in the form of a network of propositions instead of a visual image.

There are two kinds of spatial information—stored and computable. Stored spatial information is already stored in memory as a proposition (that is, Paris is in France). The knowledge that Paris is north of Marseilles is not stored directly but can be deduced logically from a set of propositions. New information also can be figured out by analysis of existing knowledge, such as finding a new route to a destination.

To remember places one visits, one must look at the scene with interest, identifying anything that is peculiar, and dwell on strong images, flashing back to them occasionally for the job of mentally traveling back there. The more one involves the senses, the stronger the memory trace will be.

memory for rote movements New studies suggest that the cerebellum may house the memory of rote movements, such as touch typing or violin fingering. Interestingly, this is the same part of the brain that controls balance and coordination.

memory for stories It appears that there is a general rule allowing the meaning of stories (the most important, most relevant facts) to be preserved in memory, along with a few specific details that also are stored for a fairly short period of time. (The exception to this is material that has been deliberately memorized; in this case, verbatim memory can persist as long as a person lives, although it may take many repetitions to acquire this lifetime memory.)

In one study of students who had years ago memorized certain famous writings (the 23rd Psalm, the Preamble to the Constitution, and Hamlet's soliloquy), the students revealed similar characteristics in what they remembered using very long-term verbatim memory.

There were very few constructive errors—either recall was perfect or it completely failed. For Hamlet's speech and the Preamble, most people showed a marked PRIMACY EFFECT; they could recall about the first 20 words and then memory completely broke down. Recall of the psalm did not show such a strong primacy effect, probably because its rhythmic structure made recalling the entire thing easier.

Researchers conclude that recall is organized in terms of surface structure, since the breakdown of memory occurred at syntactic boundaries. The surface units are remembered as associative chains, and if a part of the chain is broken, the rest is usually lost.

memory for taste While all of the senses of a human being can evoke memory, taste is one of the most powerful aids to remembering, partly because the olfactory fibers make an immediate connection with memory structures in the brain—they interact directly with the hippocampus and AMYGDALA, whereas vision requires several intermediate cell connections. (See also PROUST, MARCEL.)

memory for voices   While it is not unusual to be able to identify the voice of a friend not heard for many years over the telephone, identification of once-heard voices is not nearly as good. In one study, subjects were 98 percent correct in identifying the familiar voices of coworkers, but much less for strangers. And the memory for the unfamiliar voices decreases rapidly as time passes.

In addition, accuracy of voice recognition is reduced if the voice is whispering. Even the determination to remember an unfamiliar voice does not help recall after two or three days.

memory games   See MEMORY EXERCISES.

memory in infancy   For many years, researchers were convinced that infants had no memory because they had no language, but recent research has discovered otherwise. In fact, scientists have found that babies have very specific memories and can slowly retrieve seemingly forgotten information when given a retrieval cue. Infants' memories of events in which they have actively participated are quite enduring and they become even more so after repeated retrievals, including repeated encounters with reminders.

New research has revealed that infants' memories are highly detailed and include information about the incidental context in which events occur. Infants are so sensitive to their learning environment that when anything about it changes, they aren't able to remember what they had previously learned, according to research at Rutgers University.

Not long ago, most scientists believed that early memories are short-lived, highly generalized and diffuse, without any place information for most of the first year of life.

For many years, experts did not believe that infants who had no language could remember over the long term. This belief is rooted in the phenomenon of INFANTILE AMNESIA (adults' inability to remember events before age three or four) and the belief that the brain mechanisms necessary for long-term memory are functionally immature in infancy.

At various times, memory experts believed infants were capable only of automatic memory for motor skills or procedures, unable to recognize stimuli or remember specific events. Infants were likened to aging amnesics, Korsakoff syndrome patients or monkeys with brain lesions. In fact, however, more and more evidence suggests that even before infants possess language skills, they can remember for days, weeks or months the events in which they actively participate. Researchers also have discovered that older infants remember longer and retrieve memories more quickly than younger infants.

While scientists have long believed that basic language skills are a prerequisite for memory development, new research at Rutgers University suggests that even very young infants less than six months old may be able to store information about their surroundings in a systematic way. Scientists tied a ribbon from a baby's ankle to a mobile hanging over the crib. Within a few minutes the babies learn that kicking the foot moves the mobile. The researchers then measure how often the babies will kick when the mobile is not attached to the child's foot. The tests are performed in the child's home and so far have included more than 1,500 infants. Regardless of socioeconomic background, race or gender, babies of similar ages tend to perform about the same on the basic test.

Researchers found that infants rely on specific aspects of their surroundings (such as the color or design of a crib liner) to retrieve memories of a simple learned task. This so-called place information seems to be the first level of retrieval for memories among infants and adults. Scientists tested how infants learned to move a mobile by kicking it, how long they remembered it and what changes in their environment affected their memories.

While the six-month-olds remember how to move the mobile up to two weeks after training sessions, they remember only if the background design of their crib liner remains the same. Even three-month-olds learn that kicking sets the mobile in motion, and they retain this knowledge for up to five days. But a three-month-old who trains in the bedroom and gets tested in the kitchen, or who goes from crib training to testing in a lower portable crib, stares blankly at the previously encountered mobile. Apparently, researchers say, young infants learn what happens in what place long before they are able to move from one place to another or learn the spatial relations between those places.

Scientists theorize that the context information serves as an "attention gate"; the context during learning matches context at recall, and recognition of basic perceptual cues (such as color or form) permits attention to focus on memories for a learned task. This theory suggests that sensory receptors and the brain break information down into elementary perceptual units and then put them back together to form a coherent perception.

As language develops, the child practices his or her descriptive skills. Spontaneous strategies to recall information (active intervention) don't develop until about age 9 or 10. By then the child has learned, for example, that she can boost her memory by placing her clarinet next to her school bag to remember to take it to band practice. The adolescent years are the most important for the development of learning strategies, and memory development peaks with cognitive development.

Adler, Tina. "Infants' Memories May Be Specific, Retrievable." *APA Monitor* (November 1990): 9.

Lapp, Danielle. *Nearly Total Recall: A Guide to Better Memory at Any Age.* Stanford, CA: Stanford Alumni Association, 1992.
Rovee-Collier, Carolyn. "The Capacity for Long-Term Memory in Infancy." *Current Directions in Psychological Science* 2 (August 1993): 130–35.

memory in myth Myths involving memory and forgetting are found throughout history in all parts of the world and play a role in many cultural traditions.

In cultures where the idea of reincarnation and rebirth are strong, the mythology of memory is very important. For example, some North American medicine men claim to remember a prenatal existence, a memory they believe is lost to "common" people. Many practicing Buddhists claim to remember many lives, and a few—including Buddha himself—remember their very first existence.

In Indian myth, the veil of *maya* (illusion) prevents a person from remembering his or her true origin. The ancient Gnostics also warned of a similar forgetfulness, which they believed should be resisted. The ancient Greek goddess of memory, MNEMOSYNE, was believed to know the past, present and future and formed the basis of all life and creativity.

Forgetting this true origin of things was believed to be tantamount to death, as illustrated by the Greek's idea of the river of death (Lethe), which destroyed memory.

In the Christian religion, the anamnesis (commemoration or recollection) is one of the crucial aspects of the celebration of the Communion, through which the passion and death of the Lord is "applied" to the congregation.

memory palace One of the most ancient mnemonic strategies known, in which items are mentally placed in a huge architectural edifice; to recall the item, a person recalls the location where the object or words are placed. The use of memory palaces (part of the METHOD OF LOCI) was the most popular artificial memory system until the middle of the 1600s, when other strategies were introduced.

To make use of a memory palace, a person begins (preferably) with an architectural edifice that is already well known. The person visualizes a series of locations within the palace in a consistent order, beginning at the front door, and then continues logically from room to room. The person visualizes all of the contents in each room and holds these locations clearly in the mind's eye, making sure that a set of locations has been established that will always be seen in the same order.

To remember an object, a person simply associates the object in the order it must be remembered with a location in the palace. It is important to associate each object in as colorful, brash and dramatic a way as possible. To remember a shopping list, one could imagine a large Bermuda *onion* reclining on the front porch of the palace wearing sunglasses; upon entering the hall, one could picture a loaf of *bread* loafing on the umbrella stand; upon entering the living room, one could see a carton of *milk* toasting *marshmallows* over the fireplace, and so on.

To remember words (such as a speech), the person should begin again in the memory palace, but instead of objects associate words that sound the same or chunks of words that will serve as a memory cue to the next words that are to be remembered.

With a memory palace, the individual can be certain of remembering the correct thing at the correct time since the order is fixed by the sequence of places in the building.

memory pill See MEMORY ENHANCEMENT.

memory practice Practicing memorization can help improve memory, but what a person does during that practice is more important than how much time is spent in practice. There is no substantial evidence that practicing alone makes a significant difference in the function of memory. One study found that three hours of general memory practice did not improve long-term memory, but three hours of practicing using certain techniques did do so.

The idea that the mind can be strengthened through exercise in much the way that the body's muscles can be improved was an idea popular in educational circles in the early 1900s. This belief of the memory as muscle was behind the impetus to teach Greek and Latin in the schools, on the theory that studying these subjects exercised and disciplined the mind. But follow-up studies on thousands of high school students found that the reason why students who took Greek did better in school than those who did not was because brighter students took Greek in the first place. The study of Greek did not make them more intelligent.

In the late 1800s psychologist William James tried to test whether he could improve his memory through mental exercise. He memorized some works by Victor Hugo and then went on to memorize Milton for 38 days. After this, he memorized more from Hugo, and discovered that he was actually memorizing more slowly than he had before the memory practice. Several other subjects James tested reported similar results.

We remember a wide variety of different kinds of things: events, such as our 40th birthday party; facts, such as the capital of France; and procedures, such as how to bake a cake. While there is no substantial evidence that practice, by itself, significantly improves memory, it is possible to help improve memory by the *way* a person tries to remember something.

Improving overall memory involves three basic principles: concentration, visualization and association.

Concentration It's impossible to remember much of anything while juggling four or five activities at once. The best way to remember a fact, an event or a face is to focus on the information during learning.

Writing is one of the best ways to do this, but repeating information out loud or leaving a visual reminder (such as a string tied around finger) is also effective.

Visualization The more absurd or silly an image, the better it will be remembered.

Association Linking what must be remembered with something else provides a memory "hook" that may help retrieve it from storage.

Absentmindedness is another form of forgetting that really is tied to a failure to pay attention in the first place.

If a person is struggling with the TIP-OF-THE-TONGUE PHENOMENON, the best approach is to relax and try filling in the details of the context so it can be visualized clearly. The harder a person tries to remember in this instance, the more anxiety will be generated, and the word will not be retrieved.

People who forget what they came for when they arrive in a room or a store should repeat out loud whatever it is that is needed as they head to the location where it is found. Repeating "I'm going to the store to get some milk" as they drive toward the store will help.

Study Aids Several shorter study sessions rather than one marathon session are more useful to those who are trying to master new material. The methods used to learn should be varied—notes may be taken one day, an outline made the next, the material spoken out loud the next, then discussed with another person.

memory prodigies Individuals with exceptional memories. Very few have been studied very intensively. One such person was the Russian mnemonist known only as "S," who was studied and treated by the psychologist Aleksandr Luria. S's exceptional mnemonic ability depended on an outstandingly vivid, detailed visual memory with an unusual degree of SYNESTHESIA (stimulation in one sense activates other senses). Although S had a highly developed concrete visualization that allowed him to perform astounding feats of memorization, his abstract thinking was weak and he was only marginally successful in life.

Exceptional memory capacity sometimes also is found among mathematicians and others with talent for fast calculation. Some composers and musicians have an exceptional auditory memory, capable of remembering incredibly complex scores of music. AUTISTIC SAVANTS often are capable of prodigious feats of calculation or memory despite being developmentally disabled in every other facet of life. (See also LURIA, ALEKSANDR R.)

memory questionnaires There are two types of memory questionnaires: *Memory questionnaires* ask subjects about world knowledge or events and assess a person's memory performance; *metamemory questionnaires* ask about a person's memory functioning and assess beliefs about his or her memory performance.

Traditionally, clinical assessments of memory problems are carried out with a standardized laboratory memory test, such as the WECHSLER MEMORY SCALE, which consists of a series of tests in several intentional verbal learning paradigms. Memory questionnaires and laboratory memory tests may draw on different memory skills and are not regarded as equivalent measures of a single memory aptitude.

Memory questionnaires test two types of memories—semantic and episodic. Within each type of memory questionnaire, different questions address either a different body of knowledge (such as historical facts) or personal experiences (high school performance, hospitalizations).

Metamemory questionnaires, on the other hand, can be used to investigate the relationship between a person's self-knowledge and performance. These tests ask questions about a person's memory performance as a way of eliciting a subject's beliefs about his or her own memory. These questionnaires use self-reports to assess one or more aspects of people's memory performance—how often they forget, how well they remember, how memory changes, how easily they learn, what memory strategies they use and how they feel about personal memory performance.

While both these questionnaires may not be reliable enough to assess how well a person remembers, they can indicate how people process information in memory tasks, since beliefs affect performance. A person's beliefs about personal memory may affect whether he or she chooses to do something or how he or she performs a memory task. Research has shown that those who believe their memory is poor are more likely to have cognitive problems when stressed.

memory quotient (MQ) An assessment of memory that is measured like IQ on a scale in which 100 indicates average performance. The WECHSLER MEMORY SCALE is the most widely used clinical memory test.

memory span The amount of information that can be held in our short-term memory storage, also called the span of awareness. Memory span is measured by the DIGIT SPAN technique, which measures the number of randomly arranged digits that a person can repeat in the correct order immediately after hearing or seeing them. Normal subjects can recall about seven digits (plus or minus two). (See also MULTISTORE MODEL.)

memory stages The three stages of remembering material—acquisition (also called encoding), retention (or storage) and retrieval (or recall). Encoding is the act of learning the material; storage is keeping that information "on file" in the brain until it is needed; retrieval is finding the information and getting it back when it is needed.

If a person can't remember something, it may be because the information was never recorded in the first place (a failure of encoding); it could be that the information was never stored; or it might be that the information was not stored in a way that makes it easy to find. Most problems in remembering occur in the retrieval stage, not the storage or encoding level. While there is not much to be done to improve retrieval directly, it is possible to improve it indirectly by polishing the methods of recording and retaining. Such polishing usually involves some type of mnemonic method that stores information in a way designed to improve its retrieval.

memory systems controversy While some scientists postulate the existence of distinct short-term and long-term memory systems of unlimited capacity, others believe that there is only one system, with short-term phenomena attributed to very low levels of learning.

Those who support the idea of two separate memory systems bolster their claim with evidence from those who have sustained hippocampal injury. These patients retain information stored before the damage but seem incapable of new long-term storage; their short-term memory function appears to be unimpaired, and they perform as well as ever in tests of immediate memory. It appears that the damaged hippocampus somehow interferes with the transfer of information from short-term to longer-term storage.

Those who favor the idea of a single memory system note that research into RECENCY EFFECTS suggests that a single memory function may be involved. When a subject has seen a new list of words, the first words on the list tend to be recalled best (primacy effect) and those at the end next best (recency effect), as long as the recall begins immediately after presentation of the last word. If the subject must wait briefly (as short a time as 15 seconds) before recalling the words and cannot rehearse them, the recency effect seems to evaporate completely, but the words at the beginning of the list are still remembered.

memory trace   See ENGRAM.

meningitis   An acute infection and inflammation of the meninges (the membranes that cover the brain and spinal cord) that can cause symptoms of DEMENTIA. Meningitis is usually caused by infection from a variety of microorganisms; while viral meningitis is fairly mild, untreated bacterial meningitis can cause brain damage and dementia; it also can be fatal.

Organisms that go on to infect the brain usually travel through the bloodstream from an infection somewhere else in the body. The most common form of bacterial meningitis is meningococcal meningitis, which sometimes occurs in small epidemics and affects primarily youngsters under age five.

Symptoms include fever, severe headache or vomiting, confusion or drowsiness and stiff neck—and sometimes seizures. All of these symptoms may not develop early. To diagnose the disease, a physician will examine the head, ears and skin (especially along the spine) for sources of infection, together with samples of pus from the middle ear or sinuses, take X rays of chest, skull and sinuses (or a computerized tomography scan to detect abscess or deep swelling). The definitive diagnosis is made by analyzing spinal fluid extracted by lumbar puncture for low glucose level and increased white blood cell count.

Meningitis is considered to be a medical emergency and is treated with large doses of antibiotics. In some cases, treatment for brain swelling, shock, convulsions or dehydration may be necessary. (See also CRYPTO-COCCOSIS.)

Mesmer, Franz Anton (1734–1815)
An Austrian physician who first practiced a form of hypnotism called "mesmerism" in the 18th century.

While still a student at the University of Vienna in 1766, Mesmer began studying the works of the Renaissance mystic physician Paracelsus, developing theories based on what he thought were the astrological influences on human health as the result of planetary forces transmitted through an invisible fluid. Nine years later, he revised his theories, asserting that some occult force—which he called "animal magnetism"—flowed through the hypnotist into the patient.

He designed therapeutic interventions based on these theories loosely resembling a seance in which patients sat around a vat of dilute sulfuric acid while holding hands or grasping iron bars sticking out of the vat.

Unfortunately, it was a treatment method his fellow physicians felt was uncomfortably close to black magic, and Mesmer was forced to leave Vienna in disgrace. He settled in Paris, where he built up an extensive practice until once again his medical colleagues turned against him. So controversial were his methods that in 1784 King Louis XVI of France appointed a scientific commission (including statesman and inventor Benjamin Franklin, guillotine inventor J.I. Guillotin and French chemist Antoine Lavoisier) to investigate Mesmer's theories.

Although the committee concluded that Mesmer's methods were worthless, his practice was destroyed not by ridicule but by politics: the French Revolution forced him to flee the country and resettle yet again, this time in London.

Despite his unhappy experience with the animal magnetism method, his theories continued to interest other physicians. In his absence from France, his disciples continued to practice mesmerism. Among his former students was the Marquis de Puysegur of Buzancy, who treated a young peasant who went into a state that would today be described as a hypnotic trance. Because the peasant's condition was similar to sleep but more like sleepwalking, Puysegur called the state *artificial somnambulism;* the term later became associated with a highly hypnotizable person. Despite the peasant's alertness during the trance, when he awoke he had no recollection of what had happened—the first case of posthypnotic amnesia.

After Mesmer died in 1815, his followers became known as "mesmerists" and their technique was known as mesmerism. The practice was renamed "hypnotism" after Hypnos, the Greek god of sleep, but it was not fully understood until the mid-19th century.

mesmerism   Also known as animal magnetism, this 18th-century system of treatment was the forerunner of modern-day HYPNOSIS. Mesmerism was named for its creator, Austrian physician Franz Anton Mesmer, who developed the practice while trying to uncover a link between astrology and health.

Mesmerism was based on the theory that there were astrological influences on human health as the result of planetary forces transmitted through an invisible fluid.

Therapeutic interventions based on these theories loosely resembled a seance in which patients sat around a vat of dilute sulfuric acid while holding hands or grasping iron bars sticking out of the vat. Mesmerists believed that a person may transmit universal occult forces to others in the form of "animal magnetism" during these sessions. (See also MESMER, FRANZ ANTON.)

metamemory   The overall knowledge and understanding of our own memory processes—that which allows us to know that we know something.

metamemory   questionnaires   See MEMORY QUESTIONNAIRES.

Metrodorus of Scepsis   Counselor of kings and world famous in his time, this Greek rhetoric expert devised a secret mental writing system that was used to jog the memory. Called "almost divine" by the Roman orator Cicero, Metrodorus used not only architecture but the 360 degrees of the zodiac to place memory images. By placing images on a circle, he opened up new ways to make associations in the memory systems of his day.

Astrologers divided the zodiac not only into 12 signs but also into 36 decans, each covering ten degrees. It is believed that Metrodorus grouped ten artificial loci under each decan figure; he would thus have a series of loci numbered one to 360 in which to place information. Since all were arranged in numerical order, he could ensure against missing a locus.

It is believed that Metrodorus wrote several books on mnemonics that were subsequently lost; it is also conjectured that these lost works were part of the Greek memory system the unknown author of *AD HERENNIUM* consulted. (See also LOCI, METHOD OF.)

Yates, Frances. *The Art of Memory.* Chicago: University of Chicago Press, 1966.

milacemide   (2-n-pentylaminoacetamide)   A drug shown in some studies to improve human selective attention, word retrieval, numeric memory and vigilance. Milacemide crosses the blood-brain barrier, where it is converted in the brain to glycinamide and then glycine, and interacts with brain receptors associated with long-term potentiation of memory.

In one study, milacemide enhanced the speed and accuracy of word retrieval in healthy humans, although the effect was selective. Source memory (memory of the context in which a fact was learned) improved significantly, but item memory (memory of the fact itself) did not.

However, the drug appears to enhance memory only in normal subjects; according to studies, it was not effective in the treatment of ALZHEIMER'S DISEASE patients. It is not currently approved by the Food and Drug Administration for use in the treatment of age-associated memory impairment.

Dysken, M.W. "Milacemide: A Placebo-controlled Study in Senile Dementia of the Alzheimer Type." *Journal of the American Geriatrics Society* 40 (1992): 503–6.

Rosse R.B., et al. "An Open-label Trial of Milacemide in Schizophrenia: An NMDA

Intervention Strategy." *Clinical Neuropharmacology* 13 (1990): 348–54.

Saletu, B., Grunberger, J., and Linzmayer, L. "Acute and Subacute CNS Effects of Milacemide in Elderly People: Double-blind, Placebo-controlled Quantitative EEG and Psychometric Investigations." *Archives of Gerontology and Geriatrics* 5 (1986): 165–81.

Schwartz, B., et al. "Glycine Pro-drug Facilitates Word Retrieval in Humans." *Neurology* 41 (1991): 1341–43.

———. "The Effects of Milacemide on Item and Source Memory." *Clinical Neuropharmacology* 15 (1992): 114–19.

Mind of a Mnemonist, The A book written by Aleksandr Luria, one of Russia's greatest neuropsychologists, describing his 30 years of work with "S," a patient with a prodigious memory. Published in 1968, the book describes S, who appeared to have a limitless memory and was synesthetic—that is, he experienced sensations (such as taste or color) in response to the sound of words. (See also LURIA, ALEXANDR R.)

mirror drawing A motor task used in AMNESIA assessment in which subjects must trace between the two lines of a star while looking at their hands in the mirror.

misidentification syndromes A group of syndromes characterized by the delusion that objects or individuals are something other than what they appear to be. Familiar people may be considered to be imposters (as in CAPGRAS SYNDROME), strangers are believed to be persecuting the patient (as in Fregoli's syndrome) or individuals in the patient's vicinity can be misconstrued as other individuals (a nurse is believed to be a first-grade teacher). All of the misidentification syndromes are usually part of one of the psychotic disorders and are not diagnostic categories themselves.

mixed amnesia The complex intermingling of a true organic memory defect with psychogenic factors that prolong or reinforce the memory loss. It is quite common for a brain-damaged patient to experience a hysterical reaction as well. For example, one patient who developed a severe amnesia that impaired the formation of new memories after carbon monoxide poisoning went on to develop a hysterical amnesia that continued to sustain the memory loss. (See also PSYCHOGENIC AMNESIA.)

mnemonics The art of improving short-term recall that depends on strong visual images and meaningful associations—sort of a cross-index for memory storage.

The term was derived from the Greek MNEMOSYNE, the goddess of memory, and its techniques have been practiced since 500 B.C. Mnemonics can be verbal or visual; verbal mnemonics make word associations, and visual mnemonics use visual imagery to associate the information.

Mnemonic techniques work because they seize the attention and demand concentration. Some of the more common techniques include:

Loci (Latin for "place") One of the oldest methods (devised by Roman orators) that relate facts to various rooms or places a person knows well. For example, to remember points in a speech, the subject would match each fact to a specific site that can be visualized—a living room, bedroom or street. When giving the speech, the person would move mentally around the living room, picking up the "facts" where they had been "placed." (See also MEMORY PALACE.)

Rhymes Nobody likes grammar, but a rhyme makes it easy: "I before E, except after C."

Mental Pictures This is particularly helpful in trying to remember names: When meeting Art Black, for example, one might picture a large black painting.

Repeat Facts Another easy way to remember names is simply to repeat a person's name when introduced. For example, when someone is introduced to the new vice president, Bob Green, at a business meeting, he or she would say: "Hello, Bob," and a few seconds later repeat the name silently: "That's Bob Green." A minute or two later, the person should use Bob's name again out loud.

Chunking   While it's hard to remember a number of ten digits, everyone can remember a telephone number because it's grouped in threes: (800) 555–2222.

Acronyms   An easy way to remember a string of words is to use acronyms. To remember the six New England states, one might try: Maybe No-one Visits Mary's Red Car (Maine, New Hampshire, Vermont, Massachusetts, Rhode Island, Connecticut).

Lists   While it's helpful to write a list and refer to it, many people find that the act of writing something down fixes it in the memory.

Structure   If a person always places his eye glasses into a glass by the door, that's a mnemonic—by structuring activities so they don't have to be thought about, the person is better able to remember.

mnemonic strategies   Techniques (usually verbal) to aid memory, such as "Thirty days hath September . . ." Most mnemonic strategies do not have any inherent connection with the material to be learned, but they impose meaning on material that is otherwise disorganized. In general, these strategies usually involve adding something to the material to be learned to make it easier to remember and are referred to as "elaboration" by memory experts.

mnemonist   A person who has achieved spectacular mastery of mnemonic encoding strategies.

Mnemosyne   The Greek goddess of memory (and origin of the word MNEMON-ICS), she is the Memory that is the basis of all life and creativity and is said to know everything: past, present and future. In Greek mythology, Mnemosyne was a Titan, daughter of Uranus (heaven) and Gaea (Earth) and the mother (with Zeus) of the nine Muses. Tradition holds that after the Olympians defeated the Titans, they asked Zeus to create divinities who were capable of celebrating their victory. Zeus then went to Pieria and stayed with Mnemosyne nine consecutive nights, after which she gave birth to the Muses. Some experts argue that Mnemosyne is memory personified and as a pure abstraction could not have been a Titan.

Still, her art was of profound importance to the ancient Greek culture, and every one of the educated class practiced mnemonics. The memory palaces built by these early memory experts allowed them to perform outstanding feats of memory. Many believed memory was the path to immortality itself. (See also LETHE; MEMORY IN MYTH.)

mnemotechnics   Invented by the Greeks, this is the art of memorization by using a technique of impressing places and images on memory. Such techniques were critically important in an age before printing.

mnestic syndromes   A mixed group of disorders in which memory disturbances are the dominant clinical problem. The disturbances may be of different kinds (AMNESIA, DYSMNESIA or HYPERMNESIA) due to organic damage that is specific rather than generalized and usually involves lesions in the HIP-POCAMPUS or the MAMMILLARY BODIES. People with a variety of mnestic syndromes show intellectual impairment as well; there may be clouding consciousness, loss of abstract reasoning or mental confusion. The best known of the mnestic syndromes is KORSAKOFF'S SYNDROME. (See also AGNO-SIA; AGRAPHIA; ALEXIA; ALZHEIMER'S DIS-EASE; ANOSOGNOSIA; APHASIA; APRAXIA; BROCA'S APHASIA; CRYPTOMNESIA; DIENCE-PHALIC AMNESIA; DISSOCIATIVE DISORDERS; DYSMNESIA/DYSMNESIC SYNDROME; DYSPHA-

SIA; HYSTERICAL AMNESIA; ISCHEMIC AMNE-
SIA; MIXED AMNESIA; ORGANIC AMNESIA;
RETROGRADE AMNESIA; SELECTIVE AMNESIA;
TRANSIENT GLOBAL AMNESIA.)

Moniz, Egas (1874–1955) A Portuguese neurologist who performed the first
LEUCOTOMY (the severing of nerve tracts
connecting the frontal association cortex
with deeper structures in the brain). Moniz
was deeply interested in the practice of psychosurgery (another term he invented), and
he won the 1949 Nobel Prize in Physiology
and Medicine for his leucotomy work.

The term "leucotomy" is derived from
two Greek words meaning "white" and "to
cut." In leucotomy, the skull of a person is
opened and the white fibers connecting the
frontal lobe to the rest of the brain are cut.
Moniz developed the idea after hearing of
experimental lobectomies performed on
chimpanzees. His work inspired American
neurologists Walter Freeman and James
Watts to perform the first American leucoto-
mies in 1936.

Moniz described his procedure in the 1936
textbook on psychosurgery, *Tentatives Op-
eratoires dans le Traitement de Certaines
Psychoses (Experimental Surgery in the
Treatment of Certain Psychoses)*. In 1955,
he was beaten to death in his office by
one of his patients. (See also FREEMAN,
WALTER.)

**Moreau de Tours, Jacques Joseph
(1804–1884)** A French *alieniste* (psychiatrist) who was the first to mention DISSOCIA-
TION in his book about ALTERED STATES
OF CONSCIOUSNESS, published in 1845. The
book described his experiences with hashish
and cannabis, and he is considered to be
the first experimenter to use drugs to study
artificial psychosis.

motor association The type of memory
responsible for the fact that once a human
learns certain motor skills—say, to ride a
bicycle—the motor memory of the experience is never forgotten. It is the oldest form
of memory in the biological world.

Birds and mammals can remember both
sensory and motor associations, but animals
farther down the evolutionary ladder (such
as fruit flies, cockroaches and flatworms)
can form only motor associations.

Research with cabbage butterflies in 1986
revealed that motor associations enhance
survival; while individual butterflies visit
flowers of one species, the motor memories
of experienced butterflies enable them to
work more quickly and obtain more nectar
from flowers. Because a different method is
required to obtain nectar from different types
of flowers, cabbage butterflies that can select
one single species are more productive. Scientists know that recognition depends on
memory and not on instinct because different
cabbage butterflies favor different species;
experiments have shown that if necessary,
cabbage butterflies will change to a new
species and become faithful to those flowers.

MQ See MEMORY QUOTIENT (MQ).

MRI See MAGNETIC RESONANCE IM-
AGING (MRI).

multi-infarct dementia One of the two
most common incurable forms of mental
impairment in old age, caused by a series of
small strokes that result in widespread death
of brain tissue. Multi-infarct dementia
causes a step-by-step degeneration in mental
ability, with each step occurring after a
stroke; memory (especially of recent events)
is affected first.

Multi-infarct dementia accounts for about
20 percent of the irreversible cases of mental
impairment. In the early stages before severe
damage has been done, the person usually
is aware of impaired ability, which can lead
to frustration and depression. Multi-infarct
dementia (and the strokes that cause it) is
usually the result of an underlying medical
condition, such as high blood pressure and
artery damage.

Those who are suspected to have multi-infarct dementia should have thorough physical, neurological and psychiatric evaluations, including a complete medical exam and tests of mental state together with a brain scan. The brain scan can rule out curable diseases and also may show signs of normal age-related changes in the brain, such as shrinkage.

Treatment   Prevention is really the only effective treatment for multi-infarct dementia; patients with high blood pressure, transient ischemic attacks or earlier strokes should continue treatment for these diseases to minimize the chance of developing dementia.

While there is no cure for multi-infarct dementia, careful use of drugs can lessen agitation, anxiety and depression and improve sleep. Proper nutrition is especially important, and patients should be encouraged to maintain normal daily routines, physical activities and contact with friends. Patients should be stimulated with information about time of day, place of residence and what is going on in the home and the world; this can help prevent brain activity from failing at a faster rate. Memory aids, such as a visible calendar, lists of daily activities, safety guidelines and directions to commonly used items, also may help people in their day-to-day living.

multiple personality disorder   A disorder in which a person has two or more distinct personalities, each of which dominates at a different time. The personalities are almost always very different from each other and are often total opposites. While the personalities may have no awareness of each other, each is aware of lost periods of time. Multiple personality is often the mind's response to trauma in childhood, often including severe sexual or physical abuse.

An expanded diagnosis of multiple personality disorder was published in the third edition of the *Diagnostic and Statistical Manual of Mental Disorders* (DSM-III)

(1980) as one of the new category of mental disorders known as DISSOCIATIVE DISORDERS. Before 1980, multiple personality was believed to be rare; a total of only about 200 cases had been reported in the mental health literature. Since then it is estimated that more than 6,000 cases have been diagnosed.

Multiple personality disorder was not always considered to be a rare disorder, however; before 1910 it had been widely recognized, but between 1910 and 1975 its description disappeared from psychiatric literature. Some experts suggest this was because most people with multiple personality disorder were misdiagnosed as schizophrenics. In fact, a 1988 study found that 41 percent of 236 people with this disorder had previously been diagnosed with schizophrenia.

Because the nature of the condition is so dramatic, multiple personalities have been the subject of books and movies for some time, including *The Three Faces of Eve* (1957), a book later made into a movie.

Evidence of multiple personality also has been used as a criminal defense, such as in the case of the Hillside Strangler in Los Angeles. When Kenneth Bianchi strongly denied his guilt of rape and murder of several women, under hypnosis another personality called "Steve" emerged. This Steve was very different from Ken, and he claimed responsibility for the murders; even after returning to consciousness, Ken remembered nothing of the conversations between "Steve" and the hypnotist.

The presence of another personality inside Ken involved a moral dilemma for the court, which had to decide on the criminal responsibility of Ken, although it apparently was "Steve" who committed the crimes. In this case, the court refused to accept that Bianchi was a genuine multiple personality, because the second personality emerged only during hypnotic sessions after the examiner had already informed him that he would reveal another part of himself. (See also AMNESIA AND CRIME.)

multiple sclerosis   A degenerative disease of the central nervous system believed to involve the immune system, which attacks the myelin (protective covering of nerve fibers), disrupting function and causing paralysis and, in some patients, memory loss. It is believed that this memory loss is a result of dysfunctioning frontal and temporal lobes. The severity of the disease varies considerably among patients.

Cause   The cause of multiple sclerosis (MS) is unknown, but it is thought to be an autoimmune disease in which the body's own defense system treats myelin as an invader, gradually destroying it. There seems to be a genetic factor, since relatives of affected people are eight times more likely than others to contract the disease, although the environment also may play a part. (MS is five times more common in temperate zones. including the United States and Europe.) Some researchers believe it may involve a slow virus, picked up during a susceptible time of early life. The disease occurs in one in every 1,000 people in temperate zones.

Symptoms   The disease usually appears in early adult life, with brief periods of remission; symptoms vary depending on the part of the brain that is affected. Memory loss often does not appear immediately but may occur years later.

Diagnosis   Confirmation of the disease usually comes only after other diseases have been ruled out; a neurologist may perform tests to help confirm the diagnosis, including lumbar puncture (removal of a fluid from the spinal canal for lab analysis) or testing electrical activity in the brain.

Treatment   At present, there is no cure. Corticosteroid drugs may alleviate some acute symptoms, and other drugs may help incontinence and depression.

multistore model   The theory that memory is a series of "stores," each representing a different stage in the processing of information.

New information first enters a "sensory store" via the nervous system and one or more of the senses. Researchers have found that the pattern of stimulation set up remains for a short period after the stimulus itself ceases. For visual information, for example, this type of sensory storage is called ICONIC MEMORY: When subjects are shown three rows of letters (such as PDT, ZRT, SNR) for 50 milliseconds, afterward they could name only four or five sets of them. But when subjects were shown the letters and immediately afterward were given a signal indicating which of the three rows should be reported, they named all three letters correctly most of the time. Since subjects weren't warned ahead of time as to which row they would have to name, they must have had the whole sequence available when the signal was given, even though the stimulus itself was no longer visible.

During sensory storage, information is identified before it passes into short-term store (or "primary memory"), the basis of conscious mental activity. Short-term store determines what information is attended to and how information is processed; it also is responsible for retrieving existing memory. Short-term store can hold only so much information—called the "span of awareness," or memory span.

This short-term type of memory storage is necessary in order to perform many tasks; for example, when reading a book, the beginning of the sentence must be kept in mind while reading the last part of the sentence in order for the whole phrase to make sense. However, research suggests that the information in short-term storage is highly vulnerable to distraction or negative interference (for example, when a person loses his train of thought during a conversation after being interrupted).

Once placed in short-term storage, information can be either transferred into long-term store (or "secondary memory") or forgotten. If data are to be transferred into long-term store, a permanent memory trace is formed that provides the basis for restoring the information to consciousness.

However, these early memory processes are extremely complex and require word identification and object recognition. By the time information has reached short-term store, a great deal of processing has already occurred of which we are not consciously aware. What passes into consciousness and short-term store is simply the result of those unconscious processes. Researchers suggest that only information that has been consciously perceived is transferred from short- to long-term store. (See also ENGRAM.)

N

Nakane's mnemonics   Extensive mnemonic programs based on stories, rhymes and songs, developed by Japanese educator Masachika Nakane for learning mathematics, science, spelling and grammar and the English language.

This system has been used for children as young as kindergarten age for solving algebraic problems, performing calculus, generating formulas for chemical compounds and learning English.

In the United States, Nakane's system has been used for more basic learning. One group of third graders using his mnemonic devices learned all of the mathematical operations with fractions in three hours—just as well as sixth-grade students had learned the same calculations in three years. Extensive mnemonic programs have also been developed in the United States for reading, spelling, grammar and basic math skills.

narrative chaining   A type of mnemonic strategy in which items to be remembered are incorporated into a story.

neocortex   The part of the brain that lets us store logic, language, mathematics and

speculation about the future and enables us to change the behavior patterns that are set in motion by the more primitive parts of our brains.

nerve growth factors   Also called neurotrophic factors, this is a naturally occurring hormone that stimulates the growth of neurites (tiny projections growing from each neuron that carry information between cells). Nerve growth factor is one of the human growth factors currently being studied for its potential to restore function in the aging. Human growth hormone, another growth factor, also is being investigated for its potential to strengthen the memory in the elderly.

Nerve growth factors (at least eight different varieties currently are being studied) each have a different target cell in the body, and each has a possible role in protecting the body's nerve cells against damage from diseases such as Alzheimer's, Parkinson's and amyotrophic lateral sclerosis (Lou Gehrig's disease).

Scientists at the University of California at San Diego found that in a variety of learning and memory tests, infusions of nerve growth factor into the brain could improve learning capacity and increased the size of brain cells that had previously shrunk. In Sweden, a human Alzheimer's patient is reportedly being treated with a similar approach.

Some scientists are now developing a new class of drugs called K252 compounds, which are designed to boost the body's production of nerve growth factor. Other studies are investigating a possible treatment for Parkinson's disease, Lou Gehrig's disease and stroke patients. (See Box.)

The problem with using the different nerve growth factors is that most of the molecules are large and difficult to handle, and must be pumped directly into the brain because they will not cross the blood-brain barrier. Researchers hope that new kinds of drug delivery systems, such as patches and

Potential Uses for Nerve Growth Factor Hormone	
Nerve Growth Factor	*Used for*
Nerve growth factor	Alzheimer's disease
Basic fibroblast growth factor	Wound healing and Parkinson's disease, stroke
Brain-derived neurotrophic factor	Parkinson's disease
Neurotrophin-3	Nerve damage following trauma, chemotherapy or diabetes, and in the treatment of Alzheimer's disease
Neurotrophin-4/5	Alzheimer's and Parkinson's diseases
Ciliary neurotrophic factor	Lou Gehrig's disease
Glial growth factor	Peripheral neuropathy
Glial maturation factor	Nerve injuries

nasal sprays, may simplify research and treatment with these growth factors.

Chase, Marilyn. "Nerve-Growth Factors Brighten the Medical Horizon." *Wall Street Journal*, March 12, 1992.
————. "Scientists Work to Slow Human Aging." *Wall Street Journal*, March 12, 1992.

neurite   A tiny projection growing from each nerve cell that carries information between the cells. A nerve cell may have more than 100,000 neurites growing from it, each connected to another nerve cell.

neurofibrillary tangles   Abnormal accumulations of fibrous filamentary material within the brain's neurons are one of the hallmarks of ALZHEIMER'S DISEASE. The tangles were first described by German neuropathologist Alois Alzheimer in 1906, who realized that the tangles differentiated Alzheimer's disease from other problems. Because Alzheimer's first diagnosis was of a fairly young patient, the disease was regarded for a long time as a form of presenile dementia. It is now recognized as the same pathological brain atrophy present in many patients as they age. (See also ALZHEIMER, ALOIS.)

neuron   Another name for nerve cell, the neuron is the basic functional unit of the nervous system. Neurons carry on information processing in the brain. Each consists of a relatively compact cell body containing the nucleus, several long branched extensions (DENDRITES) and a single long fiber (the AXON) with twiglike branches along its length and at its end.

Dendrites lie adjacent to one another in a gigantic web; to send a signal, one neuron squirts out a chemical (called a neurotransmitter) that crosses the gap (synapse) between adjacent dendrites. The receiving dendrite has receptors that recognize the chemical transmitter and speed the signal through the neuron. In a series of complicated steps, the receptor changes shape and opens a channel. Information in the form of electrically charged molecules passes through the channel and into the neuron. There the information can be either stored or passed along. At the same time, the first neuron emits substances that terminate the transmission and reabsorb any excess transmitter chemicals left in the synapse.

The amazing ability of brain cells to make just the right connections may have been gained at the expense of their ability to reproduce; almost all other cells in the body can divide, and when they die they are replaced by others. Only in the brain are cells irreplaceable; we are born with almost all of the brain cells we will ever have, and those that die (about 18 million a year between age 20 and 70) are lost forever.

The average human brain contains many billions of brain cells, each with up to 60,000 synapses, but the average number of neurons varies dramatically and seems to have nothing to do with intelligence. (Some animals have more neurons than humans do.) Apparently, quantity is less important than the quality of the connections between them. (See also NEUROTRANSMITTERS.)

neurons and memory Neurons (another name for nerve cells) are the basic functional unit of the nervous system; in the brain, they carry on information processing. It also appears that memories are encoded in the brain's neurons, which convert chemical signals to electrical signals and then back to chemical signals again.

A neuron consists of a relatively compact cell body containing the nucleus, several long branched extensions (DENDRITES) and a single long fiber (the AXON) with twiglike branches along its length and at its end. Each neuron receives electrical impulses through dendrites, which lie adjacent to one another in a gigantic web whose tiny branches direct signals into the body of the nerve cell. If enough arriving signals stimulate the neuron, the neuron fires, sending its own pulse down its axon, which connects by a synapse into the dendrites of other cells.

Information is carried inside a neuron by electrical pulses, but once the signal reaches the end of the axon, it must be carried across the synaptic gap by chemicals called NEUROTRANSMITTERS. On the other side of the synapse is another dendrite, containing "receptors" that recognize these transmitting molecules and speed the signal through the neuron. In a series of complicated steps, the receptor changes shape and opens a channel. Information, in the form of electrically charged molecules, passes through the channel and into the neuron; information can be either stored or passed along. If enough stimulating signals are received, the second cell fires. At the same time, the first neuron emits substances that terminate the transmission and reabsorb any excess transmitter chemicals left in the synapse.

A single neuron can receive signals from thousands of other neurons, and its axon can branch repeatedly, sending signals to thousands more. While researchers have long understood the mechanism of neurons, only recently have they begun to understand how these cells might be able to store memories.

Most agree that when a person experiences a new event, a unique pattern of neurons is activated in some way and, within the entire configuration of brain cells, certain cells "light up." In order to store a new memory, there must be a way to save the memory—to forge connections between neurons to create a new circuit that acts as a symbol of something in the outside world. By reactivating the circuit, the brain can retrieve the memory—a replica of the original perception. The memory can be evoked again when the person encounters something that brings up a neural pattern similar to the one that was already stored in the brain.

Unlike the wiring in a home, however, the brain's circuits are not permanent; as knowledge is acquired, circuits break apart and reform, constantly rewiring themselves and influencing our representations in the world.

The amazing ability of brain cells to make just the right connections may have been gained at the expense of their ability to reproduce; almost all other cells in the body can divide, and when they die they are replaced by others. Only in the brain are cells irreplaceable. We are born with almost all of the brain cells we will ever have, and those that die (about 18 million a year between age 20 and 70) are lost forever.

The average human brain contains many billions of brain cells, each with up to 60,000 synapses, but the average number of neurons varies dramatically and seems to have nothing to do with general intelligence. (Some animals have more neurons than humans do.) Apparently, quantity is less important than the quality of the connections between them.

Any one memory can be found not in one particular neuron in one particular place, but

---

Frequently Used Neuropsychological Tests

General Intelligence
Wechsler Adult Intelligence Scale Revised (WAIS-R)

Reading, Writing, Arithmetic Skills
Wide Range Achievement Text Revised
Woodcok-Johnson Revised Test of Academic Achievement

Memory
Wechsler Memory Scale Revised
Buschke Selective Reminding Test

Visual Perception Processes
Hooper Visual Organization Test
Judgment of Line Orientation Test

Visual Form Discrimination Test
Visual Scanning and Speed
Halstead-Reitan Trailmaking Test

Abstraction and Problem-Solving
Wisconsin Card Solving Test
Receptive Listening/Vocabulary
Peabody Picture Vocabulary Test Revised

---

along a neuronal circuit within the vast, weblike structure of neurons sprawling throughout the brain. Memory, then, is not found in one place but everywhere throughout the brain.

neuronal plasticity A neuron's ability to change structurally or functionally, often in a permanent way. Plasticity is responsible for a wide variety of events, including drug tolerance, enzyme induction and axon terminal sprouting after a brain lesion. If scientists could figure out just how the nervous system performs these examples of plasticity, they would uncover valuable clues to the way that the nervous system learns and remembers. Because one of the most distinctive features of learning is persistence, an analysis of a neuron's plasticity is important to the study of learning.

Electrical stimulation, neuronal disuse and enriched learning environments have all shown the ability to produce changes in the brain's synapses. (See SYNAPTIC CHANGE AND MEMORY.)

neuropeptides Building blocks of proteins that are made of amino acids. Normally they are produced by the pituitary gland and function as neurotransmitters. They include adrenocorticotrophic hormone (ACTH), melanocyte-stimulating hormone (MSH) and vasopressin. Some researchers believe ACTH improves sustained attention and diminishes depression in dementia patients. Vasopressin is being studied as a possible memory enhancement drug.

neuropsychological assessment Tests that can evaluate the extent of brain damage and memory deficits, including assessment of language, memory, perception, reasoning, emotion, self-control and planning. (See Box.) This kind of testing was first used as a way to distinguish between those whose abnormal behavior was caused by brain dysfunction and those whose problems were caused by psychological factors. Disorders caused by brain dysfunction are called organic; psychological disorders are referred to as functional or psychogenic.

Early tests were based on the assumption that there were common characteristics in all organic impairments. These tests gave a general assessment of "organicity" instead of details about the status of different mental functions.

Although the idea of "brain damage" as a single concept persists, in fact there is no one simple test that can uncover the often-diffuse problems experienced by those who have brain problems. Because brain damage may be caused by lesions of different sizes and shapes in different parts of the brain, uncovering the exact source of brain damage requires a more sophisticated, comprehensive assessment. In order to rehabilitate patients with brain deficits properly, it is imperative to have a clear picture of their cognitive strengths and weaknesses, to help choose the treatment technique and to measure response to treatment. (See also ASSESSMENT OF MEMORY DISORDERS.)

neurosis and memory Neurosis is a term often used to describe a range of relatively mild psychiatric disorders in which the patient remains in touch with reality; memory problems are primary symptoms in several neurotic disorders.

The major neurotic disorders include mild forms of depression, anxiety disorders (including phobias and obsessive-compulsive disorder), somatization disorder and DISSOCIATIVE DISORDERS and psychosexual disorders. Of these, both depression and dissociative disorders feature memory loss as a primary symptom.

Repression—an explanation of forgetting that suggests unpleasant memories may be forgotten intentionally—was the underlying theme of the theories of Sigmund Freud; he considered repression the keystone to his entire theory of neurosis. According to Freud, to enable people to survive mentally, unacceptable, traumatic or unpleasant memories are forgotten intentionally by being pushed into the unconscious on purpose.

Repression is a form of coping and often occurs, Freud believed, during childhood. He also believed that childhood amnesia is caused by the repression of infantile sexuality; many modern memory researchers now say it is due to the lack of early development of various mental abilities (such as language) used to cue memory.

neurotransmitters Specialized chemical messengers synthesized and secreted by neurons that affect most connections between the nerve cells. A neurotransmitter is released into the synapse (space between neurons), moves across the space and attaches to a receptor in the outer wall of a neighboring neuron. Some neurotransmitters stimulate the release of neurotransmitters from other neurons, while others inhibit the release of other neurotransmitters.

Many different neurotransmitters appear to be involved in the memory process, including ACETYLCHOLINE, CALPAIN, NOREPINEPHRINE, DOPAMINE, ACTH, VASOPRESSIN, endorphins and the opioid peptides.

Gazzaniga, Michael. *Perspectives in Memory Research*. Cambridge, MA: MIT Press, 1991.

New Adult Reading Test A list of 50 increasingly difficult words that can indicate premorbid intelligence in those of high-average or superior intelligence. Psychologists who are trying to test for brain damage face a problem in quantifying loss in the absence of evidence of how well the person performed before deterioration began. For example, a person with an IQ of 140 could lose 20 or 30 points and still test as "average," but if the person's previous intellectual ability had been known the comparison would reveal a significant loss of intellectual ability.

Studies have found that, in fact, language skills seem to deteriorate more slowly than other memory aspects; a group of patients with dementia retained their ability to pronounce unusually spelled words despite gradual deterioration in other intellectual areas.

The New Adult Reading Test (NART) was developed to take advantage of this persistence of language skills; scores on this test are considered to be a good predictor of intelligence before deterioration took place in those with high-average or superior intelligence.

next-in-line effect   A phenomenon related to attention in which self-concern erases memory for events immediately preceding a person's own performance. In one experiment, scientists assembled groups of subjects to read word lists. The group of subjects who knew the order of performance showed a marked next-in-line effect; that is, they could recall the performances of those who came before the person immediately preceding them but retained no memory of the person who read the word list immediately before their own performance. When told that subjects would have to report on the list read immediately before their own, the next-in-line effect was abolished simply because subjects had a reason to pay attention.

niacin   Also called vitamin B_3, this vitamin has shown in some studies to be a memory enhancer. In one double-blind study, normal healthy subjects improved their memory between 10 and 40 percent after taking 141 milligrams of niacin daily.

Niacin should never be taken without a physician's approval by those with diabetes, high blood pressure, ulcers or porphyria. Some patients experience skin flushing or dizziness shortly after taking niacin; flushing is more likely to occur when taken on an empty stomach.

The principal dietary sources of niacin include liver, lean meat, poultry, fish, whole grains, nuts and dried beans. (See also MAL-NUTRITION; MEMORY ENHANCEMENT; XANTHINOL NICOTINATE.)

nicotine and memory   While smoking may give the impression of sharpening concentration, in fact studies have shown that smokers puffing on a regular nicotine cigarette fared 24 percent worse than subjects smoking nonnicotine cigarettes on a memory test of item recall. Similarly, a British study paired 37 smokers and 37 nonsmokers in another study and asked them to remember a list of a dozen names. Ten minutes later the nonsmokers could recall significantly more names than the smokers.

In fact, smoking cigarettes can impair memory performance about as much as several alcoholic drinks. Nonsmokers are able to remember lists of numbers more quickly than smokers, and they also score higher on the standard Wechsler Memory Scale.

In addition, research indicates that smokers who want to remember something should put off lighting up right before a memory task—but putting off smoking too long beforehand can make a person so jittery that it distracts from the task.

Scientists suspect that the nicotine may interfere with the blood supply carrying oxygen to the brain, resulting in poorer memory efficiency.

Minninger, Joan. *Total Recall.* Emmaus, PA: Rodale Press, 1984.

nimodipine   (Nimotop)   A possible "memory drug" that has been used successfully to treat stroke victims and is being studied for the treatment of ALZHEIMER'S DISEASE and age-associated memory impairment. The drug is a calcium-channel blocker, which means it alters the flow of calcium ions through cell membranes, increasing brain blood flow and blocking excess calcium in the part of the brain associated with memory and learning. Nimodipine also seems to increase ACETYL-CHOLINE levels.

It was approved by the Food and Drug Administration in 1989 to treat hemorrhagic stroke, as it improves blood flow in the brain and lessens oxygen deprivation.

Italian researchers noted a 69.5 percent increase in mental performance among 40 patients age 65 and 80 years old suffering minor to medium signs of mental aging. Twenty percent showed no change, and 9.5 percent worsened slightly.

Other studies have found that nimodipine improved acetylcholine levels in young rats, which learned more quickly than those rats that were not treated. Vanderbilt University researchers found that nimodipine was effective in improving memory, depression and general state of mind in 178 elderly patients in cognitive decline. (See also MEMORY ENHANCEMENT.)

Bower, Bruce. "Boosting Memory in the Blink of an Eye." *Science News* 135 (February 11, 1989): 86.

Deyo, R.A., Straube, K.T., and Disterhoft, J.E. "Nimodipine Facilitates Associative Learning in Aging Rabbits." *Science* 243, no. 4892 (February 1989): 809–11.

Grobe-Einsler, R., and Traber, J. "Clinical Results with Nimodipine in Alzheimer's Disease." *Clinical Neuropharmacology* 15 (suppl. 1, pt. A) (1992): 416A–17A.

Langley, M.S., and Sorkin, E.M. "Nimodipine: A Review of Its Pharmacodynamic and Pharmacokinetic Properties, and Therapeutic Potential in Cerebrovascular Disease." *Drugs* 37 (1989): 669–99.

Parnetti, L., et al. "Mental Deterioration in Old Age: Results of 2 Multiclinical Trials with Nimodipine." *Clinical Therapeutics* 15, no. 2 (March/April 1993): 394–406.

NMDA receptor The best-known receptor for the amino acid GLUTAMATE, NMDA is named after a synthetic form of glutamate (N-methyl-D-aspartate) used in research. Glutamate is a protein component found in every cell in the body and plays a central role in the workings of the brain. Recent research suggests that glutamate also may play an important role in the destruction of the brain in the wake of oxygen deprivation after a heart attack or stroke.

nominal aphasia Difficulty in naming objects or finding words, although the person may be able to choose the correct name from several offers. Nominal aphasia may be caused by generalized cerebral dysfunction or damage to specific language areas. While some recovery is usual after a stroke or injury, the more severe the type of aphasia, the less the chance of recovery. (See also APHASIA; BROCA'S APHASIA; GLOBAL APHASIA; WERNICKE'S [RECEPTIVE] APHASIA.)

nootropics A new class of drugs designed to improve learning, memory consolidation and memory retrieval without other central nervous system effects. Nootropics are considered to be low in toxicity even at extremely high doses. The name "nootropic" was taken from the Greek words *noos* (mind) and *tropein* (toward).

Although there is some disagreement among researchers on which medications should be considered nootropics, they generally include the pyrrolidone derivatives (PIRACETAM and analogues OXIRACETAM, PRAMIRACETAM, ANIRACETAM).

The mechanism by which these drugs seem to improve memory is unknown, although most studies suggest they work by affecting the cholinergic system (the part of the nervous system that uses acetylcholine as a neurotransmitter). In addition, there appears to be some involvement with adrenal steroid production in the adrenal cortex.

While physicians prescribe nootropics to patients outside of the United States, none of the nootropic drugs have been approved by the U.S. Food and Drug Administration.

Dean, Ward, and Morgenthaler, John. *Smart Drugs and Nutrients.* Santa Cruz, CA: B&J Publications, 1991.

Giurgea, C.E., and Salama, M. "Nootropic

Drugs." *Progress in Neuropsychopharmacology* 1 (1977): 235–47.

Pepeu, G., and Spignoli, G. "Neurochemical Actions of Nootropic Drugs." In *Advances in Neurology*. New York: Raven Press, 1990.

norepinephrine A chemical messenger in the brain (also called noradrenalin) involved in alertness, concentration, aggression and motivation, among other behaviors, which also seems to be associated with memory. Norepinephrine is made in the brain from the amino acid phenylalanine.

Some scientists believe that this chemical triggers long-term memory; when we have an experience that strongly affects us, norepinephrine may tell the brain to save the memory. In studies at the University of California at Irvine, researchers gave rats a shock when they stepped on a shelf. When the rats were placed in the cage weeks later, they remembered not to step on the shelf; when their production of norepinephrine was blocked, however, the rats forgot what they had learned about the shelf and endured repeated shocks.

Alterations in this neurotransmitter also have been implicated in several mental disorders. (See NEUROTRANSMITTERS.) Neurons in the locus coerulus (the source of the forebrain norepinephrine system) appear to alert the forebrain to incoming stimuli such as lights, tones and skin contact; norepinephrine, therefore, could be expected to influence learning and memory.

Minninger, Joan. *Total Recall*. Emmaus, PA: Rodale Press, 1984.

Squire, Larry. *Memory and Brain*. Oxford: Oxford University Press, 1987.

normal pressure hydrocephalus (NPH) Also known as water on the brain this uncommon disorder involves an obstruction in the normal flow of cerebrospinal fluid, causing it to build up in the brain. It is called "normal pressure" hydrocephalus because the pressure in the spinal fluid is normal, unlike most cases of water on the brain.

Symptoms A person with NPH may show all of the symptoms of classic Alzheimer's disease, especially the dementia. However, a computerized tomography (CT) scan will show that the ventricles of the brain are enlarged from an excessive amount of fluid. Other symptoms include urinary incontinence and difficulty in walking. Presently, the most useful diagnostic tools include imaging techniques.

Cause While the exact cause is unknown, NPH may be associated with the interference of circulating fluid in the brain as a result of meningitis, encephalitis or head injuries. It may also be caused by a brain hemorrhage.

Treatment In addition to treating the underlying cause, the condition may be corrected by a neurosurgical procedure called ventricular-atrial shunt, which will divert excess fluid from the brain. About 50 percent of cases are cured with this treatment. Patients whose NPH is caused by a brain hemorrhage or inflammation do not usually benefit from shunting.

Kra, Siegfried. *Aging Myths*. New York: McGraw-Hill, 1986.

nuclear magnetic resonance (NMR) See MAGNETIC RESONANCE IMAGING (MRI).

O

occipital lobes Located in the hind region of the brain, these lobes receive sensory information from the eyes. Damage to the occipital lobes causes blindness.

ondansetron A new drug that increases the release of ACETYLCHOLINE, a neurotransmitter in the brain linked to improved learning and memory. Acetylcholine deficits often are found in most forms of memory impairment. By selectively blocking serotonin, a brain substance that inhibits the release of acetylcholine, ondansetron increases acetylcholine release and enhances memory and performance, according to some research.

According to Glaxo, the British drug company that manufactures ondansetron, the drug increases acetylcholine only in parts of the brain concerned with memory; this fact might eliminate the side effects associated with acetylcholine release in other parts of the body.

Initial research suggests that drugs like ondansetron may improve memory in some healthy older adults with AGE-ASSOCIATED MEMORY IMPAIRMENT. In one study, memory improvement still occurred after three months of ondansetron administration on tests of immediate and delayed name-face recall. In studies of 250 subjects with age-associated memory impairment sponsored by Glaxo, 12 weeks treatment significantly improved the patients memories as compared to a placebo. The extent of the improvement in memory function was about equivalent to the amount of memory that is lost every six years with aging.

Other studies have found that ondansetron improves memory and learning ability in marmosets, rats, mice and primates. In some studies, scientists first injected SCOPOLAMINE to induce memory impairment and then employed ondansetron to reverse the cognitive deficits. Still other studies are investigating another serotonin antagonist, ZATOSETRON, available in tablet form in England and suspected to improve cognition in older adults with age-associated memory impairment. (See also MEMORY ENHANCEMENT.)

The drug (trade name: Zofran) is approved by the Food and Drug Administration for use only as an antiemetic (antivomiting/nausea) medication for use following chemotherapy.

Carey, C.J., et al. "Ondansetron and Arecoline Prevent Scopolamine-induced Cognitive Deficits in the Marmoset." *Pharmacology, Biochemistry of Behavior* 42, no. 1 (1992): 75–83.

optical aphasia   The inability to name the object that one sees. Recognition survives, because if a victim of optical aphasia sees a bowl of soup she can lick her lips or smile, but she cannot name what she sees. And other recognition survives, so that if she can taste or smell the soup, she can name it; it is only the visual recognition that is lacking. (See also APHASIA.)

oral traditions   The memory feats of storytellers and singers in nonliterate societies are impressive; these memory experts do not recite verbatim, letter-perfect tales, but they provide reconstructions according to formulaic rules. The storyteller introduces new ingredients to suit the current audience while adhering to a traditional structure. In oral traditions long stories usually are told in verse instead of prose because the rhythm makes verse easier to remember. Storytellers also make use of group chanting to aid retrieval.

organic amnesia   Amnesia due to brain dysfunction. Organic memory disorders can be either global or specific; that is, they can affect either a large part of memory (global) or only particular memory bits (specific).

organic brain syndrome   A disturbance of consciousness, intellect or mental functioning of physical (organic) as opposed to psychiatric origin. Possible causes include degenerative diseases such as ALZHEIMER'S DISEASE, metabolic imbalances, infections, drugs, toxins, vitamin deficiencies or the effects of brain trauma, stroke or tumor.

In the acute phase of the condition, symptoms can range from a slight confusion to stupor or coma and may include disorientation, memory impairment, hallucinations and delusions. The chronic form of the syndrome causes a progressive decline in intellect, memory and behavior.

Treatment is more likely to be successful with the acute form of organic brain syndrome if the underlying cause can be identified; in chronic cases irreversible brain damage may already have occurred. (See also BRAIN TUMOR.)

organic mental disorders   The generic name for a group of mental disorders with a known or presumed organic cause, such as alcohol withdrawal delirium and multi-infarct dementia. Physicians generally make a distinction between organic mental disorders and ORGANIC MENTAL SYNDROMES, whose origins are unknown.

organic mental syndromes   A cluster of psychological or behavioral signs and symptoms with unknown cause, but associated with brain dysfunction.

A person could be diagnosed with an organic mental syndrome upon admission to the hospital with delirium or dementia from an unknown cause. These symptoms could be due to a stroke, substance abuse, poisoning, brain tumor or neurological disease.

Once the source of brain dysfunction is discovered, the problem is rediagnosed as an ORGANIC MENTAL DISORDER.

organization and memory   Organizing material so it is easier to learn and remember is one of the best ways to improve the memory. In fact, this is such an effective strategy that many people spontaneously organize material as they memorize it.

When researchers gave a list of 24 pairs of scrambled words that were actually highly associated (such as "sleep" and "dream" or "cart" and "horse"), despite the scrambling subjects tended to recall the words in associated pairs. But when information has no inherent organization, subjects often will impose their own subjective organization. That is, they will remember a list of words in order, even though there is no logical reason to do so.

In fact, it is easier to learn any facts if there is some link between them, so that remembering one word automatically drags along its link (called "cueing"). In addition,

our ability to learn is based on what we already know about the subject.

The importance of organization rises as the information to be learned becomes more detailed and complex. While learning a simple list of words is not too difficult, digesting and understanding the contents of a book chapter is more difficult. One approach, according to memory experts, is to imagine a tree and place the organization of the book chapter on that tree.

orientation reaction   The Russian physiologist Ivan Pavlov was the first to describe the sudden arousal of orientation reaction, in which trained dogs would turn to investigate a new person entering a room instead of behaving properly. This "investigative" behavior (what Pavlov called the what-is-it reaction) has biological significance for survival, he believed.

Arousal usually changes to fear, aggression or indifference—usually indifference, which means that on the level of factual memory, we have decided the stimulus is not worth paying attention to. (See also PAVLOV, IVAN PETROVICH.)

overlearning   An important aid to LONG-TERM MEMORY, overlearning is what occurs when a person remembers something over a long period of time despite the fact that it no longer serves any useful purpose (such as a person's childhood phone number). Overlearning occurs when information has been thoroughly memorized first, and then periodically rehearsed, even though it is already well known. (See also REHEARSAL.)

oxiracetam   One of a class of nootropic drugs and an analog of PIRACETAM. Findings from a variety of studies suggest that oxiracetam enhances vigilance and attention, with some effects on spontaneous memory and improvements in concentration.

In one Italian mice study, researchers assessing the drug's potential for birth defects gave pregnant mice oxiracetam from the beginning of their pregnancies until birth. But instead of toxicity, the drug appeared to benefit the offspring of the treated mothers. These offspring—which had never received oxiracetam directly—showed signs of being more curious at one month of age than the offspring of controls that had received a placebo. At three months, the treated offspring performed significantly better in memory tests than the control offspring.

In a test of 272 humans, demented patients who received oxiracetam showed significant improvements in memory and concentration after three months of therapy.

Oxiracetam currently is being investigated for the treatment of Alzheimer's disease at a number of centers around the country, but it is not currently available in the United States for other than experimental use. (See also MEMORY ENHANCEMENT.)

Itil, T.M., et al. "CNS Pharmacology and Clinical Therapeutic Effects of Oxiracetam." In *Clinical Neuropharmacology*, vol. 9, suppl. 3. New York: Raven Press, 1986.
Maina, G., et al. "Oxiracetam in the Treatment of Primary Degenerative and Multi-infarct Dementia: A Double-blind, Placebo-controlled Study." *Neuropsychobiology* 21, no. 3 (1989): 141–45.

P

paired-associate learning   A type of test that assesses the retention of novel information. In the test, a subject is given a list of word pairs to learn. The next day he is shown one word from each pair and told to supply the missing words.

Pappenheim, Bertha   See ANNA O.

paramnesia   Errors of memory. The term was introduced by German psychiatrist Emil Kraepelin in 1886, who divided paramnesia into three main types: simple memory decep-

tions (when a patient remembers a hallucination or imagination as real); associative memory deceptions, or reduplicative paramnesia (when a patient fails to recognize well-known people or places, believing that doubles have replaced them); and identifying paramnesia, or DÉJÀ VU (in which a new situation is experienced as duplicating an earlier situation in every detail). (See also AGNOSIA; CAPGRAS SYNDROME.)

parietal lobes   The parts of the cerebral brain hemispheres that are covered by parietal bones. The parietal lobes, together with the upper temporal and OCCIPITAL LOBES, seem to serve as a short-term memory bank for auditory, visual and motion perception impulses. (See also TEMPORAL LOBES.)

Parkinson's disease   A brain disorder that causes muscle tremor, stiffness and weakness; there is evidence that motor deficits may be accompanied by cognitive problems including poor memory. It was first described by physician James Parkinson (1755–1824) of London.

Parkinson's disease is caused by atrophy of nerve cells in the BASAL GANGLIA of the brain and a resulting decrease in activity of the neurotransmitter dopamine. About one in 200 people (mostly elderly) are affected by the disease, with 50,000 new cases each year. Incidence of Parkinson's disease is lower among women and smokers.

Symptoms   Parkinson's disease usually begins with slight tremor, followed by a stiff, shuffling walk, trembling, a rigid stoop and a fixed expression. The intellect is unaffected until late in the disease, although speech may become slow; depression is common.

Diagnosis   Symptoms mimic a wide range of other disorders, including adverse drug reactions, carbon monoxide poisoning, stroke, head injury and brain tumors. While initial symptoms are so mild they may be easily overlooked, as the disease progresses it becomes so clear-cut that a physician may be able to diagnose the condition by a simple examination. However, other possible disorders may be excluded via tests in computerized tomography (CT) or magnetic resonance imaging (MRI) scans or blood work.

Treatment   Although there is no cure for Parkinson's disease, physicians usually prescribe exercise, special aids and encouragement. Drugs may minimize symptoms but cannot halt the degeneration of the brain. LEVODOPA (L-dopa), which the body converts into dopamine, is usually the most effective drug and is often the first one tried. But the beneficial effects of L-dopa often wear off suddenly; when this occurs, another drug may be given for several weeks, followed by the reintroduction of L-dopa. Other drugs sometimes prescribed to treat this disorder include bromocriptine and amantadine.

Patients also may receive anticholinergics; however, patients who exhibit dementia have been shown to have a deficiency in their cholinergic system. The use of anticholinergics can worsen their symptoms of the dementia.

Sometimes a surgical operation on the brain may reduce the tremor and rigidity, but the procedure is reserved for young, active sufferers who are otherwise in good health.

Without treatment, the disease progresses over 10 to 15 years to severe weakness and incapacity; about one-third of patients eventually go on to develop dementia. Experiments with transplants of dopamine-replacing fetal adrenal tissue are now being conducted.

Pavlov, Ivan Petrovich (1849–1936)
A Russian physiologist best known for his development of the theory of the conditioned reflex. In his classic experiments, he trained dogs to salivate when they heard a bell previously associated with food. This is his best example of an after-the-fact association (when one thing reminds a person or animal of a second thing and the creature responds as if to the second thing). Pavlov developed a similar concept (emphasizing the importance of conditioning) in his pioneering studies of human behavior and the nervous system.

The eldest son of the village priest, Pavlov attended theological seminaries in his native Russia, then in 1870 abandoned his ideas of entering the priesthood to enter the University of St. Petersburg to study chemistry and physiology. After receiving his medical degree, he began his first independent research into the physiology of the circulatory system. He married a student and friend of the author Fyodor Dostoyevsky, and he later attributed all of his success to his brilliant wife. While studying digestion he began to formulate his ideas about conditioned reflexes, widening his theories by 1930 to explain human psychoses in these terms. He believed that the excessive inhibition characteristic of a psychotic patient served to protect him or her from injurious stimuli that earlier had caused excess stimulation.

Pavlov also believed that sleep reflected a widespread inhibitory process in the brain, and concluded that hypnosis is a similar state.

peg words   A type of mnemonic strategy in which items to be remembered are mentally "pegged" to (associated with) certain images in a prearranged order. (See PEG WORD SYSTEM.)

peg word system   A type of VISUAL IMAGERY technique for improving learning in which a standard set of peg words are learned and items to be remembered are linked to the pegs with visual imagery. The system can be traced to the mid-1600s, when it was developed by Henry Herdson, who linked a digit with any one of several objects that resembled the number (for example, 1 = candle, 3 = trident).

The peg system gets its name from the fact that the peg words act as mental "pegs" or hooks on which a person hangs the information that needs to be remembered. It is probably one of the most famous mnemonic devices, popular with entertainers and students of memory training. The peg word system gets its name from the "pegs" on which a person hangs unrelated words or ideas that need to be remembered. The peg words help organize material that needs to be remembered, and act as reminders to recall that material.

The best known of the peg methods is the "rhyming-peg method" in which numbers from one to ten are associated with rhymes: one-bun, two-shoe, three-tree, four-door, five-hive, etc. The first item to be remembered is linked with a bun, the second with a shoe, the third with a tree, and so on. When the list needs to be remembered, the pegs are called up first and then the mental images that are linked to those pegs are recalled. This system was introduced in England about 1879 by John Sambrook.

The rhyming scheme is easy to learn, and many people already know many of the rhymes from the nursery rhyme "One-two, buckle my shoe." When learning the rhyming method, each peg word noun should be imagined as vividly as possible: The bun should be a sesame seed bun, a hot cross bun, a toasted and buttered bun. The tree should be specific—an oak, a spindly pine tree, a birch.

1. One is a bun
2. Two is a shoe
3. Three is a tree
4. Four is a door
5. Five is a hive
6. Six are sticks
7. Seven is heaven
8. Eight is a gate
9. Nine is a vine
10. Ten is a hen

The object that each word represents should be visualized; then a picture of each word (bun, shoe, etc.) is drawn. The act of drawing helps to fix the words in the mind, creating a strong mental association between the numbers and the words that rhyme with them.

If a person had a list of groceries to remember, the grocery names could simply be attached to the pegs. To remember ten items, such as peas, pork chops, milk, bread, eggs, butter, tomatoes, soap, peanut butter and swiss cheese, a person would visualize the list of rhyming words, making them as vivid and ridiculous as possible.

The first item *(peas)* would be visualized wearing leotards and tap shoes, tap dancing on a bun. To remember *(pork chops),* a person might think of a pig in tennis shoes. The sillier the image, the more easily it will be recalled. The peg words can be used over and over; with each new list, the previous words will be erased. Each peg is a clue to an association with the item, and to recall the item, all that has to be remembered is the peg.

The phonetic-peg system is more flexible than the rhyming system, but also more complex. This system relies on the relationship between numbers and their consonant sounds; "0" is remembered as "Z" (the first sound in "zero"); "1" is remembered as "T" (both 1 and T have one downstroke). In addition, each sound is remembered as a word; 1 ("T") is also remembered as "ties," and 2 ("N") is remembered as "Noah."

While many people consider the phonetic-peg system as too cumbersome and difficult to bother to learn, it has been used successfully with brain-damaged patients. In at least one study, four out of seven patients with severe verbal-memory problems were helped to learn experimental material and practical information with the system, although it took a long time to learn the system. Others believe that the system may be of some help to those with mild head injuries, but would probably not help those with more severe memory impairments.

There are still other peg word systems. Peg words can be selected on the basis of meaning: 1 = me (there is only one me), 3 = pitchfork (three prongs), 5 = hand (five fingers).

The system is limited, however, in that it is hard to find good peg words to represent numbers beyond ten.

Numbers make a good peg system because they are naturally ordered and everyone knows them. For this reason, the alphabet also makes a good peg system. In order to make the letters concrete, each of them either rhymes with the letter of the alphabet it represents or has the letter as the initial sound of the word. An example of an alphabet peg system would be: A-hay, B-bee, C-sea.

The peg system is similar to paired-associate learning except that the learners provide their own peg words. In a variety of research studies, people have been able to use the peg system effectively on lists up to 40 words. It can also be used to help form concepts in tasks requiring high memory demands, remembering ideas, etc.

Peg words are helpful in remembering lists for shopping or errands, in organizing activities and in giving people a sense of being in control. (See also LOCI, METHOD OF; PHONETIC SYSTEM OF MNEMONICS; REHABILITATION OF MEMORY; VISUAL-IMAGERY METHOD; VISUAL-PEG SYSTEM.)

Gose, Kathleen, and Levi, Gloria. *Dealing with Memory Changes as You Grow Older*. New York: Bantam Books, 1988.

Higbee, Kenneth. *Your Memory*. New York: Prentice-Hall, 1988.

Penfield, Wilder (1891–1976) The Canadian surgeon who discovered during the 1950s that stimulating various areas of the cortex produced a range of responses from patients; however, only stimulation of the temporal lobes elicited meaningful, integrated experiences, including sound, movement and color. Interestingly, some of these memories that popped up during stimulation were not remembered in the normal state. Furthermore, the memories Penfield stimulated appeared to be far more detailed, accurate and specific than normal recall.

Penfield did not set out to study memory; he wanted to reduce seizures in epileptic patients by removing the damaged tissue in the brain that triggered the seizures. Penfield knew that the seizures always were preceded by a "mental aura" (a warning sensation the patient experiences before a seizure). He hoped to open the skull of fully conscious patients, moving a stimulating electrode across the brain to deliver a weak electrical shock to various areas to find the site that produced the mental aura. If he found such a site, he reasoned, he could destroy it and end the seizures.

While his technique was often successful, his discovery of the ability to stimulate memories radically altered ideas popular at the time of how the brain worked. Stimulating one side of the brain brought back a certain song to one patient, the memory of a moment in a garden listening to a mother calling her child. Interestingly, stimulating the same point elicited the same memory every time. It seemed that Penfield had found an engram—the site in the brain where memory was stored.

As a result of his findings, Penfield believed that the brain makes a permanent record of every item to which a person pays conscious attention, although this record may be forgotten during day-to-day life. (See also HOLOGRAM THEORY OF MEMORY.)

personal memory All the happenings and occurrences that make up a person's own life history—everything from the first day of school to the most important moment of one's life. This type of memory brings together all the sense impressions and emotions that make up a continuous life, recording all the changes and happenings that make up a person's inner and outer worlds.

Because personal memory is recording a constant flow of change, it doesn't retain many details. And with increasing age, memory problems are often those of recent personal memory. (Personal memory from the past is likely to be intact.)

For most people, their general knowledge memory (where the sun sets, who is president of the United States) as well as memory from their early life is well organized and stable because it has been rehearsed over and over for a long period of time. Because it is history, it has remained unchanged. On the other hand, information from the recent personal memory (lunch menu from last Monday) may not be so easy to retrieve, because there has been less opportunity to rehearse it.

PET (positron emission tomography) scan   An imaging technique that creates computerized images of the distribution of radioactively labeled glucose in the brain in order to show brain activity. The more active a part of the brain is, the more glucose it uses.

PET sensors are located around the head of a patient, who sits behind black felt to eliminate distractions. The scan can pinpoint the source of the radioactivity and any corresponding heightened activity. These data are sent to computers that produce two-dimensional drawings showing the neural "hot spots"—areas of the brain that are working the hardest at that particular time. In addition, PET scans of the brains of subjects who have been injected with labeled drugs that attach to specific receptors can show the distribution and number of those receptors.

While PET scans accurately track brain function and provide the first pictures of a working brain, they also have drawbacks; principally, they can't be used for high-quality visualizations of brain structures, since they can't resolve brain structures less than .5 inches apart. (See also BRAIN SCANS; COMPUTERIZED TOMOGRAPHY (CT) SCAN; MAGNETIC RESONANCE IMAGING; SQUID; SPECT.)

Peter of Ravenna (Petrus Tommai)   The Italian author of *The Phoenix* (1491), the best known of all early memory-training books, which brought the art of memory training into general knowledge. The book was extremely popular, reprinted in many editions and translations, and made Peter of Ravenna's name known throughout all of Europe's educated classes for a century. Many other books on the subject followed during the next two centuries.

In his book, Peter gives practical advice to everyday people, full of details such as how to choose a building to establish the method of loci. He is said to have been able to accomplish astonishing feats of memory, including repeating 300 philosophical sayings, 200 speeches of Cicero and 20,000 legal points. (See also LOCI, METHOD OF.)

Petrarch (Francesco Petrarca) (1304–1374)   An Italian scholar and poet and an important authority on ARTIFICIAL MEMORY, who wrote "Things to Be Remembered" (Rerum memorandarum libri) in the mid-1300s.

phenylalanine   An amino acid from which the brain manufactures norepinephrine, which plays a major role in learning and memory. Phenylalanine is contained in cheese, milk, eggs and meats, and some research is investigating whether this substance might boost or sharpen memory. (See also MEMORY ENHANCEMENT.)

phenytoin   See DILANTIN.

phonetic mnemonic   One of the most sophisticated and versatile of all the mnemonic systems, this "mental filing system" is better than the PEG WORD SYSTEM because it allows construction of more than ten to 20 peg words. Other names for this system include number-alphabet, hook, number-consonant, digit-letter, number-to-sound and figure-alphabet. In the system, each of the digits from 0 to 9 is represented by a consonant sound; these consonant sounds are then combined with vowels to code numbers into words, which are more meaningful—which makes them easier to remember than numbers.

The phonetic mnemonic system was first developed more than 300 years ago by Winckelmann, who introduced a digit-letter

Digit-Sound Equivalents of the Phonetic System

Digit	Consonant Sound	Memory Aid
1	t, th, d	"t" has one downstroke
2	n	two downstrokes
3	m	three downstrokes
4	r	last sound for the word four in several languages
5	l	Roman numeral for 50 is "L"
6	j, sh, ch, soft g	reversed script "j" resembles 6
7	k, q, hard c, hard g	"k" made of two 7s
8	f, v	script "f" resembles 8
9	p, b	"p" is mirror image of 9
10	z, s, soft c	"z" for "zero"

system where the digits were represented by letters of the alphabet. His system was refined and then published by Richard Grey in 1730.

In these early systems, both consonants and vowels represented digits and the letters representing each digit were chosen arbitrarily. The mnemonic was further refined in 1813 by Gregor von Feinaigle, who chose to represent digits by consonants only—vowels had no numerical value. Further, the consonants were not selected arbitrarily, but were selected on the basis of their similarity to or association with the digits they represented. So "t" became a "1" because of the physical similarity; "n" is "2" because it has two downstrokes, and so on.

The system was modified still further during the 19th century. By the end of the 1800s, it had evolved into its present form. William James briefly described it in his psychology textbook written in the 1890s; the digits were represented not by consonants themselves but by consonant sounds. This version has remained basically the same in memory books and courses through the 20th century.

In the phonetic system, the consonant sounds are important, not the letters themselves. Different letters or letter combinations can take on the same sounds. For example, the "sh" sound can be made by the "c" in ocean or the "s" in sugar.

Each digit is represented by only one sound or family of similar sounds. Further, all of the consonant sounds in the English language are included, except for "w," "h" and "y," which can be remembered easily by the word "why."

When a repeated consonant makes only one sound, it counts as only one digit (mutton is 312, not 3112). A silent consonant is disregarded, because it has no value if it isn't heard when pronouncing a word.

phonetic system of mnemonics   A sophisticated, versatile mnemonic system that is more flexible than the rhyming peg system, but also more complex. This system relies on the relationship between numbers and their consonant sounds; "0" is remembered as "Z" (the first sound in "zero"); "1" is remembered as "T" (both 1 and T have one downstroke). In addition, each sound is remembered as a word; 1 ("T") is also remembered as "ties," and 2 ("N") is remembered as "Noah."

The technique is superior to the PEG SYSTEM because it allows construction of more than 10 to 20 peg words, yet it retains the peg system's advantage of direct retrieval.

This system has been referred to by a variety of names, including figure-alphabet, digit-letter, number-alphabet, hook, number-consonant and number-to-sound. It was developed more than 300 years ago when

Winckelmann introduced a digit-letter system in which the digits were represented by letters of the alphabet. These letters were used to form words to represent a given number sequence. In the early systems, the digits were represented by both consonants and vowels, but in 1813 Gregor von Feinaigle refined the system so that digits were represented by consonants that were selected on the basis of their similarity to or association with the digits they represented. The system was further refined during the 1800s, and by the end of the nineteenth century it had evolved into its present form—represented not by consonants but by consonant sounds.

While many people consider the phonetic-peg system too cumbersome and difficult to learn, it has been used successfully with brain-damaged patients. In at least one study, four out of seven patients with severe verbal-memory problems were helped to learn experimental material and practical information, although it took them a long time to learn the system. Although some researchers believe that the system may be of some help to those with mild head injuries, the phonetic-peg method probably would not help those with more severe memory impairments.

phosphatidylserine A component of brain cell membranes that keeps fatty substances soluble and cell membranes fluid; some studies suggest it also seems to boost brain glucose metabolism and increase the number of neurotransmitter receptor sites.

It appears that memory improvements last as long as one month after administration of phosphatidylserine. In one study of the substance on 149 subjects with AGE-ASSOCIATED MEMORY IMPAIRMENT, those on the drug improved on a series of tests designed to measure performance related to learning and memory tasks; those who had functioned worst initially improved the most. It also has been reported that phosphatidylserine

alleviated depression in some elderly patients.

A U.S. study of 51 Alzheimer's patients showed that improvements in cognitive performance were strongest among those who had the least cognitive problems to start with.

Amaducci, L. "Phosphatidylserine in the Treatment of Alzheimer's Disease: Results of a Multicenter Study." *Psychopharmacology Bulletin* 24 (1988): 130–34.

Amaducci, L., et al. "Use of Phosphatidylserine in Alzheimer's Disease." *Annals of the New York Academy of Science* 640 (1991): 245–49.

Crook, T.H., et al. "Effects of Phosphatidylserine in Alzheimer's Disease." *Psychopharmacology Bulletin* 28 (1992): 61–66.

Crook, T.H., et al. "Effects of Phosphatidylserine in Age-associated Memory Impairment." *Neurology* 41 (May 1991): 644–49.

photographic memory The long-term persistence of mental imagery, technically known as eidetic memory. (See also EIDETIC IMAGERY.)

phrenology The belief that there is a relationship between mental abilities and physical appearance. Phrenology, which became popular in psychiatric circles in the early 1800s, was popularized by Franz Joseph Gall. He believed that the structure of the skull was related to structural characteristics of the brain. Gall came up with this theory based on his observation that students with good memories often had prominent eyes. He traveled to hospitals, schools, prisons and asylums in search of people with either exceptional talents or terrible disabilities to test his theories. All his life, he insisted that observing the bumps on the skull was virtually the same thing as looking at the brain itself.

While much of his theory was baseless, it did introduce the then-radical idea that the mind was primarily based in the brain.

physiological causes of memory loss
Because the brain is susceptible to fluctuat-

ing levels of fluids, oxygen and nutrients, anything that affects the physiological health of the body may affect memory systems as well.

Fluid Imbalances Too much or too little water in the body can disturb brain function, because water contains electrolytes (potassium, sodium, chloride, calcium and magnesium) that are crucial to the function of cells that make up the memory system.

Hypoglycemia Because brain cells require an adequate amount of sugar (glucose) to maintain metabolic activity, a drop in the body's blood sugar level can lead to a host of memory problems.

Malnutrition Dementing brain disease can be produced by a diet that lacks enough of the B-complex vitamins (especially NIACIN, thiamine and B_{12}). This is one reason behind the memory problems of serious alcohol abusers, who typically lack thiamine because they don't eat properly. Vegetarians who don't get enough vitamin B_{12} also may experience symptoms of memory deficits; recent research suggests that those with low-normal levels of B_{12} in their blood tend to experience depression with memory problems. A more serious lack of this vitamin can lead to spinal cord degeneration and associated brain diseases, including memory loss.

physostigmine A drug used as eye drops in the treatment of glaucoma (high pressure in the eyeballs). Researchers have shown that administration of physostigmine may produce mild improvement in memory loss among ALZHEIMER'S DISEASE patients. In addition, in normal subjects physostigmine reverses memory loss following the administration of SCOPOLAMINE.

In one study, scientists tested physostigmine with 20 Alzheimer's patients as they performed a "famous faces" test, digit span and recognition of verbal and pictorial information. Physostigmine enhanced performance on the recognition task but not on the

"famous faces" or digit span tests. These findings are similar to others that found only a modest improvement in memory with physostigmine.

One drawback to the drug is that it has a very narrow therapeutic window (that is, the dose range over which it has beneficial effects). It works by inhibiting acetylcholinesterase, which breaks down ACETYLCHOLINE, important in a range of memory processes.

Piaget, Jean (1896–1980) The Swiss psychologist who was the first to study the acquisition of understanding in children systematically. Best known for his work on the IQ test, Piaget also wrote *Memory and Intelligence* (1973), based on his ideas about memory in children.

He received his doctorate in zoology in 1918 at the University of Neuchatel (Switzerland) and soon afterward became interested in psychology. He studied psychology under Carl Gustav Jung and Eugen Bleuler, and then began studying at the Sorbonne in Paris in 1919. There he began his work administering reading tests to children. As part of his work in standardizing IQ tests, he noticed that children at certain ages consistently gave the same wrong answer to a particular question. Although most would consider that a wrong answer is simply wrong, Piaget wondered why children gave that particular wrong answer.

As a result, he abandoned IQ research and began studying the qualitative changes in growing children; by the end of his life, he had moved on to the study of memory. As part of his research, he discovered that children's memories for a particular event can improve over time; a child may not remember an event very well after one week but six months later may have a much better memory of the same occurrence.

Piaget taught at the University of Geneva as professor of child psychology until his death; writing more than 50 books and monographs, he continued to develop the theme that the mind of the child evolves through a series of set stages to adulthood.

He believed in the fundamental unity and the common nature of the memory and the intelligence, not only because both pass through the same stages but also because the evolution of the mnemonic code is a direct function of the construction of operational schemata.

Piaget's work shows the interdependence of memory and understanding—the capacity to learn about the present implies a capacity to learn about the past as well. He believed that memory depends on a person's capacity to construct an experience. He did not believe in a storehouse or file cabinet where memories are preserved; instead, he thought that we construct a memory and remember the construction rather than the original event. When a person recalls items grouped together, they are reorganized because the person has constructed the list in his or her own way.

He tested children's recall for a demonstration in which one rolling ball transferred its energy to a second ball, but the second ball couldn't transfer its energy to a third. The age at which children correctly explained this varied, but most could think of some explanation and they remembered something of the experiment that emphasized their own explanation. Piaget believed that memory depends on a capacity to construct an experience. Theories that try to explain memory as retrieval from storage deny that such improvement can happen.

He also studied memory in infancy and believed that mental development begins with sensory and motor associations. His first was the "sensory-motor stage," which lasted for the first two years of life, during which children grow into active toddlers. He believed the child's exploration and remembering was a circular reaction that develops in accordance with the development of emotional memory, beginning with motor associations and progressing to sensory associations.

The best known of the early circular reactions (Piaget called them primary reactions) was thumb sucking, which depended on motor memory; the baby accidentally inserts a thumb, sucks on it and likes the sensation, and therefore repeats it. The repetition of the behavior, Piaget said, occurs because of a remembered motor association (hand motion associated with pleasure).

Secondary circular reactions such as rattle shaking, Piaget believed, depend on sensory memory and appear at about four months of age. The motor activity (shaking) leads to an objective event (rattling), and the sound causes pleasure. Piaget believed that a four-month-old baby's memory already matches or supersedes the memory of most animals.

As children grow older, interpreting their mental state becomes more difficult, and this is where Piaget's theories become more controversial. After the first birthday, children begin to speak single words (a sign of factual memory), and they associate things with sounds. By two years, children's vocabulary reflects more than factual memory—they can form sentences, showing an ability for complex factual association.

Pick disease   A type of dementia almost impossible to distinguish from ALZHEIMER'S DISEASE except on autopsy, although it occurs far less frequently. In Pick disease, brain cells have "Pick's bodies," which consist of a miscellaneous collection of parts of the normal cell. Although the parts are recognizable, their normal relationships have been disrupted.

On average, patients contract this disease at about 55 years, with death following within seven years. New cases of Pick disease are infrequent in patients over mid-50s, there have been only three cases of Pick disease in the United States in patients over 70.

The disorder usually begins in the frontal lobes. Early changes of personality and social behavior take place, instead of the memory changes usually noticed in Alzheimer's disease patients, although these will eventually follow. Some patients become mute. The spatial problems often seen in Alzheimer's disease are not usually present in early stages of Pick disease, although they will develop eventually.

Wilson, Barbara. *Rehabilitation of Memory*. New York: Guilford Press, 1988.

piracetam   A drug belonging to a group of drugs called NOOTROPICS; piracetam appears to improve the learning ability of animals and protect against memory loss in the absence of oxygen (ANOXIA) by improving the transmission of impulses between neurons. In addition, some studies indicate that mixing piracetam with CHOLINE may boost the brain's metabolism and improve memory function.

In a recent study of 84 geriatric patients with nonvascular senile cognitive deterioration, piracetam was found to be better than a placebo at enhancing several cognitive abilities, including attention, memory and behavior, especially at doses of 6 grams per day.

Scientists are studying how piracetam works; it may stimulate glucose metabolism, enhance phospholipid levels or protein biosynthesis, or increase cholinergic and dopaminergic stimulation.

When older mice were given piracetam for two weeks, scientists discovered they had a 30 to 45 percent higher density of receptors for choline in the frontal cortex than before. According to the study authors, this also could explain why mixing choline with piracetam enhances its memory attributes. Researchers concluded that piracetam, unlike other drugs, appears to have a regenerative effect on the nervous system. While piracetam is derived from the neurotransmitter GABA (gamma aminobutyric acid), there is no evidence that piracetam works through the GABAergic system; in fact, some research suggests that the GABA system may inhibit memory.

Piracetam also seems to produce resistance to several neurotoxic substances and stimulate learning through influences on the hippocampus and cortex while enhancing oxygen utilization.

Outside the United States, piracetam is used to treat alcoholism, stroke, vertigo, senile dementia, sickle-cell anemia, dyslexia and a wide variety of other health problems. It is not available in the United States.

Bartus, R.T., et al. "Profound Effects of Combining Choline and Piracetam on Memory Enhancement and Cholinergic Function in Aged Rats." *Neurobiology of Aging* 2 (1981): 105–11.

Bylinsky, G. "Medicine's Next Marvel: The Memory Pill." *Fortune*, January 20, 1986.

Friedman, E., et al. "Clinical Response to Choline Plus Piracetam in Senile Dementia: Relation to Red-cell Choline Levels." *New England Journal of Medicine* 24 (1981): 1490–1.

Plato (428/427 B.C.–348/347 B.C.)   An ancient Greek philosopher and developer of a wide-ranging system of ethical philosophy who also believed that memory was the "highest of talents," which allowed him to recall knowledge gained before his own lifetime. Possessing a prodigious memory, he was interested not in the "superficial" field of MNEMONICS but in the very essence of memory itself.

Plato believed that memory was the mother of all arts and that it could lead people back to the realization of their own divinity and wholeness. He also thought that humans have an innate memory of the realities beyond this world—a memory of ideal form. The real art, he believed, is to recover this divine memory and fit sensory impressions into this larger framework. His art of memory, therefore, was really an art of enlightenment.

Pliny the Elder (Gaius Plinius Secundus) (A.D. 23–79)   A Roman savant, author of the celebrated *Natural History*, used as an authoritative review of scientific matters up to the Middle Ages. Pliny, whose son attended QUINTILIAN's rhetoric school, discussed memory in *Natural History* in the form of an anthology of memory stories.

The art of memory was invented by Simonides Melicus, Pliny wrote, and perfected by Metrodorus of Scepsis, who could "repeat what he had heard in the very same words." Pliny went on to catalog a list of luminaries and their feats of memory: Mithridates of Pontus knew all 22 languages that were spoken in his area; Charmadas knew the contents of all the books in a library; Lucius Scipio knew the names of all the Roman people; Cyrus knew the names of all the men in his army.

Pollyanna hypothesis   The Freudian hypothesis (also called hedonic selectivity) that unpleasant memories are harder to remember than pleasant ones. (See also FREUD, SIGMUND; REPRESSION.)

poriomania   An impulsive tendency to wander aimlessly for long periods, usually experienced by epileptics who suffer from complex partial seizures. (See also FUGUE.)

positron emission tomography   See PET (POSITRON EMISSION TOMOGRAPHY) SCAN.

postencephalic amnesia   See ENCEPHALITIS AND MEMORY.

posterior cerebral arteries, infarction of   Stroke originating in the posterior cerebral arteries. Patients who have had infarctions of the posterior cerebral arteries (stroke) may experience problems in short-term memory, inability to learn new facts and skills and RETROGRADE AMNESIA. Often memory problems are associated with visual-field defects. (See also CEREBROVASCULAR ACCIDENTS [CVAS]; SUBARACHNOID HEMORRHAGE.)

posthypnotic amnesia   Memory of a hypnotic trance is often vague, similar to how a person remembers a dream upon awakening. While in the hypnotic state, if a subject is told that he will remember nothing upon awakening, he will experience a much more profound posthypnotic amnesia. However, if the subject is rehypnotized and given a countersuggestion, he will awaken and remember everything; therefore, experts believe this phenomenon is clearly psychogenic.

Memory for experiences during the hypnotic state also may return, even following a suggestion to forget, if the subject is questioned persistently upon awakening. This observation led Sigmund Freud to search for repressed memories in his patients without the use of hypnosis. (See also FREUD, SIGMUND.)

posthypnotic suggestions   Instructions or suggestions given in a trance and intended to be carried out at a later date after awakening from the hypnotic state. The use of posthypnotic suggestions offers extensive opportunities for directing and guiding behavior without depending on immediate guidance or relationships.

The phenomenon can be used to control weight or stop smoking, for example, by giving a hypnotized subject a series of suggestions about behavior and feelings in response to food or cigarettes. (See also HYPNOSIS; SUGGESTIBILITY.)

posttraumatic amnesia   See TRAUMATIC AMNESIA.

posttraumatic stress disorder   A disorder that can occur after any life-threatening traumatic event that threatens a person's existence. Posttraumatic stress disorder (PTSD) can leave long-lasting scars, including anger, guilt, insomnia, loss of appetite, extreme fatigue, recurrent dreams, nightmares, hypersensitivity and—above all—memory loss and concentration problems.

Recent research has found that many patients with PTSD can develop memory problems that are equivalent to the classic signs of ALZHEIMER'S DISEASE. While eventually (over a period of years) the memory problems may improve, symptoms also are greatly relieved with antidepressants and psychotherapy.

In addition, recent research suggests that excessive and prolonged sensitizing stimulation may lead to changes in the synapses and an oversensitivity to certain stimuli. When scientists exposed 18 PTSD sufferers to 30 seconds of combat sounds while under the influence of anesthetic pentobarbital, 14 immediately reexperienced a Vietnam combat experience with intense emotional fear, rage, indignation, sadness and guilt. (See also COMBAT AMNESIA.)

posture Good posture can pay off with sharper memories, according to research. When the upper body sags, rounding the shoulders, hanging the head and jutting out the chin, it creates kinks in the spine that squeeze the two arteries passing through the spinal column to the brain. These kinks cause an inadequate blood supply, resulting in "fuzzy thinking" and forgetfulness—especially in older people.

potentiation An increase in the intensity of a behavioral response that occurs after a stimulus has been repeated many times. Learning that a particular stimulus poses a threat, the subject becomes more aroused each time the stimulus is presented. Potentiation is the opposite of HABITUATION.

PQRST method One type of memory technique widely used as a study method in trying to remember facts. This acronym stands for "Preview, Question, Read, State and Test."

Preview Preview (skim through briefly) the material that must be remembered.

Question Ask important questions about the information. "What are the primary points in the text? How does the action occur? Who is involved?"

Read Read the material completely.

State State answers to key questions.

Test Perform self-test often to ensure the information has been retained.

While the method was developed as a study technique, it also has been reported to be of at least some benefit for memory-impaired patients to acquire new information.

Researchers suggest that this method might work better than simple REHEARSAL because it provides better retrieval cues. It also may employ the idea of ENCODING SPECIFICITY; that is, a person may remember better if the recall situation is similar to the situation during original learning. With the PQRST method, subjects may be able to answer questions about material because the questions themselves were part of the original learning experience.

Researchers also suggest that the method may work because of the LEVELS-OF-PROCESSING; that is, that deeper processing leads to better retention. PQRST appears to involve deeper processing than simple rehearsal because subjects must think about what they are listening to in order to complete each PQRST step. On the other hand, rehearsal doesn't require so much thought. (Subjects just listen and repeat back.)

To use the PQRST method, scientists suggest that ideally subjects should make up their own questions, since this will lead to better retention.

Glasgow, R.E., et al. "Case Studies on Remediating Memory Deficits in Brain-damaged Individuals." *Journal of Clinical Psychology* 33 (1977): 1049–54.

practice and memory To retain information in the memory, the material must be practiced before it is firmly entrenched. The question that has plagued researchers is whether learning is most effective with practice in short, concentrated bursts or spread over a long period of time.

The effects of "massed" versus "distributed" practice has been studied for many years, and scientists have concluded that distributed practice is more effective in memorizing information.

While repetition improves memorization, spacing repetitions is far more effective than repeating recalled items immediately. Some researchers believe that immediate and spaced repetition produces differently encoded memory traces. Immediately repeating information may cause the subject to perform exactly the same encoding operations when the information is repeated. But when repetition is delayed, the first presentation is less accessible and the second encoding is probably different. This encoding variability hypothesis stresses that the more differently information is encoded, the more easily it will be remembered because there are more ways the information can be accessed during retrieval.

pramiracetam   This nootropic drug enhances the functioning of the cholinergic system in much the same way as its relative, PIRACETAM, but it is effective at much lower doses. (See NOOTROPICS.) In one study, subjects with ALZHEIMER'S DISEASE showed enhanced intelligence and memory following administration of pramiracetam. However, the drug is not available in the United States.

preconscious   The initial momentary impressions made by sensory stimuli.

pregnancy and memory   Many women experience memory lapses during pregnancy, probably because of emotional and hormonal conditions—although, because of a lack of studies, scientists don't really know why.

The physical symptoms that occur during pregnancy (such as nausea and fatigue) can be emotionally disruptive and could cause forgetfulness. Also, the powerful hormonal changes that take place during pregnancy alter the brain's chemistry, which could reduce the capacity for remembering.

The situation is not permanent, however; women who experience memory loss during pregnancy usually report that the problem fades away a few weeks after delivery at the latest.

pregnenolone   A simple steroid that, in recent research trials, seems to enhance memory in rats and restore normal levels of memory hormones (such as ACETYLCHOLINE) that decline during aging. The steroid also facilitates rats' ability to remember learned tasks, according to scientists at the City of Hope Medical Center in Los Angeles and St. Louis Veterans Administration Medical Center in Missouri. The drug has been tested in humans as a treatment for arthritis and was found to produce no side effects.

Pregnenolone is one of several steroid drugs researchers are investigating for possible memory enhancement properties; among the most promising is DHEA (dehydroepiandrosterone), although research trials are not yet complete. It is produced from the metabolism of cholesterol in the body and then converted into all of the other steroid hormones. However, the naturally occurring form of the hormone is not known to have any effects at all.

One study has looked at the administration of pregnenolone and other steroids in mice trained to avoid having their feet shocked; researchers found that virtually all of the steroids significantly reduced the number of runs needed for the mice to relearn the footshock avoidance after a week off from training, and pregnenolone was effective at lower doses than any other compound. But scientists could not identify any relationship between the different steroids and memory-enhancing activity; the mechanism by which steroids influence memory and learning remains little understood.

The hormone was used during the 1940s to treat rheumatoid arthritis, but was aban-

doned when physicians discovered that cortisone was far more effective.

Scientists suggest pregnenolone might enhance memory because it serves as a raw
material for the production of all steroid
hormones used in storing information in
memory. Concentrations of many of these
steroids decline with age; by restoring these
levels, pregnenolone may bring back memory abilities that had begun to erode.

Neurologists in California are currently
studying pregnenolone's effects on Alzheimer's disease patients with mild to severe
memory problems and older people with
age-related memory impairment.

Maugh, Thomas H., 2nd. "Steroid Found to Aid
Memory in Lab Mice; Human Tests Planned."
Los Angeles Times, March 21, 1992.

premorbid period   The period of time
before injury or damage to the brain.

presenile dementia   In the past, this was
the other name for ALZHEIMER'S DISEASE,
used to differentiate it from the SENILE DE-
MENTIA that affects elderly people. However, most experts now believe that this
division is based on age only and that the
two forms of dementia really reflect the
same disease.

primacy effect   The tendency for the first
words on a list to be recalled better than any
of the others. While the first words on a list
are usually recalled best, the last few words
are usually recalled almost as easily (RE-
CENCY EFFECT), while the words in the middle are usually forgotten.

It is possible to disrupt the recency effect
by requiring the subject to wait a brief time
(as little as 15 seconds) without rehearsing
before recalling the list. After the interlude,
the recency effect has evaporated, while
the first words of the list are still remembered. (See also STORAGE VS. RETRIEVAL
FAILURE.)

primary memory   See SHORT-TERM
MEMORY.

priming   Facilitation of the ability to process a stimulus due to prior presentation of
the stimulus. In other words, a person who
has seen a word, picture or some other
stimulus in the past hour may have no conscious recollection of it, but still will retain
that image in memory.

In an experiment illustrating this phenomenon, a person would be presented with 30
words and then be distracted. After several
minutes, the subject would be given a list
of ten word beginnings and asked to complete the words, saying the first word that
comes to mind. For the word segment
"m-o-t" the subject could reply "motive" or
"motor," but those who had previously been
shown the word "motel" on the list of 30
words would be very likely to recall it,
probably without knowing why. This ability
to recall a word without realizing it had been
stored in memory is evidence of priming.

proactive inhibition   One type of forgetting due to the "interference" phenomenon,
in which material already learned interferes
with the acquisition of new information. It
is "proactive" because the interference is in
a forward direction. In other words, if a
person studied an anatomy textbook chapter
last week and then studied for a physiology
test last night, proactive inhibition would
be taking place if the anatomy terms kept
popping into the person's mind when he or
she tried to recall the physiology terms. (See
also EBBINGHAUS, HERMANN E.; INTERFER-
ENCE THEORY; RETROACTIVE INHIBITION.)

Higbee, Kenneth. *Your Memory.* New York:
Prentice-Hall, 1988.

proactive interference   One of two
forms of interference that results in forgetting, in which older memories impair subsequent learning.

Experts agree that all learning involves the formation of associations; as more learning takes place, some of the new associations have elements in common with those already formed. This interference, called proactive interference, will lead to forgetting.

The other form of interference is retroactive interference, where subsequent learning impairs recall of older memories.

procedural memory   Remembering how to do something, such as typing or solving an algebraic equation. This is the type of memory responsible for skills and habits, which may underlie the simple, unconscious learning that extends from lower animals to humans. Scientists believe there are two basic kinds of memory networks—procedural memory and DECLARATIVE (or factual) MEMORY. (See also HM.)

prosopagnosia   A form of AGNOSIA in which patients have special difficulty recognizing human faces. However, this definition may be too narrow, since these patients also may have problems in recognizing certain other classes of objects, such as species of birds.

protein kinase C (PKC)   A molecule found on the surface membrane of all animal nerve cells; it plays a role in growth, blood clotting and the action of hormones. This molecule was first discovered in the early 1970s by a Japanese scientist.

PKC acts by attaching a phosphate group onto specific sites on the other molecules, changing the function of those molecules, increasing or decreasing their level of activity.

Scientists first realized the potential of PKC in 1986, when Princeton University researchers noted that the protein mimicked cellular changes that occur during learning. Scientists already knew that the electrochemical current in neurons changes as an animal

learns and that a protein requiring calcium is involved.

When researchers realized that a single molecule was responsible for learning and memory, they reasoned that its appearance should coincide with learning and its disappearance would indicate forgetting. Research suggests that PKC orchestrates neuronal functions necessary for learning and memory.

Researchers also have discovered that chemicals that block PKC prevent short-term (but not long-term) memory in snails, which suggests that other mechanisms might be responsible for memories that last more than a few minutes.

Scientists also are investigating the role of PKC in memory disorders such as ALZHEIMER'S DISEASE. One recent study at the University of California at San Diego found that the brains of 11 Alzheimer's victims contained only half as much PKC as the brains of seven people who had died of natural causes.

Ezzel, Carol. "Memories Might Be Made of This." *Science News 139* (May 25, 1991): 328–330.

Proust, Marcel (1871–1922)   The novels of this French writer proved that memories are much more enduring than many of us believe; as he grew older, his childhood memories remained crystal clear. Proust is considered to be the greatest creative writer to explore memory and the mystery of recall. His masterpiece, *Remembrance of Things Past* (1913–27), analyzes memory and exalts the miracle of its mechanism.

The experiences that helped Proust remember were sensory ones—smell, sound and the feel of a certain piece of pavement or the sight of a room, almost physically transporting him backward in time to his childhood. Once amid these memories, he found other memories came rushing back, leading him to conclude that each person can develop the negatives of such memories and bring into focus dim pictures of the past. In fact, Proust believed that the only way to find meaning in life is to see what all one's past experiences really meant.

His rumination on madeleines and tea in *Remembrance of Things Past* provided one of the first clues about the relationship between sensation and recollection:

> One day in winter on my return home, my mother . . . offered me some tea . . . She sent for one of those squat, plump little cakes called "petites Madeleines," and soon after a dreary day . . . I raised to my lips a spoonful of the tea in which I had soaked a morsel of the cake. No sooner had the warm liquid mixed with the crumbs touched my palate than a shudder ran through me and I stopped, intent upon the extraordinary thing that was happening to me. An exquisite pleasure had invaded my senses, something isolated, detached, with no suggestion of its origin. Whence could it have come to me, this all-powerful joy? I sensed that it was connected with the taste of the tea and the cake. . . The taste was that of a little piece of Madeleine which on Sunday mornings at Combray . . . my Aunt Leonie used to give me, dipping it first in her own cup of tea . . .
>
> —*Remembrance of Things Past*

After this passage, Proust wondered about the origin of this memory and what it meant. He takes the rest of the novel to explore that memory and how it might have been formed. (See also PROUSTIAN MOMENT.)

Proustian moment   The experience of a sudden flash of recall of some memory apparently forgotten long ago, taking a person completely by surprise. The term gets its name from famed French writer Marcel Proust, author of *Remembrance of Things Past,* a paean to the miracle of memory.

pseudodementia   A disorder that mimics DEMENTIA but that includes no evidence of brain dysfunction. Although both dementia and severe depression feature memory loss and intellectual impairment, nearly one out of ten of those thought to be suffering from true dementia in fact have a depressive illness. Unlike dementia, depression is treatable; many people respond well to antidepressant drugs. Not surprisingly, pseudodementia is found most often in elderly patients.

Like HYSTERICAL AMNESIA and FUGUE, pseudodementia is a defense reaction. In the elderly, it is believed to be a way of avoiding depression or asking for help. When it occurs after a minor brain injury, it is often linked to the patient's desire to avoid an unpleasant experience.

Pseudodementia also can be found among those patients who have experienced a minor organic brain injury that produces a degree of impairment in excess of what would be expected after recovery. For example, one young patient experienced pseudodementia after being involved in a car accident shortly before he was due to be transferred to a dangerous military post abroad. Unconscious for just two minutes, he showed no signs of neurological problems, but he seemed to have lost his personal identity and had a dense RETROGRADE AMNESIA. He appeared to be unable to perform simple motor skills or recognize objects, but over the next six months he relearned his former skills and remembered information about his past life. When interviewed under amylbarbitone narcosis, he revealed that his psychological functions, including memory for his accident, were normal.

pseudopresentiment   Related to both DÉJÀ VU and JAMAIS VU, pseudopresentiment occurs when a person witnessing an event feels that he or she has previously foretold it. There is never any indication that there was actually a prophecy before the event, nor does the person usually claim to have done so. Instead, the dreamlike feeling of pseudopresentiment usually occurs at the moment the person watches the event unfold, suggesting to the person that perhaps the presentiment was revealed in a dream.

pseudosenility   A reversible condition caused by a range of factors including DE-PRESSION, medication or disease. (See also AGING AND MEMORY; PSEUDODEMENTIA.)

psychoanalysis   A treatment for mental illness developed by Sigmund Freud at the beginning of the 20th century as a result of his experiences with hypnosis in treating "hysterical" patients. Freud believed that re-called experiences and ideas were related to other symbolically and emotionally im-portant thoughts and feelings and that much of what a person forgets is simply repres-sion. We remember something, he wrote, because it is meaningful to us and signifi-cant, although that significance may be hid-den. He believed we eliminate from the conscious mind everything that makes us anxious, which he thought explained the loss of memories during the first six years of life.

For this reason, a patient undergoing psy-choanalysis is encouraged to reenact the first years of childhood and verbalize any prob-lems so that internal strife could be un-covered and resolved. (See also FREUD, SIGMUND.)

psychogenic amnesia   Loss of memory arising not from physical illness or trauma but from psychological causes. Psychogenic amnesia almost always is caused by some traumatic or emotionally painful event; the degree of impairment varies from one patient to the next. Some patients' amnesia may be limited to a specific episode or event, whereas others may experience a total loss of personal identity and a complete RETRO-GRADE AMNESIA.

Although psychologically based amnesias which include HYSTERICAL AMNESIA, FUGUE, PSEUDODEMENTIA, MULTIPLE PER-SONALITY DISORDER and MIXED AMNESIA, are completely reversible, they have never been fully understood or explained.

Most psychogenic memory disorders are defense reactions, in which various devices are used to repress part or all of a person's memory. It appears that episodic memory is most vulnerable, but other aspects of long-term memory (particularly in pseudodemen-tia) also may be affected. While in hysterical amnesia only one part of the memory is inaccessible, in fugue there is a complete loss of memory. Multiple personalities di-vide up episodic memory, so that different personalities remember different bits of epi-sodic memory.

In psychogenic amnesia, there is no fun-damental impairment in the memory process or registration or retention—the problem lies in accessing stored or repressed (usually painful) memories. This inability to recall painful memories is a protection against bringing into consciousness ideas associated with profound loss or fear, rage or shame. Under traumatic conditions, memories can become detached from personal identity, making recall impossible.

Psychogenic amnesia usually can be treated successfully by procedures such as hypnosis.

Hysterical Amnesia   Hysterical amnesia is a type of psychogenic amnesia that in-volves disruption of episodic memory. Un-like organic amnesia, this type of forgetfulness is restricted just to specific emotionally laden groups of memories and is usually linked to a patient's needs or conflicts. During a traumatic event, memo-ries can become detached from personal identity, interfering with recall. Sigmund Freud attributed hysterical amnesia to the need to repress information injurious to the ego. This explains why hysterical amnesia appears only after a traumatic event.

Fugue   Frequently caused by psy-chogenic reasons, fugue is a period during which a person forgets his or her identity and often wanders away from home or office for several hours, days or even weeks. Some researchers believe that the tendency to wan-der away from home while experiencing an attack of amnesia often occurs together with other symptoms, including a history of a broken home, periodic depression and predisposition to states of altered consciousness. On the other hand, psychoanalysts see the fugue state as a symbolic escape from severe emotional conflict. In a fugue of long duration, behavior may appear normal, but certain symptoms, such as hallucinations, feeling unreal or unstable moods, may accompany it.

Pseudodementia   Pseudodementia mimics DEMENTIA but includes no evidence of brain dysfunction; it is found most often in elderly patients. Like hysterical amnesia and fugue, psychogenic amnesia is a defense reaction. In the elderly, it is believed to be a way of avoiding depression or asking for help.

Pseudodementia also can be found among those patients who have experienced a minor organic brain injury, which after recovery appears to produce a degree of impairment in excess of what would be expected. For example, one young patient experienced pseudodementia after being involved in a car accident shortly before he was due to be transferred to a dangerous military post abroad. Unconscious for just two minutes, he showed no signs of neurological problems, but he lost his personal identity and had a dense retrograde amnesia. He was unable to perform simple motor skills or recognize objects, but over the next six months he relearned his former skills and remembered information about his past life. When interviewed under amylbarbitone narcosis, his psychological functions, including memory for his accident, were normal.

Multiple Personality Disorder   In multiple personality disorder a person has two or more distinct personalities that are almost always very different from each other and are often total opposites. Multiple personality is often the mind's response to severe sexual or physical trauma in childhood. Before 1980, multiple personality was believed to be rare; since then, more than 6,000 cases have been diagnosed.

Mixed Amnesia   Psychogenic amnesia also may be found in those with organic (physical) brain problems. In this type of mixed amnesia, an accurate diagnosis may be difficult. This complex intermingling of a true organic memory defect with psychogenic factors can prolong or reinforce the memory loss. It is quite common for a brain-damaged patient to experience a hysterical reaction in addition to brain problems.

psychological testing of memory   See ASSESSMENT OF MEMORY DISORDERS.

psychometry   "Reading" the memory of events embedded in objects, such as a watch, a ring or a photograph.

psychosurgery   See LEUCOTOMY; LOBOTOMY.

"punch drunk" syndrome   A problem resulting from multiple repeated blows to the head (such as those experienced by boxers or football players) that can result in a short-term memory problem and other abnormal findings on neuropsychological tests.

The condition was first described in 1928, when it was noted that a patient's brain under microscope showed many signs in common with ALZHEIMER'S DISEASE: widespread neurofibrillary tangles and scarring. It is believed that the brain damage and resulting memory loss is caused by rapid movements of the head, causing hemorrhages and damaged brain cells. In particular, the brains of boxers often exhibit nerve degeneration and loss of nerve fibers in the hippocampus to a degree far exceeding the brains of Alzheimer's disease patients.

pursuit rotor task   A type of memory assessment in which a subject maintains contact with a revolving target by using a hand-held stylus. Performance is measured as the percentage of time the subject can stay on the target.

pyroglutamate   (2-oxo-pyrrolidone carboxylic acid, or PCA)   An amino acid that is an important flavor enhancer found naturally in a wide variety of fruits and vegetables, dairy products and meat, and in large amounts in the brain, cerebrospinal fluid and blood. It also is suspected to enhance cognitive ability.

PCA is able to penetrate the blood-brain barrier, where some researchers believe it stimulates cognitive function, improving memory and learning in rats. At least one study has shown it is effective in improving alcohol-induced memory deficits in humans and in patients suffering from multi-infarct dementia. Administration of this amino acid increased attention and improved short- and long-term retrieval and long-term memory storage.

When compared with a placebo in studies of memory deficits in 40 aged patients, results indicated that PCA improved verbal memory functions in those who were already affected by an age-related memory decline.

One form of the substance already is being used in Italy to treat senility, mental retardation and alcoholism. It is found in health food and vitamin stores in a variety of preparations under several names. (See also MEMORY ENHANCEMENT.)

Pepeu, G., and Signoli, G. "Neurochemical Actions of Nootropic Drugs." *Advances in Neurology.* New York: Raven Press, 1990.

pyrrolidone derivatives   A class of nootropic drugs including PIRACETAM and its analogs OXIRACETAM, PRAMIRACETAM, ANIRACETAM and others. While the mechanism behind their memory-enhancing properties is unknown, most research suggests that the drugs affect the cholinergic system and the adrenal cortex in the brain.

Q

Quintilian (Marcus Fabius Quintilianus) (c. A.D. 35–c. A.D. 96)   This Latin writer and teacher was the author of an important book on rhetoric, *Institutio oratoria,* a major contribution to educational

theory and literary criticism that came more than a century after Cicero's *De oratore.* He also provided important developments on memory systems.

Born in northern Spain, he was educated in Rome and trained by the leading orators of the time. He first worked as a lawyer and then as a teacher of rhetoric, eventually educating the two heirs of Emperor Domitian. An excellent scholar and a sensible, moral man, he was considered to be one of the best teachers of rhetoric in Rome during the first century A.D.

His *Institutio oratoria* is really 12 books, which were published shortly before he died. The books begin with general observations on educational principles, continuing on with the usual departments of rhetoric: invention, arrangement, style, memory and delivery. In the book series, he introduces the topic of memory with the story of Simonides at the banquet, and then goes on to discuss the method of loci as a way of impressing details in memory.

Quintilian wanted to replace the art of memory with simpler precepts of memory training. He gives very clear directions about how to establish places for lodging information to be remembered, and gives very rational reasons as to why the places may help memory. It is now known from experience that a place does, in fact, call up associations in memory.

Quintilian said, in part, that people would have never realized how powerful the art of memory was except for the fact that "it is memory which has brought oratory to its present position of glory." (See also HISTORY OF MEMORY; LOCI, METHOD OF.)

R

Ramus, Peter (1515–1572)   A French dialectician who completed the fragmentation of rhetoric theory by splitting the five "sections" of rhetoric into separate studies, jettisoning the art of memory completely. He was quite aware of the art of ARTIFICIAL MEMORY and supported—as did QUINTILIAN—the idea of dividing and composing the material to be memorized rather than linking the material with places and images. For Ramus, the true art of memory lay in his dialectical method for memorizing, and elocution became the center of rhetorical theory almost solely concerned with figures of speech.

reality monitoring   The ability to assess objectively the external world and to distinguish it from the internal state. The term, invented by Sigmund Freud in 1911 *(Realitatsprufung)*, also involves the ability to discriminate ego boundaries and understand the difference between self and nonself.

recall   The patching together of clues from stored memories to reconstruct an item of consciousness. In a free-recall test, a subject might be asked to write down as many words as possible on a list first memorized the day before.

recency effect   As common sense tells us, recall is best for the most recent experiences. Most people know that, if given a list of words, it's easiest to recall the last few names on the list. This enables people to think about experiences that have just passed.

What is unusual, however, is that it is almost impossible to disrupt the recency effect. Ordinary verbal recall can be confused if all the words begin with the same letter, if words are repeated or words are very similar to each other. However, no matter what confusions are introduced in the last few words, people almost always can name them all correctly.

Normally, the recency effect works for a maximum of four items; paying attention does not enhance this ability. However, if the subject is required to wait for a brief time (even as short as 15 seconds) before recalling the list, the recency effect com-

pletely disappears. (See also PRIMACY EFFECT.)

receptive aphasia   See WERNICKE'S (RECEPTIVE) APHASIA.

receptors   Brain receptors are bits of protein embedded in the wall of nerve cells that bind neurotransmitters. Each receptor binds a specific neurotransmitter, turning a particular biochemical or cellular mechanism on or off. Receptors are generally found in the DENDRITES and cell body of NEURONS. In order to record a memory, the recording agent must be able to respond within a fraction of a second to a stimulus and then keep the information indefinitely.

When scientists at the University of California at Irvine electrically stimulated the synapses found in the HIPPOCAMPUS, they uncovered receptors and made synapses in this region more active for months. Once the receptors are uncovered, they pass information back and forth and keep their neighboring neurons healthy and functioning.

Some scientists believe that some older people lose their memory abilities because their bodies have stopped producing the enzymes that keep their receptors receptive.

recognition   Another name for perceptual memory. One of the ways to measure how much a person remembers is by picking out the items he remembers from a group.

People may not be able to remember something but may show some evidence of remembering if recognition is used as the memory measure. A person recognizes something by acknowledging that it is familiar and that it has been seen before. (The word "recognition" means "to know again.")

An example of the test of recognition would be a multiple-choice test question: Which of the following was the first president of the United States? (a) Abraham Lincoln (b) George Washington (c) Colonel Sanders (d) John F. Kennedy.

Recognition is usually easier to do than recall, since subjects do not have to come up with the information on their own; all that is required is that it be recognized as something that has been learned.

In one study, subjects were shown 600 pairs of sentences, words and pictures. Later they were shown some of these items paired with new items and had to indicate which pair member had been seen before. Most subjects were able to identify correctly sentence pairs 88 percent of the time, words 90 percent and pictures 98 percent. Most elderly subjects performed as well as young adults in these tasks.

The reason that most people can remember a face but may have trouble with the name is that remembering a face is a task of recognition, whereas attaching the name to that face involves the more complex memory task of RECALL. (See also MEMORY FOR FACES.)

recognition memory test See ASSESSMENT OF MEMORY DISORDERS.

reduplicative paramnesia See AGNOSIA; CAPGRAS SYNDROME.

rehabilitation of memory One of the greatest problems in treating organic memory loss is the fact that the brain cannot regenerate very well. When particular areas of the brain are damaged, other regions do not always take over the function of the disabled section. The ability of a brain-damaged patient to recover memory will depend on the cause and site of the damage, the individual's personality and how motivated he or she is to recover. Indeed, researchers agree there is little evidence that practice by itself will significantly improve a brain-damaged person's memory.

Internal Aids Internal aids include MNEMONICS, rehearsal strategies or anything a patient does mentally to organize the information to be remembered.

External Aids External aids include diaries, notebooks and calendars, alarm clocks, gadgets and computers. Environmental aids, such as painting lines on the ground to help patients find their way around, also may be used to help mold behavior in patients with severe memory problems. One of the most effective external aids is the combination of a digital alarm watch and a notebook listing the day's activities; whenever the alarm goes off, the patient consults the notebook.

The effectiveness of external aids depends on how the patient feels about using them. Some patients may benefit from counseling in order to accept use of external aids.

Brain Transplants Initial research with rats has suggested the possibility of restoring some types of memory using brain tissue transplants. However, the moral and philosophical issues surrounding the use of brain tissue in humans presents many problems, and the fact that successful transplants depend on the availability of fetal brain tissue adds to the ethical and legal dilemma.

Rat studies have suggested that fetal brain grafts became effective parts of the grafted animal's memory system. Other studies have shown that the neural tissue taken from the same brain region in rat fetuses could improve the age-related learning impairments in rats.

Medication While many medications and substances have been implicated in MEMORY ENHANCEMENT, the following medications actually have been studied as a treatment for memory problems.

TETRAHYDROAMINOACRIDINE (THA), also known as tacrine or Cognex, is currently being tested for use in the treatment of Alzheimer's disease and is expected to be approved for public use in the near future. In several studies, memory loss improved in those with the disease. It is believed that THA works by increasing the production of ACETYLCHOLINE.

The anti-inflammatory drug INDOMETHACIN used to treat arthritis shows promise for slowing the advance of Alzheimer's disease. In a recent study of 44 patients mildly to moderately affected with Alzheimer's disease, 24 patients given indomethacin showed an average memory improvement of 1.8 percent; 20 control patients continued to deteriorate an average of 8.4 percent. No patient taking indomethacin showed any memory loss during the six-month test period.

The drug NIMODIPINE, which blocks excess calcium in the part of the brain associated with memory and learning, has been used successfully to improve memory loss in stroke victims.

CENTROPHENOXINE (trade name: Lucidril) is believed to improve various aspects of memory function and may help patients whose brain's are not getting enough oxygen (such as after stroke). Researchers believe the drug removes lipofuscin deposits, which increase with age and interfere with learning ability. However, the drug has not been effective in the treatment of Alzheimer's disease.

DILANTIN (phenytoin) is a well-known treatment for epilepsy that is also reputed to improve long-term memory and verbal performance in young and old alike.

HYDERGINE, an extract of the fungus ergot, is a widely used treatment for all forms of senility in the United States. It is said to increase memory, learning, recall and intelligence, inhibit free radicals, enhance brain cell metabolism, and increase blood supply and oxygen to the brain. Hydergine was the first drug that showed promise in use against Alzheimer's disease.

PHYSOSTIGMINE, a drug used to treat glaucoma (high pressure in the eyeballs) may produce mild memory improvement among Alzheimer's patients. In addition, physostigmine reverses memory loss following the administration of SCOPOLAMINE in normal subjects. It works by inhibiting acetylcholinesterase, which breaks down acetylcholine, important in a range of memory processes.

Memory Strategies   There must be about as many memory strategies as there are things to forget. They include external aids—lists, appointment diaries and calendars, "safety drills," alarms and notebook combinations. Memory strategies also can include Mnemonics—rhymes ("Thirty days hath September . . ."), patterns (in birth dates, license plates, and so on), acronyms (NATO) and sayings ("Spring forward, fall back" for setting clocks to daylight savings/standard time).

Visualization and association are other types of mnemonic techniques. In the method of loci, a person links something to be remembered with a specific place and then remembers the place to recall the item. The PEG WORD SYSTEM provides pegs on which to hang unrelated words or ideas that need to be remembered. (See also LOCI, METHOD OF.)

rehearsal   The repetition of information, which is necessary for it to move from short-term to long-term memory. The importance of rehearsal in memory has been known since 400 B.C., when the Greeks advised memory students to repeat what they hear, since hearing and saying the same things transfers learning into memory.

According to researchers, rehearsal lengthens the time that information remains in short-term memory, and it appears to be the major way of transferring data into long-term memory. Often rehearsal codes information for memory by translating it into auditory images instead of visual ones. In other words, a person trying to remember a telephone number often will repeat it aloud several times before dialing. Researchers also believe that most people remember the sound of a word and not its printed shape. Studies have shown that, given a series of letters to memorize that includes the letter Q, subjects often recall the letter U instead, which sounds like Q, instead of the letter O, which looks like Q.

The best way to rehearse information to be learned is to concentrate fully, without any interfering background noise; attention is crucial to memory formation. Researchers also have found that it's better to "warm up" gradually to a task requiring concentration;

therefore, before sitting down to memorize information, the subject should first read a magazine article or short story for about ten minutes. Such a warm-up session improves concentration on the more difficult task.

relaxation and memory Trying to recall information is easier when the person is relaxed than when he or she is nervous, according to research at Stanford University School of Medicine in Palo Alto, California. In one study, people over age 55 showed improved concentration and better success at recalling faces and names after learning relaxation techniques, such as deep breathing and progressive relaxation.

relearning as a memory test A person who cannot recall information or even recognize that she has seen it before may still show evidence of remembering some portion of it through a measure of memory called relearning. If a person learns something and then learns it faster the second time, researchers suggest that the person must have some memory of the material. For example, a person who had once studied a foreign language and then forgot most of it will find much of the material "coming back" to her during the relearning phase.

In one study, a psychologist read his son Greek passages from the age of 15 months to three years, and tested the boy for retention at ages eight, 14 and 18 by having him memorize the original passages and some new material. At age eight, the boy could memorize the passages he had been exposed to already more quickly than those passages he had never heard. However, this ability decreased at 14 and again at 18, from 27 percent quicker to 8 percent to 1 percent at age 18.

remembering The process of bringing forward memories. Remembering occurs in three stages—acquisition/encoding/recording, storage and retrieval/recall.

Encoding is the act of learning the material; storage is keeping that information "on file" in the brain until it is needed; retrieval is finding the information and getting it back when it is needed.

If a person cannot remember something, it may be because the information was never recorded in the first place (a failure of encoding); it could be that the information was never stored; or it might be that the information was not stored in a way that makes it easy to find.

Most problems in remembering occur in the retrieval stage, not the storage or encoding level. While there is not much to be done to improve retrieval directly, it can be improved indirectly by polishing the methods of recording and retaining. Such methods usually involve some type of mnemonic method that stores information in a way designed to improve its retrieval. (See MNEMONICS.)

In addition, there appear to be at least two different processes involved in memory: SHORT-TERM MEMORY (or "working" memory) and LONG-TERM MEMORY. The difference between these two types of memory is more than in the amount of time information is available. Most researchers believe these two types of memory involve two separate methods of storage or different levels of processing.

Short-term memory refers to how many things a person can pay attention to—similar to the idea of attention span. The hallmark of this type of memory is its rapid rate of forgetting; information stored in short-term memory is forgotten within 30 seconds if it is not rehearsed. In other words, a person may remember an unfamiliar telephone number from the time it is read in the phone book until it's dialed, if the number is repeated during that time. A few seconds after dialing, most people would have to look the number up once more in order to dial it again. Short-term memory also has a limited capacity, usually about seven items.

The art of remembering lies in organizing the storage of trace memories so they will be easy to find with the right cues. First, it's important to perceive in a sensory mode, integrating all five senses so that the thought processes follow categories. When there is something to be remembered, it is important to observe, select, focus, analyze and comment.

repressed memories   Memories that are unconsciously "forgotten." (Usually they are traumatic ones.) The topic of repressed memories has become controversial, because it is difficult to establish their validity. (See also FREUD, SIGMUND; FUGUE; MULTIPLE PERSONALITY DISORDER; PSYCHOGENIC AMNESIA; REPRESSION.)

repression   The intentional forgetting of unpleasant memories. Repression was the underlying theme of the theories of Sigmund Freud, the father of psychoanalysis; he considered repression to be the keystone to his entire theory of neurosis. According to Freud, a person purposely pushes unacceptable, traumatic or unpleasant memories into the unconscious, where they can be forgotten. Repression of these memories is necessary to enable the person to survive mentally.

Repression is a form of coping and often occurs, Freud believed, during childhood. He also believed that childhood amnesia is caused by the repression of infantile sexuality. Many modern memory researchers say that infantile amnesia is due, instead, to the lack of early development of various mental abilities (such as language) used to cue memory.

Freud assumed that everyone stores all memories somewhere in the brain, and those who couldn't remember important things simply were not able to retrieve those hidden memories. He assumed there must be an active but known agent repressing the memory. He also assumed that if a patient could

overcome a block to memory, the person would automatically remember and the memory would be accurate.

Today, researchers aren't so sure this is true. They believe that while patients may possess the courage and strength to remember, they will not necessarily be successful—especially for memories they have refused to think about for years. Also, when at last some long-buried fact is recalled, patients and therapists can't assume that the memory is historically correct. Many scientists believe that the memory will be a mixture of fact and fiction that cannot be untangled. If a person deliberately refuses to remember an episode, he or she probably will experience a lifelong amnesia for the event. If an emotional association is particularly frightening, a person can halt at memory's emotional level and remember no more, these researchers believe.

While Freud usually obtained his examples of repression from psychoanalytical interviews with mentally ill patients, he believed that the concept also applied to normal forgetting. He noted in his book *The Psychopathology of Everyday Life* (1960) that the tendency to forget what is disagreeable is universal, and the capacity to forget is probably developed to different degrees in different people.

In the early 20th century researchers tried to confirm Freud's hypothesis (the HEDONIC SELECTIVITY or the POLLYANNA HYPOTHESIS) that unpleasant memories were harder to remember than pleasant ones. The problem with the studies was that the greater recall of pleasant experiences might reflect response bias instead of a difference in the ability to recall the memory. Scientists reasoned that the fact that people remember pleasant experiences instead of unpleasant ones may be due to their reluctance to report unpleasant things, and not a failure of memory at all.

Although some parts of Freud's theories are not widely accepted today, most memory experts do believe that such motivated "forgetting" can occur.

Repression also is believed to be the unconscious defense mechanism responsible for DISSOCIATIVE DISORDERS, which segregate a group of mental or behavioral processes from the rest of a person's psychic activity. The amnesia found in these disorders is a repression of disturbing memories; once these memories are repressed (or "forgotten"), access to them is cut off temporarily. (See also FREUD, SIGMUND; FUGUE; INFANTILE AMNESIA; MULTIPLE PERSONALITY DISORDER; PSYCHOGENIC AMNESIA.)

response bias   A person's reluctance to report unpleasant experiences to an experimenter due to his or her reluctance to discuss them.

retention   See STORAGE.

retrieval   The searching and finding process that leads to recognition and or recall.

Mnemonists teach a variety of "retrieval strategies" to bring up deeply buried memories. These strategies work by bringing a memory trace (or ENGRAM) from long-term memory into consciousness by stimulating the surrounding traces of that memory. Quite often, a person who is able to retrieve part of a memory eventually can bring the full information into consciousness. If a person's face is remembered, the name should follow eventually.

There are a number of strategies that help in retrieval:

Alphabet Search   Go through the alphabet to recall which letter the name or thing starts with.

Free Association   Think up everything possible associated with the information.

Questions   To remember details about a complicated event, a series of questions should jog memory: Who? What? Where?

When? Why? How? How often? How many? How long?

Guessing   Think of the length of the word, with any unusual features (double letters, funny spelling) to concentrate on?

Mood   Imagine the feeling when memory was experienced?

If the memory trace is almost nonexistent, it may be possible to recall it by associating it with other information.

Retrace   Go over everything that happened just before or right after the event you want to remember. If it's a thing you're trying to find, retrace all the steps you took right before you lost the object.

Causation   Think of the circumstances that might have prompted the memory.

Surroundings   Imagine the place where the memory was registered. What was being done, thought or said.

Return to the Scene   Go to the place where the information was first learned; try to come up with features of the site that connect with the memory itself.

retroactive inhibition   A type of mental interference that impedes successful memorization; it is called retroactive because the inhibition is in a backward direction. In other words, if a person studied for an anatomy test last week and studied for a physiology test last night, when he or she tries to remember the facts from the anatomy lesson, the physiology terms might get in the way. This is retroactive inhibition.

If a psychologist asked a group of subjects to memorize a string of words on list A and then asked part of the group to rest while the others memorize list B, when the time comes for the entire group to write down the remembered words from list A, the group that rested will do better. This is because the words on list B retroactively inhibited the memorization of list A. Results from studies like this have shown scientists that a key factor in successful memorization is time. A person memorizing material should rest in between task A and task B in order to give the mind time to consolidate the material, moving at least some of it from short-term to long-term memory. (See also EBBINGHAUS, HERMANN E.; INTERFERENCE THEORY; PROACTIVE INHIBITION.)

Higbee, Kenneth. *Your Memory.* New York: Prentice-Hall, 1988.

retrograde amnesia A type of AMNESIA in which the patient has a gap in memory extending back for some time from the moment of damage to the brain. This type of amnesia is principally a deficit of recall and recognition of information, and the memory gap usually shrinks over time. Retrograde amnesia also usually causes an inability to remember personal and public events instead of loss of language, conceptual knowledge or skills.

Retrograde amnesia appears to be most pronounced for the period immediately before the onset of amnesia, with less disruption of more remote memories. This means that patients with retrograde amnesia probably can describe their high school graduation but would have trouble talking about their career just before the onset of amnesia.

This phenomenon of losing most recent memories first, called RIBOT'S LAW, was first reported by Theodole-Armand Ribot in 1882 when he described his law of regression. He noted that the destruction of memory follows a logical order from the unstable to the stable.

Retrograde amnesia may occur following stroke, head injury, administration of electroconvulsive therapy or in cases of psychogenic amnesia.

Psychologists have developed tests for retrograde amnesia that can measure a patient's memory for events. By compiling a life history of the patient from relatives and friends, the tester can compile a series of questions about each period of a patient's life. The examiner also can use an autobiographical cueing procedure involving the recall of personal events in response to specific words. If the patient can recall events only from certain periods of his or her life, a diagnosis of retrograde amnesia can be made. However, this procedure may be unreliable because it is hard to determine whether the patient's memories are accurate. Retrograde amnesia also may be tested by measuring a patient's ability to remember public events, since it is assumed that memory for public and personal events has a common basis.

The most extensive test for retrograde amnesia is the BOSTON REMOTE MEMORY BATTERY, which has three parts with easy and hard questions. The easy questions may be answered on the basis of general (publicly rehearsed) knowledge, and the hard questions reflect information requiring remembering a particular time period. Unfortunately, this test is culture specific and cannot be used effectively outside the United States.

Generally, retrograde amnesia is less of a problem for patients with memory deficits than is ANTEROGRADE AMNESIA (problems acquiring new information after trauma or an illness). (See also RIBOT, THEODULE-ARMAND; SHRINKING RETROGRADE AMNESIA; TEMPORAL LOBECTOMY.)

rhetoric The ancient practice of communication that included extensive tutoring in the art of memory. Students studied rhetoric in their training as lawyers or politicians. In modern times, however, rhetoric has shifted its emphasis from the speaker or writer to the listener or reader.

Traditionally, rhetoric is limited to the insights and methods of public speaking developed by rhetoricians in the classical period of ancient Greece (about the 5th century B.C.). Rhetoric was the center of a learning process in Europe for about two millennia, well into the 19th century. The most influential book on education ever written, *Institutio oratorica (The Training of an Orator),* by the Roman rhetorician QUINTILIAN of the first century A.D. was actually a text on rhetoric.

In early Athens, rhetoric teachers (called Sophists) offered rhetoric as a profoundly important educational discipline. By CICERO's time (106 B.C.–43 B.C.), rhetoric was divided into five sections (called "offices"): invention, disposition, elocution, pronunciation and memory. By the Middle Ages, rhetoric had moved into religion, where church fathers were interested in marrying rhetoric with Christian oration.

rhymes   Using a rhyme to help remember information can be a very effective method in retaining data. For example, many people remember grammatical rules by recalling "*I* before *E* except after *C*." Most people also remember which months have 31 days by the rhyme: "Thirty days hath September . . ."

Basically, learning a rhyme to remember something is a way of imposing meaning as a way to enhance memory. Many people find that recalling a word that rhymes with a sought-after word is an effective cue to recalling the original word. (See also MEANINGFULNESS EFFECT; PEG WORD SYSTEM.)

rhyming-peg system   See PEG WORD SYSTEM.

Ribot, Theodule-Armand (1839–1916)   A French psychologist who described memory loss as a symptom of a brain disease by discussing principles of the evolution of memory function in the individual.

His book *Les Maladies de la memoire (Diseases of Memory),* published in 1881, was an influential attempt to analyze abnormalities of memory in terms of physiology. In it, he outlines what came to be called

RIBOT'S LAW of regression of memory (or progressive destruction), which was popular at the time and still influences contemporary thought on memory today. His law states that the destruction of memory follows a logical order, beginning with the most recent memories and ending with instinctive memory.

Ribot taught at the Sorbonne from 1885 to 1888, moving onto the College of France, where he chaired the department of experimental and comparative psychology. In later years, he became interested in affective and emotional factors in psychology.

Ribot's law   An explanation of the progressive destruction of memory described by French psychologist Theodule-Armand Ribot in his book *Les Maladies de la memoire (Diseases of Memory)* (1881). Ribot's law held that the destruction of memory follows a logical order that advances progressively from the unstable to the stable. The memory destruction begins with the most recent recollections because, since they were only lightly impressed on the "nervous elements," they were rarely repeated. Therefore, these memories had no permanent associations and represented organization in its feeblest form. The last type of memory to be lost is sensorial, instinctive memory, which, having become a permanent and integral part of a person, represents organization in its most highly developed stage.

This theory was quite popular for its time and has been applied to explain phenomena from the breakdown of memory for language (aphasia) to the gradual return of memory after a concussion. The theory also helped to strengthen the idea that as time goes on, the neural basis of memory is strengthened or consolidated.

Still, researchers investigating RETROGRADE AMNESIA (memory loss for old events) agree that Ribot's law has many exceptions. For example, patients recovering from a concussion do not always recover their most recent memories first, as Ribot's law stipulates they should. It is also difficult to separate the effects of the passage of time from those of repetition or rehearsal. (See also RIBOT, THEODULE-ARMAND.)

Ricci, Matteo (1552–1610)   A 16th-century Italian Jesuit priest and master of mnemotechnics. Born to a noble family in central Italy, Ricci left for law school in Rome at age 16, but joined the Jesuits as a priest in 1571. Inspired by his superiors in the order who dedicated themselves to priestly initiative, he volunteered for work overseas and was sent to China. On a trip to convert the Chinese, he shared the European art of building MEMORY PALACES as a way of gaining his hosts' attention and respect. After building his own memory palace filled with the difficult-to-learn Chinese characters, he asked his hosts to write down a large number of different characters in no order and with no relation to each other. After reading it once, he recited the characters in perfect order—and then recited them all by memory, backward.

Ricci lived in China for 30 years, adopting the language and culture of the country and traveling to the interior, which was normally closed to foreigners.

While trying to win converts, Ricci also taught the Chinese Euclidean geometry, western chemistry, astronomy, optics and clockmaking, wrote books and composed lyrics, and created an annotated map of the world. But he left no record of the kinds of memory palaces he created in his own mind.

Rivermead Behavioral Memory Test
One of the more realistic memory tests that measures everyday aspects of forgetting and monitors change following treatment for memory deficits. It was designed to bridge the gap between laboratory-based and more natural measures of memory.

Although it is administered and scored in a standardized way, the Rivermead subtests try to provide an analog of a range of everyday memory situations that appear to cause trouble for certain patients with acquired brain damage. Its subtests include measures of remembering a name, a hidden belonging, and an appointment. The Rivermead Behavioral Memory Test also tests picture and face recognition, immediate prose recall, orientation and remembering a route and delivering a message.

These subtests were chosen on the basis of the memory problems reported by head injury patients. The items require that patients either remember to carry out some everyday task or retain the type of information needed for everyday functioning, and are combined with some conventional memory measures.

Immediately after the test items are administered, the patient is given a paired-association learning test in which six paired associates are presented verbally; patients are retested in three trials, which provides a test of long-term verbal learning. This is followed by the standard Wechsler Adult Intelligence Scale (WAIS) Digit Span (a subtest of the WAIS) in which subjects are required to repeat back sequences of digits until a point is reached at which they consistently make errors.

The Rivermead test was developed as a way of predicting which brain-damaged people are most likely to encounter everyday memory problems. Although patients with severe amnesia probably will fail all parts of the test, less-impaired patients should exhibit patterns that may correlate with various neuropsychological dysfunctions. The test is particularly useful in measuring improvement (such as in head injury) or deterioration (as in Alzheimer's disease) since it can be administered in four parallel versions, which lower the practice effects through repeated testing.

Wilson, Barbara. *Rehabilitation of Memory.* New York: Guildford Press, 1987.

Roman room system   One of the most popular of the Roman mnemonic techniques. In this system, mnemonic experts imagined the entrance to their house and their room, and then filled the room with as many objects and items of furniture as they chose. Each object or piece of furniture served as a link image onto which they attached things they wanted to remember. They were particularly careful to bring order and precision to their rooms, which is essential to the proper functioning of this system. The benefit of this system is that it requires very precise structure and ordering, imagination and sensuality. (See also LOCI, METHOD OF; MEMORY PALACE.)

rosemary   *(Rosmariinus officinalis)* This small, perennial evergreen shrub of the mint family is known as the herb of memory. In ancient Greece, students believed that entwining a spring of rosemary in their hair would improve their memory, so they wore rosemary garlands while studying for exams. At funerals, mourners tossed fresh sprigs into the grave as a sign that the life of the departed would not be forgotten.

"I lett it runne all over my garden wall," wrote Sir Thomas More, "not onlie because my bees love it, but because 'tis the herb sacred to remembrance."

Native to the Mediterranean region, rosemary has been naturalized throughout Europe and temperate America. It is widely grown in gardens in the warmer parts of the United States and Great Britain, where an old legend states that where rosemary thrives, the mistress is master.

rote learning   Remembering information by repeating it over and over without making any of the details meaningful or using any mnemonic device to boost memory storage. The opposite of meaningful learning, since information needs to be meaningful in order to be remembered best. (See also MEANINGFULNESS EFFECT; MEMORY FOR STORIES.)

S

schizophrenia   The most common form of psychosis, affecting about 1 percent of the population, resulting in a break from reality involving delusions, illogical thinking, incoherence and hallucinations. Studies suggest that schizophrenia also interferes with the ability to concentrate on and think about incoming information, but it is unclear to what extent this depends on the subtype of the disorder and the patient's problems with paying attention to outside events.

Recent Swiss research suggests that training to improve attention, memory and basic reasoning skills may play a role in treating many cases of the disease. The Swiss approach of cognitive rehabilitation differs from other more traditional programs, which focus on teaching social skills. In studies at the University of Bern, researchers emphasize thinking abilities by having patients sort cards containing geometric shapes, colors and days of the week. Training then advances to word problems and interpreting the meaning of social interactions and other complex social skills. As many as 18 months after the program, participants showed substantial improvement on tests measuring attention and overall mental condition. However, these patients still are not capable of complex thought and social skills.

Schizophrenic children also suffer from attention and memory problems that undermine their ability to communicate with others. In recent studies at the University of California at Los Angeles, while their motor and perceptual skills remain intact, these youngsters fail at tests of rapid mental activity and have significant problems copying a remembered shape. In addition, tasks that normally would spark an electrical surge in one or both brain hemispheres have no effect on schizophrenic youngsters.

Bower, Bruce. "Schizophrenic Kids Memory Muddle." *Science News*, May 23, 1992.

"Cognitive Help for Schizophrenics." *Science News*, April 11, 1992.

scopolamine   An antispasmodic drug that blocks neurotransmission of certain chemicals in the brain, including ACETYLCHOLINE, important in the normal function of memory. If given to normal subjects, the drug causes a severe memory loss that is reversed by the administration of PHYSOSTIGMINE. Under the influence of scopolamine, retention remains intact, but effortful retrieval is impaired. Scopolamine appears to disrupt efficient encoding processes leading to a deficiency in effective retrieval of information. It has a more potent effect than sedatives or tranquilizers on human cognitive abilities, but the strength of the amnesia following scopolamine administration depends on the memory task used to define it.

Pettinati, Helen. *Hypnosis and Memory*. New York: Guilford Press, 1988.

screen memories   Early memories that, according to psychoanalyst Sigmund Freud, are usually fabricated to block out the emotionally painful, repressed memories of infant sexuality.

For example, one subject recalled the sharp memory of a cobblestone sidewalk in front of his house when he was two years old. While he had no idea why he should remember the cobblestones, he also noted that he had contracted polio at that age, but insisted he had no memory of the onset of the illness—just the cobblestones. It could be that the image of the cobblestones was a FLASHBULB MEMORY of the moment when the reality of the illness struck him; the image persisted while the association did not. But Freud would have called this memory a screen memory, suggesting that the apparently trivial memory obscured a more painful truth as part of a deliberate repression. (See FREUD, SIGMUND; INFANTILE AMNESIA; MEMORY IN INFANCY.)

secondary memory   See LONG-TERM MEMORY.

selective amnesia   A type of PSYCHOGENIC AMNESIA in which a patient fails to recall some, but not all, of the events occurring during a certain period of time. (See also HYSTERICAL AMNESIA.)

selective attention   Defining what one wants to remember, why and for how long.

self-testing   A powerful storage aid to mentally test retention of information, especially if used soon after first seeing or hearing the information and then at gradually lengthening intervals.

semantic memory   Memory for facts, such as the information that would be contained in a dictionary or encyclopedia with no connection to time or place. People don't remember when or where they learn this type of information.

Semantic memory is one of the five major human memory systems (the others are episodic, procedural, perceptual representation and short-term memory) for which evidence now exists.

Semantic memory registers and stores knowledge about the world in the broadest sense; it allows people to represent and mentally operate on situations, objects and relations in the world that aren't present to the senses. A person with an intact semantic memory system can think about things that are not here now. Because semantic memory develops first in childhood, before episodic memory, children are able to learn facts before they can remember their own experiences.

The seat of semantic memory is believed to be located in the medial temporal lobe and diencephalic structures. (See also EPISODIC MEMORY; SHORT-TERM MEMORY.)

semantic network   Chunks of information connected into networks by associated meanings. Activation of any one chunk automatically "readies" others that are closely associated with it, with lessening degrees of activation spreading from one network to another. Some scientists believe the semantic network may be the main structural component of long-term memory.

senile dementia   In the past, DEMENTIA was divided into two forms; presenile (affecting people under age 65) and senile (over age 65). These designations are no longer used today.

Senile dementia (or "senility") is a catchword that has been used for many years to label almost any eccentric behavior in the elderly. It has sometimes been equated with such terms as "chronic brain failure," "chronic brain syndrome," "organic brain syndrome" or "ALZHEIMER'S DISEASE."

Between 50 to 60 percent of older people with impaired memories have Alzheimer's disease; approximately 20 to 25 percent of brain impairment is caused by STROKE, and the remainder is the result of other causes.

There are a number of reasons for confusion, forgetfulness and disorientation besides Alzheimer's disease. These problems could be caused by overmedication or medication interaction, chemical imbalances (lack of potassium, abnormal sugar levels, and so on), depression, sudden illness, malnutrition and dehydration or social isolation.

senility   A term that once referred to changes in mental ability caused by old age. However, the term "senile" simply means "old." Therefore, senility does not really describe a disease; many people considered it to be a derogatory or prejudicial term.

Most people over age 70 suffer from some amount of impaired memory and reduced ability to concentrate. As a person ages, the risk of DEMENTIA rises to affect about one in five over age 80. Depressive illness and confusion due to physical disease are also common.

The terms "chronic ORGANIC BRAIN SYNDROME" and "acute or reversible organic brain syndrome" have been used respectively to refer to those dementias that cannot be treated (chronic) and to those that respond to treatment (acute). (See also AGING AND MEMORY; ALZHEIMER'S DISEASE.)

senses and memory   All of the senses of a human being can evoke memory—sight, sound, touch, taste or smell—but none of them accomplish this with equal ability. Taste and smell are particularly powerful aids to remembering, partly because the olfactory fibers interact directly with the HIPPOCAMPUS and AMYGDALA. Vision requires several intermediate cell connections, whereas smell makes an immediate connection with memory structures in the brain.

sensory memory   The holding of a sensory impression for a short time after it has been perceived. This type of MEMORY takes in a vast number of impressions, lasting about one second each (although the time varies for each sense); it can hold information for a maximum of about four seconds, to enable a person to select what to pay attention to for further processing in SHORT-TERM MEMORY.

sensory store   The initial stage of memory that works chiefly when the sense organs (eyes, ears, skin, tongue and nose) are stimulated. Before something can be remembered, information must be input. If it is a series of numbers, the sensory input will be visual; if it's the odor of cinnamon buns, the sensory input will be smell. Once sensory input enters the brain, it then enters short-term memory, where it is retained just long enough to be remembered briefly. From there, selected bits of information may enter long-term memory if an event called REHEARSAL takes place (that is, if the information is repeated) or if there is a strong sensory or emotional component.

serial position effect The ability of people to remember serial information is affected by where in the series the information appears. Items in the middle of a list take longer to learn and are more difficult to recall than items at the beginning or end of the list. For example, the names of the first few presidents and the last few presidents are easy for most people to recall, but those who served in the middle of the list are far more difficult to remember.

In addition, the length of time after learning can affect which part of the list is the most difficult to remember. If a person tries to remember the names of the presidents immediately after learning them, she will be able to remember the last few names better than the first few. When there is a delay between learning and recall, she will be able to remember the first few presidents better. But no matter how long the interval between learning and recall, those presidents in the middle of the list still will be the most difficult to remember.

This phenomenon can be manipulated to help people remember. If items don't need to be memorized in order, arranging them with the more complex ones at the two ends of the list and the simpler ones in the middle will make the task easier. If the order can't be changed (such as in the list of presidents), people should take more time to memorize the information in the middle of the list.

sexual abuse and traumatic memory Children who are repeatedly abused often bury their traumatic memories until they are unleashed by a seemingly inconsequential situation in adulthood. In most cases, the children first dissociate from disturbing events, distancing themselves from sensations, thoughts or emotions; this often results in memory gaps. The memories remain buried until adulthood, when the victims suddenly experience "spontaneous recall" of the childhood trauma.

This spontaneous recall played an important part in a much-publicized court case

in early 1992, when a 28-year-old woman claimed she suddenly remembered witnessing her father murder one of her playmates 20 years earlier. The woman, who said she was raped repeatedly by her father as a child, recalled the murder when she looked into her own daughter's eyes and realized that they resembled the eyes of the murder victim. The memory resurfaced when the woman severed all ties to her father after he made sexual advances to her daughter. The woman's description of the crime closely matched police evidence on the victim's wounds and the nature of the attack.

While some researchers question the accuracy of spontaneous recall, noting that memories tend to blend together and change over time, corroborating evidence and repeated behaviors or dreams that reflect traumatic events can be valuable checks on spontaneous recall. (See also CHILD ABUSE, MEMORY OF; FREUD, SIGMUND; POSTTRAUMATIC STRESS DISORDER; PSYCHOANALYSIS.)

Shass Pollak The technical term used by Jews for a memory expert (usually from Poland) who has memorized the entire contents of the Talmud (the writings constituting the body of early Jewish civil and religious law). The Talmud was memorized not just literally (that is, word for word) but also typographically (as a set of printed pages). *Shass* is the abbreviation for the Hebrew terms for the Talmud, and *Pollak* is Pole.

All modern editions of the Talmud are paged alike and printed alike, with each page having the same number of words and each page beginning and ending with the same word in all editions.

Sheldrake's hypothesis The idea that the world is kept running by nature's memory that exists as "morphic forms," not by immutable law. These forms, according to cell geneticist and Royal Society fellow Rupert Sheldrake, are patterns without energy that link to the world through resonance.

Every person has his or her own morphic form, and each person resonates to other larger memory patterns in the world memory.

Morphic forms shape us, Sheldrake believes. He was fascinated by what it is that makes an oak tree an oak tree and a horse a horse. A memory pattern or morphic form rises with the first horse, and each succeeding horse resonates to the form and is shaped by it. Yet at the same time, the horse gives back its own bit of idiosyncrasy, allowing change and growth.

short-term memory   Another word for consciousness, short-term memory has a range of other names: Primary memory, immediate memory, working memory. But while some researchers describe a distinct short-term memory system of limited capacity and a long-term system of relatively unlimited capacity, others don't distinguish between the two. Instead, they suggest there is only one system with what appears to be "short-term" memory as only memory with very low levels of learning.

This type of memory storage is necessary in order to perform many tasks; for example, when reading a book, the beginning of the sentence must be kept in mind while reading the last part of the sentence in order for the whole phrase to make sense.

Short-term memory receives information from sensory memory. If not processed further, the information quickly decays; among typical subjects without any memory training, short-term memory seems as if it can deal only with about six or seven items at once for about 15 to 30 seconds at a time. Research suggests that the information in short-term storage is highly vulnerable to distraction or negative interference. (For example, when you lose your train of thought during a conversation after being interrupted.)

Once placed in short-term storage, information can then either be transferred into long-term storage (or "secondary memory") or it can be forgotten.

If a person looks up a number in a phone book, sensory memory registers the number and passes it into short-term memory. As the number is repeated over and over while dialing, it is retained in short-term memory. The limited capacity of short-term memory determines how much information a person can pay attention to at any one time. Going over information keeps it in short-term memory; after a person has looked up an unfamiliar phone number and repeated it over and over, the person could probably make a phone call without having to look up the number again in the book. However, if the person was interrupted while dialing, it is likely that the number would be forgotten when the person tried to redial.

Short-term memory also is limited in capacity to about five or ten bits of information, which can be enlarged by using MNEMONICS—strategies to help remember information. For example, grouping a phone number into segments of three, three and four makes it much easier to remember than if the number was remembered as one long continuous line of ten digits.

If data is to be transferred into long-term store, a permanent MEMORY TRACE is formed that provides the basis for restoring the information to consciousness. To remember a phone number for a long period of time, it must be "encoded" and moved into LONG-TERM MEMORY—preferably using sight or sound to help remember it. A person could sing the number or think about a picture of the number to help retrieve it from long-term memory.

Short-term memory is an important part of a person's memory in that it serves as a sort of temporary notepad, briefly retaining intermediate results while we think and solve problems. It helps maintain a concept of the world by indicating what objects are in the environment and where they are located, keeping visual perceptions stable.

A person's visual perception darts around a scene taking about five retinal images per second and integrating information from all the snapshots into one sustained model of the immediate scene. New changes are included in an updated model, while old ones are discarded, thanks to short-term memory.

Short-term memory maintains the file of our intentions in "active" mode, guiding behavior toward those goals. It keeps track of topics that have been mentioned in conversations. If two friends are discussing a third acquaintance, they can refer to the person as "she" without using her name, and each will know whom the "she" refers to, because of short-term memory.

However, these early processes are extremely complex, including the necessity of word identification and object recognition. By the time information has reached short-term store, a great deal of processing has already occurred of which people are not consciously aware. What passes into consciousness and short-term store is simply the *result* of those unconscious processes. Researchers suggest that only information that has been consciously perceived is transferred from short- to long-term store.

Many researchers liken a person's short-term memory to a computer's central processing unit (CPU). Almost all computers are designed with a sort of "short-term memory" within its CPU, which receives data, stores it in memory, retrieves it and can display it on a screen or print it out. These functions are strikingly similar to short-term memory.

short-term store (STS) See SHORT-TERM MEMORY.

shrinking retrograde amnesia The gradual recovery from RETROGRADE AMNESIA with older memories returning first. The existence of the phenomenon of shrinking retrograde amnesia is not surprising, considering that earlier memories can be derived from a different source from that needed to recall more recent experiences.

As recovery occurs, more and more of the episodic record becomes available and more recent memories can be recalled. Researchers believe that older experiences are more broadly distributed than newer events, and a gradual recovery process will restore some component of older memories before it restores more narrowly distributed newer memories.

Simonides of Ceos (c. 500 B.C.–c. 468 B.C.) The father of the art of trained memory, this Greek poet invented the use of loci (or place) in association with words and images to improve the memory. (See LOCI, METHOD OF.)

According to the great Roman orator Cicero, Simonides was sitting at a banquet table of the mogul Scopas, who had asked the poet to compose a lyric in his honor. Simonides informed Scopas that he would recite if he was paid (the first time a poet ever requested payment to perform); but after the recitation, in which Simonides had praised the gods Castor and Pollux, Scopas paid Simonides only half his fee. "Let the twin gods pay the rest," he retorted. Suddenly a servant appeared and told Simonides that two young men wanted to speak with him in the street; as soon as Simonides left the room, the ceiling collapsed, crushing everyone at the banquet table. (Legend holds that the two young men who saved Simonides were Castor and Pollux, come to pay their debt.)

Although the bodies were damaged beyond recognition, Simonides was able to identify all of them through his memorization of the places where they had been sitting around the table. With this experience, he realized the value of organizing a pattern in the mind. He recognized the value of this system to orators who gave speeches from memory. He invented the art of MNEMONICS and became one of the leading consultants to orators of the day.

Yates, Frances. *The Art of Memory.* Chicago: University of Chicago Press, 1966.

sleep and memory In order to function with peak memory skills, it is essential to get enough sleep and rest the brain, which can be taxed by too much work during the day and poor sleeping at night.

While we sleep, our brain revises, manipulates and stores information. Anyone who has ever gone to sleep with a problem and awoken with the solution has experienced the way the brain can work out difficulties during sleep.

Of course, sleep is not the same, continuous process throughout the night. Instead, according to researchers at France's National Center for Scientific Research, consolidation of memories takes place during paradoxical sleep, which lasts for just about 20 minutes and occurs every 90 minutes in human beings. During this portion of sleep, all the senses are put on hold, disconnecting the brain from the outside world. It is then, these scientists believe, that the maturation of the memory takes place and the brain processes, reviews, consolidates and stores information.

Research has shown that depriving subjects of sleep after learning a task causes their performance to deteriorate.

But although people can't learn effectively without sleep, this doesn't mean that they can learn while sleeping. Because both the conscious and subconscious play a role in the memory process, one cannot work without the other.

Insomnia—the inability to sleep—deprives a person not just of the valuable memory consolidation periods during rest but also interferes with learning during waking hours as well. This problem affects the elderly in particular; often they have more sleep problems and get very little fourth-stage or "deep" sleep, during which the brain recharges itself. After a while the person lives in a chronic state of fatigue and finds it difficult to pay attention or register information.

sleep learning While popular theory holds that a person can learn better while sleeping, in fact research has proven that people do not learn while they are soundly

asleep: When a person is truly asleep, learning does not take place. If a person plays an educational tape while sleeping and learns some of the material, he or she actually has remembered what was heard during a waking period.

There is, however, some evidence suggesting that people can learn while they are very drowsy or even in a very light sleep. The material must be presented at just the right time: not sleepy enough and the material will wake up the subject, and too deeply asleep and the material won't make an impression at all. In addition, complex material involving reasoning or understanding can't be learned. What can be learned during this very drowsy state are nonsense syllables, Morse code, facts, dates, foreign languages and the like. Finally, sleep learning during this one period is still not enough on its own; it is effective only if used together with daytime learning.

However, some research indicates that falling asleep immediately after learning something helps someone retain the information better than if he or she stays up and engages in some activity. Further, a good night's sleep will help make people alert for memory tasks the next day.

Yet sleeping pills will not ensure that people wake up refreshed and ready to learn. The carryover effect of these drugs makes a person less able to register new memories the next day and less susceptible to stimulation that can assist in remembering already learned information. (See also SUBLIMINAL LEARNING.)

Higbee, Kenneth. *Your Memory.* New York: Prentice-Hall, 1988.

slow viruses of the brain A group of viruses of the central nervous system (including the brain) that cause symptoms of memory loss and dementia ten or 20 years after the initial infection. The diseases take a slow course, the end of which is usually fatal. Included among diseases suspected to be caused by such a slow virus may be syphilis, at least one type of ALZHEIMER'S DISEASE, CREUTZFELDT-JAKOB DISEASE, kuru, a rare complication of measles called subacute sclerosing panencephalitis, MULTIPLE SCLEROSIS and possibly the brain disease that occurs in some people infected with the HIV virus.

Smith, Edwin, Surgical Papyrus of

An Egyptian medical treatise written between 2,500 and 3,000 years ago that describes how head injury can have effects throughout the body. The papyrus contains information about 48 cases; eight describe head injuries that affect other parts of the body.

Apparently intended as a textbook on surgery, the papyrus begins with the clinical cases of head injuries and works its way down the body, describing in detail the examination, diagnosis, treatment and prognosis in each case.

The papyrus was acquired in Luxor in 1862 by the American egyptologist Edwin Smith, a pioneer in the study of Egyptian science. After his death in 1906, the papyrus was given to the New York Historical Society, which turned it over for study to the Egyptologist James Henry Breasted in 1920. Breasted published a translation, transliteration and discussion in two volumes in 1930.

smoking and memory

While some studies have shown that nicotine can improve factual recall, smoking cigarettes containing nicotine also cuts down on the amount of oxygen that reaches the brain and·in this way can interfere with memory. Studies have shown that smokers consistently score lower than nonsmokers on a wide variety of memory tests. Research at the University of Edinburgh on tests of name and face recall has found that both visual and verbal memory is impaired in those who smoke more than one pack of cigarettes a day.

However, in another study, smoking a cigarette just before presentation of a 50-word list improved recall after ten and 45 minutes; higher-nicotine cigarettes were more effective than lower-nicotine brands.

Socrates (c. 470 B.C.–399 B.C.)

An ancient Athenian philosopher who directed philosophical thought toward analyses of the character and conduct of human life, and who is remembered for his direction to "know thyself." He is best known for his method of teaching that involved a way of jogging innate memory by questioning his students in such a way that he drew information from them that they didn't know they possessed. The hidden agenda of this "Socratic method" is to draw forth the innate divine memory.

Socrates, who lived during the chaos of the Peloponnesian War, served as an infantryman during the war. Later, married with three sons, he was a conspicuous figure in Athens, where he seemed to spend all his time in the streets, the marketplace and the gymnasia. He enjoyed speaking with young men of promise and with politicians, poets and artisans about their work and their notions of right and wrong.

According to Socrates, people carried a block of wax within their soul of varying quality in different individuals—the "gift of Memory, the mother of the Muses." He believed that whenever someone hears or thinks something, this wax is held under the perceptions and thoughts, where they are imprinted upon it.

In Plato's *Phaedrus*, Socrates tells the story of the inventor of the alphabet, who believed his invention would make the Egyptians wiser and improve their memory. But according to Socrates, the god Thamus was horrified at this invention, predicting that the alphabet would only enhance forgetfulness. Thamus reasoned that when people relied on written words, they would no longer rely on improving their memory. "You have invented an elixir not of memory but of reminding," Socrates quotes Thamus in *Phaedrus*, "and you offer your pupils the appearance of wisdom, not true wisdom." Thamus warned that these students would read information without instruction, seeming to know many things but in fact being ignorant.

It has been suggested that this passage may represent a survival of the tradition of oral memory, of the time before writing was commonly used; others believe it is a description of the ancient Egyptian practice of memory as a profound discipline.

In 399 Socrates was arrested on two counts of "impiety," "corruption of the young" and "neglect of the gods whom the city worships and the practice of religious novelties." He was sentenced to death, declined an opportunity to escape and drank a fatal concoction of hemlock.

Socrates wrote nothing himself. Information about his personality and doctrines is found primarily in the words of PLATO and Zenophon's *Memorabilia*.

sodium amytal (amylbarbitone)   Also called truth serum, this drug facilitates the recall of emotionally disturbing memories. Scientists believe sodium amytal reduces anxiety so that the patient can tolerate the recollection of experiences that are too painful to recall in the normal conscious state.

sodium pentothal   A drug used to uncover buried traumatic memories of known origin (such as amnesia following combat trauma) by first sedating the patient via slow intravenous injection. This relieves any anxiety the patient may have and is followed by the onset of drowsiness. At this point, the injection is halted and the interview begins.

Because the interviewer knows the circumstances of the trauma, he or she can start to cue the patient about the incident. As the patient begins to remember, he or she may become agitated to the point of collapse; the patient usually is able to resume the story at a more neutral point. (See also BARBITURATES; SODIUM AMYTAL [AMYL BARBITONE].)

somnambulism   A phenomenon that sometimes occurs during HYPNOSIS, in which the subject can have the outward appearance of ordinary awareness, but in fact is deeply hypnotized.

source amnesia   Loss of memory for when and where particular information was acquired.

spacing effect   Recall of items repeated immediately is far worse than spaced repetitions. This is related to the *lag effect*, in which the recall of items given spaced repetition increases as the interval between repetition increases.

SPECT (single-photon emission computerized tomography)   A type of brain scan that tracks blood flow and measures brain activity. Less expensive than PET (positron emission tomography) scans, SPECTs may be used to identify subtle injury following mild head trauma.

SPECT is a type of radionuclide scanning, a diagnostic technique based on the detection of radiation emitted by radioactive substances introduced into the body. Different types of tissue take up different radioactive substances (radionuclides) in greater concentrations; SPECT gives a clearer picture of organ function than other systems.

The radioactive substance is swallowed or injected into the bloodstream, where it accumulates in the brain. Gamma radiation (similar but shorter than X rays) is emitted from the brain. It is detected by a gamma camera, which emits light, and is used to produce an image that can be displayed on a screen; using a principle similar to CT (computerized tomography) scanning, cross-sectional images can be constructed by a computer from radiation detected by the gamma camera that rotates around the patient. Moving images can be created by using a computer to record a series of images right after the administration of the radionuclide.

Radionuclide scanning is a safe procedure requiring only tiny doses of radiation. Because the radioactive substance is ingested or injected, it avoids the risks of some X ray procedures in which a radiopaque dye is inserted through a catheter into the organ (as in angiography). And unlike radiopaque dyes, radionuclides carry almost no risk of toxicity or allergy.

SQUID (superconducting quantum interference device) A type of brain scanning device that senses tiny changes in magnetic fields. When brain cells fire, they create electric current; electric fields induce magnetic fields, so magnetic changes indicate neural activity.

state-dependent learning The theory that a person performs better if learning and recalling information takes place in the same state (such as under the influence of alcohol) and poorer when trying to recall a memory when in a state different from the one in which it was registered. Therefore, a person who learns something after a few drinks can recall that information better while drunk than while sober. Or a person who learns while sober may then have difficulty recalling it when drunk. (See also ALCOHOL AND MEMORY.)

steroids See PREGNENOLONE.

stimulus-response memory The kind of memory involved when a dinner bell makes a trained dog salivate. This type of memory uses brain areas below the outer cortex and survives damage to regions of the brain essential for other kinds of memory.

storage The ability to hold information in memory for a brief period of time. Traditionally, researchers have believed that in memory, the most critical problems are concerned with the physiological mechanism by which events and experiences can be retained so they can be reproduced. Most researchers believe that anything that influences the behavior of an organism leaves a trace in the central nervous system. Theoretically, as long as these traces last, they can be restimulated and the experience that established them will be remembered.

In studying retention, researchers test how well subjects learn words or sets of letters, obtaining a retention score. Future forgetting will be measured against this score. Subsequent tests of retention are then given to measure the rate at which the person forgets.

storage-deficit theories Two types of theories explain storage deficits in memory: One states that AMNESIA is due to more rapid forgetting; the other, that amnesia is caused by a failure of consolidation. Neither of these theories, scientists say, adequately explains human amnesic syndrome.

The rapid-forgetting theorists assume that a memory is formed but that it simply decays more rapidly among amnesic patients, although research in general appears not to support this view. The second storage-deficit theory states that failure to consolidate memory is the underlying cause of amnesic syndrome.

storage vs. retrieval failure Forgetting can occur either because information was not properly stored or because of a problem in retrieval. "Storage" refers to keeping information "on file" in the brain until it is needed; "retrieval" is finding the information and getting it back when it is needed.

If a person cannot remember something, it may be because the information was never stored or because the information was not stored in a way that makes it easy to find. Most problems in remembering occur in the retrieval stage, not in storage. While there is not much to be done to improve retrieval directly, it is possible to improve retrieval indirectly by polishing the methods of recording and retaining. Such methods usually involve some type of "mnemonic method" that stores information in a way designed to improve its retrieval.

stress and memory There appears to be a relationship between stress and problems in remembering information. In rat studies, researchers at the University of California at Berkeley noted a relationship between endorphins, which are produced by the body's major stress systems and impaired learning and memory.

In the study, a rat's level of endorphins was related to how well the rat could escape an avoidance task. If endorphins were injected into the rat's bloodstream before a learning task, the animal did not learn as well as those who were not injected. Injections given to trained rats as much as five days before a new trial produced learning deficits. (See also EYEWITNESS TESTIMONY; MEMORY FOR EVENTS.)

stroke Damage to the brain caused by an interruption to its blood supply or leakage of blood outside of vessel walls. A stroke may be caused by cerebral thrombosis (clot), cerebral embolism or hemorrhage. Any area in the brain damaged by the stroke will affect further brain function, including sensation, movement and memory.

Following a stroke, serious memory problems can be caused when a large group of cells in a concentrated area die and break a memory circuit. The effects of stroke are random and depend on where the stroke occurs. Sometimes a stroke damages an area but the brain quickly recovers because the corresponding circuit in the other hemisphere continues to function. In other cases, the circuits in the two hemispheres don't appear to have developed equally, and the damage is lasting. Many causes of AGNOSIA and APHASIA are caused by stroke.

Causes Cerebral thrombosis is a blockage by a clot that has built up on the wall of a brain artery, depriving the brain of blood; it is responsible for almost half of all strokes. Cerebral embolism is a blockage by an embolus (usually a clot) that is swept into an artery in the brain and deprives the brain of oxygen; it accounts for 30 to 35 percent of strokes. Hemorrhage is the rupture of a blood vessel and bleeding within or over the surface of the brain; it accounts for about a quarter of all strokes.

Strokes are fatal in about one-third of cases and are a leading cause of death in developed countries. In the United States, stroke will occur in about 200 out of every 100,000 people each year; incidence rises quickly with age and is higher in men than women.

Certain things can increase the risk of stroke, including high blood pressure, which weakens the walls of arteries, and atherosclerosis (thickening of the lining of arterial walls). Stroke also can be caused by conditions that cause blood clots in the heart that may migrate to the brain: irregular heartbeat (atrial fibrillation), damaged heart valves or heart attack. Conditions that increase the risk of high blood pressure and or atherosclerosis also can cause stroke; these include hyperlipidemia (fatty substances in the blood), polycythemia (high level of red blood cells in the blood), diabetes mellitus and smoking. Oral contraceptives also increase the risk of stroke in women under 50.

Symptoms A stroke that affects the dominant of the two cerebral hemispheres in the brain (usually the left) may cause disturbance of language and speech. Symptoms that last for less than 24 hours followed by full recovery are known as TRANSIENT ISCHEMIC ATTACKS (TIAs); such attacks are warnings that part of the brain is not receiving a sufficient supply of blood.

Treatment Unconscious or semiconscious hospital patients require a clear airway, tube feeding and regular changing of position. Any fluid accumulation in the brain may be treated with corticosteroid drugs or diuretics. A stroke caused by an embolism is treated with anticoagulant drugs to help prevent recurrences. Sometimes aspirin is prescribed or vascular surgery performed to reduce the risk of subsequent stroke.

While about half of patients recover more or less completely from their first stroke, any intellectual impairment and memory loss is usually permanent. (See also CEREBRAL VASCULAR ACCIDENTS [CVAS].)

Stroop, J. Ridley   One of the most unusual figures in the history of experimental psychology, Stroop devised the "gold standard" of attention measures in 1936—a color word test that bears his name.

When his doctoral dissertation appeared in the *Journal of Experimental Psychology*, Stroop earned immediate prominence for his test of attention. But he published only four studies between 1932 and 1938, finally retiring from the psychology laboratory in favor of teaching, preaching and writing about the Bible at a small Christian college in Nashville, where he served as head of the psychology department. (See also STROOP COLOR WORD TEST; STROOP EFFECT.)

Stroop Color Word Test   The best known of all the focused-attention methods, in which subjects must sort cards on the basis of ink color. Subjects have a harder time concentrating if the ink forms the name of a different color than if the ink forms just nonsense letters. (See also STROOP, J. RIDLEY; STROOP EFFECT.)

Stroop effect   The inability of subjects to perform quickly a task in which they are asked to read a list of color words printed in a color different from the word. (For example, to say "green" in response to the word "purple" written in green ink.) But when asked to simply read the list of words (to say "purple" in response to the word "purple" printed in green ink), subjects can complete the task easily. This phenomenon has never been adequately explained.

More than 700 studies have investigated some aspect of the Stroop effect. Since 1969, about 20 papers a year have examined the phenomenon without reaching any concrete conclusions.

The studies have found that the Stroop effect occurs with exposure to lists of words (or other stimuli) presented singly that require variations in response. Not just colors, but also things such as the word "horse" inside a drawing of a bear interferes with the person's ability to name the pictures.

Researchers also found that words closely associated with the colors in the Stroop test interfere more with color identification than unassociated words. For example, "purple" printed in red slows down the respondents' ability to say "red" more than the word "house" printed in red.

People can name colors faster when the color words ("red") are printed in the same color ink than when color words are printed in black ink. But this effect is weaker than the disturbance in color naming caused by mismatches of words and ink colors.

If the test presents colors and color words in different locations (such as a blue bar above the word "red" in black ink), subjects still have trouble naming the colors, but not as much as they do for the standard Stroop test.

Subjects' ability to name colors quickly slows down when a color word on one trial matches the ink color on the next trial, as when "red" in green ink precedes "purple" in red ink. Researchers believe that subjects consciously suppress the reading response "red" on the first trial, making it harder to say "red" in response to the ink color in the next trial.

However, if subjects are allowed to practice naming incompatible ink colors of various color words, they slowly can improve their ability to name colors—but they also have a harder time in reading color words printed in nonmatching colors.

Even young children experience the Stroop effect, and the effect peaks during the second and third grades as reading skills are strengthened. The amount of time it takes to name the colors then continues to decline until about age 60, when it starts to increase again. There are no differences between men and women's experience of the Stroop effect.

Some scientists believe that people read words faster than they identify colors, so when different words and colors collide in the same test, the reading response interferes with the slower color-naming response, especially when the faster response has to be ignored. But others have found that presenting various colors just before incompatible color words doesn't interfere with naming. (See also STROOP, J. RIDLEY; STROOP COLOR WORD TEST.)

subarachnoid hemorrhage A fairly unusual type of cerebral vascular accident (or STROKE) that can cause either a temporary or a permanent memory impairment. This type of hemorrhage usually affects younger patients who are less likely to suffer from widespread cerebral vascular disease. About 8 percent of all stroke patients have this type of hemorrhage, which usually is caused by the rupture of an intercranial aneurysm that bleeds into the subarachnoid space around the brain. Common sites for these ruptures include the ANTERIOR COMMUNICATING ARTERY lying between the frontal lobes, the middle cerebral artery and the posterior communicating artery.

Shortly after the hemorrhage, the patient often will experience symptoms similar to Korsakoff's syndrome—disorientation, confabulation and memory problems. Some patients do not develop amnesia until several days or weeks afterward.

Gade, A. "Amnesia After Operations of Aneurysms of the Anterior Communicating Artery." *Surgical Neurology* 18 (1982): 46–49.

subconscious A term describing mental events such as thoughts, ideas or feelings that normally remain below the threshold of awareness and that a person may be unaware

of temporarily, but that can be recalled under the right circumstances. In psychoanalytic theory, the subconscious refers to that part of the mind through which information passes on its way from the unconscious to the conscious mind. (See also FREUD, SIGMUND.)

subliminal learning A type of learning that takes place below the level of consciousness and involves messages or information that is too fast or too weak for normal awareness. The idea of subliminal learning is related to sleep learning, in which material is presented when the subject is asleep.

The existence of subliminal advertising became publicized during the 1950s, when some outdoor movie theaters reported huge spurts of concession business when messages saying "Eat popcorn" and "Drink Coca-Cola" were flashed very briefly on the screen over a six-week period. Popcorn business reportedly increased 50 percent, and soda sales rose 18 percent.

Some research supports the notion that in a laboratory, subjects can process limited sensory information without conscious awareness if they are paying close attention to the task. But no scientist has succeeded in duplicating the subliminal advertising effect reported during the 1950s; other studies have found no evidence to support the ability of subliminal messages in ads or music to have any significant effect on behavior or learning.

Scientists have concluded that it is unlikely that anyone could learn or remember information if he or she is not aware that it is being presented.

substitution hypothesis A theory about eyewitness memory that explains why people report incorrect facts after an event they have witnessed. The hypothesis holds that false information presented to a witness after an event replaces or transforms the person's original memory, which is then irretrievably lost. This theory, which is supported by eyewitness expert Elizabeth Loftus's research, assumes a destructive updating mechanism in the brain and assumes that the subject would have remembered the correct information if the knowledge hadn't been replaced by false postevent information. (See also AGE AND EYEWITNESS ABILITY, EYEWITNESS TESTIMONY; MEMORY FOR EVENTS.)

substitution mnemonics A type of memory aid that substitutes words rich in images for information to be remembered. For example, to remember that Mt. Fuji is 12,365 feet tall, one might simply think of the mountain as "calendar mountain" and a calendar as 12 months and 365 days. This method also can be used to remember a person's name, by taking the name apart and linking it with a strongly visual image.

suggestibility A state of greatly enhanced receptiveness and responsiveness to suggestions and stimuli. It is characterized by the facility with which the subject can respond to either external stimuli or those from inner experience. But suggestions must be acceptable to the subject, who can just as easily reject them. By accepting and responding to suggestions, the subject can become psychologically deaf, blind, anesthetized or dissociated, and suffer from hallucinations or amnesia, or he can develop various special types of behavior (provided that he doesn't object). (See also HYPNOSIS; POSTHYPNOTIC SUGGESTION.)

surgical anesthesia and memory See ANESTHESIA, MEMORY WHILE UNDER.

surroundings and memory A person remembers better when placed in the same conditions (a place or a mood) as those in which the learning occurred. In one study, researchers found that a group of subjects who learned a list of words underwater re-

membered more of the list when they were underwater than when they were on dry land.

In the same way, when a person feels depressed, all the memories that rise to consciousness are colored by this emotion. This is one reason why it is so difficult to "shake off" depression; all a person's associations are negative. (See also STATE-DEPENDENT LEARNING.)

synapse The point at which a nerve impulse passes from the axon of one neuron (nerve cell) to a DENDRITE of another. To send a signal, one neuron squirts out a chemical messenger (called a neurotransmitter) that crosses the synapsic gap between adjacent dendrites. (See NEUROTRANSMITTERS.) The receiving dendrite has receptors that recognize the chemical transmitter and speeds the signal through the neuron. Many neurons have as many as 60,000 synapses.

Scientists have long believed that changes in the brain's synapses are the critical events in information storage. But researchers do not agree about how synaptic change actually represents information. One of the most widely held ideas is that the specificity of stored information is determined by the location of synaptic changes in the nervous system and by the pattern of altered neuronal interaction that these changes produce.

synaptic change and memory The theory that memory occurs as a result of functional changes in the brain's SYNAPSES caused by the effects of external stimuli prompted by training or education. Nerve cells (NEURONS) connect with other cells at junctions called synapses; they transmit electrical signals to each other by firing across this junction, which triggers the release of NEUROTRANSMITTERS (special signaling substances) that diffuse across the spaces between cells, attaching themselves to receptors on the neighboring nerve cell. The human brain contains about 10 billion of these nerve cells, joined together by about 60 trillion synapses.

Researchers generally have agreed that anything that influences behavior leaves a trace (ENGRAM) somewhere in the nervous system. As long as these memory traces last, theoretically they can be restimulated, and the event or experience that established them will be remembered.

synesthesia A sensation in another sensory modality that arises when one sensory modality is stimulated. For example, a person experiencing synesthesia would see a visual image such as colors, whenever someone else speaks. While many people feel a relationship between certain sounds and light, one subject (called "S" by Russian neuroscientist Aleksandr Luria) had an incredible case of lifelong synesthesia that began at age two or three. For example, when hearing one tone, S reported that he saw a brown strip against a dark background that had red, tonguelike edges. Also, a sense of taste similar to sweet-and-sour borscht gripped his entire tongue. Although S's descriptions were often poetic (he told one psychologist he had a crumbly yellow voice), he was not speaking metaphorically—he actually saw yellow and felt a crumbly sensation when he heard the psychologist speak.

S's synesthesia provided not an enriched existence but a tortured one, alienating him from experience and providing a hallucinatory substitute for reality. S would get so interested in the sound, sight and taste of a person's words, for example, that he would completely lose the thread of what the person was saying. His experiences dissociated him from the world, and without interpretive memory, his dissociations grew bizarre. (See LURIA, ALEKSANDR R.)

syphilis A sexually transmitted (or congenital) disease that can have devastating effects on the brain, including dementia. Syphilis of the brain, called neurosyphilis, also can cause paralysis (once called "general paralysis of the insane") in addition to dementia. Neurosyphilis is caused by the spirochete (a type of bacterium) called *Treponema pallidum*. Usually transmitted by sexual contact, the organism enters the body via minor cuts or abrasions in the skin or mucous membranes. It also can be transmitted by infected blood or from a mother to her unborn child during pregnancy.

Neurosyphilis usually occurs 10 to 20 years after the initial infection; it is considered the tertiary (end) stage of the disease. Rarely seen today, it is encountered in elderly demented patients who were never treated properly for syphilis in their youth.

Symptoms include subtle changes in personality, lack of attention, poor judgment, aggression, bizarre behavior, mood swings and problems in concentration. Some patients experience delusions of grandeur, but about 50 percent have a simple dementia.

Tertiary syphilis can be diagnosed with tests such as the Venereal Disease Research Laboratory test or the fluorescent treponemal antibody absorption test; it may be necessary to perform these tests on a sample of cerebrospinal fluid.

The disease is not nearly as deadly as it once was, due to the introduction of penicillin; however, treatment of tertiary-stage syphilis takes longer. More than half of those treated suffer a severe reaction within six to 12 hours because the body reacts to the sudden annihilation of large numbers of spirochetes. Brain damage already caused by the disease cannot be reversed.

Infection can be avoided by maintaining monogamous relationships; condoms offer some measure of protection, but do not offer absolute protection. People infected with syphilis are infectious during the primary and secondary stages, but not during the tertiary stage.

T

Tacrine   See   TETRAHYDROAMINOACRIDE (THA).

temporal lobe   The part of the brain that forms much of the lower side of each half of the cerebrum (main mass of the brain). The temporal lobes are concerned with smell, taste, hearing, visual associations and some aspects of memory. Abnormal electrical activity in a lobe (such as in temporal lobe epilepsy) may cause peculiarities in any of these functions, and some scientists suspect that the phenomenon of DÉJÀ VU represents a disturbance of the temporal lobes.

While stimulating various areas of the cortex produces a range of responses from patients, only stimulation of the temporal lobes elicits meaningful, integrated experiences (including sound, movement and color) that are far more detailed, accurate and specific than normal recall. Canadian surgeon Wilder Penfield stimulated the temporal lobe area of patients during the 1950s, eliciting a range of integrated memories. Interestingly, some of the memories that popped up during stimulation were not remembered in the normal state, and stimulation of the same spot in the temporal lobe elicited the exact same memory again and again.

Research also has suggested that removing the left temporal lobe causes verbal memory deficits and removing the right lobe impairs nonverbal memory (such as remembering mazes, patterns or faces).

Direct and diffuse effects from a HEAD INJURY may cause memory deficits, and there is some evidence that the tips and undersurface of the temporal lobes are particularly vulnerable to trauma; if so, then memory problems after diffuse brain damage may indicate hippocampal damage.

temporal lobectomy   The surgical removal of both TEMPORAL LOBES. This operation is associated with a severe AMNESIA when the HIPPOCAMPUS also is removed. Amnesia does not develop following surgery or damage involving the uncus or AMYGDALA as long as the hippocampus is not removed.

Removing one of the temporal lobes results in a material-specific memory deficit. (That is, patients whose left temporal lobe is removed suffer a verbal memory deficit, while those with whose right temporal lobe is removed have more problems in remembering nonverbal material, such as faces, patterns and mazes.) Left temporal lobectomies result in more problems in learning and retaining verbal material (such as paired associates, prose passages or Hebb's recurring digit sequences). In addition, stimulation of the left temporal lobe leads to a number of naming errors and impaired recall.

Patients who have undergone removal of the right temporal lobe can usually perform verbal tasks, but have problems with learning visual or tactile mazes or in figuring out whether they have seen a particular geometric shape before. They also have problems recognizing tonal patterns or faces. But those with right temporal lobectomies are impaired in maze learning and recognition for photographs only if extensive hippocampal lesions existed.

In fact, researchers have found that the more extensive the section of hippocampus removed, the greater the memory deficit. Among those whose left temporal lobe was removed, those with extensive hippocampus involvement had more problems with short-term verbal memory than those with no or little involvement.

temporal lobe epilepsy   A form of epilepsy in which abnormal electrical discharges in the brain are confined to the temporal lobe, which forms much of the lower side of each half of the cerebrum. This type of epilepsy differs from the generalized disturbance found in those with grand mal or petit mal seizures.

Temporal lobe epilepsy is usually caused by damage in one of the temporal lobes due to birth or head injury, brain tumor or abscess, or stroke. Because the temporal lobes are concerned with smell, taste, hearing, visual associations and some aspects of memory, seizures in the temporal lobes can disrupt any of these functions.

Symptoms People with temporal lobe epilepsy suffer dreamlike states ranging from partial to total loss of awareness; they may have unpleasant hallucinations of smell or taste, or experience DÉJÀ VU. Patients may perform tasks with no memory of them after the attack, which can last from minutes to hours. In some cases, a temporal lobe seizure progresses to a generalized grand mal seizure.

Treatment Treatment is the same as in other types of epilepsy. Surgery has been used in some cases to remove the part of the lobe containing the irritating focus for the attacks. Operations are performed only in severe cases that have not responded to medication, because of the danger of affecting other important brain functions.

tetrahydroaminoacridine   (THA)
Also known as tacrine or its trade name, Cognex, this drug is currently being tested for use in the treatment of ALZHEIMER'S DISEASE. In several studies, memory loss improved in people with the disease; a large clinical trial was underway until side effects (such as impaired liver function) became too serious.

It is believed that THA works by increasing the production of the brain chemical ACETYLCHOLINE, which is deficient in Alzheimer's patients. However, the drug does not halt degeneration of brain tissue and therefore cannot cure the disease.

THA which was denied approval by an advisory committee to the U.S. Food and Drug Administration in 1991 because of its negative side effects on the liver in some patients. While the FDA acknowledged that tacrine did benefit Alzheimer's patients, it was concerned over reports of liver damage; the damage is reversible once detected, but frequent blood tests are required. The risk of permanent damage from long-term treatment is unknown.

At present, there is no drug on the market to treat Alzheimer's disease, which afflicts 4 million Americans with memory loss, confusion, disorientation and death.

"Alzheimer's Report in Dispute." *Philadelphia Inquirer*, January 31, 1991.

THA See   TETRAHYDROAMINOACRIDINE (THA).

thyroid function and memory See HYPOTHYROIDISM.

thalamus The crucial brain structure in the factual memory circuit, the thalamus (named for the Greek word meaning "chamber,") serves as the entrance chamber to the perceptual cortex. All sensory organs (except for smell) enter the cortex via the thalamus.

One of the main parts of the diencephalon, the thalamus is active during memory and is involved in many cases of memory disorder—particularly in Wernicke-Korsakoff syndrome patients. One of the best-known cases of thalamic damage and memory problems is N.A., a man who was stabbed in the thalamic region at age 22 and suffered significant memory problems.

Other cases of memory problems involving the thalamus have been reported, primarily due to tumors, which can lead to a rapidly developing dementia.

TIA See TRANSIENT ISCHEMIC ATTACK.

tip-of-the-tongue phenomenon An acute form of "feeling of knowing," which is a situation where we are unable to recall a piece of information, but we know that we have memorized it. Sometimes a person can recall related facts but not the specific information required. In this phenomenon, searching activates networks in a way we can feel.

The brain contains a tremendous store of information, some of which cannot be retrieved at any given moment. Problems in recovering this information is called a tip-of-the-tongue experience; a person can picture the person in the mind, or remember some part of the name or a name like it, or other related information.

For example, in trying to remember the name "MacDuff," a person might think of Scotland or Shakespeare, because of the Scottish association of the prefix "Mac" and of MacDuff, a character in Shakespeare's *Hamlet.*

The brain's internal monitor will continue working on an unconscious level long after the attempt to remember has been abandoned, and the correct name or word will be remembered suddenly about 97 percent of the time, according to research.

The first research into this widespread sensation was published in the 1960s and then duplicated in the 1970s. Scientists studied the phenomenon by reading aloud definitions of unfamiliar words (such as *sampan* or *sextant*). Subjects were asked to tell what the word was or everything they could about the word. Some subjects reported words with a similar meaning or sound, or they remembered the first or last letter of the word. When given the definition of the word *sampan* (a small Chinese boat), they came up with *Siam, sarong* and *Saipan.* They also thought of words that mean nearly the same, such as *junk* or *barge.*

People in their 30s and 40s generally experience this phenomenon somewhat more often than 20-year-olds, and those over 70 have slightly more tip-of-the-tongue experi-

ences than the middle-aged. Proper names are the biggest problem, according to research.

This phenomenon indicates that memory is a matter of degree, that it exists on a continuum—a person may remember a piece of something. Information in long-term memory may not be stored as it is expected to be. The fact that a person tries to remember something by picking up different clues about the word suggests that people remember information in pieces. Although it's possible to remember something only in part, through a series of clues, it's often possible to reach more of what has been stored. Scientists suspect older people often have the tip-of-the-tongue problem because their slower mental processing rate delays retrieval.

In addition, memory is not some sort of automatic photo-snapping process; most memories are not complete representations of information that has been learned, but are a result of the process of reconstruction.

The tip-of-the-tongue phenomenon suggests that memories are not stored in only one way; they may be filed away as an auditory memory (how many syllables a word has or how it is pronounced), in visual terms (first and last letters) or by meaning (and cross-referenced with other words similar in meaning).

To avoid the problem, one might try running through the alphabet to find a "sound trigger" for the word; if that doesn't work, one might stop thinking about it for a while. The memory may well pop into one's mind.

topectomy A more conservative type of psychosurgery that destroys parts of the frontal cortex itself instead of the white fibers below it, as in LEUCOTOMY. The operation was designed to avoid the problems of hemorrhage, memory loss and vegetative states that often occurred after other more radical types of LOBOTOMY.

The procedure was developed by research scientist J. Lawrence Pool at Columbia

University in 1947 and performed on patients at the New Jersey State Hospital in Greystone Park. (See also FREEMAN, WATER; MONIZ, EGAS.)

trace decay The basis of forgetting, this theory states that anything that influences the behavior of an organism leaves a "trace" (or ENGRAM) in the central nervous system that gradually erodes as time passes, in much the way a meadow bordered by forest eventually will return to forest if it is not used. The basis of this FORGETTING is disuse; a person who has moved to a foreign country and uses that language exclusively eventually will forget most or all of the native language.

The theory of trace decay is one of the oldest, most popular explanations of forgetting. Theoretically, as long as memory traces last, they can be restimulated and the experience that established them will be remembered.

training and eyewitness ability While a witness's prior knowledge and expectations can influence perception and memory, researchers found there were no significant differences between the number of true detections of people and actions between police officers and civilians.

Specific face-recognition training is not effective either, according to studies of one such course. In the course, students attended three days of intensive training (lectures, slides and film demonstrations, discussions, and so on). They were taught to break the faces down into components to better discriminate among faces and better remember a face later; the best way to remember a face is to ignore any movement in the facial pattern.

But when these students were tested on their ability to remember photographed faces, results showed that the training course had no effect. When the photographed face was changed in either pose or expression, recognition dropped to 60 to 70 percent, and when the faces were disguised, performance was poor—about 30 percent. (Students who simply guessed should have been right 50 percent of the time.) Recognition training did not produce any improvement whatsoever in ability to match different versions of the same face. But surprisingly, the course did not improve either matching ability or memory ability either.

Researchers believed this particular course wrongly emphasized the importance of selecting individual facial features rather than considering the face as a whole as a way to remember it. Some evidence suggests that, in remembering a face, the basic facial framework and arrangement is even more important than individual physical features.

Many investigators have found that people are better at paying attention to the face as a whole rather than paying attention to a specific feature of a face. (See also AGE AND EYEWITNESS ABILITY; CROSS-RACIAL WITNESS IDENTIFICATION; EYEWITNESS TESTIMONY; GENDER AND WITNESS ABILITY; MEMORY FOR EVENTS; MEMORY FOR FACES.)

transient global amnesia An abrupt loss of memory lasting from a few seconds to a few hours without loss of consciousness or other impairment that was first described in 1964.

During the period of amnesia, the subject cannot store new experiences and suffers a permanent memory gap. At the same time, the subject may also lose memory of many years prior to the amnesia attack; this retrograde memory loss gradually disappears, although a permanent gap in memory that usually extends backward no more than an hour before onset of the amnesia attack results.

Attacks of transient global amnesia may occur more than once and are believed to be caused by a temporary reduction in blood supply in areas of the brain concerned with memory, sometimes heralding a stroke, although several toxic substances have been associated with transient global amnesia.

Victims are usually healthy and over age 50; an attack may be precipitated by many things, including sudden changes in temperature, physical stress, eating a large meal and even sexual intercourse. This type of amnesia is not common, and it disappears within a day or two. It was first described in 1964. (See also RETROGRADE AMNESIA.)

transient ischemic attack (TIA)   A temporary impairment of the brain caused by an insufficient supply of blood, which can result in brief memory problems. Other symptoms include speech problems, weakness, paralysis, dizziness and nausea lasting only a few minutes or hours.

Unlike a STROKE, which may have the same symptoms but involve a lasting deficit, TIA symptoms fade without lasting damage. However, these attacks should be regarded as possible forerunners of stroke and should be reported to a physician.

transient memory disorders   A group of temporary memory disorders in which a person's memory stops functioning normally for a certain period of time. Causes include vascular disorders, closed HEAD INJURY, medications, or aftereffects of electroconvulsive therapy (ECT). Psychogenic disorders also may be of a transient nature. (See also ELECTROCONVULSIVE   THERAPY   AND MEMORY.)

Transient Global Amnesia   A form of sudden-onset ANTEROGRADE AMNESIA, coupled with RETROGRADE AMNESIA for recent events, disorientation in time and no loss of personal identity. Attacks may last from minutes to days and can be set off by many things, including temperature change, toxins, physical stress or even sexual intercourse. The underlying dysfunction is believed to be a temporary drop in blood supply to the memory centers of the brain.

Posttraumatic Amnesia   Most victims of closed head injury suffer only a temporary memory loss from between a few seconds to several months. It is believed that the injury interferes somehow with the transfer of information from short- to long-term memory.

ECT and Memory Loss   Many patients who undergo ECT report a temporary anterograde or retrograde amnesia that gradually fades away.

translogic   A phenomenon experienced during HYPNOSIS in which the subject shows a decrease in critical judgment. For example, during age regression to childhood, a person exhibits translogic when she takes down a complicated dictation in childish scrawl but spells all the words perfectly, beyond the capability of any child. An adult who is consciously trying to mimic a child would not copy a complicated paragraph without remembering to insert some spelling errors. (See also AGE REGRESSION, HYPNOTIC.)

transorbital lobotomy   See LOBOTOMY.

traumatic amnesia   The inability to store new memories between an hour and a few weeks following a blow to the head. This posttraumatic confusional state also can induce a RETROGRADE AMNESIA that may extend backward for a few hours to many years; the duration of this amnesia depends on the severity of injury and the subject's age.

As the person recovers, memories often return in chronological order (as in RIBOT'S LAW), but sometimes memories return in no particular fashion and gradually become interrelated again in the brain. At times, there may be a permanent memory loss for a period of time during the injury and immediately preceding it; some researchers believe this permanent memory loss is an indication that the head injury was severe.

About 10 percent of patients admitted to a hospital following severe closed head injury suffer severe memory problems.

traumatic automatism   A dazed response following a mild head injury without loss of consciousness and no apparent change in ordinary behavior; however, the person is going through the motions of everyday life automatically and may have no memory whatever of his or her actions after the injury. (See also TRANSIENT GLOBAL AMNESIA.)

U

unclassified dementias Diseases producing dementia that are indistinguishable from ALZHEIMER'S DISEASE or PICK DISEASE in life; upon autopsy, no specific disease can be identified from the inspection of brain tissue. In some of these cases, depression may be the cause of the dementia; others are probably extremely rare diseases or unusual variants of more common diseases.

unconscious transference A phenomenon in which a person seen in one situation is confused with or recalled as a person seen in a second situation. For example, in one case a railroad ticket agent misidentified a sailor in a lineup as a robber. When it was later determined that the sailor had a solid alibi and could not have been the robber, the agent explained that the sailor had looked familiar. In fact, the sailor lived near the station and had purchased tickets from this agent three times before the robbery. The agent experienced unconscious transference; he mistakenly linked the familiarity of the sailor to the robbery instead of the times he sold the man tickets.

Unconscious transference is a result of the malleable nature of the human memory; a brief exposure to another person can make that person seem familiar when seen later. Unfortunately, in any given criminal case, it is almost impossible to tell whether unconscious transference has taken place. (See also AGE AND EYEWITNESS ABILITY; CROSS-RACIAL WITNESS IDENTIFICATION; EYEWIT-NESS TESTIMONY; GENDER AND EYEWITNESS ABILITY; MEMORY FOR EVENTS.)

unitary theory The idea that short-term, long-term and any other type of memory are all part of one system.

use-it-or-lose-it hypothesis The idea that patients can minimize losses to body and mind through vigorous mental and physical exercise. At the University of California at Berkeley, scientists discovered that rats housed in stimulating cages with plenty of interesting toys have larger nerve cells in the cerebral cortex (the thinking part of the brain) and more dendrites, or projections, from these cells. Further, researchers discovered that neuron size can be enlarged by living in a stimulating environment at any age.

Similar findings came from research at the University of California at Los Angeles, where autoposies of 20 men and women aged 18 to 79 found that those with more education and a busier social and intellectual life had longer dendrites in part of the brain than people with less stimulation. And people with more education who remain mentally active seem to have fewer cognitive declines as they get older.

V

vacant slot hypothesis A theory about eyewitness memory that explains why people report incorrect facts after witnessing an event. The hypothesis holds that the original information was never stored, so that false information presented after the event was simply popped into a "vacant slot" in the memory representation.

However, many leading experts in the field, including witness expert Elizabeth Loftus, reject this hypothesis on the grounds that 90 percent of subjects who are tested immediately after witnessing an event and aren't exposed to postevent information are correct. (See also AGE AND EYEWITNESS ABILITY; CROSS-RACIAL WITNESS IDENTIFICATION; EYEWITNESS TESTIMONY; GENDER AND EYEWITNESS ABILITY; MEMORY FOR EVENTS.)

vanishing cue technique   A variant of the DIRECT PRIMING procedure, this learning method gives a patient a definition with a cued instruction; each subsequent time, the instruction is presented with one less letter than needed for the last successful recall.

vasopressin   Another name for ADH (antidiuretic hormone), this chemical functions as a neurotransmitter in the brain and acts as the body's diuretic—and it also may be part of the ink with which memories are written. (See NEUROTRANSMITTERS.)

Vasopressin is released from the pituitary gland and acts on the kidneys to increase their reabsorption of water into the blood. It reduces the amount of water lost in the urine and helps control the body's overall water balance. Water is continually being taken into the body in food and beverages and also is produced by the chemical reactions in cells. At the same time, water always is being lost in urine, sweat, feces and breath; vasopressin helps maintain the optimum amount of water in the body.

Its production is controlled by the HYPOTHALAMUS (located in the center of the brain), which detects changes in the concentration and volume of the blood. If the blood concentration loses water, the hypothalamus stimulates the pituitary gland to release more vasopressin, and vice versa.

External vasopressin is approved for treatment of diabetes as a way of preventing the frequent urination common in this disease. It is given via the nose or by injection; high intravenous doses cause a narrowing of blood vessels. Vasopressin also has been used to treat memory deficits of aging, senile DEMENTIA, ALZHEIMER'S DISEASE, KORSAKOFF'S SYNDROME and AMNESIA.

Research has shown that when subjects are given vasopressin, they remember long lists of words better and seem to chunk and encode better. (Chunking, or grouping, words together is a trick that memory experts teach to improve memory.) Vasopressin also is being studied as a possible memory enhancement drug.

Because cocaine, LSD, amphetamines, Ritalin (methylphenidate) and Cylert (pemoline) cause the pituitary to step up the release of natural vasopressin, abuse of these drugs can result in a depleted pool of vasopressin and a resulting mental slowness. On the other hand, alcohol and marijuana cause mental slowness by suppressing the *release* of vasopressin.

Vasopressin is available on doctor's prescription in the United States. It is available in a nasal spray bottle, and produces noticeable effect within seconds because it is absorbed by the nasal mucosa. However, it can produce a range of side effects, from congestion to headache and increased bowel movements, abdominal cramps, nausea, drowsiness and confusion. It has not been proved safe during pregnancy. Because it temporarily constricts small blood vessels, it should not be used by anyone with hypertension, angina or atherosclerosis, and should be used cautiously by epileptics. (See also ENCODING; MEMORY ENHANCEMENT.)

Dean, Ward, and Morgenthaler, John. *Smart Drugs and Nutrients.* Santa Cruz: B&J Publications, 1990.

verbal elaboration   Comments, analysis, judgments and so on that act to enhance the recording of a memory trace, or ENGRAM. Verbal elaboration gets a person involved emotionally and intellectually, ensuring a vibrant memory trace. (See also TRACE DECAY.)

verbal memory   Also known as semantic memory, this type of memory makes it possible for a person to embrace organized bodies of knowledge. Verbal memory can be divided into two systems, active or short-term memory and long-term memory. Active memory is a transient form of remembering that includes all of the impulses that pass through the mind during the day. Long-term memory is responsible for retaining material for years—or a lifetime. This type of memory makes learning possible.

verbal memory strategies Internal methods for remembering. Some of the best-known strategies include ALPHABETICAL SEARCHING and FIRST-LETTER CUEING. These strategies often are helpful in coming up with something in the wake of the TIP-OF-THE-TONGUE PHENOMENON, when something to be recalled is partially remembered. The provision of the first letter for a word not remembered may prompt memory of the entire word; thus first-letter cueing is a valuable retrieval strategy. First-letter cueing is easy to apply, since the alphabet is usually well known, and it can be written down if necessary.

Examples of first-letter cueing include remembering the notes on the stave lines by recalling "Every Good Boy Does Fine."

verbal process One of two ways that information can be recorded, using words, numbers or names; it is opposed to the imagery process, which records information in a visual form of pictures, scenes or faces.

It's possible to see in the mind's eye a mental picture (or visual image) of a bed, or one can think of the word "bed." Thinking of the word is an example of the verbal process.

The verbal process is best suited to represent abstract verbal information such as the word "nourishment," whereas the visual process works better in representing a concrete form of nourishment, such as "banana." (See also IMAGERY PROCESS AND MEMORY; VERBAL MEMORY STRATEGIES.)

vincamine An extract of periwinkle, this drug is a vasodilator (widens blood vessels) and increases blood flow and oxygen use in the brain. It has been used with some benefit for the treatment of memory defects.

In some studies, vincamine has been shown to cause some memory improvement in ALZHEIMER'S DISEASE patients, and it normalizes the brain wave patterns in elderly people with memory problems or with alcohol-induced ORGANIC BRAIN SYNDROME.

Vincamine also has been used to treat a variety of problems related to poor blood flow to the brain, including Meniere's syndrome, vertigo, sleep problems, mood changes, depression, hearing problems, high blood pressure and others.

However, there has been very little research on the drug and cognitive enhancement in normal subjects. (See also MEMORY ENHANCEMENT; VINPOCETINE.)

Casale, R., Giorgi, I., and Guarnaschelli, C. "Evaluation of the Effect of Vincamine Teprosilate on Behavioral Performances of Patients Affected with Chronic Cerebrovascular Disease." *International Journal of Clinical Pharmacology Research* 4, no. 4 (1984): 313–19.
Saletu, B., and Grunberger, J. "Memory Dysfunction and Vigilance: Neurophysiological and Psychopharmacological Aspects." *Annals of the New York Academy of Sciences* 444 (1985): 406–27.

vinpocetine This derivative of VINCAMINE, a periwinkle extract, has fewer adverse effects and more benefits in memory enhancement, according to research. Marketed in Europe as Cavinton, the drug improves brain metabolism by improving blood flow and enhancing the use of GLUCOSE and oxygen.

It often is used to treat memory problems and other cerebral circulation disorders, such as STROKE, APHASIA, APRAXIA, headache and others.

In one Hungarian study involving 882 patients with a range of neurological disorders, significant improvements were noted in 62 percent of the patients, including memorization of word lists. In addition, at least one double-blind study of normal subjects indicated that subjects seemed to show significant short-term memory improvement within one hour after taking the drug. (See also MEMORY ENHANCEMENT.)

DeNoble, V.J., et al. "Vinpocetine: Nootropic Effects on Scopolamine-induced and Hypoxia-induced Retrieval Deficits of a Step-through Passive Avoidance Response in Rats." *Pharmacology Biochemistry and Behavior* 24 (1986): 1123–28.

violence and memory   According to experts, experiencing or watching violence can be so stressful that it negatively influences the ability of an eyewitness to recall the events accurately. Research has indicated that EYEWITNESS TESTIMONY about an emotionally volatile event may be more likely to be incorrect than such testimony about a less emotional incident.

In one study, subjects were shown a video of two police officers finding a criminal with the help of a third person. In the nonviolent version, there is a verbal exchange between the three people and a weak restraining movement by one police officer. In the violent version, one of the police officers physically assaults the third person. Both men and women who saw the violent version were significantly less able to recall events accurately. (See also AGE AND EYEWITNESS ABILITY; CROSS-RACIAL WITNESS IDENTIFICATION; EVENT FACTORS; GENDER AND EYEWITNESS ABILITY; MEMORY FOR EVENTS.)

visual alphabet   A way of representing letters of the alphabet by images formed in various ways, such as a picture of an object whose shape resembles letters of the alphabet. Visual alphabets are very common in memory treatises, and have come down to us from a very ancient tradition.

visual association   A memory strategy used to help make image associations in order to improve recall for many different types of information. By associating images with many contexts, it is possible to improve recall.

Visual imagery by itself is not that effective. Visual associations are most effective if they interact and if they are vivid.

To be really memorable, the two associated images must be imagined as interacting in some way with each other rather than simply sitting near each other. For example, to associate the words "horse" and "mop," it would be better to imagine the horse mopping a floor instead of simply standing beside the mop. Researchers suggest that this interaction boosts memory because the separate interacting images are combined into one single unit; therefore, each part of the image is a cue for remembering the entire unit. However, studies show that this interactive imagery isn't much better than separate images for word pairs that are already meaningfully related, probably because they are already remembered as a unit.

In order to best remember, the images should be as clear and vivid as possible, as much like a real picture as possible. To visualize the horse with the mop, a person should try not just to think about the image, but to truly *see* the horse mopping in as detailed a picture as possible. (See also ASSOCIATION).

visual imagery method   A type of memory technique that is basically "remembering by pictures"—either mental images or actual drawings. Visual imagery techniques include the method of loci, the VISUAL-PEG SYSTEM and the FACE-NAME ASSOCIATION METHOD.

There are a range of methods; sometimes words or sentences are read and patients are asked to make a mental image. For paired associates, a picture linking the two words is drawn for the subjects or they imagine the objects depicted by two words interacting in some way. Other procedures link the first word with the second word, the second and third with the fourth, and so on.

The visual-peg system is one popular type of visual imagery procedure that has been used since ancient times. In this system, the numbers one through ten are associated with words. (One of the best-known lists is one-bun, two-shoe). The items to be remembered are then placed on the pegs.

The face-name association method was designed specifically for learning names. In this procedure, when a subject wants to remember a name, he or she first chooses a distinctive feature of the person's face. Then the name is transformed into one or two common nouns—"Tunney" would be "ton" "knee." Finally, the distinctive features are linked with the transformed name. If the distinctive feature of Mr. Tunney is his mouth, the subject would picture Mr. Tunney with his knee shoving a ton weight into his mouth.

Research has indicated that amnesic patients can learn some paired associations more easily than others; the pairs should be based on a logical association (that is, if they rhyme or are phonetically similar). Face-name learning is one such paired associate task. In research with Korsakoff patients, subjects who were taught the face-name method were able to learn names.

A simpler type of visual imagery is simply to turn the name to be remembered into a picture, which is then drawn on a card. For example, Bill Smith could be drawn as a blacksmith with a long, rounded nose like a duck's bill. This type of system does not require mental imagery, and a person doesn't need to have any distinctive features.

Research suggests that a patient with memory problems with bilateral brain damage may be successful in using the visual imagery technique; severe damage, however, appears to interfere with successful use of visual imagery.

Research also suggests that imagery is probably of limited value in a patient's day-to-day life; it works best when patients are taught just the names of those who are regularly contacted.

The method of loci visual imagery method uses different locations to remember items. Used by the ancient Greeks and made fa-mous by SIMONIDES OF CEOS and by ALEX-SANDR R. LURIA's famous mnemonist, "S," the method is used by normal and brain-damaged patients alike.

The mental retracing of events involves retracing of a sequence of past events or actions in order to jog the memory of something that happened or to remember when someone last had something that is now lost. (See also LOCI, METHOD OF; VISUAL-IZATION.)

visualization   By picturing an image in one's mind, remembering it becomes easier. The more vivid, striking, silly or funny the image, the better. If a man always leaves his car keys on the counter, he might imagine the keys hopping off the counter and running after him as he heads toward the car. (See also FACE-NAME ASSOCIATION METHOD; IMAGERY PROCESS AND MEMORY; METHOD OF LOCI; SIMONIDES OF CEOS; VISUAL IMAGERY METHOD; VISUAL-PEG SYSTEM.)

visualizers   Individuals who have a good ability to visualize.

visual memory   A phenomenally vivid type of memory for images that capture a person's attention. Most people almost never forget a face (although they may well forget the name attached to that face), even if they saw the person only once, ten years before.

Most people (about 60 percent) are pre-dominantly visual when it comes to memo-rizing: They can easily visualize places, objects, faces, the pages of a book. The other 40 percent have stronger verbal memo-ries. (They remember sounds or words, and the associations that come to their mind are often puns or rhymes.)

visual method   A type of memory learn-ing technique used by those with memory deficits. Visual methods include ALPHABETI-CAL SEARCHING; ELABORATION; FIRST-LET-TER CUEING; METHOD OF LOCI; PQRST

METHOD; VERBAL MEMORY STRATEGIES. (See also VISUAL IMAGERY METHOD.)

visual-peg system   One popular type of VISUAL IMAGERY METHOD that has been used since ancient times. In this system, the numbers one through ten are associated with words. (One of the best-known lists is one-bun, two-shoe.) The items to be remembered are then placed on the pegs; for example, if the first thing a subject has to remember to do is mail a letter, the image could be a mailman sitting on top of a bun. If the second thing is to file some papers, the subject could imagine filing a shoe under "S" in a big filing cabinet. The visual-peg method may not work for patients with memory problems caused by brain damage on one side, as it requires remembering in two distinct stages, one involving the left hemisphere and the other, the right. (See also FACE-NAME ASSOCIATION; METHOD OF LOCI; SIMONIDES OF CEOS.)

visual process   See IMAGERY PROCESS AND MEMORY.

vitamins and memory   While the link between vitamins and cognition and memory is controversial, some studies have shown that better nutrition can lead to improved learning, IQ and behavior.

In a 1988 study, California researchers and a British research team both found that vitamin supplementation of schoolchildren boosted nonverbal IQ an average of six points; in 1991 the California team replicated their findings with an expanded study of 615 schoolchildren from six different schools and varied socioeconomic profiles. The children were randomly assigned to one of four different groups that received different vitamin-mineral supplements or placebo on a triple-blind basis. (Students, testers and scientists did not know which child belonged to which group.)

The group receiving vitamins at 100 percent recommended daily allowance scored a 3.7 point increase in nonverbal IQ scores in three months; the 50 percent and 200 percent RDA groups experienced smaller but significant increases of 1.2 and 1.5 points respectively. The results indicate that more is not necessarily *better* however. Not every child's IQ rose, but one-third experienced a dramatic 10-point jump, suggesting that some apparently normal children may in fact be subclinically nutritionally deficient.

Schoenthaler, S.J. "Diet and IQ." *Nature* 352 (1991): 292.
Schoenthaler, S.J., et al. "Controlled Trial Vitamin-mineral Supplementation: Effects on Intelligence and Performance." *Personality and Individual Differences* 12, no. 4 (1991): 351–62.

vitamin B₃   See NIACIN.

vocalizers   People who remember things better in words than in images. Words (especially a statement or proposition) may be more efficient for abstract material, but a combination of words and images is considered to be the most effective memory system of all.

W

Wechsler Memory Scale (WMS)   A widely used pencil-and-paper test of memory functions designed to be used together with the Wechsler Adult Intelligence Scale (WAIS). It includes a group of six subtests used to test memory in brain-damaged patients and evaluates general knowledge, personal orientation, mental control, short-term memory, copying drawings from memory, story recall and paired associate learning. In the test, the ability to remember names is tested by showing a photo of a person and asking patients to remember the name; retention is tested 20 to 25 minutes later. Patients also are asked to remember a hidden belonging by hiding the possession and then asking for its location.

To test ability to remember an appointment, an alarm clock is set to ring 20 minutes later, and patients have to ask a specific question when the bell rings. To test picture recognition, patients are shown ten line drawings of common objects; five minutes later patients must pick out target pictures from the sequence of 20 pictures. To test face recognition, patients view five faces; five minutes later they pick out targets from a sequence of ten faces. To test ability to remember a route and deliver a message, the tester traces a route around a room and leaves a message at a particular point; patient's try to repeat the route.

Devised by David Wechsler in 1945, the WMS rapidly gained acceptance and is still the most widely used clinical memory test. Its value as an assessment procedure has been questioned for several reasons, however. Critics question its value as a test for organic amnesia, since it contains subtests of abilities that are not likely to be disrupted in amnesia and because it examines recall but not recognition.

The value of the WMS for measuring memory function is lessened to some extent by the fact that the test measures cognitive functions rather broadly; a low score on the test can indicate dementia rather than specific memory problems. Amnesia is diagnosed when the intelligence score exceeds the memory score. Despite its disadvantages, the WMS still is used because it has value as a quick screening procedure. (See also ASSESSMENT OF MEMORY DISORDERS.)

Parkin, Alan. *Memory Disorders.* Oxford: Basil Blackwell, 1987.

Wechsler Adult Intelligence Scale (WAIS)

The best-known and commonest test used to assess general intellectual ability in adults (and also the cognitive ability of brain-damaged patients). The WAIS consists of 11 subtests, including two verbal and performance scale subtests that assess several distinct cognitive functions. The verbal scale contains tests of common knowledge, vocabulary, comprehension of common situations, arithmetic, short-term memory and abstract-thinking ability. The performance scale contains more timed tests, and high scores here depend less on previously established knowledge and problem-solving strategies.

Wernicke, Carl (1848–1905)

A 19th-century German neurologist who related nerve diseases to specific areas of the brain and also investigated the localization of memory. Wernicke is best known for his descriptions of the aphasias (disorders interfering with the ability to communicate in speech or writing).

Wernicke studied at the University of Breslau before entering practice in Berlin. He joined the faculty at Breslau, where he remained until the year before his death. He tried to relate the various aphasias to impaired psychic processes in different parts of the brain and included the first accurate description of a sensory aphasia in the temporal lobe. Wernicke showed that auditory word images appear to be located in a memory bank separate from that containing the images of the articulated words. He also noted a second language center farther back in the brain known today as Wernicke's area, which contains the records of individual words.

Wernicke went on to elaborate on different clinical syndromes in terms of damage to either Wernicke's area or the area of the brain discovered by Paul Broca.

In his *Textbook of Brain Disorders (Lehrbuch der Gehirnkrankheiten;* 1891), Wernicke tried to illustrate cerebral localization for all brain disease. Among the disorders he described was Wernicke's encephalopathy, which is caused by a thiamine deficiency. (See also WERNICKE-KORSAKOFF SYNDROME; WERNICKE'S [RECEPTIVE]) APHASIA.)

Wernicke's encephalopathy See WER-NICKE-KORSAKOFF SYNDROME.

Wernicke-Korsakoff syndrome This acute neurological condition is an uncommon brain disorder almost always due to the malnutrition that occurs in chronic alcohol dependence, although it also can occur in other conditions, such as cancer with malnutrition. The disease consists of two stages: Wernicke's encephalopathy followed by Korsakoff's psychosis, each characterized by separate symptoms.

In the first stage (Wernicke encephalopathy), the patient usually develops symptoms suddenly, including abnormal eye movements, problems in coordinating body movements, slowness and confusion. There are also signs of neuropathy, such as loss of sensation, pins and needles or impaired reflexes. The level of consciousness progressively falls, and without treatment, this syndrome may lead to coma and death.

The second stage (Korsakoff's psychosis, or Korsakoff's syndrome) may follow if treatment is not instituted soon enough. In this stage, sufferers experience severe amnesia, apathy and disorientation. Recent memories are affected more than distant memory; often patients cannot remember what they did even a few moments before and they may make up stories to cover for their loss of memory.

Causes The disease is caused by a deficiency of thiamine (vitamin B_1), which affects the brain and nervous system. This deficiency is probably caused by poor eating habits or an inherited defect in thiamine metabolism.

Treatment Wernicke's encephalopathy is a medical emergency requiring large doses of intravenous thiamine if the diagnosis is even suspected. Often such treatment can reverse the symptoms within a few hours. In the absence of treatment, however, the disease will progress to Korsakoff's psychosis and at this stage is usually irreversible. Patients will experience permanent impairment of memory and are in need of constant supervision.

Wernicke's (receptive) aphasia A type of comprehension problem caused by damage to Wernicke's area in the brain, a particular area in the dominant cerebral hemisphere. Speech is fluent, but "internal speech" is impaired because of the impaired comprehension, and speech content includes many errors in word selection and grammar. Writing also is impaired, and spoken or written commands are not understood. Wernicke's aphasia is associated with difficulty in accessing the meaning of words such as nouns.

William's Scale for Measurement of Memory See ASSESSMENT OF MEMORY DISORDERS.

Wisconsin card sorting test One of the most common ways to assess frontal lobe damage. The subject is given a deck of cards marked by a pattern with various symbol shapes, numbers and colors. A card might have three blue stars or one red star or two green triangles.

The tester's comments provide hints as to how the cards should be sorted (such as by placing all the cards with green triangles in one pile). A normal person quickly learns what the proper sorting method is; once the subject has learned to sort by the rule, the rule is changed and the subject must figure out what the new sorting rule is. Patients with frontal lobe damage or KORSAKOFF'S SYNDROME tend to make a perseveration error at this point, continuing to sort the cards by the first rule. They have not lost the ability to understand that the rules have changed, but their understanding does not improve their behavior. They continue to sort by color although each error brings the news that the action was wrong. Their mistake is not one of imagination, reasoning or any other type of intelligence, but is an inflexibility in voluntary motor behavior. It is as if once they have decided to touch their finger, it becomes impossible to touch their nose.

They can recognize the problem because they have suffered no damage to their perceptual cortex, but purposeful action is controlled in the brain's frontal areas. When that region is damaged, they may not be able to adapt their actions no matter how normal their perceptions are. A normal interpretive memory depends on a loop that brings the separate regions of the brain into harmony. (See also ASSESSMENT OF MEMORY DISORDERS.)

witness perception See EYEWITNESS TESTIMONY.

working memory A borderline area between short-term and long-term memory where, some theorist believe, material needed only for a brief period is stored. It is sometimes confused as a synonym for SHORT-TERM MEMORY.

X

xanthinol nicotinate A form of NIACIN that passes into cells much more easily where it increases the rate of glucose metabolism and improves blood flow to the brain.

In recent studies, it was found to improve the performance of healthy elderly subjects on a variety of short- and long-term memory tasks. Like niacin, however, excess doses can cause flushing and a variety of other mild symptoms. (See also MEMORY ENHANCEMENT.)

Z

zatosetron A drug that increases the release of ACETYLCHOLINE, a neurotransmitter linked to improved learning and memory and deficient in many types of memory impairment. By selectively blocking serotonin (a brain substance that inhibits the release of acetylcholine), zatosetron increases acetylcholine release and enhances memory and performance, according to some research. Initial research suggests that zatosetron, like its cousin ONDANSETRON, may improve memory in some healthy older adults with AGE-ASSOCIATED MEMORY IMPAIRMENT.

Scientists at the Memory Assessment Clinics in Bethesda, Maryland and Scottsdale, Arizona are testing zatosetron in preliminary double-blind studies of 200 subjects over age 50 with age-associated memory impairment.

zodiac as a mnemonic device One form of ARTIFICIAL MEMORY in which the zodiac is used instead of a memory palace to remember information. The zodiac is a picture of the orbital circle of the sun, divided into 12 equal parts, or signs, each of which consists of 30 degrees. Each of these signs is subdivided into 36 "decans," each covering ten degrees; for each decan there is an associated "decan figure," such as Mars, Venus, Mercury, etc.

In order to remember information, a person would group ten artificial backgrounds under each decan figure, providing a system of associating based on 360 places. With a little calculation, any background could be found since the numerical order inherent in the zodiac made remembering much easier.

APPENDICES

APPENDIX A.
PERIODICALS THAT PUBLISH
RESEARCH IN MEMORY

American Journal of Clinical Hypnosis
American Society of Clinical Hypnosis
2200 E. Devon Ave.
Suite 291
Des Plaines, IL 60018
(708) 297-3317

American Journal of Psychiatry
American Psychiatric Association
1400 K St., NW
Washington, DC 20005
(202) 682-6020
  Presents clinical research and discussion
  on current psychiatric issues.

American Journal of Psychology
University of Illinois Press
54 E. Gregory Dr.
Champaign, IL 61820
(217) 333-0950

American Journal of Physiology
American Physiological Society
9650 Rockville Pike
Bethesda, MD 20814
(301) 530-7071

APA Monitor
American Psychological Association
750 First St., NE
Washington, DC 20002
(202) 336-5600

American Psychologist
American Psychological Association
750 First St., NE

Washington, DC 20002
(202) 336-5600

*Annals of the New York Academy of
  Science*
New York Academy of Science
2 E. 63rd St.
New York, NY 10021
(212) 838-0230

Annual Review of Neuroscience
Annual Reviews, Inc.
4139 El Camino Way
Box 10139
Palo Alto, CA 94303
(415) 493-4400
  Presents original reviews of critical literature and current developments in neuroscience

Annual Review of Psychology
Annual Reviews, Inc.
4139 El Camino Way
Box 10139
Palo Alto, CA 94303
(415) 493-4400

Aphasiology
Taylor and Francis, LTD
Rankine Rd.
Basingstoke, Hants
RG24 OPR ENGLAND
0256-840366
  Presents information on all aspects of
  brain damage–related language problems

Archives of Clinical Neuropsychology
Pergamon Press
Journals Division
660 White Plains Rd.
Tarrytown, NY 10591
(914) 524-9200

Archives of General Psychiatry
American Medical Association
515 N. State St.
Chicago, IL 60610
(312) 464-0183

Archives of Neurology
American Medical Association
515 N. State St.
Chicago, IL 60610
(312) 464-0183

Behavioral Brain Research
Elsevier Science Publishing Co.
655 Avenue of the Americas
New York, NY 10010
(212) 989-5800
    Presents articles in neuroscience, with a
    special emphasis in neural mechanisms
    of behavior

Behavioral Neuropsychiatry
Behavioral Neuropsychiatry Medical Pub-
    lishers, Inc.
61 E. 86th St.
New York, NY 10028

Behavioral Neuroscience
American Psychological Association
750 First St., NE
Washington, DC 20002
(202) 336-5600

Biological Psychiatry
Elsevier Science Publishing Co.
655 Avenue of the Americas
New York, NY 10010
(212) 989-5800
    Covers the whole range of psychiatric re-
    search

Brain Research
Elsevier Science Publishing Co.
655 Avenue of the Americas

New York, NY 10010
(212) 989-5800
    Presents information on behavioral sci-
    ence and neurology

Brain Research Bulletin
Pergamon Press
Journals Division
660 White Plains Rd.
Tarrytown, NY 10591
(914) 524-9200
    Presents a broad spectrum of articles in
    neuroscience

Clinical Neurology and Neurosurgery
Elsevier Science Publishing Co.
655 Avenue of the Americas
New York, NY 10010
(212) 989-5800

Cognition
Elsevier Science Publishing Co.
655 Avenue of the Americas
New York, NY 10010
(212) 989-5800

Cognitive Development
Ablex Publishing Co.
355 Chestnut St.
Norwood, NJ 07648
(201) 767-8450

Cognitive Psychology
Academic Press
Journals Division
1250 6th Ave.
San Diego, CA 92101
(619) 230-1840

Cognitive Science
Ablex Publishing Co.
355 Chestnut St.
Norwood, NJ 07648
(201) 767-8450

Current Opinions in Neurobiology
20 W. 3rd St.
Philadelphia, PA 19106
(800) 552-5866

Dementia
S.Kargir AG

Allschwilerstr. 10
PO Box CH-4009
Basel, SWITZERLAND
061-3061111
   Presents information on the neural bases
   of cognitive dysfunction (such as in Par-
   kinson's disease, Alzheimer's disease,
   Huntington's disease)

Developmental Psychology
John Wiley & Sons
Journals
605 3rd Ave.
New York, NY 10158
(212) 850-6000

Developmental Psychology
American Psychological Association
750 First St., NE
Washington, DC 20002
(202) 336-5600

Experimental Brain Research
Springer-Verlag
Heidelberger Platz 3
D-1000
Berlin 33 GERMANY
030-8207-1
   Presents information on the morphology,
   physiology, behavior, neurochemistry,
   development and biology of brain
   function

Experimental Neurology
Academic Press
Journals Division
1250 6th Ave.
San Diego, CA 92101
(619) 230-1840
   Presents original research in neuro-
   science

International Journal of Neuroscience
Gordon & Breach, science publishers
270 8th Ave.
New York, NY 10011
(212) 206-8900

Journal of Abnormal Psychology
American Psychological Association
750 First St., NE

Washington, DC 20002
(202) 336-5600
   Articles on basic research and theory in
   abnormal behavior

*Journal of Applied Developmental
   Psychology*
Ablex Publishing Co.
355 Chestnut St.
Norwood, NJ 07648
(201) 767-8450

Journal of Applied Psychology
American Psychological Association
750 First St., NE
Washington, DC 20002
(202) 336-5600
   Presents research on applications of psychology in work settings

*Journal of Child Psychology and Psychia-
   try and Allied Disciplines*
Pergamon Press
Journals Division
660 White Plains Rd.
Tarrytown, NY 10591
(914) 524-9200
   Primarily concerned with child and adolescent psychiatry and psychology

Journal of Clinical Psychiatry
Physicians' Postgraduate Press
Box 240008
Memphis, TN 38124
(901) 682-1001
   Presents original material on psychiatric
   behavior and neurological science

Journal of Clinical Psychology
Clinical Psychology Publishing Co.
4 Conant Square
Branden, VT 05733
(802) 247-6871

Journal of Cognitive Neuroscience
MIT Press
55 Hayward St.
Cambridge, MA 02142
   Presents research on the brain and be-
   havior

Journal of Comparative Psychology
American Psychological Association
750 First St., NE
Washington, DC 20002
(202) 336-5600
  Presents laboratory and field studies of
  behavioral patterns of various species as
  they relate to development, evolution,
  etc.

Journal of Experimental Child Psychology
Academic Press
Journals Division
1250 6th Ave.
San Diego, CA 92101
(619) 230-1840
  Covers all aspects of behavior in
  children

Journal of Experimental Psychology
American Psychological Association
750 First St., NE
Washington, DC 20002
(202) 336-5600
  Presents reports of interest to all experimental psychologists

*Journal of Experimental Psychology: Learn-
ing, Memory & Cognition*
American Psychological Association
750 First St., NE
Washington, DC 20002
(202) 336-5600
  Presents experimental studies on fundamentals of encoding, transfer, memory
  and cognition processes in human behavior

Journal of General Psychology
Heldref Publications
1319 18th St. NW
Washington, DC 20036
(202) 296-6267

Journal of Genetic Psychology
Heldref Publications
1319 18th St. NW
Washington, DC 20036
(202) 296-6267

Journal of Geriatric Psychiatry
International Universities Press
Journals Dept.
59 Boston Post Rd.
Madison, CT 06443
(203) 245-4000
  Presents research in the field of geriatric
  psychiatry, Alzheimer's disease

Journal of Gerontology
Gerontological Society of America
1275 K St., NW
Suite 250
Washington, DC 20005
(202) 842-1275

Journal of Mind and Behavior
Institute of Mind and Behavior
Box 522
Village Station, NY 10014
(212) 595-4853
  Presents articles on the theory of con-
  sciousness, mind and body epistemol-
  ogy, etc.

Journal of Nervous and Mental Diseases
Williams & Wilkins
428 E. Preston St.
Baltimore, MD 21202
(301) 528-4000
  Presents studies in social behavior and
  neurological science

*Journal of Neurology, Neurosurgery and
  Psychiatry*
BMJ Publishing Group
BMA House
Tavistock Square
London, ENGLAND WC1H 9JR
071-387-4499
  Presents reports on clinical neurology,
  neurosurgery, neuropsychology, neuro-
  psychiatry

Journal of Neuroscience
Oxford University Press
Journals
200 Madison Ave.
New York, NY 10016
(212) 679-7300

Journal of Neuroscience Research
John Wiley & Sons
Journals
605 3rd Ave.
New York, NY 10158
(212) 850-6000
Presents basic research in molecular, cellular aspects of neuroscience

Journal of Psychology: Interdisciplinary and Applied
Heldref Publications
1319 18th St. NW
Washington, DC 20036
(202) 296-6267

The Lancet
Williams & Wilkins
428 E. Preston St.
Baltimore, MD 21202
(301) 528-4000

Neurobiology of Aging
Pergamon Press
Journals Division
660 White Plains Rd.
Tarrytown, NY 10591
(914) 524-9200

Neurology
Advanstar Communications
7500 Old Oak Blvd.
Cleveland, OH 44130
(216) 826-2839
Presents information on research in neurology

Neuropsychology
American Psychological Association
750 First St., NE
Washington, DC 20002
(202) 336-5600
Presents information in clinical neuropsychology, especially neuropsychological

measurement techniques and psychosocial adjustment of patients

New England Journal of Medicine
Massachusetts Medical Society
1440 Main St.
Waltham, MA 02254
(617) 734-9800

Proceedings of the National Academy of Science
National Academy of Science
2101 Constitution Ave.
Washington, DC 20418
(202) 334-2525

Psychiatry Research
Elsevier Science Publishing Co.
655 Avenue of the Americas
New York, NY 10010
(212) 989-5800

Psychological Bulletin
American Psychological Association
750 First St., NE
Washington, DC 20002
(202) 336-5600

Psychology and Aging
American Psychological Association
750 First St., NE
Washington, DC 20002
(202) 336-5600

Surgical Neurology
Elsevier Science Publishing Co.
655 Avenue of the Americas
New York, NY 10010
(212) 989-5800

Trends in Neuroscience
Elsevier Science Publishing Co.
655 Avenue of the Americas
New York, NY 10010
(212) 989-5800

APPENDIX B.
ASSOCIATIONS DEALING WITH
MEMORY PROBLEMS

AIDS Information Hotline
Public Health Service
(800) 342-AIDS
  Provides information to the public

National Gay Task Force Crisisline
(800) 221-7044; (212) 529-1604 in NY,
  AK and HI
  Offers basic information on AIDS, provides referrals

Alzheimer's Disease and Related Disorders
  Associations
(800) 621-0379; (800) 572-6037 (in IL)
  Offers information on publications available from the association, refers callers
  to local chapters and support groups

Huntington's Disease Society of America
(800) 345-4372; (22) 242-1968 (NY)
  Provides information on disease; referrals to physicians and support groups; answers questions on presymptomatic
  testing

National Parkinson Foundation
(800) 327-4545; (800) 433-7022 (FL)
  Information, referrals, written material

Parkinson Education Program
(800) 344-7872; (714) 640-0218 (CA)
  Provides materials, publication catalog,
  support group information, physician referrals

REFERENCES

Adelson, B. "When Novices Surpass Experts: The Difficulty of a Task May Increase with Expertise." *Journal of Experimental Psychology: Learning, Memory and Cognition* 9 (1983): 422–33.

Adler, Tina. "Additional Information Can Distort Memories." *APA Monitor* (October 1989): 12–3.

———. "Memory Software Explains Failings." *APA Monitor* (December 1989): 6.

———. "Implicit Memory Seems to Age Well." *APA Monitor* (February 1990): 8.

———. "Ability to Store Memory Linked to Glucose Levels." *APA Monitor* (September 1990): 5–6.

———. "Encoding Is Achilles' Heel for Dyslexic Kids." *APA Monitor* (November 1990): 4.

———. "Infants' Memories May Be Specific, Retrievable." *APA Monitor* (November 1990): 9.

———. "Psychologists Examine Aging, Cognitive Change." *APA Monitor* (November 1990): 4–5.

Albert, M.S., and Moss, M. "The Assessment of Memory Disorders in Patients with Alzheimer's Disease." In *Neuropsychology of Memory,* ed. L.R. Squire and N. Butters, 236–46. New York: Guilford, 1984.

Alkon, Daniel L. "Memory Storage and Neural Systems: Electrical and Chemical Changes Which Accompany Conditioning Applied to Artificial Network Designs." *Scientific American* 261 (July 1989): 42–51.

Allman, W.F. *Apprentices of Wonder Inside the Neural Network Revolution.* New York: Bantam Books, 1989.

Allport, Susan. *Explorers of the Black Box: The Search for the Cellular Basis of Memory.* New York: W.W. Norton & Co., 1986.

"Alzheimer's Report in Dispute." *Philadelphia Inquirer,* January 31, 1991.

Amaducci, L. "Phosphatidylserine in the Treatment of Alzheimer's Disease: Results of a Multicenter Study." *Psychopharmacology Bulletin* 24 (1988): 130–34.

Amaducci, L., et al. "Use of Phosphatidylserine in Alzheimer's Disease." *Annals of the New York Academy of Sciences* 640 (1991): 245–49.

Anderson, J.R. *Cognitive Psychology and Its Implications.* New York: Freeman Press, 1985.

Anderson, J.R., and Bower, G.H. *Human Associative Memory.* Washington, DC: Winston, 1972.

Arnold, M.B. *Memory and the Brain.* Hillsdale, NJ: Lawrence Erlbaum Associates, 1984.

Arsten, A., and Goldman-Rakic, Pl. "Catecholamines and Cognitive Decline in Aged Nonhuman Primates." *Annals of the New York Academy of Sciences* 444 (1985): 218–34.

———.N"2-Adrenergic Mechanisms in Prefrontal Cortex Associated with Cognitive Decline in Nonhuman Primates." *Science* 230 (1985): 1273–76.

Augustine, Saint. *Confessions.* New York: Penguin Books, 1961.

Bachvalier, J., and Mishkin, M. "An Early and a Late Developing System for Learning and Retention in Infant Monkeys." *Behavioral Neuroscience* 98 (1984): 770–78.

Baddeley, Alan. *The Psychology of Memory*. New York: Basic Books, 1976.

———. *Your Memory—A User's Guide*. New York: Macmillan Publishing Co., 1982. (Reprinted 1991, Emmaus, PA: Rodale Press.)

———. "Domains of Recollection." *Psychological Review* 89 (1982): 708–29.

———. "Working Memory." *Science* 255 (1992): 556–59.

Bagne, C.A., et al. *Treatment Development Strategies of Alzheimer's Disease*. New Caanan, CT: Mark Powley Associates, 1986.

Baker, Robert A., Haynes, Brikan, and Patrick, Bonnie. "The Effect of Suggestion on Past-Lives Regression." *American Journal of Clinical Hypnosis* 25 (July 1982): 71–76.

———. "Hypnosis, Memory and Incidental Memory." *American Journal of Clinical Hypnosis* 25 (April 1983): 253–62.

———. "The Aliens Among Us: Hypnotic Regression Revisited." *The Skeptical Inquirer* 12 (Winter 1987–88): 147–63.

Barnes, C.A., et al. "Acetyl-L-carnitine, 2: Effects on Learning and Memory Performance of Aged Rats in Simple and Complex Mazes." *Neurobiological Aging* 11, no. 5 (September–October 1990): 499–506.

Barron, Susan. "Fear of Forgetting: Why You Lose Your Memory and Some Solutions." *Washingtonian* 24 (May 1989): 150–58.

Bartlett, F.C. *Remembering*. Cambridge: Cambridge University Press, 1932.

Bartus, R.T. "Four Stimulants of the Central Nervous System: Effects on Short-term Memory in Young Versus Aged Monkeys." *Journal of American Geriatrics Society* 27 (1979): 289–98.

Bartus, R.T., et al. "Profound Effects of Combining Choline and Piracetam on Memory Enhancement and Cholinergic Function in Aged Rats." *Neurobiology of Aging* 2 (1981): 105–11.

Bartus, R.T., et al. "The Cholinergic Hypothesis of Geriatric Memory Dysfunction." *Science* 217 (1982): 408.

Begley, Sharon, Carey, John, and Sawhill, Ray. "How the Brain Works." *Newsweek*, February 7, 1983.

Begley, Sharon, et al. "Mapping the Brain." *Newsweek*, April 20, 1992.

———. "Thinking Looks Like This." *Newsweek*, November 25, 1991.

Bellezza, F.S. *Improve Your Memory Skills*. Englewood Cliffs, NJ: Prentice-Hall, 1982.

Belli, R.F. "Influences of Misleading Postevent Information: Misinformation Interference and Acceptance." *Journal of Experimental Psychology* 118 (1989): 72–85.

Bennett, Dawn. "Baby's Memory." *APA Monitor* (October 1985): 25.

Bernal, J., et al. "Visual Evoked Potentials, Attention and Mnemonic Abilities in Children." *International Journal of Neuroscience* 66, nos. 1–2 (September 1992): 45–51.

Birkmayer, W., et al. "L-deprenyl Plus L-phenylalanine in the Treatment of Depression." *Journal of Neural Transmission* 59 (1984): 81–87.

Birnbaumer, N. "Slow Potentials of the Cerebral Cortex and Behavior." *Physiological Review* (January 1990): 1–41.

Birren, J.E., and Schaie, K.W. *Handbook of the Psychology of Aging*. New York: Van Nostrand Reinhold, 1977.

Blodgett, Bonnie. "Ages Birth to 1: Development of Memory in Infants." *Parenting Magazine* 6 (May 1992): 126.

Blakeslee, Sandra. "Pervasive Chemical, Crucial to the Body, Is Indicted as an Agent in Brain Damage." *New York Times,* November 29, 1988.

———. "Memories Are Made of This." *New Choices for the Best Years* 29 (November 1989): 41–45.

Bliss, E.L. "A Reexamination of Freud's Basic Concepts from Studies of Multiple Personality Disorder." *Dissociation* 1 (1988): 36–40.

Blumenthal, J.A., and Madden, D.J. "Effects of Aerobic Exercise Training, Age and Physical Fitness on Memory-search Performance." *Psychology and Aging* 3 (1988): 280–85.

Boller, K., and Rovee-Collier, C. "Contextual Coding and Recoding of Infant Memory." *Journal of Experimental Child Psychology* 52 (1992): 1–23.

Bolles, Edmund Blair. *So Much to Say.* New York: St. Martin's Press, 1982.

———. *Remembering and Forgetting: Inquiries into the Nature of Memory.* New York: Walker and Co., 1988.

Bologa, L., Sharma, J., and Roberts, E. "Dehydroepiandrosterone and Its Sulfated Derivative Reduce Neuronal Death and Enhance Astrocytic Differentiation in Brain Cell Cultures." *Journal of Neuroscience Research* 17, no. 3 (1985): 225–34.

Bompani, R., and Scali, G. "Fipexide, an Effective Cognition Activator in the Elderly: A Placebo-controlled, Double-blind Clinical Trial." *Current Medical Research and Opinion* 10, no. 2 (1986): 99–196.

Bonavita, E. "Study of the Efficacy and Tolerability of L-acetylcarnitine Therapy in the Senile Brain." *Journal of Clinical Pharmacology, Therapy and Toxicology* 24 (1986): 511–16.

Bornstein, R.F. "Implicit Perception, Implicit Memory and the Recovery of Unconscious Material in Psychotherapy." *Journal of Nervous and Mental Disease* 181, no. 6 (June 1993): 337–44.

Botwinick, Jack, and Storandt, Martha. *Memory, Related Functions and Age.* Springfield, IL: Charles C Thomas, 1974.

Bower, Bruce. "Neural Networks: The Buck Stops Here." *Science News* (August 6, 1988): 85.

———. "The Brain in the Machine: Biologically Inspired Computer Models Renew Debates Over the Nature of Thought." *Science News* 134 (November 26, 1988): 344–45.

———. "Boosting Memory in the Blink of an Eye," *Science News* 135 (February 11, 1989): 86.

———. "Investigating Eyewitnesses' Memory Mishaps." *Science News* 135 (March 4, 1989): 134.

———. "Weak Memories Make Strong Comeback." *Science News* 138 (July 21, 1990): 36.

———. "Gone But Not Forgotten: Scientists Uncover Pervasive, Unconscious Influences on Memory." *Science News* 138 (November 17, 1990): 312–15.

———. "Focused Attention Boosts Depressed Memory." *Science News* 140 (September 7, 1991): 151.

———. "Infant Memory Shows the Power of Place." *Science News* 141 (April 18, 1992): 244–45.

———. "Schizophrenic Kids' Memory Muddle." *Science News* 141 (May 23, 1992): 351.

———. "Some Lasting Memories Emerge at Age 2." *Science News* 143 (June 12, 1993): 143.

Branconnier, R. "The Efficacy of the Cerebral Metabolic Enhancers in the Treatment of Senile Dementia." *Psychopharmacology Bulletin* 19, no. 2 (1983): 212–20.

Braude, Stephen E. "Some Recent Books on Multiple Personality and Dissociation." *Journal of the American Society for Psychical Research* 82 (October 1988): 39–52.

Brayne, C., and Calloway, D. "Normal Aging, Impaired Cognitive Function and Senile Dementia of the Alzheimer's Type: A Continuum?" *Lancet* 1 (1988): 1265–66.

Bremness, Lesley. *Herbs*. Pleasantville, NJ: The Readers Digest Association, 1990.

Breuer, J., and Freud, S. *Studies on Hysteria*. In *The Standard Edition of the Complete Psychological Works of Sigmund Freud,* ed. J. Strachey, vol. 2, London: Hogarth Press, 1955. (Originally published 1895.)

Brewer, W.F., and Treyens, J.C. "Role of Schemata in Memory for Places." *Cognitive Psychology* 13 (1981): 207–30.

Brooks, D.N. *Closed Head Injury*. Oxford: Oxford University Press, 1984.

Brown, H.D., and Kosslyn, S.M. "Cerebral Lateralization." *Current Opinions in Neurobiology* 3, no. 2 (April 1993): 183–86.

Brown, N.R., Rips, L.J., and Shevell, S.K. "The Subjective Dates of Natural Events in Very Long-term Memory." *Cognitive Psychology* 17 (1985): 139–77.

Burg, Bob. "Six Steps to Remembering What's-His-Name." *ABA Banking Journal* 82 (September 1990): 92.

———. *The Memory System: Remember Everything You Need When You Need It*. Shawnee Mission, KS: National Seminars Publications, 1992.

Butters, M.A., Glisky, E.L., and Schacter, D.L. "Transfer of New Learning in Memory-impaired Patients." *Journal of Clinical and Experimental Neuropsychology* 15, no. 2 (March 1993): 219–30.

Butterworth, B., Campbell, R., and Howard, D. "The Uses of Short-term Memory: A Case Study." *Quarterly Journal of Experimental Psychology* 38A (1986): 705–38.

Buzan, Tony. *Use Your Perfect Memory*. New York: E.P. Dutton, 1984.

Bylinsky, G. "Medicine's Next Marvel: The Memory Pill." *Fortune,* January 20, 1986.

"Caffeine Can Increase Brain Serotonin Levels." *Nutrition Review* 46 (October 1988): 366–67.

Campi, N., Todeschini, G.P., and Scarzella, L. "Selegiline Versus L-acetylcarnitine in the Treatment of Alzheimer-type Dementia." *Clinical Therapy* 12, no. 4 (July-August 1990): 306–14.

Carey, C.J., et al. "Ondansetron and Arecoline Prevent Scopolamine-induced Cognitive Deficits in the Marmoset." *Pharmacology, Biochemistry Behavior* 42, no. 1 (1992): 75–83.

Carey, John, and Baker, Stephen. "Brain Repair Is Possible." *Business Week,* November 18, 1991.

Carillo, M.C., et al. "(-)Deprenyl Induced Activities of Both Superoxide Dismutase and Catalase in Young Male Rats." *Life Science* 48 (1991): 517.

Casale, R., Giorgi, I., and Guarnaschelli, C. "Evaluation of the Effect of Vincamine Teprosilate on Behavioral Performances of Patients Affected with Chronic Cerebrovascular Disease." *International Journal of Clinical Pharmacology Research* 4, no. 4 (1984): 313–19.

Cassedy, Ellen. "It Isn't Lost; I Just Can't Find It." *Woman's Day,* October 2, 1990.

Cermak, Laird S. *Human Memory Research and Theory*. New York: The Ronald Press Co., 1972.

————. *Human Memory and Amnesia*. Hillsdale, NJ: Erlbaum, 1982.

Chase, Marilyn. "Scientists Work to Slow Human Aging." *Wall Street Journal,* March 12, 1992.

Chase, W.G., and Simon, H.A. "Perception in Chess." *Cognitive Psychology* 4 (1973): 55–81.

Chi, M.T.H., and Koeske, R.D. "Network Representation of a Child's Dinosaur Knowledge." *Developmental Psychology* 19 (1983): 29–39.

Christensen, H., and Mackinnon, A. "The Association Between Mental, Social and Physical Activity and Cognitive Performance in Young and Old Subjects." *Age and Ageing* 22, no. 3 (May 1993): 175–82.

Clark, Linda. *Help Yourself to Health*. New York: Pyramid Books, 1976.

Claustrat, B., et al. "Melatonin and Jet Lag: Confirmatory Result Using a Simplified Protocol." *Biological Psychiatry* 32, no. 8 (1992): 705–11.

Cohen, Gillian. *Memory in the Real World*. London: Lawrence Erlbaum Associates, 1989.

Colombo, C., et al. "Memory Function and Temporal-limbic Morphology in Schizophrenics." *Psychiatry Research* 50, no. 1 (April 1993): 45–56.

Colombo, Michael, et al. "Auditory Association Cortex Lesions Impair Auditory Short-term Memory in Monkeys." *Science* 247 (January 19, 1990): 336–38.

Conrad, C.D., and Roy, D.J. "Selective Loss of Hippocampal Granule Cells Following Adrenalectomy: Implications for Spatial Memory." *Journal of Neuroscience* 13, no. 6 (June 1993): 2582–90.

Constantinidis, J. "The Zinc Deficiency Theory for the Pathogenesis of Neurofibrillary Tangles: Possibility of Preventive Treatment by a Zinc Compound." *Neurobiology of Aging* 11 (1990): 282.

Crook, T.H., et al. "Effects of Phosphatidylserine in Age-associated Memory Impairment." *Neurology* 41 (May 1991): 644–49.

Crook, T., et al. "Effects of Phosphatidylserine in Alzheimer's Disease." *Psychopharmacology Bulletin* 28 (1992): 61–66.

Cullum, C.M., Thompson, L.L., and Smernoff, E.N. "Three-word Recall as a Measure of Memory." *Journal of Clinical and Experimental Neuropsychology* 15, no. 2 (March 1993): 321–29.

Czerwinski, A.W., et al. "Safety and Efficacy of Zinc Sulfate in Geriatric Patients." *Clinical Pharmacology and Therapeutics* 15 (1974): 436–41.

Dantzer, R., and Bluthe, R.M. "Vasopressin and Behavior: From Memory to Olfaction." *Regulatory Peptides* 45, nos. 1–2 (April 29, 1993): 121–25.

Darling, W.G., and Miller, G.F. "Transformations Between Visual and Kinesthetic Coordinate Systems in Reaches to Remembered Objects, Locations and Orientations." *Experimental Brain Research* 93, no. 3 (1993): 534–47.

Darnton, Nina, et al. "The Pain of the Last Taboo." *Newsweek,* October 7, 1991.

Dean, Ward, and Morgenthaler, John. *Smart Drugs & Nutrients*. Santa Cruz, CA: B&J Communications, 1991.

Dean, Ward, Morgenthaler, John, and Fowkes, Steven. *Smart Drugs II: The Next Generation*. Menlo Park, CA: Health Freedom Publications, 1993.

DeAngelis, Tori. "Dietary Recall Is Poor, Survey Study Suggests." *APA Monitor* (December 1988): 14.

————. "Children in Court: Studies Explore Custody Disputes, Technique to Aid Memory of Events." *APA Monitor* (December 1990): 31.

DeNoble, V.J., et al. "Vinpocetine: Nootropic Effects on Scopolamine-induced and Hyposia-induced Retrieval Deficits of a Step-through Passive Avoidance Response in Rats." *Pharmacology Biochemistry and Behavior* 24 (1986): 1123–28.

Denton, Laurie. "Memory Subsystems in Precarious Balance." *APA Monitor* (August 1987): 26.

———. "Mood's Role in Memory Still Puzzling." *APA Monitor* (November 1987): 18.

———. "Memory: Not Place, but Process." *APA Monitor* (November 1988): 4.

Deyo, Richard Al, Straube, Karen T., and Disterhoft, John F. "Nimodipine Facilitates Associative Learning in Aging Rabbits." *Science* 243, no. 4892 (February 10, 1989): 809–11.

Diagram Group, The. *The Brain: A User's Manual.* New York: G.P. Putnam & Sons, 1982.

Dilman, V.M., and Dean, W. *The Neuroendocrine Theory of Aging and Degenerative Disease.* Pensacola, FL: The Center for BioGerontology, 1992.

Dixon, R.A., Hertzog, C., and Hultsch, D.F. "The Multiple Relationships Among Metamemory in Adulthood Scales and Cognitive Abilities in Adulthood." *Human Learning* 5 (1986): 165–78.

Dobkin, Bruce. "Present Tense." *Discover* 13 (August 1992): 74–76.

Druckman, D., and Swets, J.A. *Enhancing Human Performance.* Washington, DC: National Academy Press, 1988.

Dysken, M.W., et al. "Milacemide: A Placebo-controlled Study in Senile Dementia of the Alzheimer Type." *Journal of the American Geriatrics Society* 40 (1992): 503–6.

Ebbinghaus, Hermann. *Memory: A Contribution to Experimental Psychology.* New York: Dover Publications, 1964.

Edson, Lee. *How We Learn.* New York: Time-Life Books, 1975.

Eichenbaum, H., and Otto, T. "Long-term Potentiation and Memory: Can We Enhance the Connection?" *Trends in Neuroscience* 16, no. 5 (May 1993): 163–64.

Eisdorfer, Carol, and Friedel, Robert O., eds. *Cognitive and Emotional Disturbances in the Elderly: Clinical Issues.* Chicago: Year Book Medical Publishing, Inc., 1977.

Erdelyi, M.H. *Psychoanalysis: Freud's Cognitive Psychology.* New York: W.H. Freeman, 1985.

Erikson, G.C., et al. "The Effects of Caffeine on Memory for Word Lists." *Physiology and Behavior* 35 (1985): 47–51.

Evans, C.D., ed. *Rehabilitation After Severe Head Injury.* Edinburgh: Churchill Livingstone, 1981.

Ezzel, Carol. "Memories Might Be Made of This: Closing in on the Biochemistry of Learning." *Science News* 139 (May 25, 1991): 328–330.

———. "Monitoring Memories Moving in the Brain." *Science News* 141 (May 2, 1992): 294.

Finali, G., et al. "L-deprenyl Therapy Improves Verbal Memory in Amnesic Alzheimer Patients." *Clinical Neuropharmacology* 14, no. 6 (1991): 526–36.

Finkel, M.M. "Phenytoin Revisited." *Journal of Clinical Therapeutics* 6, no. 5 (1984): 577–91.

Fisher, Kathy. "Studies Strengthen Role of Amygdala in Memory." *APA Monitor* (October 1984): 20.

———. "Learning and Memory: Brain Structure." *APA Monitor* (September 1990): 3, 6, 7.

Fisher, Ronald P., Geiselman, R. Edward, and Amador, Michael. "Field Test of the Cognitive Interview: Enhancing the Recollection of Actual Victims and Witnesses of Crime." *Journal of Applied Psychology* 74 (October 1989): 722–28.

Fitzgerald, J.M., and Lawrence, R. "Autobiographical Memory Across the Life Span." *Journal of Gerontology* 39 (1984): 692–98.

Flood, J.F., and Cherkin, A. "Effect of Acute Arecoline, Tacrine and Arecoline Tacrine Post-training Administration on Retention in Old Mice." *Neurobiology of Aging* 9 (1985): 5–8.

Flood, J.F., and Roberts, E. "Dehydroepindrosterone Sulfate Improves Memory in Aging Mice." *Brain Research* 447, no. 2 (1988): 269–78.

Forrest-Pressley, D.L., MacKinnon, G.E., and Waller, T.G. *Metacognition, Cognition and Human Performance*, vols. 1 and 2. New York: Academic Press, 1985.

Frankel, F.H. "Adult Reconstruction of Childhood Events in Multiple Personality Disorder." *American Journal of Psychiatry* 150, no. 6 (June 1993): 954–98.

Freeman, W., and Watts, J. *Psychosurgery*. Springfield, IL: Charles C Thomas, 1942; (2nd ed. 1950).

Freud, S. *The Psychopathology of Everyday Life*, ed. James Strachey. New York: W.W. Norton, 1960.

Friedman, E., et al. "Clinical Response to Choline Plus Piracetam in Senile Dementia: Relation to Red-cell Choline Levels." *New England Journal of Medicine* 304 (1981): 1490–91.

Frith, C., Bloxham, C., and Carpenter, K. "Impairments in the Learning and Performance of a New Manual Skill on Patients with Parkinson's Disease." *Journal of Neurology, Neurosurgery and Psychiatry* 46 (1986): 661–68.

Furst, Bruno. *Stop Forgetting*. Garden City, NY: Doubleday and Co., 1979.

Gade, A. "Amnesia After Operations of Aneurysms of the Anterior Communicating Artery." *Surgical Neurology* 18 (1982): 46–49.

Gallant, Roy A. *Memory: How It Works and How to Improve It*. New York: Four Winds Press, 1980.

Gardner, Howard. "Mind Explorers Merge Their Maps." *New York Times*, February 8, 1991.

Ghirardi, O., et al. "Active Avoidance Learning in Old Rats Chronically Treated with Levocarnitine Acetyl." *Physiological Behavior* 52, no. 1 (July 1992): 185–87.

Gilling, Dick, and Brightwell, Robin. *The Human Brain*. New York: Facts On File, 1982.

Glasgow, R.E., et al. "Case Studies on Remediating Memory Deficits in Brain-damaged Individuals." *Journal of Clinical Psychology* 33 (1977): 1049–54.

Gleick, James. "Brain at Work Revealed Through New Imagery," *New York Times*, August 18, 1987.

Glick, L.J. "Use of Magnesium in the Management of Dementias." *Medical Science Research* 18 (1990): 831–33.

Goad, D.L., et al. "The Use of Selegiline in Alzheimer's Patients with Behavior Problems." *Journal of Clinical Psychiatry* 52, no. 8 (August 1991): 342–54.

Gold, Philip E. "Glucose Modulation of Memory Storage Processing." *Behavioral Neural Biology* 45 (1986): 342–49.

———. "Sweet Memories." *American Scientist* 75 (1987): 151–55.

Goldberg, Joan. "The Cutting Edge: Peptide Power." *American Health* (June 1990): 35–41.

Goleman, Daniel. "In Memory, People Re-create Their Lives to Suit Their Images of the Present." *New York Times*, June 23, 1987.

———. "Open to Suggestion: Recall of Anesthetized Patients May Aid Recovery." *Reader's Digest* 136 (February 1990): 23–24.

Gordon, James S., Jaffe, Dennis, and Bresler, David. *Mind, Body and Health: Toward an Integral Medicine*. New York: Human Sciences Press, 1984.

Gose, Kathleen, and Levi, Gloria. *Dealing with Memory Changes As You Grow Older*. New York: Bantam Books, 1988.

Grafman, J., et al. "Analysis of Neuropsychological Functioning in Patients with Chronic Fatigue Syndrome." *Journal of Neurology, Neurosurgery and Psychiatry* 56, no. 6 (June 1993): 684–89.

Gray, J. *The Neuropsychology of Anxiety*. Oxford: Oxford University Press, 1982.

Greene, E., and Nartanjo, J. "Thalamic Role in Spatial Memory." *Behavioral Brain Research* 19 (1986): 123–31.

Grobe-Einsler, R., and Traber, J. "Clinical Results with Nimodipine in Alzheimer's Disease." *Clinical Neuropharmacology* 15, suppl. 1, pt. A (1992): 416A–17A.

Gruneberg, Michael, Morris, P.E., and Sykes, R.N., eds. *Practical Aspects of Memory*. Chichester: John Wiley and Sons, 1988.

Hales, Dianne. "Why Don't I Remember?" *McCall's*, 117 (February 1990): 75–77.

Hamilton, E. *Plato: The Collected Dialogues*. New York: Bollingen Foundation, 1961.

Handelmann, G.E., et al. "Milacemide, a Glycine Pro-drug, Enhances Performance of Learning Tasks in Normal and Amnestic Rodents." *Pharmacology, Biochemistry and Behavior* 34 (1989): 823–28.

Harris, J.E., and Morris, P.E., eds. *Everyday Memory, Actions and Absent-Mindedness*. London: Harcourt Brace Jovanovich, 1984.

Hart, R.P., and O'Shanick, G.J. "Forgetting Rates for Verbal, Pictorial and Figural Stimuli." *Journal of Clinical and Experimental Neuropsychology* 15, no. 2 (March 1993): 245–65.

Harvard Editors. "When to Worry About Forgetting." *Harvard Health Letter* (July 1992): 1–3.

Hayne, H. "The Effect of Multiple Reminders on Long-term Retention In Human Infants." *Developmental Psychobiology* 23 (1990): 453–77.

Heck, E.T., and Bryer, J.B. "Superior Sorting and Categorizing Ability in a Case of Bilateral Frontal Atrophy: An Exception to the Rule." *Journal of Clinical Psychology* 8 (1986): 313–16.

Herrmann, Douglas J. *Super Memory: A Quick-Action Program for Memory Improvement*. Emmaus, PA: Rodale Press, 1991.

Heston, Leonard L., and White, June A. *Dementia: A Practical Guide to Alzheimer's Disease and Related Illnesses*. New York: W.H. Freeman and Co., 1983.

Higbee, Kenneth L. *Your Memory: How It Works and How to Improve It*. New York: Simon & Schuster, 1988.

Hilgard, Ernest R. *Psychology in America: A Historical Survey*. New York: Harcourt Brace Jovanovich, 1987.

Hilts, Philip. "A Brain Unit Seen as Index for Recalling Memories." *New York Times*, September 24, 1991.

———. "Photos Show Mind Recalling a Word." *New York Times*, November 11, 1991.

Hines, William. "Brain Tumors and Their Many Different Paths." *Washington Post Health Magazine*, April 7, 1987.

Hirst, W., et al. "Recognition and Recall in Amnesics." *Journal of Experimental Psychology: Learning, Memory and Cognition* 12 (1986): 445–51.

Hoffer, A. "A Case of Alzheimer's Treatment with Nutrients and Aspirin." *Journal of Orthomolecular Medicine* 8, no. 1 (1993): 43–44.

Holmes, G.L., et al. "Effects of Kindling on Subsequent Learning, Memory, Behavior and Seizure Susceptibility." *Developmental Brain Research* 73, no. 1 (May 21, 1993): 71–77.

Horel, J., Voytko, M., and Salsbury, K. "Visual Learning Suppressed by Cooling the Temporal Pole." *Behavioral Neuroscience* 98 (1984): 310–24.

Hostetler, A.J. "Exploring the 'Gatekeeper' of Memory: Changes in Hippocampus Seen in Aging, Amnesia, Alzheimer's." *APA Monitor* (April 1988): 3.

———. "Try to Remember . . . A Computer Battery Is Helping Test Drugs' Effects on Alzheimer's." *APA Monitor* (May 1987): 18.

Howard Rosanne. "Mild Head Injury: Challenging Emergency Room Decisions." *Headlines* 3 (March/April 1991): 6–7.

"How the Brain Works." *New York Times,* October 9, 1988.

Impastato, D.J. "The Story of the First Electroshock Treatment." *American Journal of Psychiatry* 116 (1960): 1113–14.

Isseroff, A., et al. "Spatial Memory Impairments Following Damage to the Mediodorsal Nucleus of the Thalamus in Rhesus Monkeys." *Brain Research* 232 (1982): 97–113.

Izumi, Yukitoshi, Clifford, David B., and Zorumski, Charles F. "Inhibition of Long-term Potentiation by NMDA-mediated Nitric Oxide Release." *Science* 257 (August 28, 1992): 1273–76.

James, W. *The Principles of Psychology.* New York: Henry Holt, 1890.

Job, Eena. *Fending Off Forgetfulness: A Practical Guide to Improving Memory.* London: University of Queensland Press, 1985.

Johnson, George. *In the Palaces of Memory: How We Build the Worlds Inside Our Heads.* New York: Alfred A. Knopf, 1991.

Jones, David P. "Ritualism and Child Sexual Abuse." *Child Abuse and Neglect* 15 (1991): 161–69.

Kagan, J., and Hamburg, M. "The Enhancement of Memory in the First Year." *Journal of Genetic Psychology* 138 (1981): 3–14.

Karayamidis, F., et al. "Event-related Potentials and Repetition Priming in Young, Middle-aged and Elderly Normal Subjects." *Brain Research* 1, no. 2 (April 1993): 123–34.

Kearsley, Greg. "Think Tanks: Bell Laboratories." *APA Monitor* (November 1981): 1, 4, 12.

Klatzky, Robert L. *Human Memory: Structures and Processes.* New York: W.H. Freeman, 1980.

Klivington, K. *The Science of Mind.* Cambridge, MA: MIT Press, 1989.

Kolb, B., and Whishaw, Ian Q. *Fundamentals of Human Neuropsychology,* 2nd ed. New York: W.H. Freeman, 1985.

Knoll, J. "The Striatal Dopamine Dependency of Lifespan in Male Rats." *Mechanisms of Aging and Development* 46 (1988): 237–62.

———. "Extension of Lifespan of Rats by Long-term (-)Deprenyl Treatment." *Mount Sinai Journal of Medicine* 55 (1988): 67–74.

———. "(-)Deprenyl-medication: A Strategy to Modulate the Age-related Decline in the Striatal Dopaminergic System." *Journal of the American Geriatric Society* 40, no. 8 (August 1992): 839–47.

Kolata, Gina. "FDA Panel Rejects Alzheimer's Drug." *New York Times,* March 17, 1991.

———. "Mental Gymnastics." *New York Times Magazine,* October 6, 1991.

Kopelman, M.D. "The Cholinergic Neurotransmitter System in Human Memory and Dementia: A Review." *Quarterly Journal of Experimental Psychology* 38A (1986): 535–74.

Kra, Siegfried. *Aging Myths: Reversible Causes of Mind and Memory Loss.* New York: McGraw-Hill, 1986.

Krassner, Michael B. "Diet and Brain Function." *Nutrition Reviews:* suppl. (May 1986): 12–15.

Krauthammer, Charles. "Disorders of Memory." *Time,* July 3, 1989.

Kruck, T.P.A., et al. "Molecular Shuttle Chelation—Studies on Desferroxamine-based Chelation of Aluminum for Neurobiological Applications: Alzheimer's Disease." *Neurobiology of Aging* 11 (1990): 342.

Krupa, D.J., Thompson, J.K., and Thompson, R.F. "Localization of a Memory Trace in the Mammalian Brain." *Science* 260, no. 5110 (May 14, 1993): 989–91.

Landauer, T.K. "How Much Do People Remember? Some Estimates of the Quantity of Learned Information in Long-term Memory." *Cognitive Science* 10 (1986): 477–94.

Landers, Susan. "Memories of Elderly Found to be Accurate in Surveys." *APA Monitor* (October 1987): 15.

Langley, M.S., and Sorkin, E.M. "Nimodipine: A Review of Its Pharmacodynamic and Pharmacokinetic Properties, and Therapeutic Potential in Cerebrovascular Disease." *Drugs* 37 (1989): 669–99.

Lapp, Danielle. *(Nearly) Total Recall: A Guide to a Better Memory at Any Age.* Stanford, CA: Stanford Alumni Association, 1992.

Larkin, Marilyn. "Treating Head Pain Resulting from Subtle Brain Injury." *Headlines* 3 (March/April 1991): 14–20.

Lashley, M.E. "The Painful Side of Reminiscence." *Geriatric Nursing* 14, no. 3 (May/June 1993): 138–41.

Leiner, H., Leiner, A. and Dow, R. "Does the Cerebellum Contribute to Mental Skills?" *Behavioral Neuroscience* 100 (1986): 443–54.

Levin, H., High, W., and Eisenberg, H. "Learning and Forgetting During and After Post-traumatic Amnesia in Head-injured Patients." *Society for Neuroscience Abstracts* 13 (1987): 205.

Loftus, Elizabeth. *Eyewitness Testimony.* Cambridge, MA: Harvard University Press, 1979.

———. *Memory: Surprising New Insights Into How We Remember and Why We Forget.* Reading, MA: Addison-Wesley Publishing Co., 1980.

Loftus, E.F., and Greene, E. "Warning: Even Memory for Faces May Be Contagious." *Law and Human Behavior* 4 (1980): 323–34.

Loftus, E.F., and Loftus, G.R. "On the Permanence of Stored Information in the Human Brain." *American Psychologist* 35 (1980): 421–34.

Loftus, E.F. and Marburger, W. "Since the Eruption of Mt. St. Helens Has Anyone Beaten You Up? Improving the Accuracy of Retrospective Reports with Landmark Events." *Memory and Cognition* 2 (1983): 114–20.

Lorayne, Harry, and Lucas, Jerry. *The Memory Book.* New York: Dorset Press, 1974.

Luria, A.R. *The Mind of a Mnemonist.* New York: Basic Books, 1968.

Lynch, G. "What Memories Are Made Of: A Chemical Called Calpain Records the Events of a Lifetime." *Sciences* (September–October 1985): 38–43.

Mace, Nancy, and Rabins, Peter. *The 36 Hour Day: A Guide to Caring for Persons with Alzheimer's Disease and Related Dementing Illnesses.* Baltimore: Johns Hopkins University Press, 1991.

Maestroni, G.J., Conti, A., and Pierpaoli, W. "Pineal Melatonin, Its Fundamental Immunoregulatory Role in Aging and Cancer." *Annals of the New York Academy of Science* 521 (1988): 140–48.

Maina, G., et al. "Oxiracetam in the Treatment of Primary Degenerative and Multi-infarct Dementia: A Double-blind, Placebo-controlled Study." *Neuropsychobiology* 21, no. 3 (1989): 141–45.

Mantyla, T. "Knowing but Not Remembering: Adult Age Differences in Recollective Expression." *Memory and Cognition* 21, no. 3 (May 1993): 379–88.

Mark, Vernon, and Mark, Jeffrey P. "Why We Forget: Ten Common and Reversible Causes of Memory Loss." *Modern Maturity* 33 (August–September 1990): 70–74.

Markowitsch, H.J. "Hypotheses on Mnemonic Information Processing by the Brain." *International Journal of Neuroscience* 15 (1985): 189–287.

Martin, E.M., et al. "Speed of Memory Scanning Not Affected in Early HIV-1 Infection." *Journal of Clinical and Experimental Neuropsychology* 15, no. 2 (March 1993): 311–20.

Martinez, J.L., and Kesner, R.P. *Learning and Memory: A Biological View*. Orlando, FL: Academic Press, 1986.

Matlock, James G. "Age and Stimulus in Past Life Memory: A Study of Published Cases." *Journal of the American Society for Psychical Research* 83 (October 1989): 303–16.

Mayes, Andrew R. *Human Organic Memory Disorders*. Cambridge: Cambridge University Press, 1988.

Maugh Thomas H., II. "Researchers Observe Brain's Memory-forming Process." *Philadelphia Inquirer*, November 12, 1991.

———. "Steroid Found to Aid Memory in Lab Mice; Human Tests Planned." *Philadelphia Inquirer*, March 21, 1992.

McEnroe, Colin. "Sub-total Recall; Having Trouble Remembering Names, Faces, Facts? Welcome to Your 40s." *Men's Health* 6 (April 1991): 12.

McEntee, W.J., and Mair, R.G. "Memory Enhancement in Korsakoff's Psychosis by Clonidine: Further Evidence for a Noradrenergic Deficit." *Annals of Neurology* 7 (1980): 466–70.

McKenna P., and Warrington, E.K. "Testing for Nominal Dysphasia." *Journal of Neurology, Neurosurgery and Psychiatry* 43 (1980): 781–88.

McKenzie, Aline. "Gone to Pot: Marijuana Use and Short-term Memory Problems." *Reader's Digest/Canadian*, 137 (December 1990): 92.

Merzenich, M.M., and Sameshima, K. "Cortical Plasticity and Memory." *Current Opinions in Neurobiology* 3, no. 2 (April 1993): 187–96.

Meurs, E.J., and Hes, R. "Deja Vu and Holographic Images." *American Journal of Psychiatry* 150, no. 4 (April 1993): 679–80.

Minninger, Joan. *Total Recall: How to Boost Your Memory Power*. Emmaus, PA: Rodale Press, 1984.

Mishkin, Mortimer, and Appenzeller, Tim. "The Anatomy of Memory." *Scientific American* 256 (June 1987): 80–89.

Mitiguy, Judith. "New Applications of Diagnostic Techniques." *Headlines* 3 (March/April 1992): 2–5, 8–10.

Monzani, F., et al. "Subclinical Hypothyroidism: Neurobehavioral Features and Beneficial Effect of L-thyroxine Treatment." *Clinical Investigator* 71, no. 5 (May 1993): 367–71.

Moscovitch, M., ed. *Advances in the Study of Communication and Affect: Vol. 9. Infant Memory*. New York: Plenum Press, 1984.

"Mouse Models Created for Alzheimer's Disease."*New York Times*, July 23, 1991.

Myers, N.A., Clifton, R.K., and Clarkson, M.G. "When They Were Very Young: Almost-threes Remember Two Years Ago." *Infant Behavior and Development* 10 (1987): 123–32.

Naatanen, R., et al. "Development of a Memory Trace for a Complex Sound in the Human Brain." *Neuroreport* 4, no. 5 (May 1993): 503–6.

Nauta, Walle J.H., and Feirtag, Michael. *Fundamental Neuroanatomy*. New York: W.H. Freeman, 1986.

Neisser, Ulric. *Memory Observed: Remembering in Natural Contexts.* San Francisco: W.H. Freeman and Company, 1982.

———. "Interpreting Harry Bahrick's Discovery: What Confers Immunity Against Forgetting?" *Journal of Experimental Psychology* 113 (1984): 32–35.

Nigro, G., and Neisser, U. "Point of View in Personal Memories." *Cognitive Psychology* 15 (1983): 465–82.

Norman, D.A. *Learning and Memory.* New York: W.H. Freeman, 1982.

Ohno, M., Yamamoto, T., and Watanabe, S. "Blockage of Hippocampal Nicotinic Receptors Impairs Working Memory But Not Reference Memory in Rats." *Pharmacology, Biochemistry and Behavior* 45, no. 1 (May 1993): 89–93.

Ostrander, Sheila, and Schroeder, Lynn. *Super-Memory: The Revolution.* New York: Carroll & Graf Publishers, 1991.

Parent, M.E., Krondl, M., and Chow, R.K. "Reconstruction of Past Calcium Intake Patterns During Adulthood." *Journal of the American Dietetic Association* 93, no. 6 (June 1993): 649–52.

Parkin, Alan J. *Memory and Amnesia.* Oxford: Basil Blackwell, Ltd., 1987.

Parkinson Study Group, The. "Effect of Deprenyl on the Progression of Disability in Early Parkinson's Disease." *New England Journal of Medicine* 321 (November 16, 1989): 1364–71.

Parnetti, L., et al. "Mental Deterioration in Old Age—Results of 2 Multicenter Clinical Trials with Nimodipine." *Clinical Therapeutics* 15, no. 2 (March/April 1993): 394–406.

Pelton, R., and Pelton, T.C. *Mind Food & Smart Pills.* New York: Doubleday, 1989.

Petkov, V. "Effects of Standardized Ginseng Extract on Learning, Memory and Physical Capabilities." *American Journal of Chinese Medicine* 15, no. 1 (1987): 19–29.

Pettinati, Helen M., ed. *Hypnosis and Memory.* New York: Guilford Press, 1988.

Piaget, J., and Inhelder, B. *Memory and Intelligence.* New York: Basic Books, 1973.

Piccinin, G.L., Finali, G., and Piccirilli, M. "Neuropsychological Effects of L-deprenyl in Alzheimer's Type Dementia." *Clinical Neuropharmacology* 13, no. 2 (April 1990): 147–63.

Pipitone, Paul. "Brain Reorganization Explored in Stroke Recovery." *Headlines* 3 (March/April 1991): 27.

———. "Study on Substance Abuse and Brain Injury." *Headlines* 3 (March/April 1991): 27.

Pool, J.L. *Nature's Masterpiece: The Brain and How It Works.* New York: Walker and Company, 1987.

Poole, Robert, ed. *The Incredible Machine.* Washington, DC: National Geographic Society, 1986.

Poon, L.W. "A Systems Approach for the Assessment and Treatment of Memory Problems." In *The Comprehensive Handbook of Behavioral Medicine,* ed. J.M. Ferguson and C.B. Taylor, vol. 1. Great Neck, NY: PMA Publishing Corp., 1980.

Prevention Magazine Editors. *Future Youth: How to Reverse the Aging Process.* Emmaus, PA: Rodale Press, 1987.

Procter, A.W., et al. "Glutamate/Aspartame-Releasing Neurones in Alzheimer's Disease." *New England Journal of Medicine* 314 (1986): 1711–12.

Proust, M. *Remembrance of Things Past,* trans. C.S. Moncrieff and T. Kilmartin. New York: Random House, 1981.

Psychology Today Editors. "Buried Memories (Experiments on Memory in Infants)." *Psychology Today* 23 (April 1989): 12.

Putnam, F.W. "Dissociation as a Response to Extreme Trauma." In *Childhood Antecedents of Multiple Personality,* ed. R. Kluft. Washington, DC: American Psychiatric Press, 1985.

Raeburn, Paul. "Memory Tea." *American Health* (January–February 1990): 126.

Rai, G., et al. "Double Blind, Placebo Controlled Study of Acetyl-L-carnitine in Patients with Alzheimer's Dementia." *Current Medical Research and Opinion* 11, no. 10 (1990): 638–47.

Reason, James T., and Mycielska, Klara. *Absent-Minded? The Psychology of Mental Lapses and Everyday Errors.* Englewood Cliffs, NJ: Prentice-Hall, 1982.

Recer, Paul. "FDA Panel Declines to Support Approval for Alzheimer's Drug." *Philadelphia Inquirer,* March 16, 1991.

Reed, B.R., Jagust, W.J., and Coulter, L. "Anosognosia in Alzheimer's Disease: Relationships to Depression, Cognitive Function and Cerebral Perfusion." *Journal of Clinical and Experimental Neuropsychology* 15, no. 2 (March 1993): 231–44.

Reed, Graham. *The Psychology of Anomalous Experience: A Cognitive Approach.* Buffalo, NY: Prometheus Books, 1988.

Restak, Richard. *The Brain.* New York: Bantam Books, 1984.

Richardson, John T.E. *Mental Imagery and Human Memory.* New York: St. Martin's Press, 1980.

Richman, Barbara. "Memorable Mnemonic." *APA Monitor* (October 1986): 16.

Roberts, H.J. *Aspartame (NutraSweet): Is It Safe?* Philadelphia: The Charles Press, 1990.

Rolls, E.T., et al. "Response of Single Neurons in the Hippocampus of the Macaque Related to Reorganization Memory." *Experimental Brain Research* 93, no. 2 (1993): 299–306.

Rosenfield, Israel. *The Invention of Memory: A New View of the Brain.* New York: Basic Books, 1989.

Rosse, R.B., et al. "An Open-label Trial of Milacemide in Schizophrenia: An NMDA Intervention Strategy." *Clinical Neuropharmacology* 13, no. 4 (1990): 348–54.

Rovee-Collier, Carolyn. "The Capacity for Long-term Memory in Infancy." *Current Directions in Psychological Science* 2 (August 1993): 130–35.

———. "Infants' Eyewitness Testimony: Effects of Postevent Information on a Prior Memory Representation." *Memory & Cognition* 21 (1993): 267–79.

Rovee-Collier, Carolyn, and Hayne, H. "Reactivation of Infant Memory: Implications for Cognitive Development." In *Advances in Child Development and Behavior.* New York: Academic Press, 1987.

Ryan, E.B., and See, S.K. "Age-based Beliefs About Memory Changes for Self and Others Across Adulthood." *Journal of Gerontology* 48, no. 4 (July 1993): 199–201.

Sabelli, H.C. "Rapid Treatment of Depression with Selegiline-phenylalanine Combination." *Journal of Clinical Psychiatry* 53, no. 3 (March 1991): 137.

Sakai, K., and Miyashita. "Memory and Imagery in the Temporal Lobe." *Current Opinions in Neurobiology* 3, no. 2 (April 1993): 166–70.

Saletu, B., and Grunberger, J. "Memory Dysfunction and Vigilance: Neurophysiological and Psychopharmacological Aspects." *Annals of the New York Academy of Sciences* 444 (1985): 406–27.

Saletu, B., Grunberger, J., and Linzmayer, L. "Acute and Subacute CNS Effects of Milacemide in Elderly People: Double-blind, Placebo-controlled Quantitative EEG and Psychometric Investigations." *Archives of Gerontology and Geriatrics* 5 (1986): 165–81.

Saline, Carol. "Remembrance of Things, uh. . .uh. well, hmm. . ." *Philadelphia Magazine* (May 1992): 49–53.

Salzman, C. "The Use of ECT in the Treatment of Schizophrenia." *American Journal of Psychiatry* 137 (1980): 1032–34.

Sangiorgio, Maureen, Gutfeld, Greg, and Rao, Linda. "Aerobic Memory: Exercises and Memory." *Prevention* 44 (February 1992): 14–15.

Sartori, G., et al. "Category-specific Form of Knowledge Deficit in Patients with Herpes Simplex Virus Encephalitis." *Journal of Clinical and Experimental Neuropsychology* 15, no. 2 (March 1993): 280–99.

Schmeck, Harold M. "Study Identifies Part of Brain as Important Site for Anxiety." *New York Times*, February 24, 1989.

Schoenthaler, S.J. "Diet and IQ." *Nature* 352 (1991): 292.

Schoenthaler, S.J., et al. "Controlled Trial Vitamin-mineral Supplementation: Effects on Intelligence and Performance." *Personality and Individual Differences* 12, no. 4 (1991): 351–62.

Schooler, J., and Loftus, E. "Memory." *McGraw-Hill Encyclopedia of Science and Technology*, vol. 10. New York: McGraw-Hill, 1987.

Schwartz, B. et al. "Glycine Pro-drug Facilitates Word Retrieval in Humans." *Neurology* 41 (1991): 1341–43.

———. "The Effects of Milacemide on Item and Source Memory." *Clinical Neuropharmacology* 15 (1992): 114–19.

Schwartz, Evan I. "This Software Can Help Restore Lost Memory—for Humans." *Business Week*, December 24, 1990.

Science News Editors. "Marijuana Mangles Memory." *Science News* 136 (November 18, 1989): 332.

———. "Lights Out for Some Flashbulb Memories." *Science News* 139 (February 2, 1991): 78.

Sera, G., et al. "Effect of Fipexide on Passive Avoidance Behavior in Rats." *Pharmacological Research* 21, no. 5 (1989): 603–8.

Skinner, Karen J. "The Chemistry of Learning and Memory." *Chemical & Engineering News* 69 (October 7, 1991): 24–42.

Simons, Marlise. "Le Brain Jogging." *New York Times Magazine*, October 6, 1991.

Smith, Charles. "Your Memory: Don't Leave Home Without It." *American Salesman* 35 (October 1990): 3–5.

Smith, D.A., Browning, M., and Dunwiddie, T.V. "Cocaine Inhibition of Hippocampal Long-term Potentiation." *Brain Research* 608, no. 2 (April 16, 1993): 259–65.

Smith, M.E., and Guster, K. "Decomposition of Recognition Memory Event-related Potential Yield Target Repetition and Retrieval Effects." *Electroencephalography and Clinical Neurophysiology* 86, no. 5 (May 1993): 335–43.

Souetre, E., et al. "Abnormal Melatonin Response to 5-methoxypsoralen in Dementia." *American Journal of Psychiatry* 146, no. 8 (August 1989): 1037–40.

Spence, J.D. *The Memory Palace of Matteo Ricci*. New York: Viking Press, 1984.

Squire, Larry. R., and Zola-Morgan, Stuart. "Mechanisms of Memory," *Science*, 232 (June 27, 1986) 1612–19.

———. *Memory and Brain*. New York: Oxford University Press, 1987.

———. "The Medial Temporal Lobe Memory System." *Science* 253 (September 20, 1991): 1380–87.

Squire, Larry R., and Butters, N. *Neuropsychology of Memory*. New York: Guilford Press, 1984.

Staiger, E.H. "Probing More of the Mind." *ChemTech* (October 1986): 588–91.

Sunderland, T., et al. "Reduced Plasma Dehydroepiandrosterone Concentrations in Alzheimer's Disease." *Lancet* 2 (1989): 1335–36.

Tarazi, Linda. "An Unusual Case of Hypnotic Regression with Some Unexplained Contents." *Journal of the American Society for Psychical Research* 84 (October 1990): 309–44.

Tariiot, P.N., et al. "L-deprenyl in Alzheimer's Disease: Preliminary Evidence for Behavioral Change with Monoamine Oxidase B Inhibitors." *Archives of General Psychiatry* 44 (May 1987): 427–33.

Tortora, G.J., and Anagnostakos, N.P. *Principles of Anatomy and Physiology*. New York: Harper & Row, 1990.

Toufexis, Anastasia. "When Can Memories Be Trusted?" *Time*, October 28, 1992.

Treffert, D. "The Idiot Savant: A Review of the Syndrome." *American Journal of Psychiatry* 145 (1988): 563–72.

Trotter, Bob. "Better Memory Through Chemistry." *American Health: Fitness of Body and Mind* (April 1991): 12.

Tulving, E. *Elements of Episodic Memory*. Oxford: Clarendon Press, 1983.

———. "How Many Memory Systems Are There?" *American Psychologist* 40 (1984): 385–98.

Turkington, Carol. "Hypnotic Memory Is Not Always Accurate." *APA Monitor* (March 1982): 46–74.

———. "Disorders Highlight Differences in Learning, Memory Functions." *APA Monitor* (October 1983): 28.

———. "Memory Found Under Anesthesia." *APA Monitor* (May 1984): 33.

———. "Enkephalins Tied to Plasma." *APA Monitor* (October 1985): 10.

Ullman, Montague. "Dreams, Species-connectedness and the Paranormal." *Journal of the American Society for Psychical Research* 84 (April 1990): 105–25.

Verhaeghen, P., Marcoen, A., and Goossens, L. "Facts and Fiction About Memory and Aging: A Quantitative Integration of Research Findings." *Journal of Gerontology* 48, no. 4 (July 1993): 157–71.

Watson, Ronald R. "Caffeine: Is It Dangerous to Health?" *American Journal of Health Promotion* 2 (Spring 1988): 13–21.

Wearden, J.H., and Ferrara, A. "Subjective Shortening in Human's Memory for Stimulus Duration." *Quarterly Journal of Experimental Psychology* 46, no. 2 (May 1993): 163–86.

Weintraub, Pamela. "Total Recall: Ways to Improve Your Memory." *American Health* (March 1992): 77–73.

Weiss, R. "Human Brain Neurons Grown in Culture." *Science News* 137 (May 5, 1990): 276.

Welte, P.O. "Indices of Verbal Learning and Memory Deficits After Right Hemisphere Stroke." *Archives of Physical Medicine and Rehabilitation* 74, no. 6 (June 1993): 631–36.

"What Causes Memory Loss?" *USA Today* (magazine) 119 (October 1990): 3.

"What Does Your Memory Smell Like?" *USA Today* (magazine) 120 (January 1992): 6.

"What REALLY Causes Amnesia?" *USA Today* (magazine) 117 (April 1989): 13.

White, N.M., Packard, M.G., and Seamans, J. "Memory Enhancement by Post-training Peripheral Administration of Low Doses of Dopamine Agonists." *Behavioral and Neural Biology* 59, no. 3 (May 1993): 230–41.

Wilson, B. *The Rehabilitation of Memory*. New York: Guilford Press, 1987.

Wilson, B., and Moffat, N. *Clinical Management of Memory Problems.* Rockville, MD: Aspen Systems, 1984.

Wilson, F.A., Scalardhe, S.P., and Goldman-Rakic, P.S. "Dissociation of Object and Spatial Process Domains in Primate Prefontal Cortex." *Science* 260 (1993): 1876.

Winston, J. "Biology and Function of REM Sleep." *Current Opinions in Neurobiology* 3, no. 2 (April 1993): 243–48.

Wolinsky, Joan. "Responsibility Can Delay Aging." *APA Monitor* (March 1982): 14, 41.

Wuethrich, B. "Higher Risk of Alzheimer's Linked to Gene." *Science News* 144, no. 7 (August 14, 1993): 108.

Yalch, Richard F. "Memory in a Jingle Jungle: Music as a Mnemonic Device in Communicating Advertising Slogans." *Journal of Applied Psychology* 76 (April 1991): 268–75.

Yates, Frances A. *The Art of Memory.* Chicago: University of Chicago Press, 1966.

Yesavage, J.A., and Rolf, J. "Effects of Relaxation and Mnemonics on Memory, Attention and Anxiety in the Elderly." *Experimental Aging Research* 10 (1984): 211–14.

Young, Walter C. "Patients Reporting Ritual Abuse in Childhood: A Clinical Syndrome." *Child Abuse and Neglect* 15 (1991): 181–89.

Zatorre, R.J., and Halpern, A.R. "Effect of Unilateral Temporal Lobe Excision on Perception and Imagery of Songs." *Neuropsychologia* 31, no. 3 (March 1993): 221–32.

INDEX

Entries are filed letter-by-letter.
Boldface page numbers indicate extensive treatment of a topic.

A

abaissement du niveau mental, **1**
abreaction, **1**
absentmindedness, **1**, 152
abstract memory, **1**
acalculia, **1**, 138
accident neurosis. *See* amnesia, simulated
acetylcholine, **1–2**, 5, 16, 17, 18, 24, 51, 53, 54, 72, 73, 84, 99, 110, 124, 140, 142–43, 165, 167, 168–69, 178, 183, 191, 200, 227
  aging and, 100
  drugs that block, 26, 133
  transmission of, 100
acetylcholinesterase inhibitor, 17, 18, 110
acetyl-L-carnitine, **2**, 70, 139
acquisition, **2**, 153, 193; *See also* encoding
acronymns, 157
acrostic, **2**; *See also* first-letter cueing, mnemonics, mnemonic strategies
ACTH (adrenocorticotropic hormone), 3, 139–40, 164, 165
adenosine triphosphate (ATP), 3, 99, 141
ADH (antidiuretic hormone). *See* vasopressin
Ad Herennium, **3–4**, 29, 54
Adler, Alfred, 52, 118
adrenal cortex, 3
adrenaline, 51; *See also* epinephrine
adrenocorticotropic hormone. *See* ACTH
advance knowledge and witness perception, 4; *See also* eyewitness testimony; memory for events
age-associated memory impairment, 2, **4**, 42
  treatment for, 142, 155, 169, 177, 227
  vs. Alzheimer's disease, 14
age regression, hypnotic, **4–5**
aging and memory, **5–9**, 17, 66
  acetyl-L-carnitine, 139–140
  acetylcholine and, 51
  brain wave patterns and, 221
  calpain and, 46–47
  computer games and, 58
  declarative memory and, 100
  epinephrine and, 85
  explicit memory and, 87
  eyewitness ability and, 4, 71, 89

  folic acid and, 92
  fluid imbalances and, 92
  glucose and, 100
  implicit memory and, 87
  substantia nigra and, 69
  vasopressin and, 220
agnosia, **9**, 25, 43, 65, 104, 138, 157
  auditory, 138
  somatosensory, 138
  visual, 9, 81, 121, 122, 138; *See also* prosopagnosia
agraphia, **10**, 27, 28, 138, 157; *See also* alexia; apraxia; dysphasia
AIDS
  cryptococcosis and 61
  dementia **10–11**, 67, 69
  encephalitis and, 81
akashic records, **11**
Albert, Marilyn, 38
alcohol
  delirium and, 65, 100
  memory and, 5, 6, **11–12**, 19, 38, 67, 133, 220
  organic brain syndrome and, 221
  crime and, 21
  Wernicke-Korsakoff syndrome and, 226
alcohol amnestic disorder, **122**; *See also* Korsakoff's syndrome
alcohol idiosyncratic intoxication, **12**
aldosterone, 3
Alexander the Great, 111
alexia, 10, **12**, 27, 138, 157
alien abduction memories. *See* cryptomnesia
alphabetical searching, **12**, 146, 195, 223
altered states of consciousness, 1, **12**, 44, 111, 120, 158, 188
aluminum and memory loss, 15
Alzheimer, Alois, **12**, 14, 162
Alzheimer's Association, **12–13**, 18
Alzheimer's Association Autopsy Assistance Network, The, **13**
Alzheimer's Association Newsletter, 13
Alzheimer's disease, 6, 12, **13–18**, 43, 45, 133, 157, 168, 184, 188, 201, 219
  acetylcholine and, 1–2, 50, 54, 84
  acetyl-L-carnitine and, 2
  age-associated memory impairment and, 4
  amnesia and, 19
  assessment of, 198

  autopsy in, 13, 16
  behavioral problems, 17
  beta-amyloid and, 16
  chemical abnormality and, **16**
  choline, as treatment, 53, 54, 140
  choline acetyltransferase, 50, 53, 54
  computer games and, 58
  dementia and, 66, 68, 140, 168
  DHEA and, 63–64, 140, 183
  diagnosis of, **16**
  etiology, **15**
  excitotoxins and, 15
  gender, 17
  genetics and, 14, 15, 16, 17
  Gingko biloba, **99**, 139, 141
  hydergine, 192
  indomethacin, 191–192
  lecithin and, 124
  magnesium and, **132**
  medications for, 17–18, 24
  metals and, 16
  nerve growth factors, **161–162**
  neurofibrillary tangles, **12, 14, 16, 162,** 188
  nucleus basalis in, 54
  organic, 114, 169–170
  oxiracetam, 142, 167, 170–171, 189
  physostigmine, **178,** 192, 200
  PKC and, 185
  plaques and, 54
  pregnenolone and, 184
  PTSD vs, 182
  risk factors of, 17
  slow virus, 15, 16, 205–206
  symptoms of, 14
  tacrine, 17, 18, 110, 143, 191
  toxins, 17
  treatment, **17–18,** 42, 49, 53, 63, 69–70, 99, 109, 110, 117, 142–143, 155, 161–162, 170–171, 178, 182, 220, 221
  vasopressin and, 220
  vs. Pick disease, 179, 219
  in youth, 14, **18**
Alzheimer's Disease and Related Disorders Association, 12, **18**
Alzheimer's Disease Research Center Program, 18
aminergic, **19**
amino acids, **19**
amnesia, **19–21,** 38, 45, 54, 65, 87, 94, 97, 98, 104, 127, 134, 157
  after scopolamine, 200

255

F

facial agnosia. *See* prosopagnosia
face-name association method, **89–90**, 146, 222–223
factitious disorder, 98
familiarity, **90**
fantasy, 78, **90**
Faria, Abb, 112
"fat lady" syndrome, **90**
feeling of knowing, **90**
Feinaigle, Gregor von, 176
figure alphabet. *See* phonetic mnemonic
fipexide, **90**, 139, 141
first-letter cueing, 12, **90–91**, 146, 223; *See also* visual method
first letter mnemonic. *See* acrostic
flashbacks during surgery, **91**
flashbulb memory, 8, **91–92**, 200
flooding, 37
Flourens, Pierre, 107
flucytosine, 61
fluid imbalances and memory, **92**, 178
folic acid and memory, **92**
Food and Drug Administration, 18, 30
forebrain, **93**
forgetfulness, 182, 183, 206
    and AIDS, 10
forgetting, 1, 62, 63, 77, 93, 119, 184, 198
    vs. consolidation, 60
forgetting curve, **94**
forgetting, theories of, **93–94**
fornix, 71, **94**, 126–127
Francis I, king of France, 47
Franklin, Benjamin, 79, 154
Fregoli's syndrome, 156
free association, 195
free radicals, 5, 109, 141, 192
freezing effect, **95**
Freeman, Walter, **95**, 125, 126, 158
Freud, Sigmund, 24, 44, **95–96**
    on agnosia, 9
    on childhood memories, 52–53, 194
    on collective unconscious, 56
    on hedonic selectivity, 181, 194
    on déjà vu, 64
    on dissociation, 74
    on hypnosis, 112, 181, 187
    on hysterical amnesia, 20, 115, 187
    on infantile amnesia, 21, 35, 117, 165, 194
    on repression, 81, 115, 117, 165, 181, 194, 200
    on screen memories, 200
    psychoanalysis and, **187**
    reality monitoring, **190**
frontal association cortex, 108, 119, 138–139
frontal cortex, 44
frontal lobe, 39, 50, 70, 81, **96**, 97, 124, 128

assessment of damage in, 226
    event memory and, 86
    damage, 226
    lesions and memory, 43, 48, **96–97**
fugue, 74, **97**, 186, 188
functional amnesia. *See* amnesia, psychogenic
fuzzy trace theory, **97–98**

G

GABA. *See* gamma aminobutyric acid
Gaea, 157
Galen, 107
Galileo, 30
Gall, Franz Joseph, 177
gamma aminobutyric acid, 106
Ganser, Sigbert J. M., 98
Ganser's syndrome, **98**
generation-recognition theory, **99**
Gerstmann-Straussler syndrome, 16
Gingko biloba, **99**, 139, 141
ginseng, **99**, 139, 141
glucose, 85, 86, 99, **100**, 114, 141, 143, 147, 177, 221
glutamate, 15, **100–101**, 106, 109, 167
glycopyrrolate, 26
Gnostics, 150
Gold, Paul, 100
Graces, 110
Graf, Peter, 87, 115
gray matter, 50
Greek art of memory, 4, 29, 54, 106, 128, 155, 157, 192, 196, 204, 223
Grey, Richard, 176
Guillotin, J., 154

H

habituation, **101**, 129, 182
hallucinations, 64, 97, 98, **101**, 171, 199
haloperidol, 65, 76
Hartley, David, 32, 107
hashish, 133, 158
headache, 44, 48, 58, 102, 221
head injury, 9, 10 12, 19, 21, 27, 28, 39, **101–103**, 138, 168, 171, 196, 198, 206, 218
    postconcussion syndrome and, 58, 60, 101,
    fugue and, 97
healing temples, 111
Hebb, Donald, 60, **103–104**
Hebbian, anti phenomenon, **129**
Hebb synapse, 60, 103–104
Hebb's rule, **104**
hedonic selectivity, **104**, 194
Helmholtz, Hermann von, 120
hematoma, subdural, 67, 101, 102, 103
Hera, 110
Herophilus, 107
herpes virus, 43, 81

Hilgard, Ernest, 113
hippocampal formations, **104**, 126
hippocampus, 5, 22, 39, 41, 51, 54, 63, 101, **104–106**, 125, 126– 127, 135–136, 139, 149, 157, 190, 201
    damage and memory, 42, 49, 81, 85, 104, 108, 134, 139, 153
    development of, 117
    marijuana and, 133
    event memory and, 86
history of memory, **106–107**
hologram theory of memory, 64, 84, 108
HM, 41, 85, 104, **108**, 126, 129, 134
hook. *See* phonetic mnemonic
Hull, Clark, 112
human growth hormone, **161–162;**
    See also nerve growth factor
human immunodeficiency virus, 10
Hume, David, 32
Huntington's disease, 49, 66, 68, **108–109**, 123, 138
Huperzia serrata. *See* club moss
Hydergine, **109–110**, **139**, **141**, **192**
hydrocephalus, 14, 43, 67, 68
hydrocortisone, 3
hyperactivity, 3
hypermnesia, **110**, 111, 157
hyperzine A, 17–18, **110**
hypnopedia, **110;** *See also* sleep learning
Hypnos, **110**, 112, 155
hypnosis, 5, 19–20, 44, 56, 74, 92, 97, 110, **110–114**, 120, 155, 181
    forensic, 56, 92–93
    Freud on, 112
    long-term memory and, 128
    Pavlov on, 172
    somnambulism and, 207
hypnotic age regression. *See* age regression, hypnotic
hypnotic drugs, **114**
hypnotizability, **114**
hypoglycemia and memory, **114**, 178
hypothalamus, 3, 39, 41, 93, 220
hypothyroidism, **114**
hypoxia, 25, 40, 49, 115
hysteria, 74, 120

I

Icelus, 110
iconic memory, **115**
id, 78
idealization, 63
idebenone, **115**, 139, 141
identification, 63
identifying paramnesia, 171
ideomotor apraxia, 28
idiot savants, 35; *See also* autistic savants
Iliad, 110
image association, **115**
imagery process and memory, **115–116**, 221, 222